D0319766

Collingridge Standard Guides

The Amateur's Greenhouse

Collingridge Standard Guides

The Amateur's Greenhouse

A J Macself VMH

revised by John Warren NDH

Collingridge Books

LONDON·NEW YORK·SYDNEY·TORONTO

Published for Collingridge Books by
The Hamlyn Publishing Group Limited
London · New York · Sydney · Toronto
Astronaut House, Feltham, Middlesex, England

Set in 11/12 pt Lumitype Times
Printed and Bound in Great Britain by
Butler & Tanner Ltd.
Frome and London

First published by
W. H. and L. Collingridge Limited in 1930
Sixth revised edition, 1974
Second impression, 1975

ISBN 0 600 30151 6

ACKNOWLEDGEMENTS

The Editor would like to thank *Amateur
Gardening*, Pat Brindley, Ernest Crowson, Elsa
Megson and Harry Smith for the photographs
used in this book.

Line Drawings by Ian Garrard

Contents

CHAPTER ONE

Houses of Glass – their purposes and advantages

A well-designed greenhouse, equipped efficiently to exclude frost and maintain suitable temperatures, will add immensely to the enjoyment of a garden. In a large garden, a greenhouse becomes an economic necessity for the raising of young plants and preserving tender ones which cannot withstand frost, and in a small garden a greenhouse will broaden the scope of operations and enable the keen gardener to cultivate a wide range of plants of infinite charm and beauty which cannot be grown out of doors.

Success and satisfaction will, to a great extent, depend on the soundness of the structure and the quality of workmanship and materials used. The situation of a greenhouse will affect the health and vigour of the plants grown: maximum sunlight is essential except in the case of a house which is to be devoted to ferns. Shelter from rough winds is highly desirable but a greenhouse should never be placed where it is closely surrounded or overhung by large trees.

When it is intended to specialise in growing one particular family or class of plants, it is advisable to devote a greenhouse to them entirely. In some cases this is almost a necessity because of the special requirements of the plants in the way of atmospheric moisture, temperature, and ventilation. An example of this is the perpetual flowering carnations which never seem to flourish so well in a greenhouse of mixed plants as in a house by themselves. However, there are plenty of beautiful and useful plants which are companionable, and the majority of greenhouse owners will prefer to grow an assortment of flowering and foliage plants which will provide colour and interest for every season of the year.

For such purposes one can grow a few cyclamen and cinerarias together with *Primula obconica*, *P. malacoides* and *P. kewensis* for flowering in December and the early months of the year. These can be supplemented by spring-flowering bulbs and possibly a few forced shrubs. In summer the choice can embrace begonias, fuchsias, regal and zonal pelargoniums, *Campanula isophylla*, heliotropes, abutilons, cannas and numerous other plants selected from the very wide range recommended in the alphabetical list in this book which also gives guidance on their cultivation.

Thanks to the modern techniques of all-the-year-round production, chrysanthemums can be brought into flower throughout the year though they are still principally an attractive feature of autumn. If sufficient heat is available, winter-flowering begonias can be grown to provide colour at the end of the year and where a cooler atmosphere is maintained, zonal pelargoniums will flower until Christmas.

An ever-increasing number of greenhouse owners are taking an interest in succulent plants, especially cacti. These plants are both curious and unique in character, and many of them are particularly beautiful when in flower: the closer they are studied the more fascinating they become. Small numbers of them may be kept among a miscellaneous collection of greenhouse plants, provided they are carefully watered and given a situation in full sun, but if it is intended to specialise and form a collection of succulents they will require a greenhouse to themselves. This also applies to a collection of orchids or ferns.

To gain the maximum use and pleasure from a greenhouse, one or possibly two cold frames should be bought or constructed. Without adequate frame space it is not possible to use a greenhouse to its full capacity. Some plants require a period in the cool atmosphere of a cold frame, either during the hottest summer months or when they are dormant and resting before being started into growth. When a greenhouse is used for raising young plants or producing summer bedding plants, frames will be invaluable for hardening them off; at the same time releasing space in the greenhouse for the cultivation of other plants.

Another essential piece of equipment for the greenhouse is a propagating case for raising seedlings and rooting cuttings. Prototype propagation cases were glass-topped frames built over hot-water pipes and placed at the warmest end of the greenhouse. The introduction of electrical soil-warming cables has changed all this, and it is now possible to buy complete propagation cases with plastic domes to replace the glass, equipped with a thermostat and warming cables. Under these conditions, the correct degree of heat and humidity can be provided for the seedlings and young plants.

Some greenhouse plants are difficult for an amateur of limited experience to propagate, and in such cases it is recommended that young plants should be bought from specialist producers. The greenhouse space can then be devoted to raising seedlings and plants which can be grown successfully.

A collection of choice alpines will add distinction to the greenhouse and bring untold joy to its owner. These plants do not require, nor will they tolerate, artificial heat but, because many of them flower during the early months of the year, the fragile flowers appreciate the shelter of a glass roof. They do best in a greenhouse on their own — one which has been specifically designed to give unrestricted access to all possible daylight and well equipped with ventilators to allow for the maximum amount of ventilation.

Many gardeners prefer to use their greenhouses for growing fruit and vegetables, and a chapter is devoted to the production of salads, forced rhubarb and other edible crops. The forcing of strawberries in pots and the growing of grapes, peaches, figs and melons are also described.

CHAPTER TWO

Choosing a Greenhouse

In the past, many books on greenhouse management included chapters giving detailed instructions on how to make and erect a greenhouse. However, in these days of mass-produced, pre-fabricated buildings the most that a prospective greenhouse owner has to do is to lay a foundation and bolt together the sides, ends and top of the construction. This chapter, therefore, is devoted to discussing the selection of a greenhouse from the wide range of mass-produced types available. Before doing so, however, it might be as well to outline some of the laws relating to their installation which must be taken into account before work is started.

Tenants' Fixtures

There are one or two considerations which remain the same irrespective of the type of greenhouse erected. One of these is the law relating to tenants' fixtures.

Generally, greenhouses for domestic use, erected in sections and secured by bolts, may be removed by a tenant at any time before, but not after, the expiration of the tenancy.

A conservatory erected on a brick foundation, fixed to and communicating with the rooms of a dwelling house, cannot be removed, nor can a greenhouse erected on wooden posts and framework secured by cement or mortar to a brick foundation. A boiler which is built into the masonry of a greenhouse cannot be taken away but the hot-water pipes which are screwed to the boiler may be unscrewed and removed. On the other hand, a house may be removed if it rests on a foundation of dry bricks.

A lean-to structure with the ends of its rafters resting upon a plate secured to the wall may be removed, provided the rafters are not nailed or otherwise fastened to the wall plates, which are then left undisturbed.

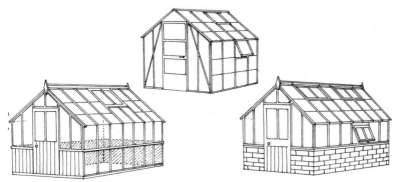

Three types of span-roof greenhouse to show the differing combinations of materials used in their construction

In most towns and urban districts it is necessary to obtain consent from the local authority before erecting a building of any sort in a garden. It is also advisable to draw up a written agreement between tenant and landlord stating clearly that the structure may be removed if the tenancy should be terminated.

TYPES OF GREENHOUSE

Briefly, the types of greenhouse may be classified as: span-roof; three-quarter span; lean-to, and Dutch light. Besides these there are a few variations such as the contemporary garden-room-cum-conservatory type of structure, and the well-known aluminium alloy house which takes the form of one half of a sixteen-sided figure. More recently, too, circular and hexagonal greenhouses have been introduced.

Span-roof

The ordinary span-roof greenhouse is by far the most useful shape, having vertical sides and a roof in the shape of a shallow, inverted V. It is available in sizes ranging from 6 to 8 ft. to the large commercial types 100 ft. long or more.

Three-quarter Span

The three-quarter span or hip-span greenhouse is built against a wall or building 8 to 10 ft. high. It has a ridge along the roof, with a foreshortened span on the wall side at the back, and a sloping one of normal height at the front. Where possible, the long slope of the roof should face due south, so that it will receive full sun in summer and maximum light during the winter. It can, of course,

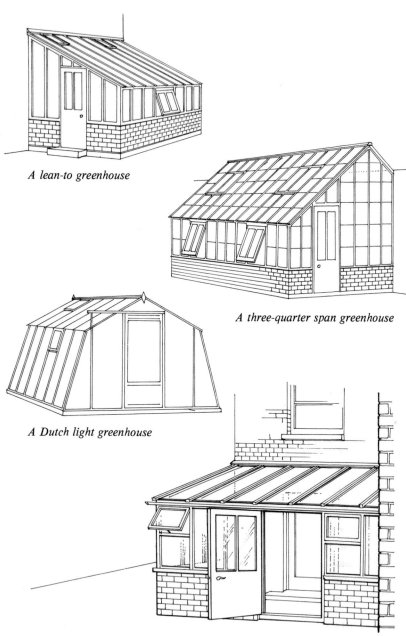

A lean-to greenhouse

A three-quarter span greenhouse

A Dutch light greenhouse

A typical conservatory

be built to face other aspects such as south east or south west, but it would not be quite so successful. Where only a northern aspect is available, a house can be built specially for raising ferns or other shade-loving plants.

The three-quarter span greenhouse once enjoyed great popularity. In the days of large private gardens it was widely used for growing vines and peaches. It has the advantage over the ordinary lean-to type of house in that it receives some light from the back as well as the front. A three-quarter span structure makes an attractive plant house, particularly when fitted with tiered staging which raises the plants at the back towards the roof where they will obtain maximum light.

Lean-to

The cheapest and most economical form of permanent greenhouse to manage is the lean-to type, built against a wall or building with a sloping roof on one side only. It has the disadvantage that light can only enter it from the front, and it must therefore have a sunny situation, preferably one facing south. An east or west aspect will be reasonably satisfactory provided it is open and not overshadowed in any way. Lean-to greenhouses are quite economical to heat – the heat loss through a wall is much lower than it would be through glass, the wall absorbing heat during the day and releasing it at night. When a lean-to is facing south, the wall or building forming the back shelters it from the north wind and minimises its chilling effect on cold nights. One drawback of a lean-to structure, however, is that it has ventilators in the front only, which means that even on bright sunny days they cannot be opened early in the year if a cold wind is blowing from that direction.

Dutch Light

Dutch lights are single sheets of 24-oz. glass measuring 56 in. by $28\frac{3}{4}$ in. and surrounded by a wooden frame made from 2 by 2-in. square-sectioned timber. They are used extensively for commercial greenhouses when they are secured to a wooden or metal framework. Recently, they have been adapted for making small and inexpensive greenhouses for the amateur. They are intended primarily for growing plants in the soil of the greenhouse border, but can be fitted with benches for growing pot plants; concrete floors can also be laid if required.

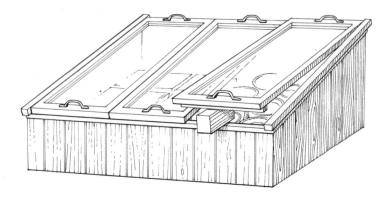

There are several styles of garden frame. This one is protected by Dutch lights. Frames provide a half-way stage between the greenhouse and garden and give extra space when the greenhouse is crowded. They can be heated or unheated. The heated frame can be used for propagating plants and for producing crops of early vegetables. Uses which an unheated frame can be put to include hardening off bedding plants, plunging bulbs and as a summer standing ground for many greenhouse subjects

Conservatory

The conservatory or lean-to greenhouse with a communicating door into the house is a very popular feature of gardens these days. It can be specially built by a local builder to fit a particular wall or corner, or it may be one of the new garden-room type of structures which gives its owner the best of both worlds in providing both an additional room and somewhere to grow plants.

MATERIALS FOR GREENHOUSE CONSTRUCTION

Wood

Because it was reasonably cheap, easily worked and readily available, wood used to be the traditional material for constructing greenhouses. It was the shortage of softwoods during the Second World War which led to the search for alternative materials. Some of these, particularly aluminium alloy, have had such a remarkable increase in popularity that the dominance of wood in the building of greenhouses is no longer secure. Not all timbers are suitable for greenhouse construction because of the rapid temperature variations and high humidities which can be highly conducive to decay in timbers which are not resistant to it. Greenhouse timber must also have a high degree of mechanical strength because glazing bars need to be fairly slender so as not to exclude valuable light, yet they must be strong enough to bear the weight of the glass, withstand wind pressures, and the added weight of several inches of snow.

Softwoods or Deal: The most commonly used softwood or deal is Baltic red wood or Scots pine. This wood has many desirable qualities but is not very durable or resistant to decay. This means that it must be treated with a wood preservative before being used and regularly painted after the greenhouse has been erected. The regular painting and maintenance of greenhouses can be quite difficult these days. If it is to be done professionally, it is not always easy to find someone to undertake the work, and if the gardener is to do the painting himself, he has to have sufficient spare time and be agile enough to climb on to the roof to carry out the work.

Western Red Cedar: Western red cedar, which is now used extensively for the construction of greenhouses, is durable and resistant to decay but not very strong mechanically so that it has to be used in larger sections. Western red cedar does not require painting but it should be oiled occasionally and the use of steel nails should be avoided — they are liable to corrode and cause structural weaknesses in the timber. Brass screws or galvanised nails are more satisfactory, as they do not corrode and damage the timber.

Oak: Although not extensively used for greenhouses, oak is strong and durable and does not require regular painting but it has a habit of twisting unless the timber is fully seasoned. Twisting of the glazing bars may cause the glass to break. At least one of the larger greenhouse manufacturers offers a good mass-produced greenhouse made in oak.

Teak: Teak has been used in greenhouse construction for many years. It is mechanically strong, has a long life, and does not need regular painting. Unfortunately, except in special cases, the cost is too high for general use. Although such timber does not need a coat of paint to preserve it, the light reflected from white-painted wood will be valuable, particularly in the winter time.

Wood Preservatives: If timber is kept dry, fungal organisms which cause decay cannot flourish. However, under the conditions of high humidity in a greenhouse, woodwork will not remain dry for long, even though it is carefully and regularly painted. Once the skin of paint is broken, moisture is rapidly absorbed which causes the wood to swell and leads to further cracking and flaking of the paint. If treated with a preservative which is toxic to decay organisms, the life of softwoods may easily be doubled. These preservatives should be applied to the timber by the manufacturer before the greenhouse is built. They are usually copper or mercurial-zinc compounds, either in a water-soluble form or in a spirit solvent, and are much more effective when forced into the wood under pressure.

Metal

There has been a great increase in the popularity of metal greenhouses in the last few years. Aluminium alloy is proving to be a most suitable material. In the days when ordinary linseed oil putty, which sets hard with age, was the only material available, it was extremely difficult to seal the joints between the glass and metal bars effectively, because of the different rates of expansion of glass and metal when subjected to temperature changes. The introduction of non-hardening sealing compounds and plastic glazing strips has changed all this, and metal greenhouses can now be made quite weatherproof under all conditions.

Aluminium Alloy: There are numerous types of aluminium alloy greenhouses in sizes suitable for the amateur. It is a relatively expensive material but the metal structure requires virtually no maintenance. It is mechanically strong so that small sections can be used offering the minimum obstruction to light. Aluminium alloy is a tractable material, easily worked into the intricate shapes required for roof bars, and in modern greenhouses the roofing bars often incorporate grooves to prevent condensed moisture dripping on to the plants, a serious problem in some of the older types of aluminium greenhouse.

Aluminium greenhouses are available in all the traditional shapes, span-roof or lean-to, and there is an extremely popular one which

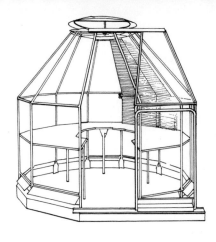

A circular greenhouse

takes the form of one half of a sixteen-sided figure. A more recent introduction is a circular aluminium greenhouse, about 8 ft. in diameter and 7 ft. high to the apex of the sloping roof. It is quite practical in its conception, and pleasingly contemporary in outline.

Steel: Being a strong material, the use of steel means that the roof members can be quite slender so that maximum light is admitted. Unfortunately, the disadvantage is that steel is highly susceptible to corrosion, and must be efficiently rust proofed when being used in greenhouse construction. Once rust is established, it builds up rapidly under the conditions of high humidity in a greenhouse, causing distortion of the bars and breakage of glass.

Glazing methods and various other considerations are much the same for steel constructions as for aluminium greenhouses. One difficulty which applies to all-metal greenhouses is the drilling of holes for fixing shelves, thermostats and other apparatus, and in the case of steel such drilling may allow rust to gain entry if the holes are not immediately treated. On the credit side, steel greenhouses are relatively cheap, strong and durable, giving a neat appearance.

Concrete

In the search for new materials during the timber shortage in the late forties, concrete was tried out as a material for constructing greenhouses, with limited success. Its chief advantages are its durability, stability and complete absence of any need for maintenance, and near the sea it has the added advantage of being unaffected by salt spray. On the debit side, the sections are large and impede light transmission; visually it tends to be rather heavy and unattractive.

17

Glass Fibre

This modern material has been tried for greenhouses, and may have a future, but its development is as yet only in its infancy.

Substitutes for Glass

The search for a substitute for glass continues. Various plastic sheets and films are being used but none of them is quite as efficient as good 24-oz. glass. However, glass substitutes are constantly being improved and it may well be that in the near future we shall have a completely satisfactory alternative, which will not be as vulnerable to stone throwing and other acts of vandalism.

GREENHOUSE DESIGN AND CONSTRUCTION

The well-designed greenhouse allows the maximum of natural light to reach the plants within it, and to do this it must have the lowest possible proportion of solid members to the area of glass it contains. This means that the glazing bars and other solid parts must be as slender as is consistent with the required strength, and they must be spaced as far apart as possible. A distance of 24 in. between bars is the ideal at which to aim.

The overall proportions should be pleasing to look at, and simple in outline. The present-day greenhouse is functional and practical without unnecessary frills and detail. It must be weatherproof and soundly constructed, the workmanship good and the fittings such as hinges, casement stays, door locks and handles of good quality.

The cost of heating a greenhouse is increased and the health of the plants impaired if badly fitting doors and windows are a permanent source of cold draughts.

Ventilation

Though greenhouse plants may not tolerate draughts, a continuous supply of fresh air is essential to their health and well being. To supply this fresh air and maintain the temperature within bounds in warm weather, the greenhouse must be adequately equipped with ventilators. The good quality, well-designed greenhouse usually has enough ventilators, but unfortunately this is not always true of a high proportion of the greenhouses offered for sale, and quite often the ventilators that are fitted are too small. A typical 12 by 8-ft. greenhouse should have at least one, or preferably two, ventilators in each side of the roof, as well as one in each side wall, or box ventilators placed low down below bench level. If, when buying a greenhouse, the one chosen does not include enough ventilators, it may be possible to have more fitted as optional extras before taking delivery. Intake of air by a thermostatically controlled extractor fan or by devices for opening and closing the ventilators is now quite common practice. Reference to both methods will be found in Chapters 3 and 4 respectively.

Most models of greenhouses are available either with glass to within a few inches of the ground or with a solid base up to bench level. Metal greenhouses with a solid base are erected on walls of brick or concrete blocks about 3 ft high. Most greenhouse manufacturers will supply a plan setting out the dimensions of these walls.

Foundations

All greenhouses require a firm and level base. A simple concrete foundation 3 or 4 in. thick with its upper surface about 6 in. below the surface of the ground will be adequate; the load to be carried is not very great. All topsoil containing organic material should be removed as organic matter oxidises and will cause the foundations to subside. This could ultimately lead to distortion of the framework and breakages of glass.

If the subsoil is firm and solid, the foundations can be laid directly on to it, but if it is soft and spongy, a layer of hard core should be put down and rammed well in before the concrete is laid. Some greenhouse owners prefer a concrete floor, and lay a concrete raft over the whole area. This has the advantages of cleanliness, durability and firmness but it also has several disadvantages. The soil in the greenhouse floor cannot be used for raising plants which will all have to be grown in pots, troughs or other containers. A concrete floor heats up rapidly in the summer and dries out quickly and though it is easy to put water down to create humidity, it soon evaporates from the surface of the concrete.

The ideal is to lay a concrete path, at least 2 ft. 6 in. wide, down the centre of the greenhouse with soil or a deep layer of gravel or ashes on either side. This provides a firm, level surface for walking on, while the porous but moisture-retentive material at the sides helps to keep the greenhouse cool and provides the correct degree of humidity.

19

Size

Modern greenhouses are available in a wide range of sizes to suit all purposes and pockets and the choice will depend entirely on the resources and requirements of the owner. There are, however, one or two general rules which should be observed. It is important to be absolutely sure that the structure chosen will be large enough. Although at the outset a greenhouse may seem too large, in a few months the keen gardener will have it full to overflowing with his favourite plants. On the whole very small greenhouses are more difficult to manage than larger ones: for comfortable working the minimum width of a span-roof structure should be at least 8 ft. This allows for a centre path 2 ft. 6 in. wide with benches 3 ft. or slightly less in width on either side. If the width is less than 8 ft., the path will still have to be the same width which leads to a serious reduction of the effective growing spaces. In a greenhouse 8 ft. wide, a 2-ft. path equals 25 per cent. of the floor area, but in one only 6 ft. wide, it will represent 33 per cent. of that area.

Height is equally important. There must be sufficient head room for taller plants, and it must be possible for the gardener to stand upright in comfort when tending the plants. An 8 ft. wide greenhouse which is 5 ft. high to the eaves and 7 ft. 6 in. to the ridge will give a height of 6 ft. 9 in. at the front of the bench which is adequate for most people. Most greenhouses are available in multiples of a unit length and this will simply be a matter of choosing a length to suit one's requirements.

Greenhouse Doors

These can be either hinged or sliding. Many of the modern greenhouses have sliding doors which are a great advantage when space is at a premium. One disadvantage of this design is that grit is liable to foul the base runners. All doors should be wide enough to allow for the passage of a wheelbarrow.

Dutch Light Greenhouses

These were originally evolved in Holland as commercial greenhouses but, like many other good horticultural ideas, they have been adopted by amateur gardeners. The lights can be clamped together with special clamps or secured to a wooden framework specially constructed for the purpose. This skeleton of uprights, rafters and ridge timbers can easily be built by the amateur gardener with a working knowledge of carpentry. On the basis of cost per square foot of growing space, the Dutch light greenhouse is the cheapest there is. Small greenhouses of this type are now made by several manufacturers, but they are mainly an adaptation of the Dutch light principle using Dutch light-sized glass. The majority are made in cedar wood, with glass to the ground, and are extremely useful for the amateur, particularly those who are interested in growing tomatoes and chrysanthemums.

CHOOSING A SITE

The position of a greenhouse is an extremely important consideration, for no matter how well designed or how well constructed it may be, if it is in the shadow of trees or buildings it cannot function properly. A greenhouse requires an open site where it can receive full sunlight but it also requires shelter from cold winds, particularly those from the north and east. In a small garden it may not always be possible to pick an ideal situation because, for the sake of appearance, the greenhouse may have to be built parallel or at right angles to the main path or boundary fence. It should, however, be given the best position available, allowing for other practical considerations. To obtain the maximum amount of light throughout the whole year, the long axis should run from north to south, but if winter light in December, January and February is the most important consideration, the greenhouse should be sited with its long axis running east to west.

There are, in addition, other factors to be taken into account. Ease of access is one; an easily accessible greenhouse is usually visited more often and is therefore better cared for than one tucked away in a corner of the garden. Supplies of electricity and mains water are highly desirable, if not essential, features of the modern greenhouse, and it will add considerably to the cost of installation if they have to be brought the full length of a long garden from the source of supply. If the greenhouse is small and heated only by one small portable oil heater journeys to attend to the heater on cold nights will be made much less willingly if it is far away from the house. Another common mistake is to build the greenhouse too close to the garden fence so that there is not enough room between them for normal maintenance to be carried out.

CHAPTER THREE

Heating Greenhouses

However well a greenhouse may be constructed, its efficiency will be seriously reduced if the heating system is inadequate. It is essential, therefore, to be quite sure that the heating apparatus installed is capable of providing sufficient heat to maintain the temperature required under the severest weather conditions likely to be experienced. To make sure of this, any calculations made to determine the size of the heater required should be based on a minimum outside temperature of $-7°C$ ($20°F$) and not $0°C$ ($32°F$), as is sometimes the case.

No heating system should have to work to its full capacity for long periods. It may shorten the life of the apparatus appreciably and lead to breakdowns just when the heat is most urgently needed. This can be avoided by installing apparatus which is large enough to maintain the required temperature at all times and still have a little capacity in reserve. Most reliable manufacturers of heating equipment will recommend a suitable apparatus which has this reserve capacity, if they are given the size and dimensions of the greenhouse. With such an apparatus the greenhouse owner will be freed from any worry or anxiety over whether the temperature can be successfully maintained on cold nights.

The amount of heat required, however, can be reduced by making sure that the structure is sound and that there are no cracks through which cold air can enter and warm air escape. The greenhouse can also be lined during the winter months with clear polythene sheeting to act as a form of double glazing. This does reduce the amount of light and the effect of this must be weighed against the substantial saving of fuel. The polythene should be attached to the glazing bars to run up and down rather than across as any condensation will then run down to the eaves instead of dripping on to the plants.

It should not, of course, be placed over the ventilators. Blinds may also be lowered at night to conserve the sun's heat in the house.

Portable Oil Heaters

Small greenhouses may be heated sufficiently to exclude frost by means of a portable oil stove, but it is too much to expect to maintain a high temperature and keep plants in a healthy growing condition with such a stove as a permanent source of heat.

Several possible dangers must be guarded against when using this type of oil heater. The use of low grade paraffin, turning the wick too high, or failing to keep the lamp scrupulously clean may cause it to smoke, giving off black oily soot with disastrous results.

The water vapour given off as a product of combustion from such stoves will saturate the atmosphere in the greenhouse during the night unless one of the ventilators in the roof is left open just the merest fraction while the lamp is burning, to allow the vapour to escape. It is important that the oil stove used is of good quality, in first-class condition, and specially designed for greenhouse use. One of these burns paraffin in a cleverly constructed lamp with a circular blue flame. It is placed under a water tank to which flow and return pipes are attached, the pipes running to a standard, which also supports a supply cistern.

Another useful pattern has the funnel of the lamp connected with the lower of two empty metal tubes, supported by hollow standards so designed that hot air passes through both pipes and standard, which combine to provide a considerable amount of radiating surface. This is of infinitely greater value for maintaining a warmed atmosphere than a hot flame ascending direct into the air. A shallow tray rests on one of the horizontal tubes, and this may, when necessary, be filled with warm water to counteract by evaporation any tendency to dry the atmosphere. Details of the heat output of such heaters are not readily available, but if the consumption of oil per hour is known, the heating capacity can be assessed. A heater which consumes $\frac{1}{4}$ pint of good grade paraffin per hour has a heat output of 3,500 BTUs per hour. One unit of electricity produces 3,412 BTUs.

Manufacturers of any of these kinds of heating apparatus will readily advise would-be buyers concerning the sizes required for safely maintaining required temperatures in houses of given dimensions. For structures which are not large enough for coal or coke

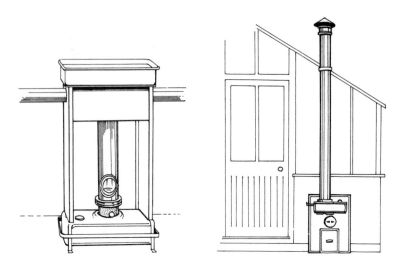

A paraffin heater   *A solid fuel boiler*

burning boilers and hot-water pipes, the foregoing types of heaters are the kinds to seek. The essentials of good management are the use of finest quality paraffin oil and scrupulous cleanliness, involving daily trimming of wicks and prompt wiping of even the smallest drop of spilled oil when refilling lamps. The latter must never be allowed to burn themselves dry, or the wicks will smoke and cause damage.

Hot-water Systems

For upwards of a hundred years, water heated by a solid fuel boiler circulating through cast-iron pipes was the only satisfactory method of heating greenhouses, but in recent years this method has become less popular. Many commercial nurseries have gone over to oil heating, and private greenhouse owners have been attracted to electrical heating because it needs the minimum of attention, and has accurate thermostatic control.

In spite of this, solid fuel is still the cheapest form of greenhouse heating, and the gardener who has a large greenhouse and can spare the time to tend a boiler would do well to consider it. It may be just as expensive or even a little more expensive to instal than electrical heating, but the running costs will be considerably less.

Several important improvements have been made in solid fuel systems for the private greenhouse during the last few years. Some boilers are now fitted with reliable thermostats which control the air inlet at the bottom of the boiler, according to the temperature of the water in the return pipe. When the temperature of the greenhouse falls, heat is given off from the pipes and the temperature of the water falls, the thermostat then opens the air inlet to the fire grate, the fire burns more quickly, and the temperature of the water is raised again.

The best of these boilers are now fitted with shaking grates, so that a few vigorous shakes of a handle will clear the fire of all rubbish and burnt material. They also have a fuel magazine which will hold sufficient fuel to last upwards of twelve hours. As it is required, the fuel trickles down by gravity from the magazine into the fire area. In those boilers of more modern design, the fire is completely surrounded by a water jacket so that every scrap of heat from the fuel is transferred to the water efficiently. These boilers are circular in shape and constructed in steel which makes them lighter and less cumbersome to instal than the cast-iron ones. With a boiler such as this there is no need for a stoke hole to house the boiler, it simply stands on the ground outside the greenhouse. The installation is relatively simple, and only a screwdriver is required to join the pipe sections together securely. In addition to the traditional 4-in. diameter, cast-iron pipes which are heavy and cumbersome, there is now also a choice of steel, or high-duty aluminium. The latter of course are much lighter and more attractive in appearance than steel or cast-iron ones.

In addition to these boilers of modern design, the well-tried traditional ones are still available. The simplest one is the saddle boiler which is suitable for the smallest installations only, and has to be completely encased in brickwork when it is installed. For larger installations the sectional boiler of the Robin Hood type, with its ingenious waterways which extract every morsel of heat from the fuel, is more suitable.

Whatever type of boiler is used, the pipe layout is the same. For mere frost exclusion, maintaining a temperature of 1–2°C (34–35°F), a pair of pipes along one side of the greenhouse will be adequate. For a cool greenhouse, where a temperature of 7°C (45°F) is the minimum, a pair of pipes along one side and across the end of the house may be adequate, but where temperatures of 13–16°C (55–60°F) are required, pipes along both sides and across the end will be necessary.

Deciding on the Size of Boiler and Length of Pipes Required:
To maintain a certain temperature within a greenhouse, the heating
system has to replace the heat lost through the fabric of the
greenhouse, that is, the glass, timber, brickwork, and, to a lesser
degree, the floor. A method of calculating this loss is given in
the section on electricity in the greenhouse, p. 30.

When this loss has been calculated in BTUs, the length of pipes
and size of boiler can be arrived at, but there is really no need
for the greenhouse owner to do this. The manufacturer of the heating apparatus will recommend a suitable installation if given the
details of the greenhouse. In the worked example on p. 30, the heat
required to raise the temperature in the greenhouse to 10°C (50°F)
against an outside temperature of −7°C (20°F) would be 13,590
BTUs per hour. The table below gives examples of the heat transmission from iron pipes in BTUs per linear ft. per hr., at a range
of temperature differences between the air in the greenhouse and
the water in the pipes. With an average water temperature of 71°C
(160°F) and an air temperature of 10°C (50°F) the difference is
61°C (110°F). The table shows that at this difference, 1 ft. of 4-in.
pipe will transmit 262 BTUs per hour.

HEAT TRANSMISSION FROM IRON PIPES IN BTUs PER LINEAR FT. PER HR.

Diam. of Pipe	Temperature difference in degrees Cent.(Fahr.) between Air and Water				
inches	27(80)	33(90)	38(100)	43(110)	47(120)
$2\frac{1}{2}$	115	135	154	174	194
3	141	165	188	212	237
$3\frac{1}{2}$	156	182	208	234	263
4	174	203	232	262	292
5	212	247	282	318	354

In the worked example, the total heat requirement is 13,590 BTUs
per hour; if we divide this total by 262 the answer will equal the
length of pipe required in feet. The greenhouse in question is 12
ft. long. Two pipes down one side and across the end would take
40 ft. of pipe which would not be sufficient. Two pipes along each
side and across the end requires 64 ft. of pipe and, although it
exceeds the necessary total by 12 ft., such an installation would
be suitable. It would give a safe working margin with adequate

reserve capacity to cope with almost any eventuality. In small, straight-forward installations the pipes form a loop. Two pipes run from the boiler into an expansion box at the far end, which acts as a supply tank and allows for the expansion of the water as the temperature rises. The top pipe, which leaves the boiler fairly high up, is the flow pipe along which the hot water flows from the boiler. In such a system the warm water flows round the pipes on the thermosyphonic principle. This is based on the fact that warm water, being less dense, rises, and cold water, which is more dense, tends to sink. To ensure this the flow pipe, along which the heated water flows, has to be arranged so that it rises steadily from the boiler to the end of the system. The return pipe along which the water flows back to the boiler to be reheated has to run downhill, the water flowing along it by gravity.

Having decided on the size of the boiler and the length and layout of the pipes, there are still one or two practical considerations concerning the actual installation. For a greenhouse running north to south, the boiler should be situated at the north end of the house. This will ensure that the shadow of the chimney will not be cast on the greenhouse. A further advantage is that the smoke and smuts from the chimney will be blown away from the greenhouse by the prevailing winds, and minimise the amount of dirt deposited on the glass. Dirty glass is a major cause of loss of valuable light to the greenhouse plants during the winter. With the boiler at the north end of the greenhouse, the water in the pipes is at its highest temperature where it is most needed at the coolest end of the greenhouse. This will help to equalise the temperature throughout the length of the greenhouse. If the greenhouse is erected running east to west, the boiler should be situated at the east end for the same obvious reasons.

Make the chimney the correct size and height for the particular boiler, and follow the manufacturer's recommendations regarding its construction very closely. The chimney is not merely a device for carrying the smoke away from the fire, it is an essential part of the boiler and the key to the efficient burning and controlling of the fire. Without a steady and sustained draught provided by a chimney of the correct height and size, the boiler cannot function properly. Always use the correct size and grade of fuel for the boiler; this may be a matter of trial and error at the outset, but once a suitable fuel has been found it should not be changed. If you live in a clean air zone, it will of course have to be smokeless fuel.

Stoking and damper setting is something which is learnt by experience, and the observant stoker will soon learn to allow for changes of wind and other variable conditions.

A flat thin fire is more efficient than one where the unburnt fuel is piled in a heap in the centre. Remember to clean out the fire at the bottom before making it up for the night, and close the fire box door properly after putting the fuel on. Set the damper carefully with due regard for the prevailing conditions. In these days of slow delivery it pays to order fresh supplies of fuel well in advance of when they are actually required. For the busy gardener who is away from home all day the boiler which offers some degree of automatic control is the most suitable, even if it costs a little more to instal.

Oil-fired Boilers

Many commercial greenhouse owners have installed oil-fired boilers, with their attendant advantages of automatic control and attention-free running. Unfortunately there is no cheap, simple, oil-fired boiler which has been designed specifically for heating the smaller size greenhouse. There is, however, a conversion unit available which enables an existing solid fuel boiler to be converted to oil burning. This is supplied with a 50-gallon fuel tank and burns domestic fuel oil of the 28-second grade.

The same manufacturer produces an oil-fired hot air heater, which is used in conjunction with perforated polythene ducting to circulate the warmed air round the greenhouse. This type of heating is valuable for plants which prefer a warm dry atmosphere, or are adversely affected by moist stagnant conditions.

Gas Heating

Although in itself coal gas is an efficient high grade fuel which will function automatically, it has not been widely adopted for greenhouse heating. This may have been because it could only be used as a fuel for traditional hot-water systems, but the conversion to natural gas has changed all this. There is now available a free-standing heater using natural gas as a fuel, which stands in the greenhouse in the same way as an oil heater, and has a flexible gas connection so that it can be moved about if required.

It is an established fact that plants make use of carbon dioxide

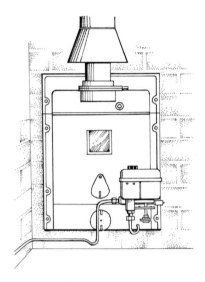

An oil-fired boiler

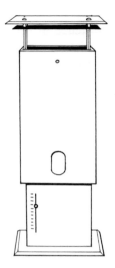

A natural gas heater

(CO_2) in their growth processes. While this heater is burning, it emits CO_2 into the atmosphere which in some circumstances could be beneficial to the plants, in addition to providing the warmth they require. This could well be an added attraction when deciding whether to instal this type of heater or not, but is not definite enough to influence the decision unduly in relation to other types of heating.

With natural gas heating, running costs will be substantially lower than with electricity, slightly cheaper than oil, but a little more expensive than solid fuel. Full details of the system including installation costs can be obtained from your local gas showroom.

ELECTRICITY IN THE GREENHOUSE

The biggest single advantage of electricity over other fuels for greenhouse heating is that, by using a thermostat, it can be made completely automatic. A thermostat is in effect a switch which maintains the correct temperature by switching the heating on and off as required, and the efficiency of the installation depends very largely upon its correct functioning. In addition to this, electrical heating has various other advantages; it is clean, there is no wearisome stoking, no ashes, and no unsightly heap of fuel, which can be a major source of irritation to a tidy gardener. There is no need to worry about ordering fuel, and the heating system will be equal to dealing with any sudden changes of weather.

Calculating the Size of Heater: The temperature at which greenhouses should be maintained will always be a controversial issue, although the fuel shortage, caused by the Second World War, taught us that many established favourites among our plants are quite happy with a minimum night temperature of 7–10°C (45–50°F). It must always be remembered that the temperature maintained, and not the size of the heater, determines the amount of electricity consumed.

The designing of a heating system is really a job for a heating engineer, but a rough guide can be given here in arriving at the approximate size of heater required. The function of a heating system is to replace the heat lost through the fabric of the house, and to determine its size it is necessary to calculate that loss. In making these calculations an outside temperature of -7°C (20°F) should be allowed for – it is a mistake to base them on 0°C (32°F). Therefore, when it is hoped to maintain a temperature of 10°C (50°F) the heating system should be capable of raising the temperature 17°C (30°F), the difference between an 'inside' temperature of 10°C (50°F) and a possible 'outside' temperature of -7°C (20°F).

This is best demonstrated by taking a worked example of a typical 12×8 ft. house, measuring 5 ft. to the eaves, 7 ft. 6 in. to the ridge, and standing on 2 ft. high brick walls. If the surface area of each material in the fabric of the greenhouse is multiplied by its particular thermal conductivity figure (1·0 for glass, 0·6 for brickwork, 0·33 for the soil forming the floor of the house), and they are added together, the resulting figure will be the heat loss per hour from the house in British Thermal Units for each half degree C (1 degree F) of difference between the inside and outside temperatures. This is the amount of heat required to maintain a $\frac{1}{2}$°C (1°F) lift within the house, but we have agreed that a 17°C (30°F) lift will be necessary, and so this figure multiplied by 17(30) will give us our total heat requirement.

Area of glass roof   = 5 × 12 ft. × 2 = 120 sq. ft.
Area of glass in sides = 3 × 12 ft. × 2 = 72 sq. ft.
Area of glass in ends = $4\frac{1}{4}$ × 8 ft. × 2 = 68 sq. ft.

Total area of glass   = 260 sq. ft.

Area of brickwork in sides = 2×12 ft. $\times 2 = 48$ sq. ft.
Area of brickwork in ends = 2×8 ft. $\times 2 = 32$ sq. ft.

Total area of brickwork $= 80$ sq. ft.

Area of floor (soil) = 12×8 ft. = 96 sq. ft.

Heat loss through glass $= 260 \times 1 = 260$ BTU/Hr./°F
Heat loss through brickwork $= 80 \times 0.6 = 48$ BTU/Hr./°F
Heat loss through soil $= 96 \times 0.33 = 32$ BTU/Hr./°F
Heat loss $= 340$ BTU/Hr./°F

Add one-third for fortuitous losses through air changes, etc. = 113 BTU/ Hr./°F

Total heat loss $= 453$ BTU/Hr./°F

Heat required for 1°F lift $= 453$ BTU/Hr./°F
Heat required for 30°F lift $= 453 \times 30 = 13,590$ BTU/Hr./°F

Electrical loading in watts $\dfrac{13,590}{3 \cdot 412} = 3,983$ watts (1 kilowatt = 1,000 watts)

A convenient size of heater would be 4 kilowatts.

N.B. In the above calculations it should be noted that, for purposes of conversion to centigrade, 1°F is approximately equal to $\frac{1}{2}$°C.

Types of Heaters

Having determined the size or electrical loading of the heater, we must now review the types available to enable us to choose one suitable for our particular requirements. It should be understood from the beginning that the output of a heater is determined by its electrical loading; any two heaters of the same loading will give out the same amount of heat, while consuming identical amounts of electricity, but with some types a slightly better distribution of that heat may be obtained.

Tubular Heaters: These are the most widely used, and there are adequate grounds for their popularity. They consist of a $2\frac{1}{2}$-in. diameter tube with a heating element running through the centre. Available in lengths from 2 to 17 ft., they make a sound, robust job when properly installed. There is a special horticultural type made of aluminium to resist corrosion, with waterproof ends, which is of paramount importance under greenhouse conditions. Operating at mains voltage, the loading is 60 watts per foot run. The best, and usually most convenient, place for mounting them is low down

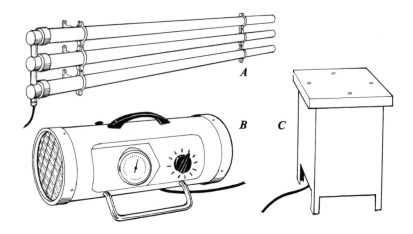

Three different forms of electrical heating. **A** *Tubular heater* **B** *Fan heater* **C** *Convector heater*

on the side walls in the traditional place for hot-water pipes. When the tubes are fitted beneath a staging, it should stand at least 3 in. away from the wall, to allow the warm air from the heaters to flow upwards between the staging and the side of the greenhouse.

Convector Heaters: Recently introduced, these are rapidly gaining popularity; they consist of a metal cabinet containing a heating element which is so arranged that air enters at the bottom, passes over the heaters to be warmed before being discharged at the top. They have the advantages of being both robust and portable, and reasonably cheap in first cost, but only those designed for the greenhouse must be used – the domestic types are not suitable for greenhouse conditions. Sizes range from 500 to 3,000 watts; the heat distribution is not quite so good as with tubular heaters, and they are inclined to get in the way in very small greenhouses.

Immersion Heaters: Existing hot-water systems can be converted to electric heating by fitting an immersion heater into the existing pipe-line. This can be done to replace a worn-out boiler where the pipes are still good, or it can be used as an auxiliary to the boiler to boost the heating on cold nights and give automatic frost protection should the fire go out. When it replaces the boiler, this is disconnected and the flow and return pipes are joined together by a small tank. The heater is fitted into the tank or direct into the return pipe – special conversion units are available in various sizes. There are also portable heaters of this type, consisting of two circular tanks connected by pipes, through which the water circulates; the water is heated by an immersion heater in one of the tanks – such a heater should stand in the centre of the house to allow free circulation of air and ensure an even distribution of heat.

Fan Heaters: These have become very popular indeed, as a quick and easy method of installing heating in a greenhouse where a supply of electricity is available. Air is blown over the heating element by a small fan; most of them have a built-in thermostat, which gives fairly accurate control of the heat, and by circulating the air the fan ensures that the heat is well distributed throughout the greenhouse. These heaters are available in a range of sizes but remember, it will be better to err on the generous side when choosing one for your greenhouse. This gives some reserve capacity for extremes of weather and will not cost any more to run if the thermostat works efficiently. With most models the fan can be used to circulate the air in the greenhouse in summer, and so produce cooler conditions.

Soil Steriliser-cum-Greenhouse Heater: A novel type of portable heater is a $1\frac{1}{2}$-k.w. soil steriliser of one bushel capacity, which can be used for heating a small greenhouse when not in use for soil sterilising.

Whatever type of heater is chosen, if it is properly installed by a competent electrician, and a reliable rod-type thermostat, with a waterproof head, is fitted, efficient temperature control will be obtained. The best position for the thermostat is one-third of the way along the house, mounted on a bracket fitted to the roof bars, about 1 ft. from the glass and one-third of the way down the roof from the ridge. It must be remembered that the temperature at which the thermostat is set has a profound influence on the amount of electricity consumed and, in view of this, unnecessarily high temperatures must be avoided; even $2\frac{1}{2}$°C (5°F) more than is necessary can almost double the bill. The installation should be large enough for the gardener to have complete faith in it without being tempted to put up the thermostat. The consumption of electricity does not depend upon the size of the heater installed, but on the area of glass and the temperature maintained.

Soil Warming in the Greenhouse

In addition to controlling the space temperature of the greenhouse, electricity can be used most effectively to control the soil temperature, which is of course the root temperature, both in the border and on the benches. This has come to be known as soil warming. Two types of equipment are available: the low voltage system which consists of a galvanised iron wire warming element, fed from a transformer at a low voltage, usually between 6 and 12 volts; and the mains voltage cable, a heavily insulated cable energised at between 230 and 250 volts.

Soil-warmed Borders: The low voltage system is usually used for soil warming the greenhouse borders, where a mains voltage cable may get damaged when cultivations are carried out. The galvanised wire, which is supplied in the correct length at the proper gauge, is laid in at about 9 in. deep, and is zigzagged over the area to give an even distribution of heat. The electrical loading is from 5 to 8 watts per sq. ft., which means that a 100-watt transformer would be capable of warming 20 sq. ft. of border. The soil provides fairly efficient thermal storage, so that it is usually sufficient to have the current switched on for only twelve hours out of each twenty-four. This system is invaluable for raising the soil temperature during the early months of the year for growing tomatoes, which, for healthy growth, require a soil temperature of $14\frac{1}{2}$–16°C (57–60°F).

Soil-warmed Benches: Mains voltage cables are more suitable for use on benches where there is no likelihood of their being damaged by digging, or other cultural operations. For providing warmth for plant propagation exactly where it is needed, in precise amounts, electricity has no serious competitors. A soil-warmed bench is constructed by placing a 2-in. layer of sand on the bench: the cable is laid on this, and covered by a further 2 in. of sand – the electrical loading is usually 5 watts per sq. ft. It can be thermostatically controlled to a required temperature, or hand switched as required. The cable warms up to 43°C (110°F), the heat is transferred to the surrounding sand, and from the sand to the soil in the pots and boxes standing on it. Such a bench can be used in a cold house or in a heated one; under any circumstances it provides a valuable source of local heat that can be utilised for raising seedlings or striking cuttings of a very wide range of plants.

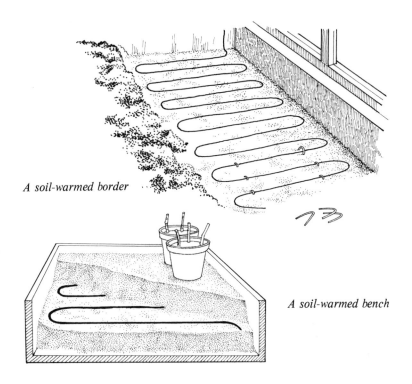

A soil-warmed border

A soil-warmed bench

Propagating Cases: To carry this development a step further, a propagating case can be built on the heated bench to conserve the heat given off by the cable, which will provide a sufficiently high temperature for normal propagation, while the main part of the house is being kept at a modest 7–10°C (45–50°F). The idea can be developed still further by fitting a soil-warming cable round the inside of the propagator to provide thermostatically controlled air warming. This is, in effect, a heated greenhouse within the greenhouse, which provides warmer conditions for the plants and seedlings that require them without having to raise the temperature of the whole house, thus a considerable saving of fuel is effected. No greenhouse installation is complete without such a propagator in which to raise seedlings and propagate plants from leaf and stem cuttings.

Intelligently used, electricity is a willing and efficient servant, but it can be wasteful and expensive if improperly used.

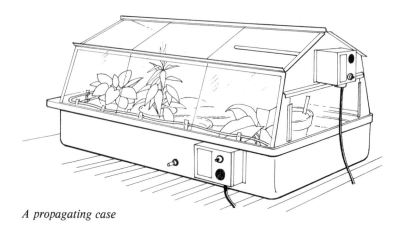

A propagating case

ARTIFICIAL LIGHT

In recent years rapid strides have been made in the use of artificial lighting in the greenhouse. Much of this progress was made possible by the introduction and development of new types of electric lamps, such as the high-pressure mercury vapour lamp and the fluorescent tube. Intensive research is still in progress to try and make further improvements.

Photosynthesis is the process whereby green plants are able to manufacture carbohydrates from carbon dioxide and water, using light as a source of energy. In the normal way, this light is provided by the sun, but from November to April in the British Isles the natural light is inadequate for maintaining plant growth, and the practice of supplementing it by artificial light is spreading rapidly. For this purpose high intensity light is required, such as that produced by the 400-watt high-pressure mercury vapour lamp, or a small bank of fluorescent tubes. The mercury lamp, mounted 3 ft. above the staging, will illuminate satisfactorily an area of $3\frac{1}{2} \times 4$ ft. – its main function will be the raising of seedlings and young plants during the winter months. The light can be switched on during the day to supplement the natural light and left on after dark to extend the day length. Alternatively, it can be switched on half an hour before sunset to extend the day by several hours, although care must be taken not to exceed 16 hours, as some subjects – e.g. tomato plants – object to this and suffer as a result. A wide range of plants have been raised successfully in this manner, but there is still much to be learnt, which only trial and error can teach.

The same technique is employed when using fluorescent tubes; 5 ft. × 80 watt, warm white reflectorised tubes are quite satisfactory, mounted at 2 ft. above the bench. One, two, three or more tubes can be used according to circumstances. A single tube will satisfactorily illuminate an area $4\frac{1}{2} \times 1$ ft; three tubes mounted on a light bracket at 8 in. apart will illuminate a bench area of $4\frac{1}{2} \times 3$ ft. Normal, or slightly reduced, greenhouse temperatures are maintained, and the plants and seedlings are pricked out and potted in the normal way.

Raising Plants Entirely by Artificial Light

By using the same lamps and employing similar techniques, plants and seedlings can be grown in a solid building such as a shed, cellar or outhouse. The same temperatures must be maintained but a very substantial saving in fuel can be effected because such a building can be thermally insulated, reducing the heat losses to a minimum. Tomatoes, cucumbers and most of the popular half-hardy bedding plants have been raised in this manner. Such plants as African violets (*Saintpaulia ionantha*) and gloxinias (*Sinningia speciosa*) can be grown throughout their lives in artificial light, and there must be many others which only need trying out.

Photo-periodism

Development of plants and formation of flowers are greatly influenced by the comparative length of day and night, the phenomenon being known as photo-periodism. This can be exploited to advantage by using artificial light to regulate the day length. Delaying the flowering of chrysanthemums by lengthening the day in August and September is the classic example. Strawberries can be persuaded to fruit a little earlier and fibrous-rooted begonias to produce cuttings earlier, but to obtain full details on the subject specialist books should be consulted.

Forcing Bulbs

The forcing of bulbs by artificial light in sheds and outhouses is now an established practice; at normal forcing temperatures tulips, narcissi and hyacinths respond quite successfully. A 100-watt tungsten filament lamp, mounted 3 ft. above the bench, will illuminate 1 sq. yd. The bulbs are boxed or potted and plunged in the normal way, being taken in for forcing at the usual stage.

CHAPTER FOUR

Routine Management of a Greenhouse

The newcomer to greenhouse management will soon gain experience and begin to appreciate the requirements of his plants if he carefully observes the conditions under which they thrive.

He will quickly realise that it is necessary to pay careful attention to watering, feeding, ventilation and pest and disease control, and that plants require clean, hygienic conditions. Hygiene is as important to plant life as it is to all other forms of life. Dust-begrimed foliage, slimy pots, walls and staging, and heaps of discarded vegetation will all invite disease and cause the loss of plants.

Arrangement

The way the interior of the greenhouse is arranged will depend on the use the owner wishes to make of it. In most cases flowering and foliage plants will be displayed on the staging on one or both sides of the greenhouse. By arranging the plants in a natural way so that they both complement and contrast with each other, an attractive display can be maintained for most of the year. Ferns and other foliage plants will act as a foil and provide a background for the flowering plants. If a plant is not tall enough for its beauty to be seen to full advantage, it can be stood on an upturned flower pot to give it extra height. The front of the staging can be clothed with trailing plants such as tradescantias, *Campanula isophylla*, *Fuchsia procumbens* and some of the more attractive ivies. Provided there is sufficient head room, one or two hanging baskets containing trailing plants such as columneas, or pendant varieties of begonia or fuchsia, add a pleasing touch in spring and summer.

Plants such as lilies, hippeastrums, tuberous begonias, freesias and achimenes which are in the resting stage can be stored underneath the staging with their pots laid on their sides so that water dripping from above falls only on to the pots.

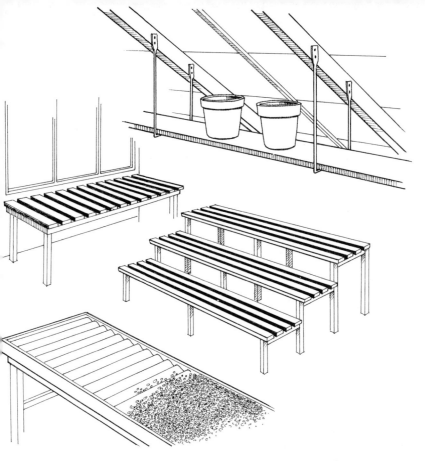

A selection of the different forms of greenhouse staging. A shelf can be suspended from the greenhouse roof for seedlings and young plants. Pot plants can be well displayed on staging and some kinds can be unbolted and removed when the greenhouse bed is needed for cultivation. Open staging does allow dry air to circulate around the plants whereas those subjects standing on a layer of gravel will have a better growing atmosphere. A level area 2 ft. above the ground is convenient for most purposes but tiered staging will give an excellent show especially in a larger house

In a span-roof house a shelf suspended a foot or so from the glass along the centre of the house will prove invaluable for holding seedlings and young plants which require a situation close to the glass to keep them sturdy.

In a lean-to a shelf can be conveniently placed on the back wall. Climbing plants can be trained to the roof but their growth should be regulated, so that they do not overshadow the plants beneath them. Quite a lot can be done to improve the appearance of the interior of a greenhouse. In some situations a large mirror at one end can create a feeling of spaciousness and improve the display by appearing to double its size, but it must be remembered that too much elaboration can cause problems. Facing the benches with cork bark and forming artificial grottoes will provide nooks and crannies which can harbour slugs and all manner of insect pests.

In larger greenhouses, from 20 ft. long and 15 ft. wide or more, pieces of stone of one of the types used for rock gardens can be arranged to support soil and form beds on the floor in which plants can be grouped in a natural way to produce a very pleasing permanent effect. Large specimens of cactus and other succulent plants appear at their best when planted in a miniature desert landscape arranged on the greenhouse floor. If such specimens are required for exhibition, the pots or pans in which they are growing can simply be immersed in the bed of sand.

Overcrowding

One of the commonest mistakes made by the novice is to overcrowd the greenhouse with a collection of plants which differ in their cultural requirements. Some may demand a low, some a high temperature; others a dry or a moist atmosphere. It is impossible to grow successfully in the same house plants needing such a wide range of conditions, nor is it wise to crowd too many plants together. Unless each plant receives its proper share of light and air the inevitable result will be weak growth. In small houses it is better to concentrate on one or two classes of plant only, for example cacti and succulents, or ferns and foliage plants, or roses, or pelargoniums and fuchsias. An attempt to grow, for instance, a Maréchal Niel rose, a grape vine, pelargoniums, fuchsias, lilies, petunias, ferns and orchids together in a 9 by 6 ft. house is doomed to failure.

Cleanliness

Next to overcrowding, cleanliness is the most important point to watch in greenhouse management. On no account must the plants be allowed to become infested with insects, which suck the sap and spread infection, or the foliage coated with dirt, which seals the breathing organs or stomata.

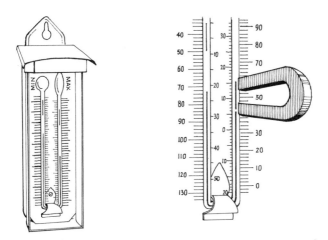

A maximum and minimum thermometer is an indispensable item of greenhouse equipment. A magnet is generally used to reset the thermometer although more expensive models have a push button readjustment

All evergreen plants should be sponged periodically with soft water or a liquid insecticide. Pots, too, should be washed frequently, lichen and slime prevented from forming on the outside, and the surface of the soil in the pots should be kept clear of moss. Dead leaves and flowers should be removed daily and in fact no decaying vegetation or other debris likely to harbour insect pests or act as a seat of infection for fungus diseases should be allowed to remain in the greenhouse. The gravel or ashes on the staging should be thoroughly washed at least once a year, woodwork and glass should also be scrubbed annually with hot water, and any wall area freshly whitewashed. The cleaner and sweeter the atmosphere, the healthier the plants will be.

Temperatures

The temperature suitable for each genus of plant is given in the later chapters of this book. Generally speaking, a cool greenhouse should be artificially heated to a temperature of 4°C (40°F) by night and 10°C (50°F) by day between October and March, with an increase of 3°C (5°F) during April and May. In summer no artificial heat will be required. A warm greenhouse should be artificially heated to 7°C (45°F) by night and 13°C (55°F) by day during the

41

winter, and 10–13°C (50–55°F) by night and 16–18°C (60–65°F) by day in spring and summer. These temperatures should never be allowed to fall below the minimum nor to exceed the maximum, and for success to be assured the plants grown should be limited to those requiring similar atmospheric conditions.

A stove house is recommended for a few of the plants mentioned in the A–Z list. The conditions in such a greenhouse should be warm and humid with a minimum winter temperature of 18°C (65°F) rising to 18–21°C (65–70°F) in spring and autumn and 21–27°C (70–80°F) in summer.

Watering

Watering is by far the most important single operation in the care of greenhouse plants. During warm spells in summer, plants growing in pots need almost constant attention to make sure they do not suffer lack of moisture, but during the winter months it is far easier to damage them by overwatering than it is by underwatering, or keeping them on the dry side, as it is termed. Experience and keen observation of the plants' needs are the best ways of learning the art of watering. Plants should never be given frequent dribbles of water. They should be watered thoroughly at any one time so that the soil in the pot is moistened throughout and then left until that water has been used up before any more is applied. A guide to the need for water is the appearance of the soil surface, which will look and indeed have become dry.

A tensiometer or soil moisture meter is a quick and easy gadget for indicating whether soil is dry, moist or wet. When the pointed probe is inserted into the soil a needle gives a calibrated reading

October to March is a critical period when water must be applied very carefully indeed, each plant receiving sufficient for its needs and no more. Where possible during this period watering should be done in the morning when the temperature of the greenhouse is beginning to rise.

From April to September watering can be much more liberal. Water during the morning as in the winter, but the plants should be examined again in the afternoon and a further supply given to any that may require it.

A good quality Haw's Patent watering can, with both oval and round roses, is the best kind for successful watering under glass. The fine, oval rose is used for watering seedlings and young plants overhead, and the slightly coarser round one for watering newly potted and established plants. Watering is made so much easier if there is a supply of water in the greenhouse either from a tap connected to the mains supply or in a tank under the staging.

Automatic Watering: During the summer watering under glass can be a time-consuming chore, and research workers have been trying for years to perfect a method of watering plants automatically. A few years ago a system of capillary watering or sub-irrigation was introduced, providing a simple but reliable means of supplying pot plants with water automatically. The greenhouse bench or staging is covered with a layer of sand which is kept evenly moist through a tank or a small cistern connected to the mains supply. The pots are placed on this moist sand and all the water required is drawn up by means of capillary attraction. The system works with plastic pots and with seedboxes, though because of their thicker bases clay pots require the aid of a wick. It is possible to buy proprietary systems complete or, with a little ingenuity, it is a simple matter for the enthusiast to instal his own.

Trickle Irrigation: This is a semi-automatic system connected to the mains water which is useful for tomatoes grown either in the soil, by the ring culture method, or in containers; it can also be used for chrysanthemums and cucumbers. The equipment consists of plastic or rubber tubing, with nozzles at regular intervals, through which the water passes, dispensing a slowly produced trickle at the base of each plant. The main tube is connected directly to the water tap which is turned on for a set time each day or whenever the plants require water.

Automatic watering by capillary action

Feeding

Both the John Innes and the various proprietary peat-based seed
and potting composts (discussed later in this chapter) contain
sufficient plant food to supply the plants with their nutritive needs
for some time. However, after a while extra feeding will be required.
Notes for guidance on feeding particular genera are given in later
chapters of this book. Both dry and liquid feeds are available
and the manufacturers' instructions should be followed as to the
amount to be applied and the way this is done. Among the
dry feeds which can be bought are those which are dissolved
in water and those which are given as a powder and watered
in. Seaweed extract is also available.

Home-made liquid feed can be obtained by suspending a bag
of well-rotted manure in a bucket of water and diluting the resulting
solution to a weak straw colour. Feed should never be applied
to a dry soil and it is better to give too little rather than too
much.

Syringing and Damping Down: The syringe and the watering can
are invaluable aids to good greenhouse management, but they can
also cause all sorts of troubles if used indiscriminately. The amount
of syringing and damping down carried out in the greenhouse should
always be related to the prevailing conditions. During warm weather

44

Trickle irrigation

in the summer it may be necessary to syringe or damp down two or three times a day, but in the winter when the atmosphere is already too moist for some plants it may not be necessary at all. When the weather is warm and sunny syringing and damping down walls, floors and staging provides humidity and creates a congenial buoyant atmosphere within the greenhouse, at the same time helping to keep the temperature within bounds, and reducing the transpiration of water from the plants. Such pests as thrips and red spider mite are kept under control, and dormant buds are softened, encouraging them to burst into growth. In the case of fruits such as peaches and tomatoes under glass, pollination is assisted, and with some plants the young, newly emerged leaves are helped to withstand high temperatures.

Syringing is usually carried out during the morning and again if necessary in the afternoon or early evening provided there is sufficient time for the drops of water to dry out before nightfall. Plants in flower must not be syringed or sprayed overhead; the spray could stain or damage the petals, and may lead to an outbreak of botrytis, causing the flowers to damp off.

Spray should not be allowed to fall on hairy-leaved plants such as gloxinias or saintpaulias, nor on the more delicate ferns. The necessary humidity can always be created by damping down floors and walls without actually spraying the plants.

45

Shading

Greenhouses which are sited so that they are in the full glare of the sun must have shade of some kind, otherwise the plants inside will be scorched and badly damaged during the summer. The glass can be painted with a proprietary or home-prepared shading material, or shade in the form of roller blinds made of wooden laths, green PVC sheeting, or plastic coated wire-netting can be used, or scrim (thin muslin) can be attached temporarily to the undersides of the glazing bars in the summer. The roller blinds are the most satisfactory since they can be rolled up out of the way when the weather is dull. Shading paint can be made by mixing whitening with cold water to form a paste, to which sufficient size and hot water are added to give the consistency of paint. This can be tinted green if required; it should be applied while still warm. Alternatively a thin wash of screened whitening and flour can be made, and sprayed or painted on to the glass. These shadings will of course have to be washed off in autumn.

Automatic roller blinds are now available. A thermostat or photoelectric cell activates an electric current which causes the blinds, made of wooden laths, to roll and unroll automatically.

Ventilation

With the exception of unrooted cuttings – most of which root more readily in a close, still atmosphere – it is essential that fresh air can circulate freely if plants are to be really healthy and strong. Greenhouse ventilation is extremely important, and to be adequate every greenhouse should be ventilated on every side, some ventilators being placed close to the top of the roof, and some in the side walls under the staging. This ensures that one always has the choice of opening those on the leeward side on windy days, thus avoiding the cold cutting draughts which are so harmful; it is bad management to open either top or side ventilators in the face of a strong wind.

Box ventilators in the walls of the house under the staging allow the fresh air to come into contact with hot-water pipes, or other heating, and become slightly warmed before it reaches the plants.

The top ventilators allow overheated air and excess water vapour to escape, so that condensation does not occur in the lower night temperatures. It is usually advisable to leave at least one of these ventilators open an inch or so day and night practically the whole year round, except during hard frost, heavy rain, or thick fog.

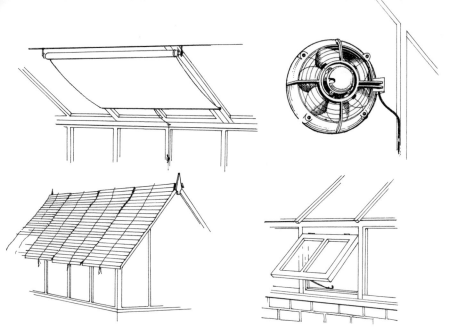

Correct shading and ventilation are very important parts of good greenhouse management

If plants of soft growth or a rather tender nature are being grown, it is wise to stretch thin muslin over the ventilator openings so as to break the force of possible gusts of wind.

Where a supply of electricity is available, one can ventilate the greenhouse automatically, by means of a thermostatically controlled extractor fan. As the temperature rises the thermostat switches the fan on, and as it falls it switches it off again. During the summer the thermostat is set at about 10°C (50°F), and in the winter 5°C (10°F) higher than the heating thermostat.

If electricity is not available, there is a special gadget for opening ventilators automatically, which consists of a cylinder filled with mineral oil. As the temperature rises, the oil expands and forces back a piston which opens the ventilator, and as the temperature falls, the reverse occurs − the oil contracts, the piston moves in the opposite direction, and the ventilator closes.

Fumigation

In recent years many new substances for controlling insect pests and fungus diseases of plants have been introduced, and it is now much easier for the gardener to keep plants clean than it used to be. In the greenhouse fumigation offers a convenient way of apply-ing these materials, provided the greenhouse is a free-standing one and not attached to a dwelling house. Many of the modern insecti-cides such as BHC (benzene-hexachloride), malathion and azoben-zene are available in the form of smoke cones or as aerosols. The well-known fungicide dinocap, for controlling powdery mildew, is also available in smoke cones for use under glass. This is a quick, simple way of treating a greenhouse full of plants and much less laborious than spraying. There is no longer any need to use noxious sub-stances such as calcium cyanide, or tetrachlorethane. For those who prefer to use nicotine to control greenfly, it is still obtainable as nicotine shreds, which are simply placed on the floor in small heaps and lit.

These substances and the specific troubles they control are dealt with more fully in Chapter 6, but there are one or two general principles of fumigation which could be usefully discussed here. Whether using smokes or aerosol canisters, in which the insecticide vapour is released by pressing a button, the manufacturer's instruc-tions must be rigidly adhered to at all times.

Obviously the greenhouse must be as air tight as possible for successful fumigation, and all doors and windows must be tightly shut. Any broken panes of glass can be covered with wet brown paper on the outside, and any gaps or openings filled with rags or paper. Newly germinated seedlings and the tender young leaves of some plants are susceptible to damage during fumigation, and should be removed from the greenhouse before the operation, or placed on the floor where the concentration of vapour is never quite as dense as it is near the roof. Before fumigation, the soil in the pots should be on the dry side, and the plants themselves should be quite dry. Where necessary the greenhouse ventilators should be opened for a few hours before fumigation to ensure that the foliage is reasonably dry. Evening is the best time to carry out fumigation, so that when the smoke cones are lit, the house can be closed up and left closed until the following morning.

Before actually lighting the smoke cones take a final look round to make sure that nothing has been left in the greenhouse, and that there are no dogs or cats asleep under the bench. Place the required number of cones along the centre path, light the one farthest from the door first, and work backwards towards the door, finally closing the door and locking it if possible. Failing this, place some obstruc-

A summer display of streptocarpus, gloxinias and coleus with fuchsias,
Begonia rex *and ivies.* Hoya carnosa *is trained along the roof*

tion across the doorway and pin a notice on the door stating that fumigation is in progress.

To arrive at the correct number of smoke cones required, the cubic capacity of the greenhouse must be known. This is easily calculated for an even span or simple lean-to greenhouse, since multiplying the length in feet by the width in feet and then multiplying the result by the average height will give the capacity in cubic feet. For an uneven or three-quarter span greenhouse, treat it as two lean-to greenhouses standing back to back, that is, calculate the capacity of the two parts separately, and then add them together. All smokes are plainly marked with the number of cubic feet for which they are sufficient.

Up to now we have been discussing fumigation to destroy pests and fungus diseases on plants in the greenhouse. There is, however, another type of fumigation, in which sulphur candles are used, for ridding the greenhouse itself of pest and disease organisms, when the plants have been removed and it is empty. All plants must be removed or the sulphur fumes will destroy them. This type of fumigation is usually carried out when the greenhouse is being scrubbed out and receiving its annual clean. A convenient time is in the autumn when the summer plants are over and before the autumn and winter ones are brought in. One pound of sulphur is sufficient for a greenhouse of 1,000 cu. ft. capacity. It should be noted that sulphur fumes can be a serious irritant, and special care must be taken to see that no one enters the greenhouse while fumigation with this material is in progress. Light the sulphur candles in the late afternoon or early evening, and leave the greenhouse tightly closed all night. Open the doors and windows the following morning, and allow several hours for the fumes to disperse before engaging in any work in the greenhouse. On no account should sulphur be used in a greenhouse which is attached to a dwelling house or other building.

Composts

A very important part in the routine work of greenhouse management is potting on young plants and repotting older ones that have outgrown their containers or have exhausted the nutrients in the soil. Beginners think that gardeners make themselves unnecessary work by potting young plants first into tiny pots and then shifting them on by small stages, instead of transferring them at once to

Top left: Agapanthus orientalis *Top right:* Agapetes macrantha
Bottom left: Ananus comosus variegatus *Bottom right: Indian azalea*

larger pots in which they may remain. However, a small plant put into a larger pot will not thrive since it cannot use all the moisture available in the compost. Consequently the roots die back, due to excess water which takes the space that might otherwise be occupied by oxygen, so necessary to root growth.

Another common mistake is to suppose that every kind of plant must be put into a larger pot at least once during the course of the year. As a matter of fact, there are some plants of slow growth which require repotting only once in three or more years, and many things grow better when their roots are restricted than when they have spare room round them.

A useful adjunct to the greenhouse is a potting shed, or a place where potting can be carried out. For the larger greenhouse it should also provide storage space for pots of all sizes, sieves, rammers, stakes for plant supports and possibly compost ingredients. For the smaller one it may just be a space on the corner of the greenhouse bench, where bought compost will be used, but provision must be made for it from the outset.

Ordinary garden soil is quite unsuitable for growing plants in pots or raising seedlings in boxes. It is not sufficiently open in texture, is usually deficient in organic matter and is likely to have faulty drainage. In addition to providing anchorage for the roots, a good compost must be open and free draining, yet reasonably retentive of moisture. It must be well aerated to provide air for the developing roots, contain a balanced supply of plant nutrients, and be free from harmful organisms which may attack and damage the plant roots. Experienced gardeners have always gone to a good deal of trouble to provide such mixtures for growing their pot plants and raising seedlings. Unfortunately in the past most of them had their own special mixtures for each particular type of plant, and in some cases the formulae were very jealously guarded secrets. This practice of using a multiplicity of mixtures led to a good deal of unnecessary complexity, and waste of time and energy.

Since the introduction of the John Innes composts which satisfy all the requirements mentioned above, the position has changed completely, and we now have these standard mixtures which have proved suitable for a very wide range of plants indeed. Much of the old complexity has as a result been swept away. Unfortunately, good fibrous loam which is the basic constituent of the John Innes mixtures is now quite difficult to obtain, and the practice of buying composts ready mixed has become firmly established. For those greenhouse owners who operate only on a small scale this is more convenient and has much to recommend it. The John Innes mixtures are readily available from nurserymen, seedsmen, garden centres and large stores, but the samples vary enormously in quality. Only when a good sample of loam is used as the basic ingredient can a good John Innes mixture be produced. It pays therefore to look for a supply which contains good fibrous loam if possible. This is easily determined by handling and examining a sample of the compost before placing an order or making a purchase.

Because of the difficulties experienced in obtaining good loam, and the wide variations in the samples which were available, investigations were started at the University of California to find a medium for growing pot plants which did not contain loam. As a result of this the U.C. mixtures or loamless composts were formulated. These consist mostly of peat which, although it does vary, is not as variable as loam and is more easily standardised. Furthermore, it does not require sterilising before being used as does loam. Loamless composts, which are now very widely used, are mixtures of peat and sand, with fertilisers and lime added to bring them up to the various grades required.

The John Innes Seed and Potting Composts, Ingredients: As previously remarked the quality of the ingredients determines the quality of the mixture as a whole. Loam for use in composts should be the best quality available, cut from the top spit of a meadow or pasture. The turves, face downwards, are built into a stack 4 ft. high and left to mature for several months, so that the turf can rot down completely, before being used. The ideal loam should be just on the heavy side of medium in texture and should contain a high proportion of root fibre. Small quantities are cut from the vertical face of the stack as the loam is required for use. To make John Innes composts strictly in accordance with the recommendations, the loam must be sterilised before being used (see p. 53).

Leafmould was formerly used almost exclusively for providing the humus in composts, but it was found to have several disadvantages. In some cases it was responsible for introducing disease into the compost, and as a result has been largely superseded by peat. Baled moss or sedge peat of the granulated type, and not the black, greasy, rhododendron peat should be used.

A proportion of sand gives the correct physical condition to the compost and improves the drainage. The sand used should be coarse and sharp; the soft, fine sands used by builders are quite unsuitable.

A good compost must contain a balanced supply of plant nutrients. This is provided for in the John Innes compost by a specially mixed fertiliser, called J.I. base fertiliser.

John Innes Seed Compost: The seed compost is used for seed sowing and pricking off the less vigorous seedlings.

It consists of: 2 parts by loose bulk medium loam
    1 part by loose bulk granulated peat
    1 part by loose bulk coarse sand

To each bushel of the above mixture add:
    $1\frac{1}{2}$ oz. superphosphate of lime (18 per cent. $P_2 O_5$)
    $\frac{3}{4}$ oz. ground chalk

Pass the loam, and the peat if it needs it, through a $\frac{3}{8}$-in. sieve. Where possible the loam should be sterilised before being used.

John Innes Potting Compost: The potting compost is used for potting into 3-in. pots and upwards, to the largest pots used. The strength is varied for larger pots and more vigorous plants by increasing the amount of fertiliser in the mixture.

The proportions are: 7 parts by loose bulk medium loam
    3 parts by loose bulk granulated peat
    2 parts by loose bulk coarse sand or grit

To each bushel of the mixture add:
    $\frac{3}{4}$ oz. ground chalk
    4 oz. John Innes base fertiliser

This is known as John Innes Potting Compost No. 1.

To make John Innes Potting Compost No. 2, for the larger pots and stronger growing plants, add:

$1\frac{1}{2}$ oz. ground chalk
8 oz. John Innes base fertiliser $\Big\}$ per bushel

For the John Innes No. 3 potting compost, which is used in large pots such as the final pots for chrysanthemums and in the rings when tomatoes are being grown by ring culture, add:

$2\frac{1}{4}$ oz. ground chalk
12 oz. John Innes base fertiliser $\Big\}$ per bushel

John Innes Base Fertiliser: This can be bought at any garden shop, but can be made by mixing:

> 2 parts by weight hoof and horn (13 per cent. N)
> 2 parts by weight superphosphate of lime (18 per cent. $P_2 O_5$)
> 1 part by weight sulphate of potash (48 per cent. K)

Sterilisation

Recently it has become standard practice for both professional horticulturists and private gardeners to sterilise all soils or composts for propagation and potting of plants. The reason is that bacteria, fungus spores, insect pests and weed seeds which would be harmful to plants are thereby destroyed. However, the soil itself is not improved by sterilisation, and unless it is very carefully done, there may be a serious deterioration in soil fertility, due to excess sterilising; inadequate treatment, on the other hand, will be a waste of time and money, and will leave the plants' enemies untouched.

Various methods of sterilising are practised, such as saturation with solutions of chemicals, e.g. cresylic acid or formaldehyde, scalding with boiling water, or heating by steam, by baking or by electricity. It should be remembered that there are drawbacks as well as advantages to each method, for instance cresylic acid and formaldehyde both impregnate the soil with fumes which are poisonous to plants as well as their enemies, and treated soil should not be used for potting or propagation until all trace of odour has vanished, or until four to six weeks have elapsed, whichever is the sooner. Moreover, both are rather unpleasant to use, and need careful handling and the use of protective clothing.

Heat sterilisation kills beneficial, as well as harmful, bacteria in the soil, and upsets its fertility, consequently it is necessary to add certain plant foods in suitable amounts to offset this temporary loss. Private gardeners who require only a few bushels at a time are better advised therefore to obtain composts ready made according to the John Innes formulae.

For sterilising by saturation, use formalin, containing 40 per cent. pure formaldehyde, at the rate of 1 part in 50, i.e. 1 pint of formalin mixed with 49 pints of water. Spread the soil on a smooth, hard floor, and apply the solution through a rosed can. Immediately shovel the soil into a conical heap and cover completely with sacking or polythene sheeting to keep the fumes in contact with the soil and prevent them escaping. After 48 hours remove the covering and spread out the soil. Turn frequently until all smell of formalin disappears.

Cresylic acid is used in the same way; it should be of 97 per cent. purity, and is used at the rate of 1 in 40 parts.

For sterilising by heat the greenhouse owner who would like to do this himself will find one of the small electric sterilisers that are available more than adequate for his needs. There are several sizes, and one of them can also be used as a standby greenhouse heater.

Alternatively, a very small quantity of soil can be sterilised by the following method, as suggested by Lawrence and Newell, the originators of the John Innes compost formulae. Into a 6-pt. saucepan place exactly $\frac{1}{2}$ pt. of water, and bring to the boil. As soon as this occurs, fill the saucepan to within $\frac{1}{2}$ in. of the top with dust-dry soil; then put on the lid and boil for exactly 7 min. Take off the heat and stand for a further 7 min., then remove the lid and spread the soil out thinly on a clean surface to cool. Afterwards, use immediately or store in a clean container, in which it does not dry out.

Pots

Clay Pots: For nearly a hundred years flower pots were made exclusively of clay, and although they are still very widely used they are gradually being replaced by pots made from other materials, chiefly plastics. Traditionally clay pots were sold in numbered sizes which indicated the number of pots of a particular size that could be made from a certain quantity of clay. The table which follows gives these sizes and the actual dimensions of the pot.

Sizes of pots (inside dimensions)	Diam. at top (in).	Depth (in).
Thimbles	2	2
Thumbs	$2\frac{1}{2}$	$2\frac{1}{2}$
Sixties (60s)	3	$3\frac{1}{2}$
Forty-eights (48s)	$4\frac{1}{2}$	5
Thirty-twos (32s)	6	6
Twenty-fours (24s)	$8\frac{1}{2}$	8
Sixteens (16s)	$9\frac{1}{2}$	9
Twelves (12s)	$11\frac{1}{2}$	10
Eights (8s)	12	11
Sixes (6s)	13	12
Fours (4s)	15	13
Twos (2s)	18	14

New clay pots should be soaked in water for at least 24 hours before being used. Pots which have been used should be washed before being used again.

Plastic Pots: These have now been available for a number of years. At first acceptance of them was very slow, but now they are being used widely, and are gradually superseding clay pots. They have several advantages, such as being easier to keep clean, breaking less easily, and holding more compost than a clay pot of comparable outside dimensions. Plants growing in them may need watering a little more carefully, but one quickly becomes accustomed to making this slight adjustment.

Paper Pots: Papier-maché and bituminised paper pots are quite cheap, and can be used successfully for propagating and raising young plants, which only remain in them for a short time; they are disposable.

Peat Pots: Peat is a very congenial material for making pots, and peat pots have had a rapid rise in popularity. They are used for propagating and plant raising very successfully on a wide scale. They have the advantage that for plants grown in them, transplanting or repotting checks are completely eliminated. The roots penetrate the sides of the pots, and the pots are transplanted or repotted along with the plant, with an absolute minimum of disturbance.

Sieves

Putting compost materials through a sieve should, on the whole, be avoided as far as possible. There are occasions, however, when it is necessary, for instance leafmould may require sieving to remove decaying wood and unrotted leaves. For this, a 1-in. square-meshed sieve is the best. Seedlings which are to be potted into thumb pots must, of course, have finely sieved loam and peat, and a $\frac{1}{4}$-in. mesh sieve is suitable in this case, with the addition of plenty of coarse sand to prevent compaction of the sieved materials. For the intermediate stages of potting, the soil and peat particles should be of such a size that they will fit between the sides of the new pot and the root ball, and a $\frac{1}{2}$-in. mesh sieve will ensure this. In all cases where large, well-rooted plants are transferred to big pots the loam or peat should be pulled or chopped to pieces rather than sieved.

One further sieve will be required: a fine-gauge wire sieve for sieving surface loam and sand for seed pans. An excellent one can be made from a piece of ordinary perforated zinc, or an ordinary household sieve can be used.

Stakes and Plant Supports

Many greenhouse plants need supporting, but it is important to use stakes which, while being strong enough to do their job, are at the same time as inconspicuous as possible. The tips of bamboo canes, stained a dull green, can be used for a good many plants such as fuchsias, schizanthus and celosias. Neat wire stakes with open ring ends are suitable for begonias, perpetual flowering carnations and pelargoniums. Balloon-shaped or pyramidal wire frames are needed for all sorts of trailing plants, which can be attractively trained to cover the supports with leaves, stems and flowers. Bougainvilleas, tropaeolums and *Diplacus glutinosus* are examples of this type of plant.

Ramming sticks with flattened ends are needed for firming the compost in large pots, and flat boards shaped to fit pots, pans and square-cornered boxes will ease the smoothing of the surface of containers intended for seeds.

POTTING PLANTS

There is a great deal more to potting plants than the mere placing of the roots in a pot and filling in with compost. In the first place, judging whether a plant even needs potting or not is a matter for knowledge and experience; it may be just as bad to disturb a flourishing specimen unnecessarily as to neglect repotting when it should be done. The general rule is that a young, rapidly growing plant should be moved into a slightly larger pot as soon as its roots have penetrated the compost in the smaller pot, but before they have become a densely tangled mass running round and round the outside of the root ball, i.e. have become pot-bound, and will then have to be maintained by watering and regular feeding.

Clean pots and crocks are highly essential, and they must be perfectly dry at the time of use. Broken clay pots, crocks, old mortar rubble, lumps of charcoal, and broken brick are all useful materials for draining pots. Pieces of the sides of clay pots should always be placed convex side uppermost; if placed hollow side up they will hold water instead of allowing it to escape. Ideally, fibrous material should be placed over the crocks in all the smallest pots, to keep fine particles of soil from filtering down and choking the drainage. Moss, fibre from loam and peat, spent hops, or flaking siftings from leafmould are all suitable. On top of this drainage layer place a little of the compost prepared for the plants. As far as plastic pots are concerned, the extra number of drainage holes, and the different reaction of the compost to watering mean that crocks and fibrous material are largely unnecessary.

Plants should be placed neither too low nor too high in their new pots, and the surface should always be levelled off at a point below the rim of the pot such that sufficient water can be added to fill the space between the compost surface and the rim of the pot at any one watering. The depth of this space will vary with the diameter of the pot, and may be as follows:

For pots	4 in. in diameter			$\frac{3}{8}$	in.
,, ,,	6 ,, ,,		,,	$\frac{5}{8}-\frac{3}{4}$	,,
,, ,,	8 ,, ,,		,,	$\frac{3}{4}-\frac{7}{8}$	,,
,, ,,	10 ,, ,,		,,	1	,,
,, ,,	12 ,, ,,		,,	$1\frac{1}{4}$	,,

Having prepared the pot to receive the plant, take the latter and turn it out of its old pot by first placing one hand across the top of the pot, and by passing two fingers on either side of the stem of the plant; then invert the plant and, if necessary, give the rim of the pot a rap on the edge of the potting bench or staging. As a rule, the plant comes out easily, but when a dirty pot has previously been used there is often difficulty, as the roots adhere to the soil particles left in the pot, to which they themselves are sticking, and the pot gets broken. A thin knife-blade passed between the ball and the pot will sometimes release the plant, but the roots will be injured in any case.

Place the plant exactly in the centre of the new pot, both for the sake of appearance and in order that it may have an equal amount of fresh compost, and therefore of fresh food, all round it. Next proceed to fill in the new compost in the space between pot and plant; press it steadily and firmly downward, either with the fingers or with a potting-stick, using the thin part of the stick when there is not space for the thick end to be inserted between the old ball and the pot. Keep adding fresh compost, pressing it down until it is level with — and equally as dense, or firm, as — the old ball of compost. Should the new compost be made less firm or dense than the old ball, the water will pass more quickly through the new compost, and the old — where all the roots are at the time — will be only partially moistened and the plant seriously deprived of water, at a time when it particularly needs it.

Stem-rooting lilies, such as *auratum* and *speciosum*, require special care in potting. The pot should be provided with a layer of crocks to serve as drainage. Over this place a layer of fibrous soil or moss, and then add about 3 in. of compost, put the bulb on top, and just cover it with fine leafmould. The pot will then be only half filled. In due course the bulb will develop basal roots, then, as the stem elongates it will produce roots also. When these begin to appear additional compost should gradually be added until the pot is filled to within an inch of its rim.

Orchids require potting in a different way from other plants. The pots for epiphytic orchids should be half filled with large crocks, placed concave side downwards. For terrestrial (cypripediums) orchids filling one-third of the pot with drainage material is enough. The potting material should be just moist, since dry, hard fibrous peat will damage the roots when firmed around them. Thereafter, when repotting orchids, remember to have all equipment as clean as possible, place the plant so that the leading growth is as near the centre of the pot as possible, so that fresh potting is not required for some time, and keep the base of the plant level with the top of the pot. The quantity of compost will be regulated by the number of roots and the vigour of the plant. Remember, also, that the fewer the roots, the less quantity of compost is needed. Use some really fresh moss when finishing off the surface, partly for appearances' sake, and partly because it supplies more uniformly moist and healthy conditions round the roots. The material used in potting can be made reasonably firm round the roots with the help of a pointed stick, so that the plants are not disturbed in the course of routine handling. It is better when planting in small pots to cut up the peat into about 2-in. lengths, so that it is more easily worked in the pots.

It is not necessary to repot orchids every year, but only when the number of roots really requires more room. At other times simply remove the old peat and moss topdressing carefully, and replace both with fresh materials.

CHAPTER FIVE

Plant Propagation

The increase of plants is one of the most interesting and skilled branches of gardening, and it is certainly of major importance as far as greenhouse work is concerned. Hence this chapter will deal with the subject as fully as possible, so that beginners can learn the correct methods from the start and thereby have the pleasure of successfully producing adult plants from their own seeds, cuttings, divisions and so on.

Equipment

One essential item of equipment is a heated propagating case, of which there are many different kinds now available. They are in various sizes, supplying varying amounts of heat, both to the air and to the compost or sand, in the latter case by means of electric cables. Some contain rod thermostats. The frame may be of wood or fibre glass with glass or some form of transparent plastic for the top, which will be movable to provide ventilation. A very simple frame can be made with a framework of soft cedar, about $2\frac{1}{2} \times 1\frac{1}{2}$ ft. with a front depth of about 10 in. and a back one of 14 in., heat being provided by a low wattage electric light bulb in a box below the frame.

Other essentials are shallow pans and boxes, either wooden or plastic, two sieves, one moderately fine, and one very fine, a fine rosed watering can, and a sharp knife. A few transparent plastic bags and rubber bands can be used with pots of cuttings to take the place of a frame. For the larger greenhouse, it will be worth installing a mist propagating unit. This is an electrically controlled piece of apparatus in which a very fine spray is turned on to the cuttings automatically at frequent, regular intervals so that the atmosphere is always humid and the cuttings never have to contend with drying out. An electronic 'leaf' is placed among the cuttings

A mist propagating unit

The propagation of plants by seeds

and as soon as its surface becomes dry, the spray is automatically turned on for as long as required, usually from 20 to 40 seconds. With such a unit shading of the cuttings is unnecessary.

Compost for Propagating

The John Innes seed compost, or one of the proprietary loamless mixtures, will be ideal for seed sowing. For rooting cuttings, a mixture of equal parts (by volume) peat and sand is very satisfactory, or one of the seed composts can be used for this purpose. Place some form of fibrous material, as for ordinary potting, on top of the crocks in the box or pan, and then fill in with the seed compost. For fine seeds, sift a portion through a $\frac{1}{16}$-in. mesh sieve, and use this for just covering the surface before sowing the seeds. As weed seeds, fungi, and insect pests are apt to be present in loam, sterilise it beforehand, as suggested on p. 53, or by scalding it with boiling water, before inserting cuttings or seeds. If the latter is used, it will be best to fill the pots, pans, or boxes with loam, then scald by soaking with boiling water, and leave for a day or two partially to dry out, finally mixing with sand and peat in suitable proportions. Heating the loam will ensure the germination of only such seeds as are sown. A little fine charcoal mixed with the compost will help to keep it sweet and encourage germination.

SEEDS

If ordinary pans or boxes 3 in. deep are used, place 1-in. crocks in the bottom, then $\frac{1}{2}$ in. of fibrous material, and fill up to within $\frac{1}{2}$ in. of the top with seed compost. Press the compost down firmly and evenly with a flat piece of board, then moisten thoroughly with warm water applied through a fine rose watering can, and leave to drain for a time. If pots are used, half fill these with crocks then fill with fibre and compost, as advised for the pans, and press down firmly and evenly with the base of another pot, and finally moisten as in the previous case. Tiny seeds, like those of the begonia and gloxinia, should be sown thinly on the surface, and afterwards lightly sprinkled with fine sand only. Seeds like those of the balsam should be just covered with very fine compost; while those of the canna should be pressed in about $\frac{1}{4}$ in. deep. Special hints for particular kinds of seeds are given under their respective headings elsewhere.

After sowing, place each pot or pan in a shallow container of water so that water does not cover the top of the seed container, and leave it there until water has gradually been drawn up to the compost surface, then withdraw it, cover with a pane of glass, and place in the propagator or frame. Most seeds germinate best in darkness; therefore shade each pot, pan, or box with paper until the seeds sprout. Whilst the sun is shining the paper should still be kept over the glass, removing it directly the sun ceases to shine.

As soon as the seeds are fairly well sprouted, tilt the glass a little on one side, and a day or two later remove it altogether, and place the pan or box on a shelf not far from the roof. Whilst in this stage of growth the seedlings must not be exposed to the sun; therefore give shade whilst the sun is bright. Black polythene sheeting can be used instead of glass and paper, but when removed, do not forget to keep the seedlings from the sun for the time being.

As soon as the seedlings can be safely handled they must be transplanted carefully to pots, pans, or boxes in similar compost, but not quite so fine. After planting put them back in the propagator or frame for a day or two until they take hold of the new compost, and then remove to the shelf again. When the seedlings have made fair progress transfer them singly to small thumb pots, shade for a few days, and then grow on in the way advised for each genus.

The temperature of the propagator or propagating frame should be not less than 18–21°C (65–70°F). Water must be applied carefully at all times. As a rule, if the containers are watered before and after sowing the seeds, no further watering will be needed till germination has taken place, and then it should be done by placing them in water till the compost is moist. The propagator and frame lights should be opened for an inch or so for a short time every morning to change the air. Care must be taken not to let the containers remain in the propagator or frame after the seeds have sprouted nicely as, if detained too long, the seedlings become attenuated and weakly, and difficult to manage afterwards. Hard-coated seeds, like those of the canna, may have a little notch filed in them before sowing, to help them to germinate more rapidly.

Although I have emphasised the advantage of raising plants from seed in a propagator and frame, it by no means follows that they are essential. On the contrary, pots, pans, or boxes of seed may be placed anywhere in a heated greenhouse, and so long as they are kept constantly shaded till the seeds germinate, plants may be successfully raised in them. The pots, pans, or boxes should be covered with sheets of glass to maintain an even degree of humidity, and if paper is placed over the glass, germination will be hastened. The covering, however, must be removed immediately growth appears on the surface, and the glass should be slightly tilted for a few days and then removed entirely.

Ferns are raised from spores, which in their case are equivalent to seeds. The spores are extremely minute, and being somewhat slow in germination it is doubly important that the soil used shall be sterilised to prevent development of mosses or lichens which will otherwise smother the minute growth of the young ferns. Many methods are adopted, with varying success, but that which I have personally found successful is to break good loam into lumps about the size of a child's clenched hand, dip them into boiling water to sterilise, allow to cool, and place them in a clean glass container to which a close-fitting lid may be attached. Cheap glass butter dishes are ideal for the purpose. While the loam is still thoroughly wet, thinly dust the fern spores over the surface and put the lid on. Do not give any more water, but keep the container tightly closed, and in a warm but shady corner of the greenhouse. In two or three months the surface of the loam will be covered with a green mass of saucer-shaped growths. These are the first obvious stages of fern development. In due time tiny fronds will rise, when it will be necessary to separate the mass into little patches and gently press them into a smoothed surface of fresh, sterilised soil.

CUTTINGS

Soft-wooded cuttings, like those of the zonal or show pelargonium or fuchsia, should be prepared so that they are about 3 to 4 in. long, have the lower leaves removed, and the base cut cleanly across close to the lower leaf joint, not above it. Hard-wooded cuttings like those of the heath or acacia, may be 2 to 4 in. long, and selected from shoots that are fairly firm. Remove the leaves from the lower half of the cutting, and see that the base is cut off close to a joint. Numerous plants of smaller proportions and softer growths are propagated from shorter cuttings, either from side growths or young shoots from the base. Such are exemplified by *Campanula isophylla*, the trailing lobelia which is so useful for hanging baskets, the large-flowered mimulus, the popular little *Panicum variegatum*, various

The propagation of a pelargonium by cuttings. The formation of roots is encouraged by dipping the base of each cutting in a hormone rooting powder before inserting it into the compost

selaginellas and so on. Quite small shoot tips of these plants will frequently root quickly and make better, neater plants than bigger, older growths with inches of naked stem. The essentials are to fix the base of the cuttings firmly into a tray or pan of light compost with a well-shaded surface. Then keep them close in a propagator to prevent their soft foliage shrivelling in a comparatively dry atmosphere.

Top left: Campanula isophylla *in hanging basket Top right:* Browallia
speciosa major
Bottom: Two fine foliage begonias

Even in harder-wooded plants there are a few of which quite small side shoots will root more easily than longer growths. The ericas (heaths) are probably some of the most quickly rooted of these, cuttings of which should be short side growths less than an inch long, peeled off the main branches and inserted in a mixture of sand and fine peat, without attempting to trim them. Nevertheless, rooting this type of plant is generally beyond the ability of the beginner, though the more experienced gardener will be successful, and it is customary to buy in such plants from specialist nurserymen. Some cuttings, like those of the plumbago, require to be removed with a thin slice of the older branch attached, technically called a 'heel'. This heel should be trimmed neatly, removing any torn end of bark at the point of the heel which might decay.

Except where otherwise mentioned under each genus, these cuttings may be inserted singly in thumb pots, filled with a compost of equal parts (by volume) of loam, leafmould or peat, and sand, or several put into 3- or $4\frac{1}{2}$-in. pots, each well drained. Free-rooting plants may be inserted an inch or so apart in shallow boxes of sandy compost. Each cutting should be inserted about an inch deep, a hole the proper depth having previously been made by a round stick called a dibber. Care should be taken to press the base of the cutting to the bottom of the hole. It is a good plan to drop a pinch of sand in the hole before putting in the cuttings. The compost in the pots or pans prepared for choice cuttings should be pressed down firmly and sprinkled freely with silver sand, then watered before the cuttings are put in. There are a few kinds of plants that root more readily in pure sharp sand rather than a mixed compost. In their case it is necessary to pot off as soon as roots appear, using a light, porous mixture of leafmould, loam, and sand, otherwise the young roots will be quickly starved to death.

Place the pots or pans in a propagator and keep the lid tightly closed for the first few days, where this is felt to be necessary. Some plants such as geraniums, to quote one example, will root quite readily without such treatment. The reason for this is not so much to ensure a high temperature as to maintain a steady unvarying degree of humidity, thus reducing the moisture loss from the cuttings through the leaves during the rooting period.

Where no propagator exists, place the pot of cuttings inside a larger empty pot, fill the space between the two pots with moist sphagnum moss or peat, and then place a pane of glass over the

The showy, curious blooms of the vigorous climber Passiflora caerulea, *a fascinating plant for the cool greenhouse*

top. This will form an excellent miniature propagator. Another method is to stand the pots inside a box large enough for the shoots to have ample head room and air space, and then cover this with one or more panes of glass. The space between the pots can again be filled with moss or peat. Yet another method is to use a transparent polythene bag, supported over the top of the pot by two short sticks, so that it is not lying on the cuttings, and secured round the pot rim by a rubber band. Rooting can be encouraged with difficult subjects by using hormone rooting powder, of which there are several proprietary brands. Cuttings of many plants can be raised thus in a cold greenhouse in late spring and summer.

Another type of stem cutting is that used in the case of the dracaena. The stems are cut into inch lengths and placed horizontally on the surface of pans of a peaty compost, when they will send out roots and a shoot from each piece to form a new plant. Warmth and humidity are of course essential.

Leaf Cuttings

Various plants, including gloxinias, ornamental-leaved begonias, streptocarpus and saintpaulia, are easily increased by leaf cuttings. The whole leaf may be laid underside downwards on the surface of a light sandy compost in a pan or box, and kept in contact with the compost by placing pebbles on top. Before laying the leaf down, cut the principal mid-ribs through, here and there, at the junction of each pair of ribs. At each of these cuts a callus will form, eventually producing tiny plants which, when rooted, can be removed and planted separately in pots. Another plan is to divide a begonia leaf into several triangular portions, each terminating at the junction of two ribs. The rib should be inserted $\frac{1}{2}$ in. deep in small pots filled with equal parts of peat or leafmould, loam, and sand, and surfaced with sand. In the case of gloxinias, a leaf is cut in two, and the stalk inserted in pots in a way similar to that used for the begonia. Saintpaulia leaves are taken with about $1\frac{1}{2}$ in. of leaf stalk left on them and inserted vertically just deep enough to hold them upright in a peaty mixture. Place the pots or pans in a warm propagator until rooting has taken place.

Leaf Bud Cuttings

A wide range of plants including such favourites as the geranium (zonal pelargonium) and the India rubber plant, *Ficus elastica*, can

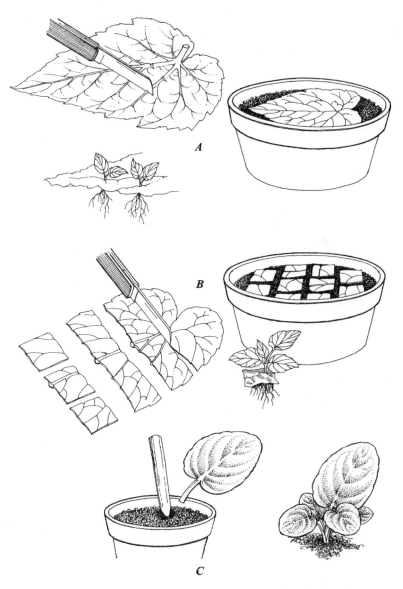

Propagation by leaf cuttings. Methods **A** and **C** are described in the text.
Method **B** is a variation of **A**. The begonia leaves are cut into small
squares, each with a main vein running through it, and they should be
rooted in the same way as described for **A**

be propagated from a short piece of stem with one leaf attached. For the sake of convenience the leaf can be rolled up and held in position by a neat stake.

AIR LAYERING

This age-old method of propagating has been given an exciting new lease of life by the introduction of semi-permeable, polythene film. Tall dracaenas, India rubber plants, aralias, and numerous others with unsightly, naked stems which have outgrown their usefulness, are easily propagated and reduced in height by this method. A slanting cut or notch is made in the stem at a convenient height, preferably just below a leaf joint. This is surrounded by a generous handful of moist sphagnum moss. A piece of polythene film is wrapped round to enclose the moss totally, and fixed firmly in position with adhesive tape a few inches above and below the cut in the stem. If it is felt to be necessary, the surfaces of the cut or notch can be dusted with hormone rooting powder before applying the moss. When a good strong growth of roots can be seen through the polythene the stem can be severed just below them and repotted into a suitably sized pot.

OFFSETS

Many ferns, especially *Asplenium bulbiferum*, produce tiny plantlets on their fronds. If the frond is bent down and pegged to a surface of sandy peat and leafmould, in a pan or box, and placed in a propagator, the plantlets will form roots. Offshoots also form on the flowering stems of *Chlorophytum comosum*, and on the creeping stems of *Saxifraga stolonifera*. These may be removed and planted in small pots and placed in a propagator till roots form; in many cases the chlorophytum plantlets will have already begun to form roots while attached to the parent plant. Offshoots from vallotas, hippeastrums and other bulbous plants may be removed and potted separately at repotting time.

DIVISION

Ferns, orchids, agapanthus, and aspidistras are examples of plants that may be increased by dividing the plants into two or more portions in spring when repotting. Some plants are strong and vigorous

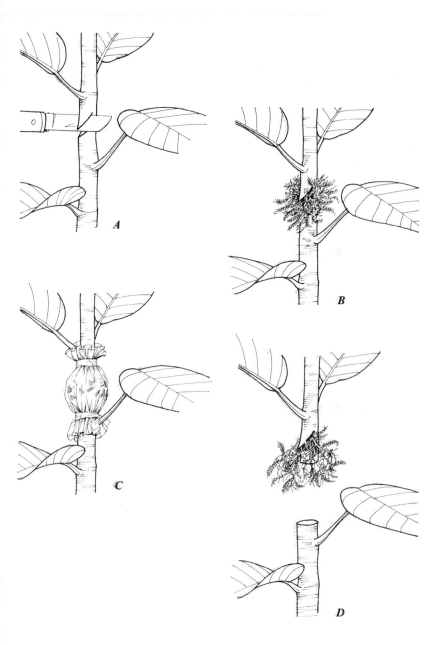

Air layering an India rubber plant

enough to withstand rough methods of tearing or cutting asunder, but others require careful treatment, and none can be roughly handled with absolute impunity. It is strongly advised, therefore, that reasonable care be taken with any kind of plant when the aim is to increase numbers or to give fresh vigour and pleasing character to an old and waning plant.

First, although various plants are capable of retaining life and making growth after division at almost any time of year, it may be taken as a rule that the best time to do this is at the start of the plant's new season of growth. It should be before that young growth is far advanced for two reasons. One is that when young growth is far advanced there is greater difficulty in avoiding damage by breaking shoots or bruising tender foliage, and the other is that young growth is apt to wilt, and perhaps collapse before roots can re-attach themselves to the fresh soil.

If the soil in a pot is very dry, soak it the day before dividing. Begin by removing drainage material, then take a skewer or a pointed stick and use this to shift the compost without breaking roots. Plants which have made definite crowns should have these crowns separated, singly, keeping their own complement of roots intact. Take it as a general rule that it is better to pot small divisions in small pots, but where it is desired to procure a few big specimens of spreading or trailing plants quickly, several divisions may be evenly spread over a wider surface.

A further good rule is to keep growing points to the surface, burying only actual roots in the soil.

GRAFTING

This is a method of propagation that the average greenhouse owner will not find necessary. Further, it requires a good deal of practice, and a great deal of skill, to perform satisfactorily, and it is therefore thought advisable not to give detailed advice regarding this method of propagation.

MISCELLANEOUS

In addition to the techniques already described, there are other methods of propagation which relate only to a few specific genera. Details are given under the propagation heading which forms part of the description of these plants

CHAPTER SIX

Greenhouse Pests and Diseases

In a practical book of this kind it is essential to include a section on the troubles and ailments to which greenhouse plants, like all others, are subject. There are a great number unfortunately, and it is most important to maintain constant vigilance and care in order to prevent outbreaks or keep them in check. This is where the observant gardener comes into his own, as a keen and experienced eye will spot trouble long before it can seriously harm the plants. Insect pests and fungus diseases cause the most trouble in gardening.

It is realised that this chapter is only a brief summary of the pests and fungal and bacterial diseases which may infest greenhouse plants. To attempt a really comprehensive survey of the whole range of ills and all the known or reputed remedies and preventives would require a complete book on the subject alone. Even so, it would not be long before detailed revision was required, since entomologists, mycologists, and chemists are constantly discovering fresh remedies and new methods of fighting plant enemies.

The greatest safety lies in cleanliness in every detail, coupled with good cultivation to keep plants growing strongly from the start. Fumigation as a preventive is a more effective measure than as a remedy when any pest or disease has obtained a foothold.

Methods of fumigation are dealt with on p. 47. When using liquid insecticides, do not let them touch the flowers and, moreover, see that they are applied to both the under and upper surface of the leaves. Such insecticides are best applied on dull days, or, failing these, in the evening – certainly not in the morning or during the middle of bright sunny days. It is necessary to apply any insecticide or fungicide in the form of a mist-like spray; therefore, the syringe must be fitted with a fine nozzle. It is sheer waste of material to use a coarse nozzle; besides, it is not certain that the whole of the leaf will be covered with insecticide.

Lime-washing brickwork, washing woodwork with warm soapy water containing disinfectant, and regular removal of all decayed or fallen vegetation are among the best means of preventing trouble from either attacks of pests or outbreak of disease. Cleanliness in the home of plants is as necessary to their health and happiness as, in our own homes, it is necessary to the well-being of its occupants.

Prompt isolation of a sickly plant is advisable because most plant troubles are capable of spreading rapidly, and it is preferable to lose one plant rather than to risk rapid spread of its affliction.

PESTS

Ants: There are two kinds of injuries for which ants are usually responsible. In the first place, the soil becomes spongy, waterlogged and sour because they live and build nests in it; secondly, they do an infinite amount of harm in carrying aphids and young scale insects to various plants in order to 'milk' them of the sugary secretions which these pests excrete. They are found in association with aphids chiefly in houses where orchids, crotons, and similar plants are grown.

REMEDIES. Ants infesting the soil in pots are best destroyed by immersing the pot entirely in water for a few hours, thereby drowning them. Dusts containing lindane (benzene-hexachloride) and trichlorphon are effective in controlling ants, and should be sprinkled on the pots, staging, and paths where these pests are troublesome.

Benzene-hexachloride effectively kills ants; if a band of this is dusted round the base of the walls and in the ventilators, it will keep them out of the house. Do not use this material on ground which will hold root crops, as it taints their flavour.

The nests can be destroyed by using one of the proprietary ant destroyers, according to the manufacturers' instructions.

Aphids: These are well known under the common name of greenflies; the term also includes blackfly. They attack all kinds of softwooded plants, but are particularly addicted to cinerarias, variegated abutilon, tradescantia, and chrysanthemums. They have pale brown antennae, transparent, irridescent wings when adult, soft bodies and long legs, and are furnished with a proboscis with which they penetrate the epidermis of the leaf or the rind of the shoot and suck the juices of the plant. Aphids are marvellously fecund. In the

72

autumn eggs are laid which lie dormant until spring, when they hatch into adult greenfly. From the latter are hatched viviparous females which go on producing generation after generation of living young until the autumn, when over-wintering eggs are laid once more in cracks and crevices, and on the bark of trees and shrubs.

REMEDIES. The best method of control is to fumigate with smoke cones, nicotine shreds, or to use aerosols. BHC smokes are usually effective against aphids: malathion, dimethoate, pirimicarb and menazon can also be used in liquid form. The dose is usually given in the instructions from the manufacturers. Fumigation is best done on a still night, and when there are flower crops in the house it is advisable to cut all the open blooms before the operation, in order to avoid injury to the petals.

When only a few plants are attacked, or spraying is preferred, the plants can be sprayed with a liquid insecticide, in accordance with the manufacturers' instructions, making doubly sure that none of the plants is susceptible to damage by the particular material being used. For example, malathion should not be used on members of the crassula family.

It is important to destroy weeds near the greenhouse as these harbour pests and supply them with food when there is no crop in the house. When a new stock of plants is bought this should be carefully sprayed with an insecticide before placing with the clean old stock.

Peaches and nectarines should be sprayed with tar oil in the winter when fully dormant to kill any eggs laid on the bark.

Capsid bugs, Leafhoppers, and Froghoppers: These are closely related, and all damage the plant by piercing the tissue and sucking the sap. The characteristic symptom of their attack is distortion of the leaves, shoot tips and flower buds; usually the punctures can be seen as minute yellow spots, and pinprick holes in the leaves, in the case of the capsid bugs. Leafhoppers produce an all-over pale yellow stippled effect on leaves, and the froghoppers are distinguished by the mass of frothy liquid surrounding the young insects. The last named can be regarded as a minor pest in general, and hand picked.

Capsid bugs attack chrysanthemums and dahlias, causing considerable malformation of the flower buds, while they are still very small, so that damage is not noticed until the capsids have long departed. A number of weeds form alternative hosts, including dock, nettle, groundsel and fleabane. Leafhoppers attack chrysanthemums, fuchsias, primulas, calceolarias, pelargoniums, *Asparagus sprengeri*, tomato and cucumber. Froghoppers may be troublesome on chrysanthemums brought indoors for flowering, and on carnations.

REMEDIES. Thoroughly drenching the plants with a nicotine, malathion or dimethoate spray will destroy these insects and, as they quickly drop to the ground when disturbed, the soil round the plants should also be treated. Fumigation with nicotine or BHC gives some control but is not as successful as spraying.

Weeds and crop refuse should be destroyed, and, by thus clearing suitable over-wintering places, sources of infestation are minimised.

Carnation Tortrix Moth (*Cacoecimorpha pronubana*): The larvae of the carnation tortrix moth will attack other plants than the carnation, including acacia, chorizema, coronilla, cytisus, grevillea and nandina.

Symptoms of attack by this pest are rotted leaves or leaves spun together with webbing at the tips of the shoots; later the leaves may be eaten and the growing tips of the shoots destroyed. The caterpillars will also, in some cases, eat into the flower buds and feed on the petals, so that the flowers are distorted.

The moths are most active at night. They may be recognised by the bright orange hind wings; the wing expanse is just less than an inch. Clusters of up to 200 eggs are laid, usually on the upper surface of the leaf, and each female may lay several batches.

REMEDIES. Where the attack is not severe, picking off the affected shoot tips and destroying the egg clusters is effective. Fumigate with BHC smokes, or spray with fenitrothion or lindane.

Chrysanthemum Eelworm (*Aphelenchoides ritzemabosi*): The damage done by this pest is well known. The first symptom is a yellowish-green blotching of the lowest leaves, followed by browning, at first in areas sharply defined by the main veins, but spreading to the whole leaf, until eventually all the leaves at the base of the stem are brown and hanging limply. When plants are badly infested, the flower buds are small and weak and the flowers may be malformed, and all the leaves will be affected.

The eelworms live in the plant tissue, which they enter through the stomata, but are only active when a film of moisture is present. They are very long lived and can withstand desiccation for three years, becoming active when sufficient moisture is available. They are often present in cuttings from infested plants and persist in the soil in dead leaves, but not for more than about three months, and in any case normally do not survive a winter out in the open.

REMEDY. At present the most effective measure in dealing with eelworms seems to be immersion of dormant stools in water heated to 45°C (110°F) for a period of 20–30 minutes. The stools should then be cooled in clean water, drained and then boxed in sterilised soil. Fuller details of this procedure are obtainable from the National Chrysanthemum Society.

Chrysanthemum Midge (*Diarthronomyia chrysanthemi*): The maggots of this small fly burrow into the tissue of the leaves, stems and bracts and cause development of galls which stand out for about $\frac{1}{8}$ in. from the surface of the leaf.

REMEDY. Because the maggots feed concealed within the galls they are difficult to control. The times when they are susceptible are when the eggs are being laid on the plant, and as the flies are emerging from the galls. The adult midges can be killed by fumigating with BHC smoke, but this treatment should be followed by fortnightly spraying with BHC, or nicotine. The tips of the young shoots should be thoroughly wetted with the spray.

Cockroaches: These are extremely lively and crafty insects which feed on seeds, seedlings and the foliage and stems of many plants. They also eat the aerial roots of orchids and damage the blooms of chrysanthemums, cinerarias and orchids. Being nocturnal feeders it is difficult to catch them; besides they have a habit of concealing themselves beneath pots, or anything else they can crawl under or into, directly light is introduced, or as soon as daylight appears. It is hardly necessary to describe them in detail; but for those who are not familiar with them they are large, light brown to dark brown, fast-moving beetles. They are little seen in the modern greenhouse.

REMEDIES. If cockroaches are present, they may be trapped in glass jars sunk to their rims in the soil and containing stale beer and treacle or peeled banana. Proprietary beetle powders are also available which give good control of this pest.

Earwigs: Every chrysanthemum grower knows very well what destructive pests these are. They need no detailed description here for they are, unfortunately, too common to be unknown. It may per-

75

haps be interesting to add that, unlike most insects, the female ear-
wig does not leave her eggs, but broods them until hatched and
afterwards, just as a bird does. Earwigs commit great havoc among
the blooms of chrysanthemums, roses and other flowers, by eating
and otherwise disfiguring the petals by means of their formidable
forceps. They are rarely met with in moist places but are found
in dry positions and in hot dry seasons, they are usually abundant.

REMEDIES. Dusting about the pots, staging and floor with BHC
or the use of BHC smoke will much reduce the numbers of earwigs,
and spraying with dimethoate or trichlorphon is also effective.
Another way of destroying them is by using traps. Boiled potatoes
enclosed in dry moss or hay in a flower pot, or pieces of hollow
bean stalk or cane laid about, or partially open matchboxes, prove
excellent traps.

Fern Eelworm (*Aphelenchoides olesistus*): This eelworm has a similar life-cycle to the chrysanthemum eelworm and is just as difficult
to control. It attacks pteris, asplenium, coleus, salvia, orchids and
gloxinias. Badly attacked plants are weakened and the leaves are
discoloured, with blackened areas in the case of ferns, and pale-
coloured, rather transparent patches in the case of begonias and
gloxinias.

REMEDIES. Small ferns can have the same hot-water treatment
as chrysanthemum stools. Large ferns and orchids should be
sprayed regularly with nicotine or malathion to check the spread
of the pest. In all cases clean stock should be potted in sterilised
composts and all pots and crocks should be sterilised. Pick off and
burn affected leaves and pull up and burn badly attacked plants,
burn the compost and sterilise the pots.

Leaf Miners: These are the larvae of two-winged flies infesting the
leaves of holly, celery, tomato, chrysanthemums and others. The
ones we are concerned with are *Phytomyza atricornis*, which tunnels
into the leaves of chrysanthemums, cinerarias and other plants of
the family *Compositae*, and *Delia brunnescens*, which attacks carnations. The flies themselves are minute and of a slatey black or ash
colour. They pierce the upper cuticle of the leaves and deposit an
egg inside, which speedily hatches into a pale green, legless maggot,
and starts to eat its way through to the inner surface of the leaf
and forms small galleries or tunnels, which show as pale green lines,

or brownish blisters. These naturally disfigure the foliage, besides rendering it unhealthy and giving a great check to the growth of the plant. In due course the maggots change into chrysalids, and ultimately develop into flies, which in their turn lay eggs and produce another batch of progeny.

REMEDIES. Regular routine spraying with nicotine or dimethoate at fortnightly intervals will keep this pest under control, and in frames and greenhouses fumigation with BHC or nicotine is effective. Careful watching for signs of the maggot in the leaf and then crushing it between the finger and thumb is a good remedy or stabbing with the point of a penknife. Badly attacked leaves should be cut off and burnt before the grubs hatch into flies.

Mealy Bug: This is a well-known pest of ornamental plants. It is the nymphs and female adults that do the damage as they feed by sucking the sap of the leaves and shoots. The eggs are laid in masses, and colonies of the pest occur; these are conspicuous by the white mealy substance covering the bodies of the insects. There are several species of mealy bug, varying in size, but all are of the genus *Pseudococcus* and are closely related to the scale insects, *Coccus* spp. The important host plants are vines, ferns, asparagus spp., gardenias, palms, jasmine, dracaenas, figs and crotons.

REMEDIES. Spraying with malathion or regular fumigation with malathion-atomising concentrate will keep outbreaks in check. Small isolated attacks can be controlled by carefully dabbing the mealy bug with a small swab of cotton wool dipped in methylated spirits. Plants which have been badly infested can be cleaned by carefully washing them in a weak solution of insecticide.

Millepedes: These occasionally find their way into potting composts, and although they feed mainly on decayed vegetable matter, they are not fastidious, when short of their natural food, about attacking the roots of plants. They are either round or somewhat flattened in shape, brown or slate in colour, and furnished with a number of fine legs along the entire length of their bodies. They are easily distinguished from wireworms – the larvae of click beetles – by the large number of their legs, by their dark colouring and by their habit of coiling themselves up when disturbed.

REMEDIES. Soil sterilisation is the most effective remedy. In small quantities of potting compost the millepedes can be carefully picked out by hand. BHC, wireworm dust or carbaryl worked into the top 4 in. of soil in greenhouse beds will give a good control of millepedes and other soil-borne pests.

Red Spider Mite (*Tetranychus urticae, T. cinnabarinus*): This is a serious pest, attacking tomatoes, arums, cucumbers, carnations, vines and peaches in particular, and many other plants also in suitable conditions. The main symptom is the pinhead-sized bleached spots showing on the upper surface of the leaf, where the mites are feeding below by sucking the sap. In a severe attack the leaves become closely mottled and then drop and shrivel. The immature mites cover the leaves with a fine web. The mites are just large enough to be seen with the naked eye; the males and young ones are a pale straw colour, the females dark red, and the eggs pink or red in the case of *T. cinnabarinus*. *T. urticae*, which feeds mainly on tomatoes, chrysanthemums and cucumbers, is mostly much paler in colour, except for the hibernating adult females which are red, and are the only survivors through the winter in cracks, crevices and litter generally.

REMEDIES. A hot, dry atmosphere is favourable to the increase of red spider; consequently the best way to keep this pest at bay is to maintain, as far as possible, a moist atmosphere by spraying and damping down the foliage, walls and paths daily. Azobenzene fumigation or aerosol gives very good control; malathion and dimethoate can also be used two or three times when controlling an outbreak.

Scale: Scale insects are small and inconspicuous, and are often the same colour as the stem on which they feed. They adhere closely to the plant on which they feed by sucking the sap. Attacked plants are weakened and stunted and the leaves turn yellow and often fall prematurely. They are often covered in a sooty substance which is a fungus growing on the secretions produced by the scale insects, and this is another indication of their presence.

Plants most commonly attacked are peaches, roses, palms, orchids, aspidistras and ferns.

After hatching, the young scales seek a suitable place to feed and then flatten themselves against the plant and begin to rob it of sap. At first their bodies are soft, but leathery scales develop and the insects feed beneath these. Eggs are laid under the scales and are protected by them; the parent dies and the newly hatched young escape and look for another place to feed, and the cycle begins again. As the insects never move very far, colonies develop and the scales gradually encrust the plant.

REMEDIES. Control is as for mealy bug, though it may be necessary to employ a pointed stick to scrape off the encrustation. Oleanders, oranges and camellias, very badly infested, may be quite cleared of scale by immersing the plants entirely in water for a day or two. This, however, should be done only in summer. Where sooty mould has appeared, it should be washed or sponged off, as far as possible, with warm soapy water.

Slugs: Slugs may be introduced to the greenhouse in turf or manure and if there are any neglected corners, they will breed rapidly and become a great nuisance. They eat young seedlings and also feed on the foliage, shoots, roots, and bulbs of mature plants.

REMEDIES. Eliminate breeding places such as weedy, neglected corners. Bait with metaldehyde and bran or one of the proprietary slug killers containing methiocarb or metaldehyde, or dust a growing crop with dry Bordeaux mixture and work this lightly into the soil round the plants.

Thrips: Thrips are serious glasshouse pests which feed on and under the leaves of many plants, sucking the sap. The adult flies are slender and only about $\frac{1}{10}$ in. long. The two pairs of wings are deeply fringed. The damage is very like that caused by the red spider mite, the attacked leaves showing bleached spots and in a bad attack being wrinkled, distorted and then blackened and wilted. Damage by this pest can be distinguished by a black sticky secretion left as globules on attacked leaves and by the absence of insects or web under the leaves. Thrips are very agile and jump away as soon as a leaf is touched, but may often be found in the flowers.

Carnation blossoms are attacked, and pink and red varieties can be ruined if the petals are mottled with tiny white specks caused by the feeding of thrips. Cyclamen flowers are also often attacked and the leaves of cucumbers, beans and many ornamental plants including palms, azaleas, smilax, crotons and clivias.

REMEDIES. Thrips are not, as a rule, troublesome in greenhouses that have a fairly moist atmosphere or amongst well-spaced vigorous plants. If plants are allowed to get over-dry or stunted in any way, an infestation quickly builds up. Syringing attacked plants forcefully with clear water is often sufficient to check an attack. A lindane smoke is effective against thrips, and so is malathion-atomising concentrate.

Vine weevil: The grub of the vine weevil (*Otiorrhynchus sulcatus*), which is about $\frac{1}{2}$ in. long, legless, white and wrinkled and has a brown head, will eat the roots of many pot plants and also vines and peaches. It will eat into the crowns and corms of primulas and cyclamen.

REMEDIES. At the roots of vines and peaches lightly work BHC dust into the surface of the soil to destroy the grubs. On aerial parts of the plant BHC can be applied. When pot plants are attacked it is sufficient to repot into clean soil after thoroughly washing the roots. The addition of BHC dust to the potting compost when making up will have no ill effect on the plants and will give good control of the grubs. Remember to destroy the old infested compost.

Whitefly: The greenhouse whitefly (*Trialeurodes vaporariorum*) can be a most troublesome pest in greenhouses, especially on chrysanthemums, fuchsias, salvias, and tomatoes. Besides whitefly, they are also commonly called ghost-flies or snow-flies. They have white, powdery wings and are only about $\frac{1}{25}$ in. long but usually occur in large colonies, and fly off the plants in cloudlike masses when disturbed. They feed by sucking the sap of the leaves and, owing to their large numbers and speed of reproduction, can become a serious menace if not dealt with.

REMEDIES. Fumigating with lindane smoke or spraying with malathion or lindane will be quite effective in controlling whitefly if repeated at 10–14 day intervals so that newly emerged young will also be killed.

Whitefly parasite (*Encarsia formosa*) has proved useful in commercial establishments, but in a small amateur's house the parasite often dies out because the fly is the only diet upon which the parasite lives.

Woodlice: These are very well known. They usually feed at night on decaying organic matter but, when their normal food is exhausted, will attack crops, and are particularly destructive to the tender roots and shoots of orchids and seedling plants.

The gloriously coloured flowers and attractive foliage of the canna or Indian shot plant make it an excellent subject for a warm greenhouse

REMEDIES. Small numbers may be trapped in inverted pots or boxes containing straw, or pieces of potato or apple scooped out and laid about the staging. These traps should be examined daily and the captives crushed. Satisfactory control is obtained by sprinkling BHC about the staging and pots; strict attention to cleanliness and the absence of litter and rubbish will help considerably in controlling woodlice. Fumigation with BHC is effective. One or more toads kept in a greenhouse will generally ensure an entire absence of woodlice.

FUNGUS AND VIRUS DISEASES

Botrytis cinerea (*Grey Mould*): Grey mould can affect every plant in the greenhouse. Symptoms are a grey fluffy outgrowth on leaves, stems and flowers, particularly if soft and fleshy. It grows rapidly in cool, humid conditions where there is little or no movement of air, and affected parts quickly rot and die. Infection is mostly through injuries already on the plant such as wounds left when faded flowers drop and when buds drop without opening as well as through injuries caused by breaking or cutting.

REMEDIES. Control by chemical means is difficult, and prevention is best. This means a thoroughly clean greenhouse, in which fallen leaves and flowers are not allowed to lie, and plant debris generally is collected and destroyed as quickly as possible. Plants should not be crowded or close together, sufficient ventilation should be given all the time, and plants encouraged to grow slightly 'hard', rather than soft and green. If the disease does appear, destroy affected plants at once, and if it still gets a hold, water slightly less, increase the ventilation and raise the temperature a little if on the cool side. Fumigate with tecnazene, or use quintozene or tecnazene dusts; spray with captan or thiram. In bad cases, sterilise the house at the end of the season with formalin.

Damping-off: This is a disease of seedlings, often found when unsterilised seed compost has been used. Seedlings topple over with a black or dark red colouring at the base of the stem. Too thick seed sowing, overwatering and watering with dirty water encourage the trouble.

REMEDIES. Clean seed trays, sterilised compost and seeds treated with a fungicidal dressing will ward off infection; if it does occur,

Top: Caladium hybrids
Bottom left: Codiaeum variegatum pictum *Bottom right:* Clianthus formosus

remove affected seedlings and the compost in which they are growing, and water with Cheshunt Compound, a copper-based fungicide.

Mildew: This disease is fairly widespread. It takes the form of a white,
powdery coating on the youngest leaves and stems at the tips of
shoots and works back down them; it may also produce small
blisters on leaves, and curled-under leaf margins. Buds and flowers
can be infected. Chrysanthemums, roses and vines in particular may
be badly infected so that growth is stunted, and fruiting and flowering poor. Dryness at the roots and stuffy conditions encourage its
appearance.

REMEDIES. At the first traces, spray or smoke with dinocap,
or use a sulphur-containing spray. Flowers of sulphur dusted on
are also effective. Vine mildew can be controlled by spraying with
a mixture of sulphur and soft soap. These controls act as protectants
– dinocap is an eradicant to some extent – and it is important
to cover the plant with the fungicide before the fungus can penetrate
and gain a hold, when control is very difficult. Removal of affected
parts before spraying is advisable.

Root Rots: These too are widespread, and consist of a complex
of soil-borne fungus diseases which infect the roots of plants so
that they become brown and stunted. The outer skin rots and can
easily be rubbed off and new root growth ceases. Tomatoes are
particularly prone to these troubles, but it is possible to obtain
stocks of plants which are resistant to them, and on to which
required varieties can be grafted. Infected plants cannot be treated,
but should be lifted and burnt, including the roots. Soils should be
sterilised, preferably before planting, if this trouble is suspected. Wet
cold soils and bad drainage exacerbate the trouble, as also does
planting small plants from a warm compost into a soil of a lower
temperature.

Rust: This is not often seen but damaging when it does appear,
quickly spreads and is destructive. It takes the form of raised, bright
ginger-brown spots on the under surface of leaves which disintegrate
into powder when touched. This powder consists of spores. A brown
felting may also be present on stems. Roses and chrysanthemums
in particular are likely to be affected, and in the last few years
pelargoniums have also become infected from imported diseased
plant material.

The accurate measurement and application of chemicals used in the control of greenhouse pests and diseases is of the utmost importance

REMEDIES. Affected leaves and stems should be destroyed, and plants sprayed at frequent intervals with a thiram or zineb spray as the makers instruct. On pelargoniums, however, these do not seem to be effective, and an affected plant is best removed immediately the trouble is seen and burnt; any close to it but not apparently infected being sprayed as a protection, and isolated for a time.

Sooty Mould: This is a minor fungus disease which in itself is harmless, growing on the honeydew excreted by sucking insects while they feed on leaves and stems. The honeydew drops to leaves below and on it a black soot-like covering may grow. Since it blocks the stomata of the leaves, it should be washed off and the insect pests destroyed. Scale insects and greenfly are the worst culprits.

VIRUS DISEASES

Since these are part of the nucleus of the plant cell, it is not possible to free a plant from a virus disease without killing the plant at the same time. The disease can be spread by insect carriers, such as thrips, greenfly and whitefly, and by handling healthy plants, but is not capable of spreading itself, as a fungus disease can, by spores. Hence, removal and destruction of such plants will eliminate the possibility of further infection.

Viruses are characterised by various symptoms, mostly discolouration of leaves in regular or irregular patterns, such as yellow rings, bands, blotches or mottling, striping or brown streaks or spots on the stems, and mottling and flecking of flower colour. There is a sharp distinction between the normal and abnormal colouring, easily recognised after a little experience. Growth may be stunted, cease altogether, or be distorted. Tomatoes, cucumbers, pelargoniums and occasionally roses are prone to viral troubles.

SPECIFIC DISEASES

Azalea Gall: Leaves, stems and flowers become thick and swollen, with a white covering. Growth is badly stunted.

REMEDY. The affected parts should be removed before the white covering appears, as this consists of spores, capable of fresh infections. After careful removal of all visible infection, spray the plants with a copper-containing fungicide.

Carnation and Tomato Wilt: This is a soil-borne fungus disease which infects the plants through the roots and stains the internal tissues of the stem brown, from the base of the plant upwards. First signs are wilting of the leaves during the day, with recovery at night. Later the lower leaves discolour brown or yellow and drop off, progressing up the plant. Eventually the affected plant does not recover from wilting during the day and dies.

REMEDIES. Affected plants are best removed, though tomatoes may sometimes recover to some extent if mulched with peat so that fresh roots can be encouraged from the stem, low down. Sterilising the soil or compost beforehand, and use of wilt-resistant stocks in the case of tomatoes are advisable. Captan can be used to prevent fusarium wilt on carnations by spraying the stock plants before taking cuttings, and by watering the cuttings in with a spray-strength solution of the same fungicide; this obviates the need for sterilising the soil in most cases.

Carnation Leaf Spot: This is characterised by light brown spots on the leaves which spread quickly and defoliate the plant. Badly ventilated houses and crowded plants are much more likely to produce a bad epidemic of the disease.

REMEDIES. Badly infected plants should be lifted and burnt, and the remainder sprayed with a copper-containing spray. Carnations in general should not be repeatedly sprayed as this destroys the natural 'bloom' on the plants, which is a protection, and once this has gone, fungi can penetrate very easily.

Peach Leaf Curl: The leaves become thickened in patches, rather like blisters, and gradually distort and curl up as the disease spreads. The blisters are a yellowish-green, gradually turning pink and then red, with a blue bloom, and at this stage are producing spores to infect other healthy leaves.

REMEDIES. Remove affected leaves as soon as they are seen, in March in most cases, and spray the remainder with captan as a protection. In autumn, as the leaves fall, apply a copper spray, repeating at complete leaf fall, and again just before the buds burst, in late winter. The last three sprays are a protection and are used at those times when re-infection of the buds is most likely to occur.

Rose Black Spot: This is characterised by fringed black spots about $\frac{1}{4}$ in. in diameter on the leaves; the latter then gradually turn yellow and fall early.

REMEDIES. Spray with benomyl, a systemic fungicide which is absorbed into the sap, or captan (protective), and collect fallen leaves. Burn all prunings.

Tomato Blight: This disease is not often seen on indoor tomatoes; it produces large, dark brown-black blotches on leaves and stems, and brown patches on fruit. It normally does not appear before July and can then spread rapidly in warm humid conditions.

REMEDY. Spray with Bordeaux mixture at half strength, or with zineb at fortnightly intervals, before it appears.

Tomato Leafmould: This can be distinguished by small yellow spots on the leaves which develop a brown growth of mould on the under-surface; the spots spread rapidly so that the whole leaf may be covered, and the plant ceases to grow. Overcrowding and lack of ventilation are conducive to its spread, so also are high temperatures and a too humid atmosphere.

REMEDY. If signs of it are seen, spray at once with a zineb-containing solution. Resistant varieties are available.

Tomato Stem Canker: The first symptom is sudden wilting of plants, followed by recovery. Dark brown or black patches on the stem at, or close to, soil level are usual but they may also be apparent higher up where the stem has been damaged. The disease can be soil borne, or carried on tools, string, straw and so on.

REMEDIES. Infected plants must be lifted and destroyed as soon as seen, and the remainder sprayed with colloidal copper; Cheshunt Compound should be applied to the soil. At the end of the season, it should be sterilised and the remaining plants burnt.

CHAPTER SEVEN

Alphabetical List
of Plants

(Ingredients for composts are always measured in parts by volume.)

Abutilon: The members of this genus of shrubby and, in some instances, semi-climbing plants, are pretty plants, very good for greenhouse cultivation. They are remarkable for their attractive leaves and beautifully veined, bell-shaped flowers. Moreover, several species are well worth growing if only for the fact that autumn and winter are their flowering seasons.

Quite good specimens can be grown in 8- or 10-in. pots, but the best results are obtained when they are planted out.

SPECIES. Several species are ideal for growing against a green-house wall, and for this purpose *Abutilon insigne* is strongly recommended. In addition to its dark purplish-crimson flowers, produced in winter, it has large, handsome, dark leaves. Another suitable plant is *A. megapotamicum* (syn. *A. vexillarium*). It is free blooming, from April onwards, and the flowers are dark red and yellow, with dark brown stamens. Plants trained against a wall will need periodical thinning.

Other good species and varieties having the distinction of handsomely marked foliage are *A. striatum thompsonii*, yellow variegated, and *A. savitzii*, with silvery-white markings, while kinds grown for their flowers are Ashford Red, *brilliantissima* (bright red), *milleri* (pale yellow), Firefly (crimson), and Golden Ball.

Abutilon hybrids can be made to bloom within six months of sowing, given sufficient heat for germination, and make very shapely plants a foot or more high within nine months. When in full bloom they are very beautiful.

CULTIVATION. The back wall of a lean-to could be covered with an abutilon, and the less robust kinds can be grown in pots.

Pruning or trimming the plants into shape should be carried out in February, and during the following month repotting can be done. Those planted out will appreciate an annual topdressing of fresh compost. This consists of fibrous loam, peat, and leafmould in equal parts. Good drainage is essential, and plenty of water is needed when the plants are active and have filled their pots with roots. At this stage a weekly application of liquid fertiliser will be beneficial. Temperature in winter should not fall below 7°C (45°F). In summer, warmth can be moderate.

PROPAGATION. By cuttings of side shoots during early spring or late summer, using semi-ripe wood about 2 to 4 in. long. They will form roots in a close propagating frame where the temperature is about 18°C (65°F). Also by seed sown in March in cold frames.

Acacia: In this genus, the mimosas, there are some very useful spring and early flowering trees and shrubs which vary in habit and in formation of flowers and foliage. The flowers are in attractive shades of yellow. All are natives of New South Wales or other temperate regions, and are well adapted for a cool greenhouse.

SPECIES. *Acacia armata, A. cultriformis, A. drummondii, A. grandis, A. hispidissima, A. pulchella, A. verticillata.* Many of the taller growing kinds are too large for the smaller greenhouse.

CULTIVATION. If frost is kept out they are easily grown. Prune immediately after flowering by thinning out and shortening back loose growths. Repot during the summer months every second or third year. The soil should be equal parts of turfy loam and leafmould or peat, with plenty of silver sand. Avoid over-potting, and make the compost quite firm.

Winter temperature 4–10°C (40–50°F) but from early June till the first week in October the plants should be placed outside with their pots plunged in ashes. Never allow the roots to become dry. If grown as climbers, plant out in a well-drained bed in March, and ventilate the house freely in summer. An occasional overhead washing with water will keep them free of insect pests.

PROPAGATION. Either from seeds or cuttings. Seeds are sown, as soon as ripe, in sandy peat, and they germinate in a temperature of 16°C (60°F). Cuttings are made from semi-ripe shoots with a heel attached. Insert in pots of peat, leafmould and sand, place under a cloche outside or in a cold frame and shade until rooted. Pot off singly, and put in a close frame until established, when cooler conditions must be given.

87

Acalypha: Greenhouse shrubs which appreciate the comfort of a warm house. They are mainly of value for their highly coloured leaves or, in some cases, for their pendant tassels of flowers.

SPECIES. *Acalypha godseffiana*, green leaves spotted white. *A. hispida*, long axillary tassels of rich red, *A. wilkesiana macafeeana*, leaves red blotched with bronzy crimson, *A. w. macrophylla*, leaves cordate, russet brown blotched with paler spots, *A. w. musaica*, leaves bronzy green variegated with orange and dull red.

CULTIVATION. Compost of a coarse nature with a little peat added to the loam, thus ensuring good drainage. Though this compost should be good it must not be over-rich or it will lead to coarse foliage. Make sure that the atmosphere is always moist, as these plants are prone to attacks by red spider mite and mealy bug.

PROPAGATION. By semi-ripe cuttings, taken in summer, in a heated frame, or by heel cuttings, taken in March from new growth, in sandy soil also placed in heat, with plenty of moisture in the atmosphere. Grow on in warm conditions till of reasonable size.

Adenandra: This is a genus of small, spring-flowering, evergreen shrubs from the Cape of Good Hope, deserving of wider cultivation.

SPECIES. *Adenandra fragrans*, with rose-coloured flowers at the tips of last season's shoots, and *A. amoena* (red) are the best. Both bloom in June.

CULTIVATION. Compost peaty, with a liberal sprinkling of silver sand. The roots are kept just moist from October till March, but otherwise plenty of rain water is essential. Spray the plants with clear water daily during the spring and summer months. Shade from strong sunlight.

After flowering cut back the shoots fairly hard, and when new growth is apparent repot. The plants may be stood outside during August and September.

PROPAGATION. Cuttings of young shoots, in sandy peat, kept in a close propagating frame will form roots during March. Seeds, when available, can be sown at any time except in winter.

Adiantum, see Ferns

Agapanthus: Known also as the African Lily, this plant has always been popular for the cool greenhouse. It is hardy in the South and other mild localities.

SPECIES. *Agapanthus orientalis* (syn. *A. africanus, A. umbellatus*), flowers of bright blue. There are several varieties, such as *alba* (white), *maximus* (large and bright blue), *giganteus* (dark blue), and *variegatus*, with blue flowers and variegated foliage. All are summer flowering.

CULTIVATION. These plants are gross feeders, and need plenty of room. Usually grown in large pots, tubs, or planted out. Frequent repotting is not conducive to free flowering; it is better to have them more or less pot-bound, and feed freely with liquid fertiliser during the growing season. Repot in March, when necessary, using a mixture of good loam, leafmould, and rotted dried cow manure, or well-rotted garden compost, if cow manure cannot be obtained. Water freely when growing and very little in winter.

PROPAGATION. By division just as growth begins in spring, keeping the young plants in warmth for a few weeks until established. Seed can also be used, sown in a temperature of 18–21°C (65–70°F).

Agapetes: Although rarely seen these days, *Agapetes macrantha* is a beautiful greenhouse climbing plant. It is not rampant, but the growths can be trained under the greenhouse roof so that the flowers are seen at their best hanging in clusters from the older shoots. They are about $1\frac{1}{2}$ in. long and have a porcelain-like texture. The colour is white with delicate red markings. It is an evergreen with narrow, leathery leaves.

CULTIVATION. As the plant belongs to the erica family, it must be grown in a compost that contains no lime. Moist peat, sand and acid fibrous loam suits it well. It needs to be grown in a warm greenhouse with a minimum temperature of 10°C (50°F), in winter. Warm, moist conditions in the summer are needed to encourage new growth with light shading from strong sunshine. Pruning after flowering will keep the plant small enough to flower in a 6-in. pot.

PROPAGATION. Cuttings can be taken in the spring and summer from shoots made in the previous year. Insert them in a compost of peat and sand in a propagating frame with a temperature of 18–21°C (65–70°F).

Allamanda: Evergreen, climbing plants which need a warm greenhouse with a minimum temperature of 13°C (55°F). They have mostly large yellow, trumpet-shaped flowers, in June.

SPECIES. Two attractive kinds from tropical America are *Allamanda cathartica grandiflora* with pale yellow flowers, and *A. c. hendersonii*, orange-yellow with white spots on the throat.

CULTIVATION. The growths should be allowed to ramble up wires under the greenhouse roof and plants are best grown in pots of well-drained compost. Pruning can be done in February by cutting back the previous year's side growths to within one or two buds of the base. Repotting should be done after pruning. Little water is required in winter, but frequent waterings should be given during the summer months.

PROPAGATION. Cuttings 3 in. long can be taken in the spring from growths made in the previous year. They will root in sandy compost in a warm propagating frame (temperature 27°C (80°F) approximately) in a greenhouse. Once rooted, pot each plant separately in a 3-in. pot, and when new growth begins pinch out the tips of the shoots.

Alonsoa (Mask Flower): A half-hardy shrubby perennial under glass, but also grown out of doors as an annual, depending on the species. Flowers are mostly red; it is a native of South America.

SPECIES. *Alonsoa acutifolia* (red, winter flowering) and its white variety *alba*; *A. incisifolia* (red, summer) and *A. meridionalis* (salmon orange, summer).

CULTIVATION. A suitable compost would be one containing 2 parts loam, 1 part leafmould and sand, or the John Innes potting compost No. 2. A sunny place is preferred, and they do not require a great deal of water – it is better given in moderate amounts. Temperature in the winter should not fall below 7°C (45°F), and 10°C (50°F) would be better still. Where grown as a perennial, repotting can be undertaken in March.

PROPAGATION. Seeds can be sown afresh each March for *A. acutifolia* and *A. meridionalis* in a temperature of 16°C (60°F); all can be grown from cuttings taken in August placed in a sandy compost.

Ananas (Pineapple): During the 19th century these were grown in greenhouses with high temperatures, but since the importation of cheap fruits and the present-day high cost of fuel, they are rarely grown, except as ornamental foliage plants.

SPECIES. *Ananas comosus* is the true pineapple, which has plain green leaves; the variegated form (*A.c. variegatus*) has yellow margins to the leaves. This variety succeeds better than the species as an ornamental plant in a living-room and, when grown in a heated greenhouse, will also produce fruit.

CULTIVATION. Plants grown for their fruits need a minimum temperature of 18°C (65°F) in winter. They like a sunny, light position in the greenhouse, and the pots are best sunk in a hot bed or stood on staging with bottom heat. Young plants should be potted on gradually until they are in 10- to 12-in. pots. Plenty of water is needed in the spring and summer, but in winter the compost in the pots can be kept almost dry; a humid atmosphere in summer is very important. Fruiting can be expected when the plants are two years old, when they should be given liquid fertiliser.

PROPAGATION. The best means is by suckers which appear around the base of the plants. These are removed and potted separately in small pots. Crowns, or the tufts of leaves at the top of the fruits, can also be removed and they will form roots if placed in a mixture of moist peat and sand in a propagating frame with a temperature of 21–27°C (70–80°F). Plants can also be raised from seed.

Anigozanthos (Kangaroo Paw): These plants have unusually shaped flowers which give them their common name, and they are natives of Western Australia.

SPECIES. *Anigozanthos flavidus* has greenish-yellow flowers, about $1\frac{1}{2}$ in. long, usually tinged with red. This species grows 3 to 5 ft. tall, but *A. pulcherrimus* does not usually grow as tall, to about 2 to 3 ft. only. The latter has yellow flowers covered with red hairs. Flowering time is May–July.

CULTIVATION. Plants are not difficult to grow provided they can be given a frostproof greenhouse, although a minimum temperature of 4°C (40°F) in the winter is adequate. A suitable potting compost consists of 3 parts moist peat, 1 part loam and 1 part coarse sand. Give plenty of water in summer, but keep the compost almost dry in winter. The best means of propagation is by division in the spring.

Anthurium: A genus of tropical plants with ornamental flower spathes or attractive leaves.

SPECIES. The most striking species is *Anthurium andreanum* with large red spathes which, at first, appear to be almost artificial. It also has large leaves carried on long stems. *A. scherzerianum* is a smaller plant with long narrow leaves, 6 to 8 in. long. The red spathe, 2 to 3 in. long, is very striking and the spadix is curled. Two species with attractive leaves are *A. crystallinum* and *A. veitchii*. The former has thick leaves, 12 to 14 in. long, and they are velvety green in colour with distinct white veins. *A. veitchii* has leaves $1\frac{1}{2}$ to 3 ft. long. They are deep green in colour. Apart from *A. scherzerianum*, anthuriums are too large for the small greenhouse.

CULTIVATION. To grow anthuriums well a greenhouse with a temperature of 16–18°C (60–65°F), is required. During the summer, when temperatures are high, regular damping inside the greenhouse is needed to create moist, tropical conditions, and shade should also be provided. The plants succeed in a compost of fibrous peat, sphagnum moss and loam, together with some charcoal. Large clay pans are suitable for big specimens. When potting, place the plant on a mound of compost and work more compost around the roots. Potting is best done in the spring and at the same time large plants can be divided. This is the most satisfactory way of increasing the plant. During the summer keep the compost around the roots evenly moist, but in winter water should be given sparingly.

Aotus: A small family of dwarf and elegant flowering shrubs belonging to the Pea family.

SPECIES. The one in general cultivation is *Aotus gracillima* with graceful spikes of yellow and crimson flowers in May. A pretty, slender plant about 3 ft. in height. Native of Australia.

CULTIVATION. Grow in equal parts of loam, sand and peat, with a little crushed charcoal added. Repot in well-drained pots in June or July every third year. After flowering, cut the shoots back to keep the plants fairly compact. Daily syringing should be practised while growth is being made. They need a light, airy position and plenty of water in summer, but only sufficient to keep the soil moist in autumn and winter. A temperature of 4–10°C (40–50°F) is ample during the winter months.

PROPAGATION. Cuttings of half-ripened shoots in sandy peat will root under a frame in spring if shaded from bright sunlight.

Aphelandra: This is a genus of ornamental tropical plants, which were once little known outside botanic gardens. *Aphelandra squarrosa* and its variety *louisae*, however, have become very popular in the last few years as house plants. The foliage is most striking and the veins of the leaves are white and distinct. The flowers at the apex of the stems are surrounded by a cone of yellow bracts.

CULTIVATION. To grow aphelandras well a greenhouse with a temperature of 16°C (60°F) is needed, and in the spring and summer a warm, moist atmosphere should be maintained. Old plants can be trimmed into shape in the spring by cutting the shoots back hard, which should encourage new growths to develop lower down the stems, for flowering later in the year. Repotting is best done in the spring, and when well established feeding with liquid fertiliser is beneficial. To preserve the flowers for as long as possible remove the plants to slightly cooler and drier conditions when they begin to flower. Indoors the plants resent hot and dry conditions and any check in growth due to draughts or faulty watering will cause the leaves to drop. They require a good deal of water when flowering and wilt quickly without it.

PROPAGATION. Cuttings can be made from young shoots in the spring. To obtain these, plants that have finished flowering are cut back and the new growths can be removed when a few inches long with a heel of older wood. They should be inserted in small pots of sandy soil, and a propagation frame with a temperature of 18–21°C (65–70°F) is needed for the cuttings to root successfully.

Aralia sieboldii, see Fatsia

Araucaria: A group of conifers of elegant proportion suitable for the greenhouse or conservatory. Small plants are the best for this purpose.

SPECIES. *Araucaria excelsa*, the Norfolk Island pine, is the most popular and the only one which is widely grown. There are several varieties such as *albo-spica*, with silver-tipped growths; *compacta*, a dwarf form; *glauca*, with pale green and glaucous foliage, and *robusta*, larger in all its parts.

CULTIVATION. Araucarias need cool treatment; a winter temperature of 4°C (40°F) will suffice, and in summer they require plenty of light and air.

Repot in March. They succeed in a good fibrous loam, 2 parts, and 1 part leafmould (by bulk) with a little sharp sand. When the pots are filled with roots they will take water freely, but specimens recently repotted will only need a moderate supply. Avoid over-potting. Allow each plant ample head room and space to develop.

PROPAGATION. The most satisfactory method is by seeds sown in pans or boxes and placed in a warm greenhouse. Germination is somewhat slow. Cuttings made from the leading shoots, inserted singly in sandy loam during autumn, will form roots in the following spring if kept in a warm greenhouse from the time of insertion.

When the centre or leading shoot has been removed, the plant will push out side growths, which can be treated as cuttings.

The soil containing cuttings or seeds must not be kept too moist.

Aristolochia: A large genus of strong-growing plants, one of which is useful as a greenhouse climber, either in pots or planted in the border.

SPECIES. *Aristolochia elegans*, the Dutchman's Pipe, a free-flowering species from Brazil, with rich maroon-purple blooms marked with white lines in August. It always attracts attention but it needs a good deal of room and is only suitable for the larger greenhouse.

There are several other handsome and strangely beautiful aristolochias, but they require high temperatures and skilful cultivation and cannot legitimately claim inclusion in this range of plants for the average amateur's greenhouse.

CULTIVATION. *A. elegans* enjoys a rich soil, and a little rotted manure can be added to the usual compost. A minimum winter temperature of 16°C (60°F) is required together with plenty of water in summer but little in winter. Little pruning is necessary beyond removal of straggling shoots. Pot in March.

PROPAGATION. Cuttings of young shoots in a close propagating frame during the summer months.

Arum, see Zantedeschia

Arundinaria, see Bamboo

Arundo: Although these are more or less hardy members of the grass family, one or two forms will be found attractive for grouping with other plants, while for exhibition on a large scale they are well-nigh indispensable. A cold greenhouse will give quite sufficient protection.

SPECIES. The European *Arundo donax*, and its varieties *variegata* and *macrophylla* are the kinds that should be thus used.

CULTIVATION. Keep in fairly small pots. Repotting is done in March. A compost of loam and leafmould in equal parts is recommended. When growing outside they prefer damp situations, so give plenty of water, especially during the spring and summer months. At no time must the roots become really dry.

PROPAGATION. By division when repotting.

Asclepias: There is one species of asclepias suitable for the greenhouse. It is *Asclepias curassavica*, which blooms from July till September. It is a native of tropical America, and should be grown in a warm greenhouse. The flowers, borne in large erect clusters, are a reddish orange-scarlet, on stems 1 to 3 ft. tall.

CULTIVATION. Keep the plants slightly on the dry side during winter and cut back the growths in early spring. Repot in John Innes No. 1 potting compost. When repotting shake out as much of the old compost as possible. Bushiness can be encouraged by tipping back the shoots.

PROPAGATION. Cuttings in spring will form roots in a propagating frame. Both cuttings and seedlings must be potted off singly directly they are ready and given larger containers as required.

Although a perennial, it can easily be raised from seeds and treated as an annual. Seeds should be sown in gentle heat about February, and if kept growing will flower in late summer.

Asparagus: These are indispensable foliage plants. All the kinds quoted are highly ornamental, and remarkable for their fern-like foliage. They make ideal house plants, and are useful for cutting for sprays, bouquets and flower arrangements.

SPECIES. One of the best is *Asparagus sprengeri*; it produces bright green sprays 1 to 4 ft. in length. On account of its drooping habit it is an ideal species for baskets, also for pots to drape the front of stages. The South African *A. plumosus* is quite distinct from *A. sprengeri*. It makes an elegant climber. The dwarf variety, known as *nanus*, is a pretty plant, and can be grown in quite small pots. The lasting properties of its cut sprays are remarkable. Other species are *racemosus*, and *scandens*. *A. medeoloides*, or smilax, produces slender green shoots 3 to 6 ft. long. The flowers are greenish or white, and of no decorative value.

CULTIVATION. All the above are strong rooting subjects and need a fairly rich compost; they will grow readily in John Innes potting mixtures. Established plants should be repotted in March. Young plants must be moved on when they have filled their pots with roots, irrespective of season. They enjoy a liberal supply of water and when well rooted will benefit from weekly applications of liquid fertiliser. All can be grown in pots, but the long trailing species, such as *plumosus* and *scandens*, may be planted out.

Smilax requires slightly more specialised treatment, as follows. It is best raised from seeds early in the year. February is a good month for sowing if a temperature of 18°C (65°F) can be maintained, otherwise operations should be deferred till March. Fill a well-drained pan with John Innes seed compost and sow the seeds thinly. Just cover with fine compost and do not over-water, although dryness is equally fatal.

When the seedlings are a few inches high, pot off singly in 3-in. pots. The John Innes No. 1 potting mixture is a suitable compost. At the next stage the plants can either be potted on or planted out in long boxes several inches in depth or in a well-prepared border. They should be given a partially shaded position. The back wall of a greenhouse is excellent, especially if cut sprays are needed. Strands of fine string or twine are fixed to nails at the top of the wall and made fast to the box or pots. One growth is attached to each length of twine, then it is an easy task to cut the twine and spray when required without injury to the plant.

During active growth plenty of water is necessary, and the foliage should be syringed twice a day when the sun is bright. Old plants are cut down each spring and repotted or topdressed with fresh compost. These will benefit by occasional application of soot or liquid fertiliser.

Cuttings of young shoots can also be used for propagation and will form roots in a propagating frame in spring or summer.

PROPAGATION. Seeds should be sown in light compost during spring or summer months, and germinated in a temperature of 18°C (65°F). Large specimens may also be divided when repotting.

Aspidistra: These were once universally grown, and commonly known as the Parlour Palm; they are now becoming popular again. Evergreen foliage plants with large wide leaves, and insignificant but peculiar flowers just showing above the compost surface.

Top: Cobaea scandens
Bottom left: Clerodendrum speciosissimum *Bottom right:* Dracaena fragrans massangeana

SPECIES. The best known is *Aspidistra lurida* from China; there is also a variegated form, *A. l. variegata*, with cream stripes on the leaves. The plant has a remarkably strong constitution and will remain in good condition for years.

CULTIVATION. They thrive for years without repotting, but when repotted should have the usual mixture of good fibrous loam, leafmould, and sharp sand. A moderate supply of water will keep them healthy. Fancy pots must be emptied of accumulated water from time to time. If a green leaf appears in the variegated varieties, it must be promptly cut out, otherwise the whole plant may in time revert to the original type. Cool greenhouse temperatures are suitable.

PROPAGATION. Increase by division between March and September. Each piece of rhizome removed should have a few roots and leaves attached. Give a little shade until established.

Asplenium, see Ferns

Astilbe: Formerly known as *Spiraea*, the correct name *Astilbe* is now generally recognised. The several species and hybrids quoted are valuable pot plants for the greenhouse in early spring. If retarded roots are obtained, the flowering period can be extended later into the year.

SPECIES. An old favourite was *Astilbe japonica* (white); another white variety is Gladstone, but it is the coloured hybrids that have made these plants so highly prized. They include Amethyst (violet-purple), Ceres (silvery pink), Fanal (deep red), Federsee (rose red), Fire (salmon red), the beautiful Gloria (rose pink), the early Koln (rose cerise), Salmon Queen, Venus (deep rose pink), Serenade (rose lilac), and others. These varieties range in height from 2 to 3 ft., and are remarkable for their graceful and elegant panicles of bloom, produced well above the attractive foliage. For late flowering the pretty dwarf *A. simplicifolia rosea* should be chosen. It has graceful arching rose-coloured plumes.

CULTIVATION. Clumps with flowering crowns should either be lifted from the open ground or purchased during the autumn months. Place in pots that will just take the roots, and use a compost of loam and leafmould.

After potting arrange in a cold frame, and introduce a few plants to the greenhouse at intervals of three weeks, with a view to pro-

Few plants surpass the merits of the tuberous-rooted begonias as greenhouse subjects for the amateur. This is the variety Lionel Richardson

longing the season of flowering. The first batch can be moved early in the New Year or during December if any have started into growth. Until the plants are growing freely a temperature of 7–10°C (45–50°F) will be ample; afterwards it may rise to 16°C (60°F) until the flowers begin to open, when cooler conditions can prevail. A fairly moist atmosphere and an abundance of water at the roots are essential. In fact, when the plants are well rooted the pots can be stood in saucers of water or weak liquid fertiliser. The last batch will produce its flowers without any forcing. If very early (mid-winter) blooms are required retarded clumps must be secured.

After flowering gradually harden off and plant outside. Choose a moist situation and give water during dry weather. The following March they can be lifted, divided and replanted in lines 2 ft. apart. If the soil is good and moist they will develop in two or three years into suitable clumps for forcing again. It is not advisable to grow them in pots two years in succession.

PROPAGATION. Named varieties are increased by division, but good forms can be raised from seeds, especially the pink shades. Sow the seeds during March in pans, and allow them to germinate in the greenhouse. When the seedlings are large enough, transfer to boxes of light compost, and in June or July transplant outside. A few may push up a spike towards the end of the summer. They will, however, make good flowering clumps for the following year.

Azalea: The azaleas belong to the hard-wooded class of plants and are botanically embraced in the genus *Rhododendron*. They are quite indispensable for decoration from December to May. There are both double- and single-flowered forms in many shades of red, cerise, pink and pretty combinations of these colours with white, while the pure white forms are valuable for various purposes. They can be grown as standards, pyramids, or quite small compact plants in 5-in. pots.

SPECIES. Three classes of azaleas are used for decoration of the greenhouse. The most popular is the azalea botanically called *Rhododendron simsii* (sometimes known incorrectly as *Rh. indicum*), the 'Indian' azalea, from Japan. A host of garden seedlings and hybrids derived from this plant constitute a most important feature in the horticultural trade. They are evergreen.

The varietal names in all the groups and sub-sections of the azalea family are legion. To print the names of a dozen, score, or even a hundred representing them to be the best choice that can be made, would be ever open to criticism and disagreement. The far better recommendation is that trade catalogues of firms handling these gorgeously beautiful plants in quantity should be consulted by intending purchasers or, better still, good collections inspected when in bloom and varieties picked out which appeal most strongly to personal taste.

Another group comprises the varieties of the Japanese *Azalea mollis (Rh. japonicum)*, which is a deciduous species, and is obtainable in various shades of rose, orange, yellow, and flame. They are useful for early spring work in pots as well as for outdoor cultivation.

The third group contains various dwarf evergreen azaleas well adapted for pot cultivation. The flowers are smaller than the Indian class. The plants are hardy so can be grown in quite a cool house. The best known is probably *A. amoena* (light crimson, correctly *Rh. obtusum amoenum*). Others of interest and distinct beauty are Hinodegiri (brilliant red), Hinomayo (bright pink), Benigiri (brilliant red), and Yasgegiri (brilliant salmon red).

CULTIVATION. Indian azaleas are imported from the Continent in the early autumn. They are usually full of flower buds, and should be purchased either in bud or flower.

After flowering they make their best growth, and form flower buds for the following season. In the first year fresh compost will not be required, but afterwards they will need attention every second year. Repot when growth begins. Perfect drainage is essential. The compost consists of good quality peat and a liberal addition of silver sand. Yellow fibrous loam, if free of lime, can also be used in conjunction with peat. Avoid over-potting and make the soil firm. While the plants are growing they enjoy a temperature of 16–18°C (60–65°F) and a buoyant atmosphere is kept up by sprinkling the paths and stages with water twice each day. Syringe the plants occasionally, especially the undersides of the leaves.

Newly potted plants need careful watering – in fact, indiscriminate application of limy water is responsible for the loss of many plants annually. When water is really required, sufficient must be given to soak the ball of soil right through. Extra care is necessary in winter to avoid waterlogging.

When the plants begin to complete their growth, admit more air, and gradually harden off with a view to standing them outside during July, August and September. Place in full sunshine, and continue the use of the syringe. Return to the greenhouse when nights become chilly, and start with a temperature of 4–7°C (40–45°F), and if kept steadily moving, without too much heat, they will bloom in the following spring and summer.

For early work select well-budded specimens, and introduce them to a slightly warmer temperature about November, gradually increasing it to 16 or 18°C (60 or 65°F). Azaleas should always be given rain water.

The amoena group enjoys the same treatment as the forms of *Rh. indicum*.

The mollis section needs somewhat similar treatment, or the plants may be hardened off and planted outside. Here they can remain until they produce a full crop of flower buds, when they may again be potted and brought into use for the greenhouse. After flowering, all seed pods must be removed.

PROPAGATION. This is seldom attempted except by the trade, who have the proper facilities for the task. The Indian azaleas are chiefly increased by grafting, but they may also be obtained from cuttings – a somewhat slow job. Select half-ripened shoots, cut to a joint, and remove the lower leaves. Fill the pots to one third of their depth with drainage material and then add a layer of sandy peat, with 1 in. of pure sand on top. Insert the cuttings in the sand. Place the pots in a frame with a little bottom heat. Seeds are sown when ripe, and kept in a warm, moist house until germination is effected. *Rh. japonicum* can also be raised from seeds, and by layering plants grown outside in spring after flowering.

Azaleas are occasionally attacked by thrips or red spider mite, especially when under glass. These pests must be destroyed either by fumigation or spraying with an insecticide, otherwise the plants will be ruined.

Bamboo: Under this heading will be found a few representatives of *Arundinaria* and *Phyllostachys* suitable for pot cultivation and greenhouse embellishment. They include the Japanese *Arundinaria variegata*, slender stemmed and with graceful foliage, the Indian *A. falcata*, 3 to 6 ft. tall, with slender, dark green stems clothed with graceful foliage and *Phyllostachys aurea* from Japan, 4 to 8 ft., whose cones are cream to dull yellow.

CULTIVATION. Repot in March. Large plants can be divided. Use compost of 2 parts loam and 1 each of leafmould and sand. They need a liberal supply of water except in winter, when the roots are kept just moist. An ordinary greenhouse temperature will suffice. Increased by offsets and division at potting time.

Beaufortia: A small group of elegant Australian evergreen shrubs, attaining about 2 ft. in height. They flower in May, June and July.

SPECIES. *Beaufortia purpurea* bears purplish-red flowers in July; *B. sparsa* (syn. *B. splendens*) is bright scarlet.

CULTIVATION. Repot in March in loam, peat and leafmould with a little sand. Provide ample drainage, and make the compost quite firm. Water freely from May to August, and sparingly at other seasons. Any pruning needed is done in March, when repotting. Cool greenhouse conditions are suitable.

PROPAGATION. By cuttings of half-ripened shoots using sandy soil. Place in a close frame in summer. Very little heat is needed.

Begonia: This is a large and widely varied genus of plants, which must be one of the most suitable and decorative of those which the amateur can grow in the greenhouse. Many years ago fibrous-rooted species, and those of which the conspicuous charm was in beauty of foliage rather than blossoms, were the highly prized occupants of practically all greenhouses and conservatories. The astonishing improvement in the tuberous-rooted section brought them into great prominence and popularity and, maybe, their development was somewhat to the disadvantage of their fibrous-rooted relatives. Some of these are so decorative and serviceable that it is to be hoped they will regain the recognition and popularity they deserve.

The family as a whole might well provide ample material for an entire book of considerable dimensions, but in this general volume covering a comprehensive range of plants for greenhouses, only brief notes on the most desirable kinds are possible.

In view of their outstanding merits first place must be given to the tuberous section. Few plants surpass these in their merits as greenhouse plants for the amateur. Both doubles and singles embrace a wide range of entrancingly lovely colours, and whilst named varieties are available in wonderful forms and distinctive colours, seedlings of superb quality will meet the needs of a large proportion of amateurs, the one limit possibly being that colours of seedlings cannot be chosen in advance of the flowering period.

CULTIVATION, TUBEROUS ROOTED. Seedlings raised in heat, by sowing seed early in the year – February is a good month for sowing – will flower in late summer and autumn of the same year. After flowering ceases the plants should be induced gradually to rest by drying them off in easy stages, but not by any means suddenly. By the time top growth has died off tubers of reasonable size will have formed in the compost. These are best stored in their pots through winter and will provide good stock to develop into bigger plants, and come earlier into bloom the following year. Tubers of more than one year's growth may be stored in their pots in the same way, or, if either room or pots are needed for other purposes, the tubers may be shaken out and stored, closely placed in trays with clean, dry sand between them. A temperature of 4°C (40°F) is safe enough for winter storage.

The correct time to start dormant tubers depends upon the command one has over temperature. If a greenhouse can be heated sufficiently to maintain a temperature between 13 and 16°C (55 and 60°F), a first batch may be started in February but where there is a risk of the night temperature falling below 10°C (50°F) it is wise to wait until mid-March and even later if the house is entirely unheated. To start the tubers into growth place them in shallow trays of moist peat. For a while no further water should be required but the peat should not be allowed to become really dry. Whenever water is used in the early stages of root formation it should be made just lukewarm. When sprouted freely pot off singly in small pots, and later on repot them into larger pots. Provide ample drainage, and use a compost of fibrous loam (3 parts) and leafmould (1 part, by bulk) with a sprinkling of sharp sand. Pot moderately firmly. Remove all flower buds until the roots are well established. Give water in moderation. Syringe between the pots daily, and shade from strong sunlight. During the summer months ventilate freely. Pick off seed pods and stake any plants that need support.

PROPAGATION. The usual method of propagation is from seeds sown from February to April. Fill a well-drained pot with light, fine compost, water thoroughly with a fine-rose watering can, and allow the pots to drain for a few hours. Sow the seeds thinly, and then add the merest sprinkling of sand. Cover the pot with glass, and remove to a temperature of 18°C (65°F). If kept moist and heavily shaded, seedlings will soon appear. When these are large enough, transplant in boxes or pans 1 in. apart. Directly the seedlings begin to become crowded pot off singly in 2-in. pots and grow on in the greenhouse until ready for potting into large pots.

When increase of stock is required of named varieties or of particular colours which cannot be relied upon to remain true to colour in young plants raised from seed, they may be propagated by means of cuttings. The procedure is first to start tubers in gentle warmth early in the year. When young shoots have made sufficient stem growth to enable them to be fixed firmly in a light compost in tiny pots, sever them cleanly from the point of origin, at the crown of the tuber, insert in the prepared compost, no deeper than is necessary to hold them steady. Plunge the pots to the rims in moist granulated peat, in a position where gentle bottom heat can be maintained, and cover with glass to ensure a still, warm, and moderately humid atmosphere.

The compost should consist of sifted peat and sharp silver sand, in equal parts. Roots should form rapidly, and as soon as signs of growth become evident the young plants must be inured to the freer atmosphere of the greenhouse, and repotting must take place before the thumb pots become crowded with roots. Such plants from early spring cuttings should flower the first summer and form good tubers by the time top growth dies away.

In addition to the normal class of erect habit, there is a group of pendant begonias, also tuberous rooted, which produce many slender, prostrate, or hanging stems with a profusion of small elegant blooms in delightful colours. Methods of cultivation for these are on the same lines as for the others, but their habit of growth adapts them for treatment as hanging-basket plants or, if grown in pots, they should stand on pedestals so that their blooms may hang clear of the staging.

CULTIVATION OF WINTER-FLOWERING HYBRIDS. Closely related to the summer-flowering section of the family, but differing in character because they are hybrids between the tuberous begonias and *Begonia socotrana*, which is bulbous rooted, there is a very attractive and useful class of winter-flowering begonia, the Socotrana Hybrids, of which there are named varieties bearing single, semi-double, or fully double flowers. The management of this class is not quite so simple as in the case of the tuberous rooted. The chief difference is that because they are only partially tuberous in character they will not endure total drying off. Furthermore, since they are blooming long after their summer-flowering relatives have gone to rest, this winter-flowering race must be kept in growth during the most difficult months of the year; their resting period begins in February and ends in May. During that period just sufficient water must be given to maintain the stems in a plump condition, while the temperature must be kept safely above freezing point, but not much higher.

About the end of April more water can be given, and when growth begins any repotting is carried out. Avoid over-potting, and use a mixture of loam (2 parts) and peat (1 part). Press the compost moderately firm and water sparingly until growth is well away. If the shoots are overcrowded, a few can be removed and made into cuttings. They will root in a close frame, and make nice little flowering plants in 3-in. pots.

During the summer months keep the atmosphere buoyant by an occasional damping of the floors and stages, but do not spray the plants overhead. A few neat stakes will be necessary, and any flower buds that appear before November should be picked off. An occasional fumigation will hold in check greenfly and the begonia mite. A stunted growth, with the undersides of the leaves brown or dark, denotes the presence of the last-named pest. Admit a little air, but avoid cold draughts over the tops of the plants. Shade when the sun is bright.

Begonia Gloire de Lorraine and others of this type can be grown in the same house. After flowering reduce the growths to encourage basal shoots. These make the best cuttings and can be inserted from February till April. They will root in sandy compost if placed in a close propagating frame. Pot on as required, and they will bloom in 5- or 6-in. pots. A little sieved manure and wood ashes may be added to the usual fare. Propagation is also effected by leaves, treated in the same way as advised for Rex varieties. Sufficient atmospheric humidity always to keep growth soft and succulent is the secret of securing abundance of bloom on the Lorraine class. The specialist nurseries which supply these plants have many new and beautiful varieties in their collections.

Begonias in hanging baskets are very effective suspended from the roof shelters of the greenhouse. Grow the plants in pots until a few inches high, then transfer to wire baskets lined with moss. These begonias can be raised from seeds.

CULTIVATION, FIBROUS-ROOTED SPECIES. These are very numerous and were once very popular, but of recent years they have been replaced by the more showy hybrids already mentioned. These should include *coccinea*, growing up to 4 ft. and bearing scarlet flowers from spring onwards; *evansiana*, a Chinese species, 2 ft. tall, autumn flowering, pink; *fuchsioides*, winter blooming, scarlet, capable of growing 6 ft. high; *manicata*, a dwarf (1 ft.), winter blooming, pink; *socotrana*, 1 to $1\frac{1}{2}$ ft., bearing pale pink flowers in late autumn; *weltoniensis*, 1 to 3 ft., an erstwhile favourite winter-flowering hybrid.

Begonia semperflorens is in a class by itself. It is perennial, but grows so rapidly from seed to flowering stage that it is treated by the trade as an annual of great service for summer bedding. It may be had in white, pink, scarlet or deeper red, and will commence to bloom when about 4 in. high, seldom far exceeding a foot under outdoor cultivation. Grown as a pot plant it makes a highly decorative winter bloomer and may exceed a foot by several more inches in height. It is easier to manage than the Lorraine class. The last few years have witnessed a remarkable improvement in these begonias, and many new varieties including F_1 hybrids have appeared.

The chief point in management of the fibrous-rooted section is the provision of a good porous compost, such as the John Innes mixtures or one of the new loamless composts. Pot with only moderate firmness. Repot before root-binding until the plants reach the size in which they are to flower. Give shade from direct sunshine, and maintain a buoyant and reasonably humid atmosphere. Do not allow roots to become really dry throughout the growing season, but reduce the water supply by gradual stages as the resting season approaches. The plants must never be completely dried as in the case of tuberous begonias.

PROPAGATION. Practically all fibrous-rooted begonias are raisable from seed, treated as advised for the tuberous class. Cuttings of young growths provide a convenient means of producing limited numbers of any special favourites. Spring is the season for propagation, and temperatures for either young seedlings or rooting cuttings should average 18°C (65°F) with a bottom heat of 21°C (70°F).

CULTIVATION OF FINE FOLIAGE BEGONIAS. Still another class of begonias consists of species and hybrids which are more remarkable for beauty of leaves than of flowers. It is customary with these to pinch out the flower buds in order to throw all energy and virtue into the foliage.

Begonia rex and its varieties may be given foremost place in this section. Well-grown plants will produce huge leaves with lovely and widely varied colouring, veining, and contrasting zones or blotches of glorious tints. Other attractive kinds are *albo-picta* and *argenteo-guttata*, both having leaves conspicuously dotted and sprayed with white on a bright green ground colour. *Laciniata* is almost black and green; *metallica* shows lovely metallic tints and sheen, *ricinifolia* is beautifully outlined with lobed margins, and *sanguinea* is rich red on the reverse of the leaf and a lovely rich shade of green above.

These begonias are grown in the same way as the other kinds, except that frequent syringing is beneficial, and leaf colouring is usually more accentuated when roots fill the pots to the point of pot-binding.

PROPAGATION. In addition to raising from seed or cuttings, the foliage begonias can usually be increased by division of the root-stock just as new growth starts in spring.

Leaf cuttings provide another means of propagation where many new plants are required. For this purpose leaves should be well developed and almost fully grown. Sever a selected leaf from a plant, bend it in two or three places so that its largest ribs crack. Spread the leaf flat upon a pan or tray of light, very sandy and well-drained compost. Weight the leaf down with pieces of tile or smooth stones so that the cracks in the leaf ribs rest in close contact with the compost. Water with tepid water, and place the container in a close propagating frame. Within 18 or 20 days a callus should form at each crack point, and soon afterwards signs of formation of tiny plants should appear. Wait until these have formed tiny young leaves and have thrust young roots into the compost, then separate and lift these with gentle care, pot separately in tiny pots of similar compost. Give them a few days' start in the propagating frame, after which inure gradually to air, and then remove to a shelf in the shady part of the greenhouse. Pot on as necessary.

Beloperone (Shrimp Plant): The most popular species grown is *Beloperone guttata*, a native of Mexico. It is a showy perennial and an excellent pot plant for a cool greenhouse. The flowers are inconspicuous as they are hidden amongst clusters of drooping, salmon-brown bracts. These are carried at the ends of the shoots. Plants grow 2 to 3 ft. tall and have soft green leaves.

CULTIVATION. Young plants can be placed in 3-in. pots in good potting compost. As they fill their pots with roots gradually repot them in 5- or 6-in. pots. Pinch out the tips of the shoots regularly to encourage a bushy habit. When established in their final pots feed the plants regularly in the summer with liquid fertiliser. Light shading from strong sunshine is advisable.

PROPAGATION. Plants flower so freely that is is often difficult to obtain young unflowered shoots for cuttings. One plant can, however, be set aside for the reproduction of cuttings. It should be cut back regularly to encourage young growths to develop. These, if removed when a few inches long, should root readily in a warm propagating box in the greenhouse. The spring and summer are the best times for rooting cuttings.

Bignonia: Usually strong-growing climbers, only two of which are recommended for the greenhouse or conservatory.

SPECIES. *Bignonia tweediana* (syn. *B. unguis-cati*) attains a height of 15 to 20 ft. It has yellow flowers produced in summer, and is native of Buenos Aires. *B. venusta* (syn. *Pyrostegia venusta*), 10 to 15 ft. high, has orange flowers, and blooms August to December. Native of Brazil.

CULTIVATION. The plants enjoy plenty of light and sunshine and, where possible, should be planted out in a narrow border. Provide good drainage. Compost should consist of 2 parts loam, 1 part peat, and sand. Make the compost fairly firm. Water liberally from March to October, and keep on the dry side during winter. Spray the foliage daily when the weather is hot and dry.

To ensure freedom of flowering the wood must be well ripened. Avoid overcrowding by removing all weak shoots as they appear. In January cut back the growths by one-third of their length.

PROPAGATION. By cuttings in spring and layering young shoots at the end of the summer.

Billbergia: These are attractive bromeliads which come from tropical America. They are popular as room plants, but do best in a heated greenhouse.

SPECIES. *Billbergia nutans*, which is nearly hardy, is the most easily grown. It has long, tapering, dark green leaves forming a rosette. The curious flower spikes appear in the spring and they are pink, yellow, green, and blue in colour. *B. windii* is similar, but has larger flowers.

CULTIVATION. A warm greenhouse with a moist atmosphere suits them well. Regular repotting is not needed, but a suitable compost to use consists of moist peat, fibrous loam, sphagnum moss and coarse sand in equal proportions. Pots should have plenty of crocks at the bottom to ensure good drainage. Water freely in summer, but sparingly in winter.

PROPAGATION. The best way of increasing billbergias is by dividing older plants into several pieces, potting each one separately in a small pot in spring.

Blandfordia: A small group of extremely showy bulbous plants hailing from Australia. They are summer blooming.

SPECIES. The best are *Blandfordia flammea aurea* (golden yellow), *B. f. princeps* (rich orange-red), *B. grandiflora* (crimson), *B. marginata* (orange-red), and *B. nobilis* (orange with yellow margins). They attain a height of about 2 ft.

CULTIVATION. Repot in spring in small pots with ample drainage. The rooting medium consists of loam and peat in equal parts with a little coarse silver sand. Give water sparingly until growth begins, then water freely while the plants are active. Arrange the plants where they will receive plenty of sunshine. Very little moisture is needed in winter. Temperature in winter should not fall below 4°C (40°F).

PROPAGATION. By seeds sown in March or offsets from old plants when repotting.

Blechnum, see Ferns

Boronia: A useful and pretty group of hard-wooded, evergreen, summer-flowering fragrant plants. They make neat, shapely shrubs in 6- and 7- in. pots, for the cold greenhouse.

SPECIES. The best are *Boronia elatior* (with pendulous rosy-red flowers), *B. heterophylla* (purplish-pink), and *B. megastigma* (brown and yellow). All are native of Australia, and under cultivation attain a height of 1 to 4 ft.

CULTIVATION. Repotting should be done directly the top growth ceases. A suitable compost is 2 parts peat and 1 part fresh loam with plenty of silver sand. The pots must be well drained, and the soil rammed firmly in the pots. They need a light, airy position and extra care in watering. Pinch the young shoots two or three times when the plants are small, and the leading shoots of old plants once, to create bushy specimens. Some growers choose a compost of fibrous peat with a liberal addition of sharp sand and powdered charcoal. The plants can be put out of doors during the summer, if liked. Moderate watering only is required in winter.

PROPAGATION. Cuttings of firm shoots 2 or 3 in. long will form roots in August. The soil should be principally sand, with a little fine peat. Cover with a hand light or polythene bag and place in a temperature of 10°C (50°F). Shade from bright sunshine, and when rooted pot off singly in small pots. Plunge in fibre and water carefully. Frequent pinching is essential during the early stages of growth.

Bougainvillea: The beauty of these deciduous plants will be found in the highly coloured bracts which enfold the small greenish flowers. They remain in bloom for a long period and are well adapted for training up a back wall, rafter, or pillar as well as for training as specimens over balloon-shaped wire frames in large pots.

SPECIES. *Bougainvillea glabra*, Brazil, has rosy bracts. Some varieties are an improvement on the type. *B. glabra cypheri* is deep rose, a free grower and profuse bloomer, while *sanderiana* has mauve bracts and is very free flowering.

Bougainvillea spectabilis, from South America, is a dull brick red shaded scarlet, but a shy bloomer; its variety *lateritia* is light red. *B. buttiana* is considered the best form in commerce. The gorgeous crimson-red bracts are produced in large trusses. Moreover, it is easily grown and will thrive in an ordinary greenhouse. A newer variety is Orange King, and its name is descriptive of its colour, this being distinct as well as lovely, and there are others such as Californian Gold, deep yellow; and W. R. Higgins, cream-variegated leaves.

CULTIVATION. Bougainvilleas are sometimes referred to as stove plants but as their resting period is in the winter there is no need for high temperatures all the time. A minimum temperature of about 10°C (50°F) is ample.

Good specimens can be grown in pots (especially *B. buttiana*, which will flower when quite small), or they may be planted to cover a wall or pillar. The root run, however, must be curtailed, then they will bloom more freely. Provide plenty of drainage and the soil should consist of 3 parts turfy loam and 1 part leafmould. If the loam is heavy, add a liberal sprinkling of sharp grit or sand.

When the plants finish flowering, usually about October or November, the water supply should gradually be reduced and withheld until February. At this time prune closely and remove all weak shoots. Any repotting or topdressing should be carried out, and pot plants can be arranged in the warmest part of the house. Syringe occasionally with tepid water. Allow the growths to develop without restriction as far as possible in a greenhouse, and do not pinch the shoots. From March to September water freely. Liquid fertiliser will be beneficial for plants that have filled their allotted space with roots. This ought only to be given during the growing season.

PROPAGATION. Bougainvilleas are increased by cuttings of half-ripened wood. If young shoots are taken in March or April with a heel of the old wood attached at the base of each cutting, they will form roots in a brisk bottom heat or close propagating frame with a temperature of about 21°C (70°F).

Bouvardia: A group of handsome evergreen plants which are capable of furnishing a persistent display from September till January. They are of easy cultivation, can be grown in fairly small pots, and are valuable for sprays and buttonholes.

SPECIES. Several are good, including *Bouvardia humboldtii corymbiflora* (white and fragrant), and *B. jasminiflora* (a charming species with fragrant white flowers). Some garden hybrids are Mary, pink; Unique, light red, and Pink Giant.

CULTIVATION. Bouvardias grow well in a warm greenhouse, with a winter temperature of about 13–16°C (55–60°F). After flowering the roots are kept on the dry side to give the plants a rest.

Towards the end of February old plants are cut back, placed in a warm, moist house and freely syringed. This will cause them to break away freely, and so provide plenty of cuttings. Repot at the end of March. Reduce the ball of soil, and use a compost of loam, peat, leafmould, and silver sand in equal parts. Arrange in a warm greenhouse, keep the roots well supplied with water, and spray the foliage once or twice daily to keep down red spider mite. Occasional pinching of the shoots is needed until the end of August, when it must cease. A cold frame is the best place for the plants from early July till September. Keep the roots moist, and syringe each evening. Return to the greenhouse, allow ample space and give weak liquid fertiliser once each week.

PROPAGATION. The usual method is cuttings made of young shoots 2 to 3 in. long. Pots about 3 in. across are filled to half their depth with drainage, the remainder being light sandy compost, with a liberal sprinkling of silver sand on the surface. Dibble the cuttings around the edge of the pot about 1 in. apart. Place the plants in a close propagating frame with a temperature of 18–21°C (65–70°F). When rooted gradually expose them to the house, and pot off singly in thumb pots.

Bouvardias may also be increased by root cuttings. Thick roots are cut into 1-in. lengths and planted $\frac{1}{2}$ in. deep in pans or boxes of sandy compost in spring.

Brachysema: A small group of elegant evergreen climbers, native of Australia, and belonging to the Pea family *Leguminosae*. They bloom in spring.

SPECIES. The chief are *Brachysema acuminatum* (red, a good pillar plant) and *B. latifolium* (crimson and scarlet), a handsome climber 8 to 10 ft. which grows best planted out.

CULTIVATION. The plants require ample drainage in large pots or tubs, and a compost of loam, peat and leafmould in equal parts with sand. Avoid over-watering, and during the dull period of the year just keep the soil barely moist. Train the shoots fairly near the roof glass. Avoid overcrowding to enable light and air to reach the plants, otherwise they will fail to bloom.

PROPAGATION. Seeds sown in March, temperature 16°C (60°F). Cuttings, if made of half-ripened shoots, will form roots in summer. Increased also by layers.

Browallia: This genus contains a few plants, valuable for the greenhouse on account of their free-flowering qualities and neat habit. They may almost be termed perpetual flowering and will grow well in the cool greenhouse.

SPECIES. *Browallia speciosa major,* a charming plant with large bright violet flowers with a white throat. It grows about 2 ft. high, and is a very floriferous perennial.

Browallia demissa (syn. *B. americana, B. elata*) is a half-hardy annual. There are two varieties, one blue and the other white; both are worth growing. Height 1$\frac{1}{2}$ ft.

CULTIVATION. Young seedling plants must be set near the glass. Pot off singly, and transfer to 5- or 6-in. containers before the young plants become starved. They will thrive in John Innes No. 1 potting compost. Pinch the growths about three times to encourage a dwarf and bushy habit.

If nice specimens are needed to bloom from Christmas onwards, seeds should be sown in early July. When the seedlings are large enough they can either be potted off singly or placed three in a pot. The latter, grown on without further division, will make fine massive flowering plants in 6-in. pots. This batch should be grown in a cold frame until the end of September, and then removed to the greenhouse. A daily spraying with clear water will keep the foliage clean and healthy. When flower buds appear and pots are filled with roots, weak liquid fertiliser will be beneficial once or twice a week.

PROPAGATION. Seeds may be sown in spring in sandy compost, or in July for winter flowering, as mentioned above.

Brunfelsia: A genus of shrubs suitable for the warm greenhouse with large, beautiful, salver-shaped flowers, formerly known as *Franciscea*.

SPECIES. *Brunfelsia calycina*, which produces its brilliant purple fragrant flowers in spring and summer, is the only one we need mention here. It reaches a height of 2 ft. and is evergreen.

CULTIVATION. Throughout the growing season the plants must be kept in a moist, warm atmosphere, cooling them off slightly when growth is finished. They like a fairly rich compost made up of 2 parts loam, 1 part peat, some rotted manure and sand.

PROPAGATION. By cuttings of soft growth, struck in a warm moist propagating frame and a very sandy compost.

Caladium: Warm-house, tuberous-rooted perennials, grown for their richly coloured ornamental foliage in summer-time. The colours are many and the leaves beautifully veined.

SPECIES. The main types of interest will be the many hybrids of *Caladium bicolor*, *C. picturatum* and *C. schomburgkii*.

CULTIVATION. These plants require warmth, and without the means to produce a temperature of 18°C (65°F) should not be attempted. Compost must be composed of equal parts loam, peat, rotted manure, and sand. The tubers are dried off in autumn, and stored in the warm for the winter. They are brought into growth again in March by placing in boxes of moist peat and keeping in

Bougainvillea is a very beautiful greenhouse climber with its highly coloured bracts retained over a long period

a warm greenhouse. Humidity in the atmosphere while growing is most important. The tubers can be divided in early spring.

Calceolaria: For cultural purposes these showy and easily grown plants must be divided into two sections, the shrubby and the herbaceous. The shrubby kinds can be grown into fine tall specimens, and their flowering period is spread over several months of the year. The herbaceous varieties are those with spreading heads of large spotted or blotched and gaily coloured flowers. A packet of seeds from a reliable firm will produce strong healthy plants fairly dwarf in habit and remarkable for the great diversity of colour. They are usually at their best in May and June, but may be flowered at different seasons by varying the time of seed sowing.

SPECIES AND HYBRIDS (Shrubby). A group of calceolarias characterised by the greater height, smaller flowers and more graceful branching habit. They only need a winter temperature just a few degrees above freezing. The forerunner and most popular is *Calceolaria profusa* (syn. *C. clibranii*), the golden-yellow flowers being produced in light sprays, and the whole plant attains a height of 2 or 3 ft. The *C. profusa* hybrids are the same in habit as the type but the flowers vary in colour, and the reddish-bronze forms are very effective.

The John Innes strain of *C. gracilis* and their various hybrids are very choice and graceful plants, about 2 ft. high. The flowers show great variation in colour, including pink, mauve and cream.

One of the best of the newer forms is a large-flowered yellow type known as *C. banksii* which not only makes a good pot plant but is also excellent as a bedding subject.

CULTIVATION. Calceolarias of the shrubby type do quite well in the John Innes composts. Good-sized specimens will flower profusely in a 6-in. pot of the No. 2 potting mixture. Rooted cuttings or seedlings are transferred to small pots and repotted as they require it. Pinch the shoots once or twice to induce bushiness, and keep the roots moist during the growing season.

PROPAGATION. This group can be increased by cuttings. Summer kinds will furnish plenty of suitable shoots in autumn, the resulting plants being grown in cool conditions throughout the winter, potting on to 6- or 7-in. pots in spring. The winter-flowering forms provide cuttings in March. It is advisable to maintain a stock of young plants, so that old specimens can be discarded.

Top: Eupatoriums are autumn and winter-flowering plants for the cool greenhouse
Bottom: Datura, an evergreen shrub which can be trained as a climber

SPECIES AND HYBRIDS (HERBACEOUS). Of little value to the amateur, who may well confine attention to good strains of hybrids. They are readily raised from seeds, which should be sown in July on a surface of fine compost in well-drained pans or shallow boxes. The merest covering of fine soil will suffice. Cover with paper and a sheet of glass or black polythene, and place in a cold frame. Keep shaded until the seedlings appear, when more light is gradually admitted. Never allow the compost to become dry. When the seedlings are large enough pot them individually into small pots of John Innes No. 1 potting compost. Grow them in a cold frame fairly near the glass, keep the roots moist, and admit plenty of air immediately the plants have taken possession of the fresh compost and are established.

About October they will need pots 5 in. in diameter, and at the final shift in February or March containers from 5 to 7 in. will be required, according to the strength of the plants.

Calceolarias enjoy a good fibrous loam and will appreciate the John Innes mixtures which contain good loam. It should be well chopped up and left rather lumpy for the final potting. The plants should pass the winter in a greenhouse where the temperature is about 7°C (45°F). When the days begin to lengthen more water and air will be necessary, and after the final potting they will need ample space to develop. Shade lightly when the sun is bright, but this ought not to be overdone, or the plants will become weak.

To grow fine specimens cool conditions must prevail at all times. They dislike excessive heat. Stand the pots on a cool bottom. Lightly fumigate occasionally, or greenfly will ruin the young shoots. Never allow the roots to become dry, while air must be admitted whenever possible. Give liquid fertiliser to well-rooted plants until the flowers begin to open.

A form of herbaceous calceolaria, ideal for growing in 5-in. pots, is *C. hybrida multiflora nana*. The cultivation is the same as for the large-flowered type, but the plants are a little hardier.

Another hybridisation has led to what are known as Albert Kent Hybrids, growing somewhat looser in style and about $1\frac{1}{2}$ ft. or 2 ft. high, with very diverse colourings in the large pouches.

Calla (Arum Lily), see Zantedeschia

Callistemon (Bottle Brush Tree): Evergreen shrubs, native of Australia, which can be grown in cool greenhouse conditions. The species of this genus are very attractive during the flowering season when the plants are well grown. They bear dense spikes of crimson or yellow flowers near the ends of the shoots.

SPECIES. The best known are *Callistemon speciosus* (syn. *Metrosideros speciosa*) crimson-scarlet, March to July, from 5 to 8 ft. high; *C. linearis*, scarlet, June flowering, 4 to 6 ft., and *C. salignus*, straw coloured, June flowering, from 4 to 6 ft. in height.

CULTIVATION. Callistemons need plenty of sunshine and free ventilation. Water freely during the growing period, but sparingly at other times. They must never become really dry at the roots.

After flowering lightly cut back the shoots, and syringe the plants daily to encourage new growth. Repotting will be needed every second or third year, when new shoots are evident after pruning. Provide good drainage, and a mixture of loam and peat in equal proportions with a liberal quantity of sand.

PROPAGATION. Cuttings of ripened wood inserted in small pots of equal parts peat and sand will root quite readily in a close propagating frame. Seeds are available but the seedlings take several years to reach flowering size.

Camellia: Camellias are not difficult plants, but they will not tolerate any neglect in regard to watering. They are beautiful evergreen flowering shrubs suitable for large pots and tubs or for planting out in cool greenhouses. Owing to their size they are not adaptable for small structures, but where there is sufficient head room a few should be grown for their early flower qualities, usually during the winter months.

SPECIES. With a few exceptions these are not in general cultivation. They embrace *Camellia japonica* and its varieties, the parent of many of the hybrids now available, and *C. reticulata*, probably the finest camellia known. This has large, semi-double, bright rose flowers, whose beauty is enhanced by the cluster of yellow stamens.

A dozen good hybrids or varieties would include *C. j. alba plena* (the old double white form); Adolphe Audusson, crimson; Contessa Lavinia Maggi, white with broad bands of carmine; Debutante, pink; *donckelarii*, red marbled white; Gloire de Nantes, carmine-rose; C. M. Hovey, crimson-scarlet; *elegans*, large blooms, semi-double, rich soft rose; Jupiter, single, bright light red; *imbricata*, formal double rose; *mathotiana*, red and *alba*, the white version of it, and Preston Rose, carmine.

CULTIVATION. Annual repotting is unnecessary, but every third year fresh soil will be needed. This consists of equal parts of loam, leafmould, and rotted manure from an old mushroom or hot bed in equal parts with a little sharp sand. Camellias will also thrive in peat and sand if never allowed to become dry. Repot during March or April, and make the compost firm around the ball, to prevent water passing freely through the fresh compost and thereby leaving the roots dry. Unthrifty specimens should have all the old compost carefully removed to the living roots, and such plants will usually go back in the same sized pot. They will generally improve if placed in a warm house for a few weeks and syringed with tepid water daily. Large plants can be kept healthy for some years by an annual topdressing of new compost.

After flowering, camellias make their growth, and throughout the period of growth daily spraying (when the weather is bright) will be helpful. Keep the roots moist, and allow plenty of light to reach the plants. Very little pruning is needed, but each spring examine the plants and curtail any shoots inclined to upset the balance of the shrub.

From June to September they may be arranged outside, choosing a position that is sheltered from strong winds but not heavily shaded. They should not, however, be placed in direct sunlight; dappled shade is best. During this period close attention must be paid to watering, and dryness at the roots must be prevented. Owing to the thick texture of the leaves the effect of drought is not shown immediately, but later on the buds will drop off in large numbers.

Return to a light, airy greenhouse during September, and if any shoots are producing two buds one should carefully be removed. Avoid both extremes of dryness and excessive moisture. The plants will be improved if the leaves are sponged with warm water two or three times each year.

PROPAGATION. Traditionally, named hybrids are raised from cuttings or layers, or by grafting on to seedling stocks of *C. japonica*. This is normally a job for the professional nurseryman but in recent years propagation from leaf-bud cuttings under mist propagation has become popular. The amateur with a small mist unit may like to try this method. The time to take the cuttings is the last two weeks of June, in general, and the cutting is rather like the bud taken when rose budding. It consists of a sliver of bark and wood, with one leaf and a bud in its axil. The leaf is cut in half and the cutting inserted for half its length in a mixture of mostly coarse sand, with a little peat, and kept in a heated propagation frame or a mist unit.

Campanula: The members of this family are chiefly plants for the herbaceous border, but those mentioned here are excellent plants for pot cultivation.

SPECIES. *Campanula pyramidalis* (chimney bellflower), a native of Dalmatia, with blue flower spikes, and its white form, *C. p. alba*, both of which flower in July. *C. isophylla*, an Italian trailing plant with lilac lavender-blue flowers, is also very attractive.

The varieties of *C. isophylla* are excellent for baskets or 4- to 5-in. pots for the front line of the staging. Repot in March, and make the soil moderately firm. This species is a favourite cottager's plant, bearing blue, starry blossoms. There is a white form (*C. i. alba*) and a lavender-coloured variety named Mayi, which has woolly, variegated leaves.

The beauty of the chimney bellflower, *C. pyramidalis*, is considerably enhanced when brought into bloom under glass. It is an erect-growing species about 4 ft. in height with numerous blue flowers. There are several varieties of this fine species, such as light blue, dark blue, and pure white, the latter being known as *alba*. Well-grown specimens will produce many spikes, which are at their best in July and August.

CULTIVATION. *C. pyramidalis* must have cool treatment after the seedlings are pricked off. Sow the seeds in February or early March, and germinate in a temperature of 16°C (60°F). When large enough the seedlings can either be pricked off in boxes or placed singly in small pots. Gradually harden off to a cold frame. About May they can be planted out in lines a foot apart, choosing fairly rich soil and an open situation. Here they will grow freely during the summer and autumn months, if kept free of weeds.

The following autumn the best of the plants should carefully be lifted and placed in pots from 8 to 10 in. in diameter. Those lifted in the autumn should be arranged in a cold frame, and taken into the greenhouse about March or April, or alternatively the plants can be grown in pots the whole time and progressively repotted as they require it.

The John Innes potting composts are eminently suitable for *C. pyramidalis*. The plants require plenty of water, and the roots should be fed with fertiliser, solid or liquid, when the flower spikes begin to push up. Specimens with several flower scapes will need staking out to get the best effect.

PROPAGATION. The only method worth adopting with *C. pyramidalis* is to raise from seed. *C. isophylla* and its varieties should be struck from cuttings annually, taking off sturdy young growths from the base and inserting in sandy compost in a moderately warm temperature.

After flowering, the old stools should be thrown away, the finest results being obtained from young stock.

Canna: The Indian shot plant enjoys plenty of heat and sunshine. The varied and brilliantly coloured flowers are produced in bold spikes, surmounting handsome broad leaves. These are often green in colour, but some varieties have coloured foliage, which is an additional charm. Cannas are highly ornamental throughout their growing period. They vary in height from 2 to 6 ft. or even more.

SPECIES. *Canna indica*, a tall plant with red and yellow flowers and the parent of the present-day race.

The plant breeder has produced a magnificent race of beautiful hybrids. Named varieties of canna are numerous and selection is difficult but outstanding are Bonfire and R. Wallace (green leaved), and America and Di-Bartolo (brown and purple leaved).

CULTIVATION. Cannas thrive in rich compost consisting of good loam (2 parts) and sifted rotted cow manure (1 part), with a little peat added. It should also be porous, so a portion of coarse grit or sand will be necessary. The pots must be well drained. The roots are started into growth in the spring by placing in a temperature of about 16°C (60°F). They appreciate a liberal supply of moisture at the base when the roots become active.

A plant with a single crown will need a 6-in. pot, but bigger clumps must be grown in 8-in. containers or even larger. It is advisable to place them in their flowering pots at once, and to make the soil only moderately firm.

When the growth is well advanced and the roots have taken possession of the soil, give all the sunlight possible and keep the roots well supplied with water. Liquid fertiliser, once or twice each week, will be of great benefit.

After flowering, growth will cease and water should be gradually withheld in order that the plants may be dried off. Store in a frost-proof shed or cellar, or beneath a greenhouse stage till the following spring.

PROPAGATION. Cannas are raised from seeds but owing to their hard texture they should be soaked in water for 24 hours before sowing. Sow singly in small pots of light compost during February and March, and place in a temperature of 21 °C (70 °F). Sow the seeds 1 or 2 in. deep, and never allow the compost to become dry. A little bottom heat will be an advantage.

They are also largely propagated by division, and this is the only method for named or choice varieties. Such work is done before the plants are started into growth, and each portion must have one or more crowns, with a few roots when possible. When potted a little extra warmth will help the divisions to form roots and grow away freely.

Carnation: Many greenhouses are devoted exclusively to the cultivation of carnations, which is the most suitable way of growing them. Almost all of those grown today are varieties of the perpetual flowering carnation. Its development has been one of the more notable horticultural achievements of this century. In the early stages varieties came to us from America, but it was not long before British raisers proved themselves capable of breeding varieties which pleased and suited British growers even more than the most popular American introductions. So rapid has been progress in this direction that lists written ten or a dozen years ago mentioning varieties which then were considered to be the very best are now hopelessly out of date. For this reason no such list is here attempted, but the reader is advised to consult the catalogues published periodically by trade specialists, and to select from them varieties to form the nucleus of a collection to which additions may be made from time to time when new varieties are seen at shows.

CULTIVATION. Whenever possible a house should be set apart for carnations only, but where this cannot be carried out the plants should be grouped at one end of the greenhouse rather than inter-mixed with other subjects.

The perpetual flowering carnation is a hardy plant, and must not be subjected to excessive heat. The winter temperature should be between 7 and 10°C (45 and 50°F) at night, with a rise of 2°C

(5 °F) during the day. These figures can be exceeded with sun heat. Avoid a close, stuffy atmosphere; ample ventilation must be provided at all seasons. The top ventilators will never be entirely closed, except during foggy weather or very cold, cutting winds. A thin shading is advisable during the hottest part of the day in summer.

Keep the roots moist, but in winter careful watering must be the rule and the atmosphere kept fairly dry, otherwise rust fungus disease may appear. A good spraying with clear water each day when the weather is bright will encourage healthy growth and help to keep down red spider mite.

To start a collection, young plants should be purchased about April. They will be in 3-in. pots with several shoots, and ready for moving into 5-in. pots. Early in July they should be placed in their flowering containers, usually 6 or 7 in. in diameter. The pots should be well drained; over the drainage place a thin layer of fibrous loam. The traditional compost is comprised of 2 parts good fibrous loam (greasy Kettering loam is ideal), 1 part well-rotted manure, 1 part sifted lime rubble and sharp sand (all parts by bulk). To each bushel of this mixture add a 3-in. potful of bonemeal. Of recent years the John Innes No. 2 potting compost has been used quite successfully for carnations.

Stand the plants in a cold frame, keep the roots moist, and ventilate freely. Stopping or pinching the growths will be necessary, but as a rule this should cease by the middle of July. In August or early September remove them to the greenhouse, wash the pots, stake and allow the plants plenty of room. Artificial heat will only be required when the night temperature is likely to drop below 7 or 10°C (45 or 50°F).

By this time a few will be pushing up their flower stems. Disbud early. As winter approaches the blooms will begin to open, and careful treatment is needed to produce good flowers with a perfect calyx. Ventilation and watering are the principal factors at this season.

To maintain a display of bloom throughout summer and autumn as well as in winter and spring it is necessary to have a second batch of plants raised from cuttings struck later in spring, and grown on in a similar manner to the earlier ones, but potted into flowering pots during the early part of the following year. When two batches have thus been formed, it is just a routine matter to propagate twice a year, thereby ensuring a constant succession of fresh young plants to take the place of an old, tired batch of plants.

During the last twenty years or so the growing of carnations in continuous troughs instead of pots has developed considerably; these are usually made of wood or concrete slabs, giving a depth of soil of 8 to 10 in. and will in the case of the amateur gardener be of a size to fit into the greenhouse space he has available.

PROPAGATION. At the beginning of December cuttings can be rooted and continued till March, unless the requisite number is obtained earlier. These will provide flowering plants the following year, and whenever possible the cuttings should be rooted by the end of January. The best shoots for cuttings are those on the lower half of the flower stem, well above the base of the plant. Pull them off and just trim the ends. Take some clean 3-in. pots, provide a little drainage, and fill with sand. Dibble the cuttings around the sides, and give each pot a label. Arrange the pots in a propagating frame, and maintain a temperature of 16 or 18°C (60 or 65°F). Wipe the glass daily, and keep the sand moist, or they can be rooted very quickly in a mist propagation unit.

In a few weeks they will be rooted. Remove the glass, and expose the plants to light and air. After three or four days stand the pots on a shelf, and see that the sand never becomes dry, otherwise the tender young plants will be ruined. When they become thoroughly accustomed to the house, each one must be potted off singly in 2- or 3-in. pots, or planted in the troughs where they are to be grown in this way. The compost consists of ashes, old soot, lime or mortar rubble, and sand. Press the soil moderately firm. They will need a temperature of about 13°C (55°F). Stand the pots on a bed of fine ashes near the glass. Pinch the centre out of each plant when it is about 4 in. high to encourage basal growths.

Aftercare is the same as advised for plants bought in April. Young plants yield the best results, therefore it does not pay to retain very old ones. Still, two-year-old plants produce a quantity of useful blooms, and the best of them should be retained and repotted in the spring. A few may require cutting back, but all healthy shoots must be left intact. This should be done three weeks prior to repotting.

CARNATIONS FROM SEED. Carnations are easily raised from seeds, and there is always a possibility of obtaining a variety of exceptional merit. Sow the seeds during the spring months in boxes of light sandy compost, and place in a warm greenhouse. Pot off when large enough and pinch the plant when a few inches high.

PERPETUAL MALMAISON CARNATIONS. This is a modern race of Malmaisons, which combines the free-flowering qualities of the perpetual flowering carnations to a marked degree, and the large flowers closely resemble the old Malmaison. They are more easily grown than the latter, and will thrive under the same conditions as the perpetual flowering carnations.

MALMAISON CARNATIONS. At one time large batches of the old blush Souvenir de la Malmaison were grown, but this has been largely superseded by improved varieties. The method of cultivation is slightly different from that required by other sections.

Although side shoots can be rooted in May and June, the best plants are obtained from layering, in a manner similar to border carnations. After flowering, old plants with plenty of healthy growths are removed from their pots and placed on their sides in a cold frame. Cover the roots with compost, so that the shoots can be brought down for layering. Strip each growth of a few basal leaves, partially sever the stem by making a longitudinal and slightly diagonal cut an inch long, and peg down in sandy soil. Keep the compost moist, and admit air each day. When rooted pot off singly. Aftercare is similar to that given to the perpetual flowering varieties, but keep the roots slightly on the dry side in winter.

Cassia: A large genus belonging to the Pea family.

SPECIES. One only calls for attention here. This is *Cassia corymbosa*, an evergreen shrub 6 to 10 ft. high, native of Buenos Aires. Its fine yellow flowers are produced in numerous corymbs during the summer and autumn months.

CULTIVATION. Repot in March, mixing loam (3 parts) and leafmould (1 part) with a sprinkling of sand. If desired this plant can be placed outside in a sunny situation from June to September. Plenty of water is needed from March till October, very little in winter. In January plants that require it should be pruned, and loose or straggling shoots can be cut back to within 2 in. of their base. Place in a frost-proof greenhouse for the winter.

PROPAGATION. By cuttings during spring or early summer months. Select half-ripened shoots, and root in a close propagating frame.

Cattleya, see Orchids

Celosia: A well-grown batch of celosia is always admired. Owing to their feathery or silky flower heads, they are quite distinct from other plants. The forms of *Celosia pyramidalis* (or *C. plumosa* of catalogues) are most varied; they are highly ornamental, and make first-class pot plants from 1 to 2 ft. high. They can be had in various shades of scarlet, yellow and crimson.

The cockscomb is *C. cristata*, and a good mixed strain would produce colours such as orange, rose, crimson, white and yellow. Dwarf crimson is only 6 in. high. The giant forms are from 9 in. to 1 ft. and the brilliant red varieties justify the popular name of cockscomb.

SPECIES. *Celosia argentea*, with white inflorescence, 2 ft., native of China; *C. cristata*, crimson, 1 ft., tropical; *C. pyramidalis*, yellow, 2 ft., native of Java. This species has given us hybrids and strains embracing shades of pink, scarlet and crimson. Recently new and improved varieties in a wider range of colours have been introduced.

CULTIVATION. Celosias are raised from seeds in spring. Well-drained pots or pans are filled with light, fine, sandy compost and made quite level on the surface. Sow the seeds thinly, and just cover with fine compost. If placed in a temperature of 18–21°C (65–70°F), the seedlings will soon appear above the soil. Stand the pots near the roof glass, and if the atmosphere is kept moist less water will be needed at the roots.

When the seedlings are large enough for removal, place them singly in $2\frac{1}{2}$-in. pots. The compost should consist of leafmould (1 part), loam (2 parts), well-rotted manure (1 part), and sand.

Frequent clear water sprayings are needed to keep down thrips and red spider. Grow on in a warm house near the glass. When the inflorescence can be detected, make a selection of the finest quality plants, and place them in pots 4 to 6 in. in diameter. Admit air on favourable occasions, and liquid fertiliser can be given after the final shift, when the pots are filled with roots. Henceforth they will occupy the side stages of the greenhouses, where they will bloom.

Celsia: A small genus closely allied to the verbascums, which contains a few species admirably suited for a cool greenhouse.

SPECIES. Two are recommended; *Celsia arcturus*, a shrubby plant with large clear yellow flowers, which are enhanced by purple-stained bearded anthers. Free flowering. Height variable from under 2 up to 4 ft. *C. cretica* will reach 5 ft. and the large soft yellow flowers continue to open for several months. As the lower blooms fade, the stems elongate, and other flowers develop. Each blossom is marked with velvety brown spots at the base of the upper petals.

CULTIVATION. An important point is that celsias enjoy cool conditions at all times. In late autumn the plants will need 5-in. pots, and a compost of 3 parts loam to 1 part leafmould. Stand the pots on a cool base, and keep them in cold frames so long as frost is excluded. Remove to the greenhouse about November. Give the plants a light position and close proximity to a ventilator. Keep the roots just moist, and directly signs of growth are apparent the final potting should be carried out. Containers from 6 to 8 in. in diameter will be needed. When these are filled with roots, plenty of water must be given and a weekly application of liquid fertiliser.

PROPAGATION. Both species can be raised from seed. They may either be sown in early spring for autumn flowering or in July or August for flowering the following summer. The latter method produces the best results. Sow the seeds in pots of light soil, and germinate in a cold frame. Pot off when large enough, return to the frame, and admit plenty of air.

Plants from a spring sowing need similar treatment. *C. arcturus* will commence to bloom in six or seven months from the sowing of the seeds, but the plants can still be grown into quite fine specimens. This species can also be increased from cuttings during the spring or summer months.

Cestrum: Although not hardy in all districts these attractive shrubs can be grown outside against a sheltered wall in favourable parts of the country. Elsewhere plants are best grown in a frost-proof greenhouse, where they should be trained up the roof or against a wall. The small tubular flowers are produced in clusters during the summer.

SPECIES. *Cestrum newellii* is one of the best species with crimson flowers. *C. aurantiacum* is also good. It grows about 8 ft. tall and has bright orange flowers.

CULTIVATION. This presents no difficulties as the plants grow happily in ordinary garden soil, provided the drainage is good. It is best to have the plants in a border in the greenhouse, but they can be grown in large pots or tubs. Water should be given sparingly in winter, but during growth keep the soil thoroughly moist. Plants can be pruned into shape in the spring by cutting back the side growths, arising from the main stems, fairly hard.

PROPAGATION. Cuttings can be made from young growths that have hardened a little at the base. Remove the shoots with a heel of older wood attached and insert in sandy soil in July or August. A heated propagation frame in the greenhouse is needed to root the cuttings successfully.

Chlorophytum: A useful ornamental foliage plant with curving green leaves, striped and marginated with white.

SPECIES. The only one for the greenhouse is *Chlorophytum comosum variegatum* from South Africa.

CULTIVATION. Repot in March or April, in John Innes No. 1 potting compost. Water freely from March till September, syringe the foliage on bright days and choose a well-lit part of the greenhouse, to ensure good colour.

PROPAGATION. Effected by division at the time of repotting, and by the small plants that form at the ends of the flower stems. When the latter have begun to form roots, they are detached from the stems and placed in small pots for growing on.

Chorizema: These attractive Australian plants are more or less trailing in habit, and for this reason they are suitable for clothing dwarf pillars and walls. Moreover, they can be trained over a balloon made of wire, or made to clothe trellis work.

SPECIES. The principal are *Chorizema cordatum splendens* (red, spring), *C. henchmannii* (scarlet, spring), and *C. varium* (shades of yellow and red, May).

CULTIVATION. Chorizemas succeed in a mixture of loam and peat, with a liberal addition of sharp sand. The best time to repot is when the plants break into new growth. Provide ample drainage, avoid over-potting, and make the compost firm. Established specimens will only need fresh compost every second year. Alternate years they may be topdressed only, with a little fresh compost.

Like other hard-wooded plants, they must have plenty of light and air. Endeavour to keep the growths short jointed. The leading shoots of young plants must be pinched once or twice to induce a sturdy foundation. Early training is essential. When any pruning is required, it should be done immediately after the plants have finished flowering. This will apply chiefly to specimens in pots; those growing against pillars or trellis work will be allowed to develop with little cutting back. Watering must be carefully performed at all times and, as is common to any plant that enjoys a peaty soil, rain water is infinitely preferable to tap water.

PROPAGATION. By seeds or cuttings. The latter do not root easily or freely. Select shoots 2 or 3 in. long and remove with a heel. Insert in pots of a sandy compost and place in a propagating frame to root.

Seeds may be sown in spring and germinated in a temperature of 16°C (60°F).

Chrysanthemum: No plant can take the place of the chrysanthemum for an autumn and early winter display. If the varieties are carefully selected, blooms will be available from early September till January or later. There are several sections of these beautiful flowers, all of which are worth growing.

JAPANESE. These are extremely popular. The flowers can be very large indeed, to as much as 12 in. wide, and vary enormously in colour and appearance. So much is involved in the successful cultivation of these large-flowered varieties that it would occupy too great a space in this volume to do justice to the subject. The National Chrysanthemum Society publishes manuals and guides to various aspects of chrysanthemum growing whether for exhibition or decorative purposes, and these will be found very helpful. In the revised classification of the National Chrysanthemum Society the term Japanese has been abandoned, this class being now called Large Flowered Exhibition.

EXHIBITION INCURVED. For a long period this section was topmost favourite among the keenest of exhibitors, the most obvious reason for that special affection being that production of a faultless bloom demanded more exacting skill than was required for production of the looser, less formal shaggy type. The incurved bloom makes a perfectly regular ball, every petal growing upward and curving inward, each filling its proper place to contribute to the perfect symmetry of the flower. Even the best will occasionally develop a superfluous petal or one or two which are malformed, and therefore create irregularity in the flower. To rectify small defects of this character a reasonable amount of manipulation or dressing of petals is allowed. Ivory tweezers are a requisite for dressing an

126

incurved chrysanthemum. It is a work of art to dress an uneven bloom so that it becomes a perfect globe. Not everybody approves of dressing or manipulating flowers in this manner, and the continual criticism, coupled with the modern style of showing in vases instead of on boards, has resulted in reducing the favour formerly bestowed upon the incurves. A few are still grown, and this type or class may yet be reckoned the acme of perfection from the standpoint of the showman.

There is another group with incurving petals, but of much looser build and usually greater size. These are now classed as Incurving Decoratives, except in the case of varieties considered to be Large Flowered Exhibition (Incurving). The National Chrysanthemum Society has been at great pains to classify all varieties to be of exhibition standard, and growers for show should consult the N.C.S. Classification to avoid risk of staging blooms out of the recognised section.

DECORATIVE. The type of flower that is in general favour today is that known as the Decorative. The plants are of bushy habit, easily grown and produce an abundance of medium-sized flowers in a great variety of colours, while their flowering period spreads over some months. The main shoot is pinched early in March and subsequent stopping will take place when the growths are about 6 in. long. The final pinching out of the shoots will be done at the end of June, but for a December display it can be deferred till the middle of July.

SINGLES. Another popular section, which includes many varieties. In recent years, they have been much hybridised, and improved forms are frequently introduced. They make good specimen plants, and are ideal for cutting purposes. They produce their greatest display in October, November and early December. The varieties with single flowers possess a charm that is characteristic of most single blooms – they vary in colour and size, are produced with extreme freedom, and are ideal for all decorative purposes.

CASCADES. Still another race or class has recently gained a degree of popularity in this country. These are known as cascade chrysanthemums. The plants produce large numbers of small, single, starry blossoms no larger, individually, than the blooms of the *stellata* forms of the greenhouse cineraria. Left to grow naturally the stems would grow erect, like other chrysanthemums, and even in this style they are daintily elegant and very decorative. From

Japanese growers, however, we have learned that by tying down the branches, either to taut cords, fixed canes, or wires, growth can be made pendant, side shoots are induced to grow from every leaf joint, and every shoot produces a loose spray of the starry blossoms, the aggregate effect of which is a veritable cascade of bloom. Such plants have a charming effect when raised on pedestals or placed to overhang the front of the greenhouse staging.

The anemone-flowered, pompons, and spidery (rayonnante) varieties also find favour with a few growers, but the singles and decorative kinds are the most serviceable for amateurs and beginners. Some years ago a completely new race of hybrids known as the charm chrysanthemums was introduced, which make very attractive pot plants for October and November. They are raised from seed sown in February or March and progressively repotted until they reach 7- or 8-in. pots in the John Innes No. 2 potting compost.

PROPAGATION. To produce exhibition blooms large-flowered and decorative varieties are raised from cuttings taken in January.

After flowering retain sufficient healthy plants to furnish a supply of cuttings. The growths are cut down to within 6 in. of their base, and the stools are arranged in a cool house. Here they will soon produce new shoots around the base of the old stem, which will make ideal cuttings. A few varieties do not produce new growths very freely, and these should be assisted by a topdressing of fresh compost. It will be a further inducement to growth if the plants are afforded a few degrees more warmth and sprayed occasionally with tepid water.

Select good cuttings only; the ideal shoot is the one that pushes its way through the soil a little distance from the old stem. Shoots produced on the stems and those with a flower bud at the top are unsuitable. Remove with a sharp knife, cut to the joint, and take off a few of the lower leaves. A good length for the cutting is 3 in.

Cuttings may be rooted singly in small pots when they are grown on without a check, or they can be rooted in boxes or pots and later on potted off singly. Shallow boxes with lid and bottom removed, if stood on the greenhouse stage and covered with a sheet of glass, make excellent propagating frames. A mixture of loam and leafmould in equal parts passed through a quarter-inch mesh sieve, and a liberal addition of coarse sand, will be suitable for the cuttings. Provide a little drainage, and cover the top of the compost

Top: Exacum affine
Bottom: The maidenhair ferns are a handsome, versatile genus

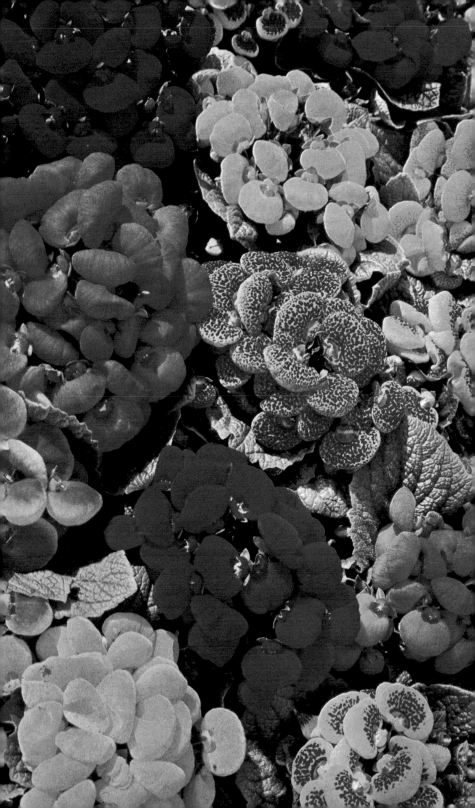

in the pots with a thin layer of sand. See that the base of each cutting rests on the compost and make them fairly firm. Label each variety. Stand the pots in the frame, giving a watering, and turn the glass daily. Maintain a temperature of about 7°C (45°F) and remove any decayed leaves as they appear. Keep the soil just moist, and when the cuttings begin to form roots admit a little air to the frame. Shade from strong sunlight to prevent flagging. As the cuttings become rooted, remove the pots to a shelf in a cool greenhouse, or a frame from which frost is excluded. A sturdy, healthy growth is very essential during the early stages.

Stocks of new varieties are ordered in autumn for delivery as young plants in spring. It used to be an established practice in large private gardens to root the tops of young shoots in April to produce small plants for flowering in 5-in. pots.

CULTIVATION. Young cuttings, rooted singly in thumb pots, will be transferred to containers $3\frac{1}{2}$ in. in diameter. Others which have been rooted in boxes or several in a pot are potted individually into $2\frac{1}{2}$ or 3-in. pots when they are nicely rooted. For all this potting the John Innes No. 1 potting compost will be adequate, although many successful chrysanthemum growers still use special mixtures.

After repotting stand the plants near the glass in a cool greenhouse. Shade from full sun until they are re-established, keep the roots reasonably moist, and allow sufficient space for each one to develop into a strong, sturdy plant. Do not forget to stop the main shoot in March.

As the weather becomes warmer, and there is no longer any danger of frost remove all the plants to a cold frame. After a few days ventilate freely, and grow the plants as cool as possible within reasonable limits. Remove the lights whenever the weather is favourable.

It is hardly possible to fix the day for the next repotting, but it should be carried out directly the pots are filled with roots. This will prevent the growths becoming spindly and the loss of lower leaves. This time 6-in. pots will be needed for most varieties, but a few of the weaker kinds will only require pots 5 in. in diameter. Use clean pots, provide good drainage and give a slightly richer compost; the John Innes No. 2 potting compost is ideal at this stage. If the loam is poor quality, rotted manure, such as from an old hot-bed or mushroom bed, can be incorporated. Rub it through a half-inch sieve, and add a 12-in. potful to every barrowful of the

The herbaceous calceolarias are easy to grow producing their unusual, gaily coloured flowers during May and June

compost. The whole should be thoroughly mixed a week before it is required. Allow plenty of space between the plants, and admit air freely both day and night.

The next shift will be the final potting, which takes place early in June or whenever the roots need fresh compost. The pots will vary in size from 8 to 10 in. and two or more plants can be placed in 12-in. pots or boxes of similar dimensions. Provide good drainage, pot firmly, ramming the compost well round the ball of the roots, but not to the extent of making it so hard that the passage of water is impeded. There is danger of this happening if the compost is too wet at potting time. For this final potting the John Innes No. 3 potting compost is quite suitable. The traditional composts are used with the loam which constitutes three-quarters of the bulk in a rough lumpy condition. The other quarter is made up of peat or leafmould and sharp sand, usually with a special chrysanthemum fertiliser, added according to manufacturer's instructions.

When the potting operation is completed the surface of the soil should be about 1 in. below the rim of the pot.

Stand the plants in the open, away from the shade of trees and buildings. Attend to staking and tying early, before the growths bend over. Cease pinching the main growths after the middle of July, but if large blooms are required do not cease to remove axillary shoots, which will absorb a lot of nourishment, but will not produce useful blooms. Small plants rooted in April will not need any stopping. Allow them to develop naturally, and flower them on first buds. All plants must be made secure against rough winds by tying the central stake to a stout galvanised wire fixed to posts at each end of the row. Watering will need close attention, especially during showery weather. There is often only enough rain to wet the surface of the soil, the lower part being quite dry.

At the beginning of August the pots will be well filled with roots, and plenty of water will be necessary, particularly if the weather is hot and dry. At this stage the application of liquid fertilisers should be made every week or 10 days, according to the vigour of the plants. Alternatively dry topdressings of a chrysanthemum fertiliser can be applied.

With a few exceptions all varieties pay for a little disbudding. If large blooms are required each shoot is disbudded until the top crown bud is left to develop. Many varieties will be improved by the early removal of all weak buds, and a few where they are overcrowded. Natural sprays are also very beautiful, especially where the flowers are on the small side. In such cases no buds are removed, except in cases where they are too crowded to permit development of all.

The first batch should be placed in the greenhouse about the end of September. Late-flowering kinds will remain outside as long as possible, but they must not be injured by frosts or subjected to cold dewy nights. Before taking the plants inside, pick off decayed foliage, remove weeds, wash the pots, and tie any growths that need it. If greenfly, leaf-miner or earwigs are present, spray with a suitable insecticide before moving the plants into the greenhouse. Also add a fungicide to the spray as a routine measure against powdery mildew. Ventilate the house freely, keep the atmosphere fairly dry, and if the weather is damp and foggy give a little heat. A temperature between 7° and 10°C (45° and 50°F) will suffice. If earwigs are troublesome these are easily trapped by placing an inverted flowerpot containing a little hay on the top of a few stakes, or controlled with a BHC dust or spray.

Marguerite: The marguerite is really a summer-flowering plant, but can also be had in bloom during the spring months. It also belongs to the chrysanthemum tribe, and is native of the Canary Islands.

SPECIES. *Chrysanthemum frutescens*, the white marguerite, of which there is also a yellow form. There are various good garden varieties, among which Etoile d'Or is yellow and one of the best. The blue marguerite is in fact *Felicia amelloides*, and is given the same treatment as the others.

CULTIVATION. For spring blooming, cuttings should be rooted about April. Pot off singly when ready, and grow outdoors from June to September. During this period they will need abundant supplies of water, potting on and pinching occasionally to produce bushy plants. They grow quite happily in the John Innes composts or the loamless mixtures. Keep the plants cool in winter but free from frost.

In spring growth will be renewed and flowers appear. If the roots are fed with liquid fertiliser the plants will prove of decorative value for several months. Another lot of cuttings should be rooted in early spring or late autumn, and if potted on as required a fine display will be obtained in late summer and autumn. Cease to stop the shoots after the end of June. Dryness at the roots must be avoided; established specimens must be watered freely during the summer.

Greenfly and the leaf-mining grub are often troublesome, especially in hot weather, and routine measures should be taken to keep them in check.

PROPAGATION. By cuttings of firm young shoots cut close beneath a joint and inserted round the edge of well-crocked pots of sandy compost. Keep close and shaded until rooted. Or sow seeds in a temperature of 13°C (55°F) in April.

Cineraria: For a spring display in a cool greenhouse cinerarias are indispensable. They are easy to grow and can be had in flower from November until May.

SPECIES. It is interesting to note that the cinerarias originated from *Senecio cruentus*, a member of the groundsel family. The most popular sections are the large-flowered type, and the star or stellata group. The species itself is of little worth.

The large single-flowered ones are dwarf, and are noteworthy for their well-formed blossoms in a variety and combination of colours. In addition to a good mixed strain, they can be obtained in such shades as blue, scarlet, white, pink, purple and colours intermediate between these.

The cactus-flowered have narrow rolled petals, which remind one of a cactus dahlia, and are similar in general habit to the intermediate hybrids. These are midway in size of flower and height between the stellata and large-flowered groups. They are graceful in appearance, nicely branched, and free flowering. Average height 2 ft. The range of colours is not so extensive, but shades of blue are lovely. The star or stellata cinerarias are characterised by their free-branching, light habit. The small star-shaped flowers are freely produced in graceful panicles, and they can be obtained in white, blue, pink and other shades. Well-grown examples, in 7- or 10-in. pots, will attain a height of 4 ft. These forms are valuable for cutting for indoor decoration. Most amateurs will only need one type of cineraria, and where space is limited the modern strains of *Cineraria multiflora nana*, with their compact habit, have much to recommend them.

CULTIVATION. When seedlings are large enough, transfer to small pots and provide ample shade until the roots are established.

The plants should be placed in a cold frame for the summer, standing the pots on a thin layer of coal ashes. Do not allow the seedlings to become starved. When the small pots are nicely filled with roots repot into 5-in. pots of John Innes No. 2 potting compost or one of the loamless mixtures.

In a cold frame the plants will soon begin to grow freely, and the soil must be kept moist. Allow ample space for development, shade from strong sunlight, and ventilate freely. During the night the frame can be drawn back; the dews will greatly improve the health of the plants. In the autumn remove to a cold greenhouse from which frost is excluded.

Any specimens that need it can then be given a final repotting. The pots will vary in size from 6 to 8 in. according to the vigour of the plant and the type. When the flower stems begin to rise, and the pots are fairly well filled with roots, weak liquid fertiliser can be given two or three times each week. Discontinue when the flowers commence to open.

Fumigate occasionally to destroy greenfly, which can be a great nuisance and are very fond of cinerarias. Keep a close watch for leaf-mining maggots. If discovered in the early stages they can be destroyed with the thumb nail. Routine fumigation with lindane smokes will keep this pest in check.

PROPAGATION. To maintain a lengthy display of flowers, two sowings, if not three, must be made. The first, in April for December flowering; the second, in early June for January and February; and the third in July for late spring. In many establishments one sowing only is practised, and this usually takes place in May. Shallow boxes or pans are filled with light compost. After having drained for a few hours the seeds are sown thinly and evenly on the surface, and just covered with fine soil. Seeds sown in April will require a little warmth, but the remainder will germinate in a cold frame. Keep the compost just moist, and shade till the seedlings appear. Gradually admit both light and air, and lightly shade when the sun is bright.

After flowering the plants are thrown away.

Cissus: This genus contains several ornamental climbers which thrive in a warm, moist greenhouse. They are grown primarily for their attractive foliage.

SPECIES. The leaves of *Cissus discolor* are velvety green on the upper surface with white blotches, and beneath they are deep red. *C. antarctica*, the kangaroo vine, is a popular room plant and has plain green, shining leaves.

CULTIVATION. A warm humid greenhouse with a temperature of 16°C (60°F) is needed to grow *C. discolor* well, and the stems can be trained up the greenhouse roof or to trellis work. Plants can be grown in large pots, but better results are obtained if they are planted in a border of good, well-drained soil. *C. antarctica* is happy in cooler conditions, but both species require ample moisture and regular feeding in the spring and summer. Water should be given sparingly in winter.

PROPAGATION. Young side shoots can be removed from the plants in the spring when they are a few inches long. They will root fairly rapidly in moist peat and sand in a propagating frame where a temperature of 18–21°C (65–70°F) can be maintained.

Citrus: Oranges, lemons, tangerines and grapefruit all belong to this genus. They are evergreen shrubs with deliciously fragrant flowers. In the last century they were often grown in a special structure called, appropriately enough, an orangery.

SPECIES. The chief species are *Citrus limonia*, the lemon; *C. sinensis*, the sweet orange; *C. aurantium*, the Seville or bitter orange; *C. aurantifolia*, the lime; *C. paradisi*, the grapefruit and *C. nobilis deliciosa*, the tangerine or mandarin. *C. mitis*, the dwarf calamondin orange, is now a popular house plant and does equally well in the greenhouse. It comes from the Philippines. There are also a number of different named varieties available from a few nurserymen in this country.

CULTIVATION. Plants grown primarily for their fruits will do well in tubs or large pots in a greenhouse with a minimum temperature of 7°C (45°F). The pots must be well drained and John Innes potting compost No. 3 is suitable. Firm potting is essential to encourage sturdy growth. Plenty of water is required in the spring and summer when growth is active, but it is better to keep the compost rather dry in winter. Fruits that do not ripen before the end of the summer will remain green during the winter and ripen the following year. The plants will appreciate light overhead sprays of water when the weather is hot. Feed weekly with liquid fertiliser during the growing season. Little pruning is required. Red spider mite can be a problem with this genus and should be watched for.

PROPAGATION. Although attractive ornamental plants can be raised from seeds of imported fruits, it is better to purchase plants of named varieties if the plants are to be grown mainly for their fruits. These are usually grafted on a suitable citrus root stock.

Clerodendrum: This genus of plants contains some species which are in the nature of hardy flowering shrubs and others which are of climbing habit and require warm greenhouse treatment.

SPECIES. For the latter purpose *Clerodendrum fragrans* is one of the most popular and decorative. It makes strong growths attaining a length of 6 ft. or more, and is a good subject to train on wire balloons or to cover trellis work on the back wall of a greenhouse or conservatory. The flowers are rose coloured and produced in autumn. Other good kinds for the greenhouse are *C. speciosum*, *C. splendens* (both of which have scarlet flowers in summer and grow up to 10 ft. or thereabouts), and *C. thomsonae* (which is also frequently named *C. balfouri*). The flowers of this species are crimson and their season is summer. A very good non-climbing species is *C. speciosissimum* (syn. *C. fallax*) which produces large, rounded, or heart-shaped leaves surmounted by loose heads of coral-red flowers. The plant attains heights varying from 2 to 4 ft. and the blooms are borne usually during summer, but it is possible to force the plants for spring flowering.

CULTIVATION. For potting a compost consisting of equal parts loam, peat, leafmould and sharp sand should be used, breaking up the loam and peat into rough lumps rather than fine particles. Early spring is the best time for potting, and the compost can be rammed firmly into pots that have been well drained with clean crocks.

Start newly potted plants in a temperature of 16–18°C (60–65°F) and maintain this by artificial heat until natural warmth is nearly equivalent to the temperature quoted. Keep the plants well syringed during the growing season until flowers expand. Keep shoots tied to some form of support, and immediately after flowering prune all growths that have borne blossoms to within 2 or 3 in. of their base. Clerodendrums will absorb liberal supplies of water throughout the growing season, but should be kept somewhat on the dry side during the resting period. Where plants are required to climb trellis work or pillars, they may be planted in a bed of good compost, well dug and drained. Established plants may be fed moderately with diluted fertiliser.

PROPAGATION. The quickest method of producing young plants is to take cuttings of pieces of the stem about 3 in. long, insert in sandy compost and place in a propagating frame with bottom heat and an atmospheric temperature of about 21°C (70°F). This may be done during the first three months of the year.

Clerodendrum speciosissimum is easily raised from seed, sown $\frac{1}{8}$ in. deep in light sandy compost, covering the pan with glass and placing in a temperature of 21–24°C (70–75°F). March is a good month for sowing the seed. The other kinds also may be raised from seed, but young plants are slow to develop, and cuttings attain flowering strength more quickly.

Clianthus: These climbing plants are very remarkable for their richly coloured blooms of typical pea-flower structure.

SPECIES. Two only: *Clianthus formosus* (syn. *C. dampieri*), from Australia; and *C. puniceus*, from New Zealand.

Clianthus formosus, the glory pea of Australia, has red flowers with a black or dark purple blotch at the base of the standard, from March onwards. A plant of climbing habit, but by no means rampant.

Clianthus puniceus is a more easily grown plant. It is known as the parrot's bill or lobster claw plant of New Zealand. The flowers are crimson, but in the variety *magnificus* the clusters of blossoms are bright scarlet, while *albus* has white ones. This plant attains a height of 6 ft. or more, and is useful for training up pillars or walls. It flowers from June onwards.

CULTIVATION. From this standpoint the two subjects are distinct. *C. formosus* is the more difficult of the two. This species should carefully be trained to a trellis or wire balloon. It may also be cultivated in a hanging basket, and the growths allowed to droop over the sides. The compost consists of equal parts peat and loam with sharp sand or grit added in sufficient quantity to ensure good drainage. Frequent disturbance at the roots is fatal, so the plants should be placed in their final stations as early as possible. These can either be large pots, baskets, or a prepared shallow border in the greenhouse. Careful watering is advisable at all times. Use the syringe freely during the summer months to keep down red spider mite.

PROPAGATION. Seeds are sown in March, singly in small pots containing peaty soil. Place them in a warm greenhouse. When the seedlings are 1 or 2 in. high, transfer them to pots $4\frac{1}{2}$ in. in diameter. Directly these containers are comfortably filled with roots the plants should be removed to their flowering quarters. At this stage a cool house or conservatory will suit them admirably.

Clianthus formosus occasionally fails on its own roots, and in consequence is grafted on to *Colutea arborescens*. If any amateur wishes to try this method he should sow the seeds of colutea three weeks in advance of the clianthus. The grafting is carried out in a warm greenhouse, and while both plants are in a young state.

Clianthus puniceus and its varieties are quite reliable, and are excellent for clothing back walls or pillars in the conservatory or greenhouse.

CULTIVATION. For this type a suitable compost consists of sandy loam 2 parts, and 1 part fibrous peat, with a liberal sprinkling of silver sand. Repot in spring. Provide ample drainage. Syringe the foliage daily throughout spring and summer when the sun is bright. The roots need plenty of water during the growing season, but less in winter. After flowering straggly shoots must be cut back.

PROPAGATION. This plant is raised from seeds, which are sown in early spring. Propagation is also effected by cuttings, which strike easily if removed with a heel, placed in pots of clean sand, and given a temperature of 16°C (65°F). Cover with a handlight, and shade until the roots are formed. Pot off singly both seedlings and cuttings, and gradually harden to a cool greenhouse.

Cobaea: An easily grown climber bearing large, bell-shaped flowers in summer. The remarkable feature about these flowers is the manner in which they change colour, being at various stages or ages green, white, pink and ultimately a rosy purple. At the height of the season blooms showing every stage of colouring may be seen simultaneously on one plant, thus creating a deal of interest. Cobaea is known by the common names of the cup-and-saucer flower and the Mexican ivy, being a native of Mexico. It is adapted for a cool house, and is most effective where there is ample space for the growths to hang in festoons.

SPECIES. The only one is *Cobaea scandens* and its variety *variegata* with prettily marked leaves.

CULTIVATION. Old plants should be pruned hard in February and the roots given fresh compost. When the growths are breaking freely, remove the weak shoots to prevent overcrowding. No pinching or stopping is needed. Water freely during the summer.

PROPAGATION. Seeds may be sown in February or March in a warm house. If kept growing and potted on as required, the plants will bloom freely towards the end of the summer. They will thrive in the John Innes mixtures. The variegated form of *C. scandens* is increased by cuttings in July or August. Select young firm side shoots, and place in a close propagating frame till rooted.

Codiaeum: The plants in this genus are commonly called crotons. Their main attraction is their brightly coloured leaves which vary considerably in shape and size. The flowers are not particularly ornamental and they are usually removed. There are a great number of different forms which are known botanically as *Codiaeum variegatum pictum*. Codiaeums were very popular in the last century and there were many named forms, but most of these have now disappeared from cultivation.

CULTIVATION. A greenhouse with a minimum winter temperature of 13°C (55°F) is needed, and in the summer temperatures of 18–21°C (65–70°F) are desirable, provided a moist atmosphere can be maintained by regular damping of the floors and stagings. Apart from this the plants also like to be syringed with a fine spray of water in hot weather which helps to keep down insect pests. An occasional sponging of the foliage with a proprietary white oil emulsion will deal with insect pests at the same time as it gives a glossy effect to the foliage. The colour in the leaves tends to fade if the greenhouse is shaded, and they should be grown in a light position. The John Innes potting composts are ideal for codiaeums, and young plants should be potted on gradually from 3-in. pots to 6-in. pots. Feeding with liquid fertiliser when the roots have filled the pots will help the plants considerably.

PROPAGATION. The tendency of the plants is to grow tall and as the older, lower leaves fall the lower part of the stems becomes bare. When this happens the tops of the plants can be removed as cuttings. Only the bottom two or three leaves should be removed so that the rooted cutting is furnished with leaves from soil level upwards. The cuttings should be rooted in a humid propagating frame with a temperature of 18–21°C (65–70°F).

Coelogyne, see Orchids

Coleus: These are highly decorative plants with bright and variously coloured leaves. Moreover, they are highly ornamental from the early stages. They are essential plants for late spring and summer decoration. Given a liberal diet and plenty of light few subjects are so easily grown. During the winter, however, they tend to lose their colour and become faded and pale, due to the weakness of the light and its short duration during the day. Hence they are best grown afresh each spring.

SPECIES. *Coleus blumei*, from Java. This plant has bronze-red foliage, and is the parent of the ornamental-leaved race. *C. thyrso-ideus* is plain leaved, but bears spikes of pretty blue flowers in winter. It is an African species.

CULTIVATION. When growing the ornamental-leaved kinds for decoration, select a few plants for stock purposes in October. These will be kept in a temperature of about 16°C (60°F), and not over-done with water. They enjoy the John Innes composts, and useful specimens can be had in pots from 3 to 8 in. in diameter. Pot on as the containers are filled with roots, and pinch the cuttings when about 6 in. high to produce bushy specimens. As a rule one stopping will suffice. Give plenty of water, allow full sunlight, and in May the plants can be transferred to an ordinary greenhouse. If properly grown stakes are rarely needed. Admit air, but avoid cold draughts. Feed the roots with liquid fertiliser two or three times a week after the final potting.

PROPAGATION. About February a few shoots will be available for cuttings, and these will readily form roots in sandy compost if placed in a close propagating frame. Cuttings can be rooted at any time, thus providing plants in various sizes. The best method of keeping plants through the winter is to strike cuttings in September and leave them undisturbed throughout the winter in a house with a temperature not below 10°C (50°F) if possible.

Seeds should be sown from the end of February onwards in a temperature of 18°C (65°F). Fill a well-drained pan with John Innes seed compost and after a good watering with tepid water sow the seeds thinly and just cover with fine soil. When the young plants are large enough to handle, pot off singly, and keep growing on a shelf in a warm house. In a few weeks it will be possible to determine which varieties are worth growing on. A few will have green leaves, others will be distorted; both are useless and can be thrown on the rubbish heap.

Coleus thyrsoideus is grown for its blossoms. It bears large panicles of deep blue flowers in mid-winter, but a warm greenhouse is necessary to grow this plant well. Cuttings are rooted in the spring, and then grown on during the summer in a greenhouse. Pinch the shoots two or three times, and flower the plants in 6- or 7-in. pots.

Columnea: These are among the loveliest of plants suitable for growing in hanging baskets in a stove greenhouse with a temperature of at least 16°C (65°F). The hanging stems carry small, regularly placed leaves along their length, and in the winter the gorgeous flowers appear in profusion.

SPECIES. The most attractive species is *Columnea gloriosa*, which has fiery red tubular flowers with yellow shading in the throat. *C. microphylla* has a similar habit, but the leaves are smaller and they are covered with purple-coloured hairs; the flowers are bright red. *C. banksii* has glossy foliage with orange-red flowers.

CULTIVATION. To be seen at their best these plants should be grown in hanging baskets suspended from the greenhouse roof. The baskets, lined with moss and filled with good, open compost, can be planted in the spring. The plants should be put fairly close to one another and the hanging stems will grow rapidly in a warm and humid atmosphere. It is best to make up a fresh basket of young plants each spring as the stems tend to become bare and leafless as they age.

PROPAGATION. Pieces of stem, cut into lengths a few inches long, will root readily in sandy compost in a warm, moist propagating case.

Convallaria: Although a hardy plant, lily of the valley (*Convallaria majalis*) is grown extensively under glass for cut flower and greenhouse decoration. In addition to the ordinary or typical plant, there is a superior variety named Fortin's Giant, with extra large bells on long, stout stalks.

About 12 crowns are placed in a 5-in. pot, and they are introduced to warmth as required. For early work, say before Christmas, retarded crowns should be obtained. They will come into bloom in three or four weeks after being placed in a temperature of 16–18°C (60–65°F). They should be kept moist. After Christmas Berlin crowns are recommended, but these require a certain amount of bottom heat with a temperature of about 27°C (80°F). For a later supply Fortin's Giant can be used, provided they are allowed to develop slowly in a temperature of 13–16°C (55–60°F).

Cordyline: Extremely handsome foliage plants, closely related to the dracaenas, requiring warmhouse temperatures, and plenty of humidity in summer.

SPECIES: Some particularly good kinds offered are the varieties of *Cordyline australis*, such as *C. a. atropurpurea*, purple midribs and bases of leaves beneath; *C. a. aureo-striata*, longitudinal yellow lines and *C. a. veitchii*, crimson midribs and bases of leaves beneath; *C. indivisa*, large leaves 3 to 6 ft. long and up to 6 in. wide; *C. stricta*, leaves 1 to 2 ft. long and only 1 in. wide, and *C. s. discolor* has dark bronze-purple leaves; *C. terminalis*, broad leaves, purplish-green; and *C. t.* Firebrand, leaves purplish-green, reddish-purple and completely cream.

CULTIVATION. During winter the temperature should not fall below 10°C (50°F).

A suitable compost consists of fibrous loam, peat, dried manure and sand. Any repotting should be carried out in the spring. Keep the roots well supplied with water, and syringe the foliage freely when the weather is hot. A little shade is necessary during the summer months. Sponge the leaves occasionally to free them of dirt and insect pests. Do not overlook the undersides, where insects congregate.

PROPAGATION. Most kinds, particularly *C. indivisa*, can be raised from seeds, which are sown in the spring. They will germinate in a temperature of 16°C (60°F). If potted on as the necessity arises they soon make serviceable plants. Cordylines are also propagated by cuttings of the tops of side shoots of old plants, by the fleshy roots, and by cutting up the stems of plants from which the tops have been removed. Stem rooting is also practised.

Bury the root cuttings in sandy peat; the pieces of stem, about 2 in. in length, are treated as ordinary cuttings. A warm moist temperature is needed for propagating cordylines.

Coronilla: In this genus there is one species suitable for the cool or cold greenhouse. This is *Coronilla glauca*, an evergreen shrub with numerous yellow flowers. It belongs to the pea family, is native of South Europe, and is in bloom the greater part of the year. The bulk, however, are produced in spring and summer. The flowers are fragrant during the day. There is also a form with foliage variegated in creamy white.

CULTIVATION. Any repotting should take place in March, using the John Innes mixtures or similar ones. About the same time pruning can be done, which consists of reducing any shoots that are likely to make the plant a bad shape. Coronillas require a light, sunny position and plenty of water. After the bulk of the flowers are over the plants can be stood outside till frosts are likely.

PROPAGATION. By cuttings from young shoots either in April or August. The former will root in a greenhouse and the latter in a cold frame. It can also be propagated from layers taken in September.

Correa: At one time the correas (Australian fuchsias) were extensively grown for greenhouse decoration. They are pretty evergreen summer-flowering shrubs from 3 to 6 ft. high., but only those amateur greenhouse owners who like something different should grow them.

SPECIES. The principal ones are *Correa harrisii*, bright scarlet, and *C. speciosa*, bright crimson tipped with green.

CULTIVATION. Give a winter temperature of 4–10°C (40–50°F) and an ordinary greenhouse temperature during the summer. The compost is made up of good fibrous peat, with a liberal proportion of silver sand. Repotting is done in summer while the plants are still growing, and sufficiently early for the roots to take possession of the compost before winter sets in. Avoid over-potting. Work the compost well down between the ball of roots and the new pot and make it quite firm. After flowering (in June and July) gradually reduce the water supply, and then cut back the old flowered shoots to maintain a well-balanced specimen.

Spray the plants freely in bright weather, and if possible the house should be closed for a few hours each afternoon to encourage new growth. Admit a little air again at sunset, and increase it the following morning. Careful watering is needed. Pinch any shoots that are likely to outstrip the remainder. A few neat sticks will be necessary. During August and September the plants may be stood outside except in heavy rain, which is detrimental.

PROPAGATION. By grafting on to *C. alba*. Side grafting is practised during the summer months, and it takes from six to eight weeks for the stock and scion to unite. A heated frame and a moist atmosphere are necessary. It is better for amateurs to purchase healthy young plants with plenty of basal shoots.

Crowea: If grown in a cool house croweas are very useful dwarf evergreen shrubs. They vary in height from 1 to 3 ft. and are natives of Australia.

SPECIES. Two only are usually grown. *Crowea angustifolia*, rose-pink to white flowers freely produced in spring, and *C. saligna* (syn. *C. latifolia*), clear pink flowers in July.

CULTIVATION. Compost consists of 2 parts peat and 1 of loam with a little sand. Repot in March or April. The plants prefer a light, airy position, and need every care in regard to watering. Very little moisture is necessary during the autumn and winter months. To keep the plants dwarf and bushy a certain amount of pinching is needed during the early stages of growth. Cuttings should have their tops pinched out soon after they have formed roots.

PROPAGATION. Cuttings of young shoots will strike if given a little bottom heat in a propagating frame in April.

Cryptogramma, see Ferns.

Cuphea: A small genus of pretty dwarf plants, a few of which are suitable for greenhouse cultivation.

SPECIES. The best is *Cuphea ignea*, a native of Mexico; the tubular flowers are bright scarlet, with a black and white tip and are freely produced during the summer months. The appearance of the flower is responsible for its common name of the Mexican cigar plant.

CULTIVATION: Cupheas need a winter temperature of about 10°C (50°F) and will grow quite happily in the John Innes composts. Keep the plants near the roof glass and spray them daily when the sun is bright until the flowers open. Remove the points of the shoots to secure bushy specimens. At the final potting make the compost fairly firm. Six-inch pots will be large enough, the plants being fed with liquid fertiliser when they are comfortably filled with roots. After flowering keep them fairly dry. Prune in January, and repot when growth begins.

PROPAGATION. Cupheas are increased by cuttings in spring or summer or raised from seed sown in early spring.

Cupressus: This genus contains at least one member admirably suited for greenhouse embellishment. Excellent specimens can be obtained in 5-in. pots, while large plants will be found useful for groups and the dwelling-house.

SPECIES. *Cupressus funebris*, the funereal cypress, a charming plant, graceful and light with grey-green foliage. Old plants produce cones and seeds freely. *C. cashmeriana* is another beautiful, slightly tender conifer, with long, pendulous branchlets in blue-grey.

CULTIVATION. When seedlings are large enough pot off, and arrange on a shelf near the roof glass. Directly they are ready transfer them to 4- and 5-in. pots, using a mixture of loam and leafmould. In these pots they will develop into nice plants suitable for house decoration and the side stages of the greenhouse. If potted on they will grow into fine specimens until too large for the ordinary greenhouse. This, however, will take a number of years.

PROPAGATION. The seeds can be sown in spring in pans of light sandy compost, but few amateurs would be interested in growing this plant in quantity. Cuttings of side growths taken in autumn will root in a propagating frame or under mist propagation.

Cymbidium, see Orchids

Cyperus: Cyperus, owing to its light and elegant growth, is almost indispensable.

SPECIES. *Cyperus alternifolius*, native of Australia, which grows to 1 to 3 ft. It produces numerous stems, each crowned by a number of long narrow leaves, fanning out round the top to form a circle, hence the name of umbrella plant. *C. a. variegatus* is a pleasing form with the stems and leaves streaked white. Another very useful species is that known as *C. natalensis* (more correctly but less usually called *Mariscus umbilensis*), the strap-like, leathery leaves of glossy green being useful as a decorative subject amongst plants.

CULTIVATION. Plants make good specimens in 5- or 6-in. pots in John Innes No. 1 potting compost.

They grow best in a warm greenhouse, where they can be frequently syringed, especially after being repotted in the spring. Shade from strong sunshine, and keep the roots well supplied with water. As the pots become full of roots liquid fertiliser can be given once each week.

PROPAGATION. The green form may be raised from seeds. They are sown in pots of sandy compost and placed in a temperature of 21 °C (70°F). When the seedlings are large enough pot off singly and transfer to a slightly cooler house.

The lovely, elegant flowers of Camellia japonica *grace the cool greenhouse during the first months of the year*

Both plants are increased by division in February or March, and also by rooting the crowns or the cluster of leaves at the ends of the stems. These are removed with an inch or so of stem and then placed in pots of light compost. Give a little bottom heat and keep well shaded until growth begins to emerge from the centre of the crown.

Cypripedium, see Orchids

Cyrtomium, see Ferns

Cytisus: Most of the members of this genus are hardy but two species are on the border line and, owing to their beauty, are largely grown for greenhouse decoration. They make compact, free-flowering shrubs, and quite small plants produce a quantity of bloom.

SPECIES. *Cytisus canariensis,* dwarf, freely branched, and bears yellow flowers from May to July; it is the 'genista' of the florists' shops. *C. fragrans* has terminal spikes of yellow, pea-shaped, fragrant flowers, and can be had in bloom from Christmas to April.

CULTIVATION. These plants will succeed in a winter temperature of 7–10°C (45–50°F), and they should be stood out in the open air from July till September. After flowering the shoots are cut back to within a couple of inches of their base. When new growth is apparent repot in a mixture of loam (2 parts) and leafmould (1 part) with a little sharp sand. Keep the plants in a growing atmosphere, and use the syringe freely when the weather is bright. They enjoy plenty of water when well rooted. Return to the greenhouse in September, and directly the flower spikes show feed the roots with liquid fertiliser.

PROPAGATION. Effected in March or August by cuttings made from young shoots a couple of inches in length. They will form roots fairly easily in a close propagating frame. Pot off singly when rooted. Occasional pinching is needed, particularly in the early stages of growth. *C. fragrans* is also raised from seeds, but as a rule the seedlings are not true to type.

Daphne: A popular genus owing to its sweet fragrance.

SPECIES. There is one suitable for greenhouse cultivation, *Daphne odora,* a small evergreen shrub with purple flowers, white in the variety *alba,* and rosy pink in *rubra.* All are sweetly scented and blossom about February.

Top left: Ficus elastica tricolor *Top right:* Gerbera jamesonii
Bottom: Gardenias are beautiful evergreen shrubs for the warm greenhouse

CULTIVATION. Pots to 6 in. diameter are big enough for moderate-sized specimens. Repot in March or April after flowering. Avoid over-potting, and use a mixture of 3 parts peat and 1 part leafmould or loam with a liberal sprinkling of sand. The daphnes do not, on the whole, enjoy soils with a high alkaline content and *D. odora* will do best if the loam used has an acid reaction. A winter temperature of 10–13 °C (50–55 °F) will suffice, and at this season water must be applied in strict moderation. To ensure a good crop of flowers the wood must be thoroughly ripened during the autumn months. Syringe daily when the sun is bright throughout summer.

PROPAGATION. Usually effected by grafting on to seedling plants of *Daphne laureola*, the spurge laurel.

It can, however, be raised from cuttings. Choose matured shoots or side growths in autumn and insert them in pots filled with sandy peat. Keep in a cool house for the winter and transfer to a warmer structure in the spring. Here the already callused cuttings will emit roots and start into growth. Pot off singly in a peaty compost.

Datura: The daturas, also known as brugmansias, are large ever-green shrubs with enormous trumpet-shaped flowers, about 7 to 8 in. long. They are suitable for large houses, where they can be trained up a back wall or around pillars. The best results are obtained if planted out or grown in large pots.

SPECIES. *Datura arborea* (white flowers, Peru), *D. cornigera* (syn. *B. knightii*) (large double white drooping flowers), *D. sanguinea*, (orange, Peru, and its yellow form known as *lutea*), *D. suaveolens* (white, fragrant, Mexico). All are summer flowering.

CULTIVATION. Any repotting or topdressing is carried out during March or when new growth begins. Daturas need ample drainage and a fairly rich compost. This consists of fibrous loam, peat, and rotted manure in equal proportions, with sufficient sand to render it porous. Spray the stems freely and give plenty of water during the growing period. Very little moisture is needed in winter. Prune the shoots well back about October to keep the plants shapely. Established examples will appreciate weak liquid fertiliser when in a state of activity.

PROPAGATION. Effected in the spring or autumn. Select shoots about 6 in. long, insert them singly in small pots of sandy compost, and arrange in a propagating frame where the temperature is about 21 °C (70 °F). Shade until rooted. Young heel cuttings can be taken.

Davallia, see Ferns

Dendrobium, see Orchids

Dicentra (Dielytra): This genus is sometimes catalogued as *Dielytra* but more accurately as *Dicentra*. There is one species, *Dicentra spectabilis*, which is very beautiful when gently forced for an early spring display. It is known as the Chinese fumitory, also bleeding heart, and *Dielytra spectabilis*. The lyre-shaped flowers are a pretty rosy crimson, disposed in graceful racemes. There is a white variety named *Dicentra spectabilis alba*.

CULTIVATION. The best way to keep up a healthy stock is to grow a batch in the open ground. Sufficient plants can be lifted in September, potted up, and placed in a cold frame. In January a few specimens should be transferred to the greenhouse, where the temperature is about 10°C (50°F). A month later a further batch can be given similar treatment. They enjoy a fairly rich compost, and plenty of water during active growth. Hard forcing will not be tolerated.

PROPAGATION. Effected by division when the roots are dormant.

Didiscus: One species only, *Didiscus caeruleus* (syn. *Trachymene caerulea*), is grown, usually known as the blue lace flower of America, where it is largely grown, although a native of West Australia. It grows from 1 to 2 ft. high, and produces its blue flowers in July. It is a charming pot plant, and when grown under glass the beauty of its flowers is considerably enhanced.

CULTIVATION. Seeds should be sown in February in pots of light compost and germinated in a temperature of 13°C (55°F). When the seedlings are large enough, pot off singly, and arrange on a shelf in a warm greenhouse. Repot before the seedlings become starved in the small pots in 5- or 6-in. pots of John Innes No. 1 potting compost. Water freely when the pots are filled with roots.

Dieffenbachia: Dumb cane and mother-in-law plant are two of the common names given to these plants because of the poisonous sap which causes extreme discomfort in the mouth. They have ornamental foliage and need a warm greenhouse to grow well. *Deffenbachia*

147

picta and *D. seguine* are two species that are fairly common. Both have oblong green leaves, pointed at the ends, and white or yellow spotting.

CULTIVATION. Although dieffenbachias have found a certain popularity as room plants, they do best when grown in a greenhouse with a temperature of 16°C (60°F). In warm, humid conditions, they will produce their ornamental leaves freely. They are not difficult to grow if they are given plenty of water in the spring and summer, but when temperatures are lower in winter much less moisture is required. Propagation is by means of suckers that appear at the base of the plants. These are simply detached and potted separately.

Dillwynia: A few of the species are very interesting. They are elegant, heath-like shrubs, natives of Australia, and are members of the pea family.

SPECIES. *Dillwynia floribunda*, yellow, blooms in April. Fairly tall, to 5 or 6 ft. *D. ericifolia*, orange and yellow. This is May flowering, and grows only 2 or 3 ft. tall. Both forms are evergreen.

CULTIVATION, see Chorizema

Diosma: At one time these were largely grown on account of their fragrant foliage, and for this reason they are recommended to amateurs. They grow from 1 to 3 ft. high.

SPECIES. *Diosma ericoides*, white tinged with red. The foliage is very fragrant when bruised. *D. capitata* and *D. gracilis* are two forms usually quoted in catalogues.

CULTIVATION. Diosmas need a winter temperature of 4–10°C (40–50°F). They thrive in a mixture of fibrous peat and sand; some growers add a proportion of loam. Repot in May or June. Keep the plants in shape by pinching the strongest shoots in summer, thus causing bushy growth. Give plenty of water in spring and summer but less in winter.

PROPAGATION. Easily raised from heel cuttings inserted in pots of sandy peat and placed in a warm propagating frame in spring.

Diplacus: The diplacus, or glutinous monkey flower, is closely related to the *Mimulus* family, and is frequently listed under that genus. They are evergreen shrubby plants, very free flowering, and suitable for clothing small pillars or supports of the greenhouse. By judicious pruning in the early spring they also make good pot plants.

SPECIES. The main ones are *Diplacus glutinosus,* orange to salmon, *D. g. aurantiacus,* orange-red, and *D. g. puniceus,* crimson.

CULTIVATION. With cool greenhouse treatment no difficulty will be experienced in growing fine plants of diplacus. Their chief requirement is a fairly rich compost, which means a small proportion of well-rotted manure added to the usual mixture.

Prune into shape about February, and repot just as new growths begin. Water freely in summer.

PROPAGATION. By cuttings during spring and summer, in moist soil.

Dizygotheca: This family contains a number of elegant foliage plants, excellent for a warm greenhouse, and ideal as room plants. *Dizygotheca elegantissima* is the only one which is very widely grown these days. It is a very elegant plant, with thin spidery leaves.

CULTIVATION. This is quite easy provided the compost is fairly rich, and a minimum temperature of 10°C (50°F) is maintained. Repot in March in equal parts leafmould, peat, and loam. Syringe the foliage daily from April to September when the days are bright, and shade from strong sunlight. An even temperature all the time is very important, and if subjected to draughts the leaves drop.

Dracaena: These are amongst the most handsome and ornamental of foliage plants, but most of them require a stove house temperature, especially those with highly coloured leaves.

SPECIES. Some of the most attractive are *Dracaena fragrans,* with shining green leaves 1 to 3 ft. long, and fragrant yellow flowers; *D. f. massangeana,* leaves with a broad central white stripe; *D. godseffiana,* 4-in. long oval leaves, heavily spotted cream; *D. sanderiana,* narrow leaves to 10 in. long, grey-green with wide white margin. See also Cordyline.

CULTIVATION, see Cordyline

Echinocactus, see Cacti

Epacris (Australian Heath): Small shrubs, which are very decorative when in bloom, also useful for cut flowers. For the most part the species of this genus are native of Australia, but a few come from New Zealand. As a rule they are more easily grown than ericas, and the flowers are in distinct shades of rose with some white.

SPECIES. *Epacris impressa*, white to red, March; *E. longiflora*, crimson and white, May and June; *E. purpurascens*, white and rose, winter. Height 1½ to 2 ft. Epacrises are no exception to the general rule for all hard-wooded plants, that both pots and drainage must be clean. Unless this is carried out, the roots will not readily leave the pots when repotting takes place making the task more difficult and possibly causing permanent damage.

CULTIVATION. After flowering, usually about the end of February and early March, the plants are pruned. The growths of the erect-growing varieties are cut back to within 1 in. of their base, the object being to secure a few strong shoots rather than several weak ones, which would produce a poor show of bloom. Spreading varieties are merely cut to shape. After pruning keep the house rather close for a few days, and when the new growths are about half an inch long any repotting can be carried out. Provide good drainage, and do not over-pot. The rooting medium consists of fibrous peat broken up rather fine and a liberal sprinkling of silver sand. Do not disturb the ball of roots except to remove the drainage. Make the soil quite firm.

When the plants have recovered from being repotted they may be transferred to a cool frame. During August and September place the plants outside, and winter in a cool house.

Epacrises need plenty of light and air in order to thoroughly ripen the growths, failing which the flowers will be few and poor in quality. See that the pots never become really dry, and for a few weeks after potting a daily spraying overhead with clear water will be an advantage.

PROPAGATION. By cuttings of the young shoots in August or April, but it is not always easy. The amateur is advised to buy his plants already rooted in small pots. Anyone, however, who wishes to try his hand at rooting epacrises should treat them in the way advised for hard-wooded cuttings, or for ericas. Seed can also be sown as soon as ripe in sandy peat and a temperature of 13 °C (55 °F).

Epiphyllum, see Cacti

Ericas (Heaths): The ericas may be divided into two groups: the harder wooded kinds, which are rather difficult to grow, and the softer wooded species and varieties, which are mostly cultivated for

Covent Garden and other markets. Most of the species suitable for the greenhouse hail from the Cape. They are evergreen, height 1 to $2\frac{1}{2}$ ft., and some forms are in bloom from October till midsummer. The free-growing sorts flower chiefly in autumn and winter. They make highly decorative plants in 4- to 6-in. pots, the growths being well clothed with foliage and flowers.

SPECIES. The principal are *Erica hyemalis*, pink, December to March; *E. gracilis*, rose, September to December; *E. g. alba*, white; *E. walkeria praestans*, red, February to June; and *E. willmorei*, pink and white, early spring. The later flowering with harder wood include *E. bowieana*, white to rose, August to October; *E. cavendishiana*, yellow, May to July; *E. mammosa*, purple, scarlet or white, late summer; *E. spenceriana*, white, June, and *E. ventricosa*, white to rose, summer.

CULTIVATION. The roots of ericas are never inactive, and must never be entirely dry. The best time for pruning is immediately the flowering period is over. The free-growing kinds, of which *E. hyemalis* may be cited as an example, have their strongest growths cut back to within 1 or 2 in. of their base. Weak shoots are just tipped. The slow growers rarely require pruning, beyond occasional pinching of a strong growth that is likely to upset the balance of the plant.

When new growth begins in the spring, or early autumn in the case of later flowering kinds, any repotting can be given attention. Young plants must not be allowed to become pot bound, but large plants may be grown for several years in the same pots. Do not disturb the roots, and avoid over-potting; also do not bury the stem of the plant. The compost consists of good quality fibrous peat, well broken or chopped up (3 parts) and clean sharp silver sand (1 part). Firm potting is essential. Grow the plants cool, and give as much air as possible the year round. Artifical heat is only required to keep out frosts and to prevent damp causing damage to the foliage. A very important factor in the successful cultivation of ericas is watering. Use rain water, and every time moisture is given see the whole ball of soil is wetted, then no more is given until it is really needed. A thin shading is only required when the sun is very strong. From July to the end of September the plants can be stood outside, choosing a sunny position, plunging the pots in ashes to preserve moisture.

Ericas are more easily managed when a house is devoted to their cultivation but with careful handling they can be grown with a certain measure of success among other plants.

As a rule it is better for the amateur to buy small plants already rooted and grow them on. Ericas are raised from seeds when the object is to obtain new varieties, but the usual method is by cuttings. The soft-wooded early flowering kinds root fairly easily, the hardwooded kinds are rather difficult. One-inch cuttings from the base of plants are taken in spring or late summer, and put in sandy peat with a temperature of about 16°C (60°F).

Eriostemon: These are handsome shrubs of easy cultivation that produce their flowers freely during the spring and early summer months. Natives of Australia, they are 1 to $2\frac{1}{2}$ ft. tall.

SPECIES. The principal are *Eriostemon buxifolius* (pink or rose), *E. myoporoides* (rosy red), *E. scaber* (white, tinged pink).

CULTIVATION. Soil consists of peat (2 parts), loam (1 part) and sand (1 part). They need little if any pruning, naturally forming nice bushy specimens. Repot in March. Keep a little close, and syringe daily while the season's growth is being made. From July till the end of September stand the plants outside in a sunny position to thoroughly ripen the growths. A winter temperature of 4–7°C (40–45°F) will suffice. Water carefully at all times.

PROPAGATION. By cuttings early in spring or in August. Choose half-ripened shoots, insert in sandy peat, cover with a hand light, and place over a little bottom heat or where the temperature is about 16°C (60°F). Keep just moist, and shaded from strong sunlight. When rooted gradually harden and pot off singly. Further pottings are required, but overpotting must be avoided.

Erlangea: This genus is closely allied to *Eupatorium. Erlangea tomentosa* is the only species met with, a native of Uganda. It is a beautiful plant with numerous heads of pale lavender-blue flowers, freely produced from Christmas till May. An additional charm is scented foliage. Cool greenhouse conditions suit it well.

CULTIVATION. This plant is a rapid grower, and must be potted on without check to progress. It will flower in 5- to 8-in. pots. A fairly light compost, such as loam and leafmould in equal parts, is recommended. Make it moderately firm around the roots. Well-rooted specimens will benefit by twice weekly applications of liquid fertiliser.

Old plants can be cut down after flowering and repotted when growth begins. These will develop into fine specimens.

PROPAGATION. By means of cuttings, which will form roots in a warm propagating frame during the spring months. When rooted, pot off singly in 3-in. pots and when established remove to the greenhouse, where the night temperature is about 7–10°C (45–50°F). Can also be raised fairly easily from seed when it is available.

Erythrina: There is one species, *Erythrina crista-gallii*, suitable for the greenhouse. It is a Brazilian plant, known as the coral tree, and bears terminal racemes of deep scarlet, pea-shaped flowers from June to August on prickly stems whose height is 6 to 8 ft.; it forms a stout rootstock, and should be treated as a herbaceous plant. The growths are cut down to within a short distance of their base in early spring.

CULTIVATION. Start roots in a warm house, and when growth is evident repot in a fairly rich compost. This consists of loam (2 parts), leafmould (1 part), and rotted manure (1 part) with a sprinkling of sand. When growth is well away a lower temperature will be better; it will cause the shoots to become strong and consequently produce finer blooms. Let plants be liberally supplied with water and liquid fertiliser when well rooted. Soon after flowering the resting period begins. Gradually reduce the water supply and finally withhold. Store the roots for the winter under the greenhouse stage away from drips.

PROPAGATION. Effected by taking a few of the young shoots with a heel attached when the plants are started in the spring. They readily form roots in a warm propagating frame.

Eucalyptus: Although several of the eucalyptus develop into large timber trees, two or three species are highly decorative in a small state for the cool greenhouse. Their chief attraction, however, is their pleasantly scented foliage.

SPECIES. The best for greenhouse decoration is *Eucalyptus globulus*, the blue gum tree of Australia; *E. multiflora* is another kind, while *E. citriodora* is citron scented. The leaves, when gently rubbed or bruised, emit a fragrance somewhat similar to the lemon-scented verbena or aloysia. Another excellent species for pot cultivation is *E. gunnii*, its silver foliage and prettily shaped leaves being very beautiful amongst all the flowering plants.

CULTIVATION. Unless large plants are required, treat as an annual. Seeds should be sown in pans of light soil in the early spring and germinated in a temperature of 18°C (65°F). If a few old plants are kept, side shoots will make good cuttings, which will form roots in gentle bottom heat. Pot off singly when rooted, and gradually harden to a temperature of 13°C (55°F). Pot on as required in a mixture of loam and leafmould. Good specimens can be obtained in 5- and 6-in pots.

Eupatorium: On account of their autumn- and winter-flowering qualities eupatoriums deserve consideration as plants for the cool greenhouse, especially the following.

SPECIES. *Eupatorium micranthum*, white and sweetly scented. This plant is quite shrubby, 4 to 8 ft. tall, and should be lightly pruned after flowering in autumn. It is a native of South America. *E. riparium*, flower heads white in early spring. It is a native of South America, and grows about 2 ft. high. *E. vernale* is a very elegant species from Mexico. The white blooms are borne in large terminal corymbs on stout stems from late January to March. Height 2 to 3 ft.

CULTIVATION. When kept in pots the year round rich compost is needed. It consists of fibrous loam (2 parts), leafmould (1 part), and rotted manure (1 part) with a little sand. Repot old plants in the spring. They need plenty of water during the summer and liquid fertiliser, when the pots are filled with roots.

PROPAGATION. Effected by cuttings of young shoots in spring and August.

Eupatorium vernale is propagated from basal cuttings in the spring in coarse sand with a temperature of 16°C (60°F). When rooted wash the sand from the roots and place them in 3-in. pots, using a light, porous compost. Grow the plants on without pinching; then each cutting will produce one fine head of bloom the following season. Large specimens are obtained by cutting back these plants after flowering and growing them on for another year. *E. riparium* needs similar treatment.

Cuttings of *E. micranthum* may be rooted in the spring or in August. The former needs a little heat, but the latter will strike in a cold frame. Pot off singly when ready, and while they are being grown on into good plants an occasional pinching of the growths will be necessary. When the plants become too large for the greenhouse they can be planted in a sheltered spot outdoors but will only survive mild winters.

Euphorbia: There are two showy species particularly valuable for a display in December and January, and a third which can be had in flower for much of the year.

SPECIES. *Euphorbia pulcherrima* is commonly known as the poinsettia and has showy, bright red whorls of bracts at the top of the stems, surrounding the insignificant flowers. *E. fulgens* is entirely different. Masses of small orange-red flowers are produced on long, arching stems, together with purple-green, willow-like leaves. *E. splendens*, the Crown of Thorns, is extremely spiny, but has small $\frac{1}{2}$-in. wide bright scarlet flowers, and attractive, fresh green leaves; it grows to about 3 ft. tall.

CULTIVATION. After flowering water is withheld so that the plants can rest and the dead flower heads cut off. They can be started into growth again in May or June and, to obtain cuttings, the old stems should be cut back to 4 in. long, and the resultant new shoots used for cuttings about 3 to 4 in. long. To prevent 'bleeding', seal the cuts with charcoal dust. *E. fulgens* is cut back in June to within 1 in. of the base. Young plants should be grown from cuttings rooted in sandy peat and a temperature of 21°C (70°F) and grown on in a cool greenhouse; they can be potted on gradually into 6-in. pots and John Innes No. 3 potting compost. Poinsettias obtained from cuttings in August make small neat plants but cuttings of the older varieties rooted earlier may grow 6 ft. tall or more. This has all been changed, however, with the introduction of the Mikkelsen strain which has a shorter, more compact habit. Due to this and for various other reasons poinsettias have become much more popular of recent years. Watering must be done very carefully, otherwise the leaves will turn yellow and fall. A warm greenhouse with a temperature of at least 10°C (50°F) is necessary to grow them to perfection. If poinsettias are brought into the home, they should not be kept in electric light during the hours of darkness from October to Christmas, otherwise they will not flower.

PROPAGATION. The three species can be increased from young shoots removed when a few inches long, from cut back plants. The ends of the cuttings need sealing with charcoal dust. Insert in a warm, moist propagating frame with a temperature of 16–18°C (60–65°F). Poinsettia stems of the previous year's growth can be cut into pieces. These will form roots and shoots if placed in a heated propagating frame.

Eurya: A showy evergreen shrub with creamy-yellow variegated foliage useful for the cool greenhouse and sometimes used as a room plant.

SPECIES. One, *Eurya japonica*, and the variety *variegata*. The latter is usually grown. It has yellow variegated foliage.

This plant will thrive in a light compost such as sandy loam and peat or leafmould in equal parts, potting it in April.

PROPAGATION. Cuttings made from ends of young shoots in pots of sandy peat will form roots in a warm propagating frame in spring.

Eutaxia: A genus of evergreen shrubs, native of Australia. They need similar treatment to *Chorizema* and kindred subjects.

Eutaxia myrtifolia has golden-yellow flowers, produced during the month of August. Height 2 to 6 ft.

Exacum: A group of pretty plants belonging to the *Gentianaceae* family. Most of the species require warmth and moisture, but the beautiful flowers are well worth some trouble being taken to grow the plants well. The scent is delicious.

SPECIES. *Exacum affine* has small, saucer-shaped purple flowers with orange stamens, making a very beautiful combination. This is best treated as an annual, but it does need a warm, moist atmosphere if it is to grow well. Flowering is from June to October. The larger flowered *E. zeylanicum* is best grown as a greenhouse biennial, sowing the seed in late summer and growing the plants throughout the winter, when flowering will start somewhat earlier.

CULTIVATION. Sow seed in a very fine soil and only slightly cover with soil. Keep in a temperature of 18°C (65°F) and make sure the soil and the propagating frame are kept moist. Prick out when quite small and grow all the time in a humid atmosphere. Prick off and pot on as required and spray frequently.

PROPAGATION. By seed sown annually in spring and summer. Specimens grown from seed usually produce more shapely plants than those from cuttings.

Fabiana (False Heath): A genus containing one species suitable for cool greenhouse cultivation, especially in northern areas. *Fabiana imbricata* is a spring-flowering subject with heath-like foliage and pure white flowers, freely produced. Native of Chile.

CULTIVATION. It will thrive in a mixture of peat and leafmould, also loam if fairly free of lime. After flowering the shoots should be lightly pruned, and when growth begins repotting can be carried out, usually in early spring. The roots are kept more or less moist throughout the year.

PROPAGATION. By cuttings of firm young shoots during April or August. Insert in pots filled with sandy peat and place in a cold frame in spring, or, if taken in late summer, place in gentle heat. Pot off singly when rooted, and pinch the tops when established to encourage a bushy habit.

Fatsia (Fig Leaf Palm): Although somewhat coarse in general habit, the fig leaf palm has always been a popular subject for greenhouse and rooms on account of its hard-wearing foliage. It is also known as the false castor-oil plant.

SPECIES. One, *Fatsia japonica*, also known as *Aralia sieboldii*. It has large leathery leaves of a deep shining green, and much-branched heads of small white flowers in clusters in October. There is a variety named *variegata*, with the leaves marked with white at the ends, and *aurea*, with leaves veined with yellow. Native of Japan.

CULTIVATION. Size varies with age and treatment. Given a liberal rooting medium and kept supplied with water, there will be no difficulty in growing good specimens of this plant. Old plants that have lost their lower leaves can be stem rooted. Minimum winter temperature should be 4°C (40°F) when grown in a greenhouse.

PROPAGATION. *F. japonica* is raised from seeds sown singly in pots. Germinate in a temperature of 18°C (65°F). Cuttings of the stems 2 in. in length will also produce plants during the spring months. Arrange them in a close propagating frame until growth is formed. The variegated form should be treated in the same way.

Felicia: A small, shrubby, half-hardy perennial suitable for pot cultivation, which can be had in bloom practically the whole year round.

SPECIES. The principal one is *Felicia amelloides*, a pleasant, interesting plant but not grown as much as it used to be, from the Cape of Good Hope, producing heads of sky-blue, daisy-like flowers. Hence its common name, blue marguerite.

CULTIVATION. When potting make the compost firm but not hard, in John Innes No. 1 potting compost. Never allow the plants to become pot-bound in the early stages of growth. Specimens being grown on for autumn flowering can occupy a cold frame during the summer months.

PROPAGATION. From seeds during the spring and summer months if placed in a temperature of 16–18°C (60–65°F). Prick off in boxes when large enough to handle and later place them singly in small pots. Grow on in the greenhouse. They will bloom in 5- or 6-in. pots. The plants should be pinched two or three times to encourage a bushy habit. Sometimes three seedlings are arranged in one container; these will require flowering pots 7 or 8 in. in diameter. Propagation is also by cuttings, and if a batch is rooted in the autumn, good plants will be available for the following summer. They will form roots in a cold frame. Pot up when ready, and arrange on the shelf of a cool house for the winter.

Ferns: Here we have a wonderful and superbly lovely class of plants which stand by themselves for inimitable beauty of foliage. To do ferns justice they should have, and richly deserve, a house devoted entirely to their cultivation. Indeed, a comprehensive collection of all classes would demand three or four houses: one for species and varieties requiring hothouse temperatures, a second for those which belong to more temperate climates and need ordinary greenhouse temperature but always safety from frost. Then there are beautiful types and varieties which are hardy so far as frost endurance is concerned, but which need shelter from rough winds because of the fragile softness of their fronds. These are admirably suited for amateurs' unheated greenhouses. For the purpose of this book it is considered sufficient to deal only with the sections of this great family which are suitable for cultivation in unheated and moderately heated greenhouses. Even so, no more can be done than very summarily to introduce useful generic groups and outstanding varieties and give a brief outline of cultural routine. Those who aim at building up a comprehensive collection of ferns will find it necessary to study books devoted solely to ferns.

SPECIES (for the heated greenhouse). *Adiantum* (maidenhair fern), of which there are very many species, including *Adiantum*

cuneatum, A. decorum, A. gracillimum and *A. williamsii;*
Asplenium, such species as *Asplenium bulbiferum, A. nidus* (the
bird's-nest fern), one of the few ferns which produces entire, undi-
vided fronds, and *A. praemorsum; Blechnum,* dwarf tree fern, the
most commonly grown species being *Blechnum gibbum* in reasonably small pots for the greenhouse staging (the giant tree ferns,
Dicksonia, are beyond the scope of most amateurs, as they require
very tall and spacious houses); *Cyrtomium,* sometimes classified as
Aspidium, the two most serviceable for the amateur's greenhouse
being *Cyrtomium falcatum,* the holly fern, and its variety *caryoti-
deum; Davallia,* most species of which bear handsomely cut fronds
on rhizomatous shoots, which add greatly to their charm and interest, for instance *Davallia bullata,* known as the squirrel's-foot fern,
D. canariensis, the hare's-foot fern, and *D. mariesii cristata,* a dwarf
form with crested fronds; *Nephrolepis,* a class of ferns which
includes some remarkably beautiful species and varieties, for
instance *Nephrolepis exaltata,* the ladder fern, which makes long,
arching fronds with narrow pinnae protruding at right angles on
both sides of the midrib, is an excellent fern for hanging baskets,
and there are others with beautifully plumose and much divided
fronds of entrancing beauty, *elegantissima, furcans* and *pluma;*
Pteris, another extensive genus among which the species *Pteris cretica* and its varieties *albo-lineata, cristata, summersii* and *wimsettii*
are popular and easy to grow. This list, although by no means comprehensive, gives a representative collection for the amateur to
choose from. To extend it would be of interest to the fern specialist
or pteridologist only.

SPECIES (for the unheated greenhouse). Among the very extensive range of ferns, many of British origin and others from high
mountain regions in foreign countries, which are hardy enough to
stand frost, there are both small kinds and larger ones, so fragile
in frond structure that they are safer and happier under the shelter
of a greenhouse. They include *Adiantum, Adiantum capillus-veneris*
and varieties of the species, *A. pedatum* and *A. venustum;*
*Asplenium, Asplenium fontanum; Cryptogramma, Cryptogramma
acrostichoides; Platycerium, Platycerium alcicorne,* the stag's-horn
fern; *Phyllitis,* some of the *crispum* and *sagittato-cristatum* sections;
Polystichum, the *gracillimum* and *plumosum* groups. This brief list
makes no pretence of embracing all that are good for greenhouse
cultivation. Their names are legion, but as already indicated, the

seeker after a good collection should study specialist books and catalogues on ferns.

CULTIVATION. Whether a fernery or greenhouse in which ferns are to be grown is to be heated or not, it should be situated so that little direct sunshine strikes upon the glass. Otherwise good daylight is beneficial and favourable to healthy growth. A position where high buildings, screens, or overhanging trees·cause perpetual reduction of daylight is conducive to weak, flimsy frond growth and poor, sickly colour. Lean-to houses against high buildings and with a northern exposure are seldom in need of shading, but where a house stands open to sunshine it is essential that blinds shall be provided or that the glass shall be coated with shading material from early spring until the passing of autumn. Ample means of ventilation without cutting draughts will be required, and it should be possible to maintain humidity of atmosphere throughout the growing season.

Practically all kinds of ferns begin to grow in the spring, and this is the time to repot. The pots should be clean and well drained. The rooting medium consists of 2 parts fibrous loam and 1 part peat or sweet leafmould, with sufficient silver sand to render the whole porous. Some growers add a little crushed charcoal. Cut off old and worthless fronds. Plants that need a larger pot are moved on without disturbance beyond the removal of the drainage and loose compost.

Make the compost only moderately firm, and see that the old ball of soil is not elevated above the new. Ferns should be grown on a cool base. This can be done by covering an ordinary stage with builder's slates, upon which ashes or fine gravel may be placed for the pots to stand on. Never allow ferns to become dry at the roots; plants not repotted will take a generous supply of water during the summer months.

From October till February no artificial shading is required, but at other seasons the delicate fronds must be well protected from strong sunshine. During the spring and summer the walls, paths, and other bare places should be syringed two or three times daily if possible, to create the moist atmospheric conditions which growing ferns enjoy. Never spray overhead unless the weather is very hot and dry. If a house or division is devoted exclusively to ferns, it should be syringed round and the ventilators closed in the afternoons. Never apply strong manures or fertilisers. Very weak, pale

Top left: Gloriosa rothschildiana *Top right:* Heliotropium peruvianum
Chatsworth
Bottom left: Ipomoea rubro-caerulea *Bottom right:* Ixora

soot-water will benefit pot-bound plants if given in moderation. In late autumn and winter little ventilation and no syringing will be needed, but the roots must be kept just moist. When fumigating be sure to do it mildly two nights in succession, rather than the full dose at one time.

If well grown, ferns in hanging baskets are very effective, and the procedure is the same as advised for *Asparagus sprengeri*. The davallias and nephrolepis are most suitable for this purpose.

PROPAGATION. Generally speaking, there are two methods of propagation of ferns, one by spores produced on the backs of the fronds, which are flowerless plant's equivalent to seeds, the other by division of the clump or root stock. This latter method ensures reproduction of the exact replica of the parent plant. Spores are always subject to variation from the normal; sometimes the variations are considered to be an improvement on type, but often they are inferior from the culturist's point of view.

Division may be attempted when the crown of the plant is visibly splitting into several distinct portions; it may be undertaken in the early autumn, otherwise it is best left until spring, just as new growth is commencing. The best method of dividing the parent root is to use two small hand forks, place them vertically in the vacant space between two young crowns, thrust them gently but firmly downward and then lever the crowns apart by slowly and gently widening the distance between the handles of the forks. Always avoid cutting roots with a knife or tearing them to pieces by brute force. Apart from the care of the roots, the folded heads of the young embryo fronds must be preserved from crushing or bruising.

In potting the divided portions, select pots which are capable of taking the roots without cramping but, on the other hand, avoid the use of too large a pot, because a great body of unoccupied compost is liable to become sour and unhealthy before new roots can work through it. Never bury the actual crown, but keep it as nearly level on the soil surface as possible. In potting most kinds of plants stress is laid on the necessity of thoroughly firming the soil, but with ferns it is seldom that the roots enjoy battling through tightly pressed earth. Anything in the way of a rammer or potting stick must not be used; usually the act of tapping the bottom of the pot on the bench, coupled with thrusting the points of the fingers round the inside of the pot, will effect the right degree of firmness of the soil.

The adaptable and indispensable fuchsias can be grown as bushes, standards, in hanging baskets, up pillars and along rafters. This is the variety Swingtime

The old idea was that fern compost should consist almost entirely of peat and leafmould. It has been proved, however, that when a moderate amount of fibrous loam is available it is an advantage for this to be used to the extent of 40 to 50 per cent. of the bulk, making up the rest with fibrous peat, pulled to bits by hand, about the same bulk of oak or beech mould, and just sufficient sharp, clean silver sand to provide porosity. Remember there is no nourishment for plants in sand, and do not use it to an excessive degree. A little crushed charcoal is always useful, as it helps to keep the soil sweet and wholesome for a prolonged time. Anything in the way of manure or fertilisers should not be used. Despite the fact that ferns require copious supplies of water, it is important that the pots should be thoroughly well drained with a sufficiency of crocks. Stagnation is abhorrent to ferns, even though they are moisture loving.

After potting, plants should be kept in the shade for a period, and, if they can enjoy a moderate degree of heat for the first few weeks it is an advantage, but otherwise high temperatures are not to be advocated for the well-being of ferns.

The germination of fern spores cannot be hastened, and it is a task requiring attention to various details chiefly concerned with avoiding the growth of moss and lichen, which will suffocate the germinating spores if allowed to grow unchecked. The best method is to take the loam from fibrous turf loam, scald with boiling water, place about two tablespoonfuls in a small glass or earthenware basin without drainage, allow the soil to stand for at least 12 hours after scalding, then scatter the spores over the surface of the turf and cover the basin with a sheet of glass. The quantity of turf mentioned is sufficient for a bowl about the size of an ordinary dessert bowl; this, by the way, is an excellent vessel for the purpose. When covered with glass, place the bowls in a position where they will get no sunshine and leave them until signs of life appear. Sometimes this will be within three months, often it will be 12 months before the spores begin to germinate.

When the first fronds rise from the lichen-like covering of the soil, tilt the glass by placing a label or other small object on the rim of the bowl and raise one side of the glass upon it; this lets in air without uncovering the tender young plants. Before growth reaches $\frac{1}{2}$ in. in height, the tiny plants need to be separated by very careful handling and pricked out into shallow pans of a light gritty compost at about $\frac{1}{2}$ in. apart. A couple of inches of compost is sufficient for the first transference, and the glass should be replaced until growth is apparent, when more air can be given until eventually the glass is removed entirely. Before they become overcrowded in these pans the young ferns should again be separated and put singly into pots of smaller size; the smaller the better so long as any danger of crushing the roots is avoided. Be very careful not to bury the crowns of the tiny plants beneath the surface of the compost. After potting, replace the glass for a week or two and keep the atmosphere humid, but not saturated with moisture, and again when growth becomes active admit ventilation until the covering glass can be removed entirely. These young ferns should be potted on before they become pot-bound in any degree.

Ficus: This genus provides some ornamental foliage plants both erect and trailing, or weeping. All are evergreen.

SPECIES. The best is *Ficus elastica*, the India rubber plant, with large leathery leaves 6 to 18 in. long and 3 to 6 in. wide. There is a variegated form known as *F. e. variegata*, and another variegated kind whose leaves are pink, cream and green, called *F. e. tricolor*. Quite distinct from these is the creeping species, *F. radicans variegata*, which is self-clinging, and has much smaller leaves, $2\frac{1}{2}$ in. long. It is often used for covering bare walls in greenhouses. Another creeper is the green-leaved *F. pumila*, also known as *F. repens*, with even smaller leaves; it can be used as a climber also. *F. benjamina* makes an attractive small weeping tree, and *F. lyrata*, with large 12-in. long leaves, shaped like a violin, giving it its common name of the fiddle-leaf fig.

CULTIVATION. Specimens of *F. elastica* can be had in 6-in. pots; in fact, larger plants are of little use in an ordinary greenhouse. Repot in March, using a compost of 3 parts loam and 1 part leafmould. Shade from strong sunlight. The plant enjoys a liberal quantity of water when well rooted and during the summer months. In winter the temperature ought not to fall below 10°C (50°F). The creeping species will succeed in ordinary compost. They will need a little support until growth begins, when the shoots will naturally cling to the wall. The remaining species will succeed in the J.I. mixtures, such as 2 and 3. In winter all the species can be allowed to dry out completely between waterings, but not for long. The large-leaved kinds respond well to regular sponging of the leaves.

PROPAGATION. The creepers are increased by cuttings in spring. *Ficus elastica* is propagated by eyes with a leaf attached and about a couple of inches of stem. These are placed in sandy compost and set in a close propagating frame until growth begins. Tall, leggy plants are usually stem rooted, and after the top is removed side growths often appear. When sufficiently advanced these may be removed and treated as ordinary cuttings. Large specimens can be reduced in size by air-layering at about 1 ft. from the top and discarding the lower portion when rooting has taken place.

Fittonia: Small trailing plants having ornamental foliage. *F. argyroneura* has white and green leaves, and *F. verschaffeltii* has red markings on the foliage.

CULTIVATION. Fittonias do best in a shaded position in a warm greenhouse with a moist atmosphere. Their cultivation presents no difficulties if they can be given these conditions, and they will grow happily under greenhouse staging. They can also be grown in small pots for decorating the edges of greenhouse staging. Cuttings taken in the spring or summer will root readily in sandy soil in a temperature of 16°C (60°F). They are extremely susceptible to slug damage.

Franciscea, see Brunfelsia

Francoa (Bridal Wreath): Largely used for groups and for mixing with other subjects, the bridal wreath is also excellent for cutting. Plants are easily grown and produce elegant sprays during the summer months. Native of Chile. Height from 2 to 3 ft. when in bloom.

SPECIES. There are several species but *Francoa ramosa*, with white flowers, is the only one widely grown. The flowers are borne on long sprays.

CULTIVATION. Good specimens can be grown in 6- or 7-in. pots of the John Innes No. 2 potting mixture. Old plants are hardly worth retaining, but examples of two or three years' standing can be repotted in the spring and summer, and well-rooted plants will appreciate weak liquid fertiliser once or twice a week. The normal flowering period is July and August, so if odd spikes appear at other seasons they should promptly be removed. A minimum winter temperature of 4°C (40°F) is appropriate.

PROPAGATION. Francoas are usually raised from seeds, but cuttings of non-flowering growths will strike in summer.

Seeds are sown in pots of fine sandy compost and placed in a temperature of 13–16°C (55–60°F). If kept moist and shaded, seedlings will soon appear, when they are potted off singly. Arrange them on a shelf, shade from strong sunshine, and pot on as they require it.

From June to September they can be grown in a cold frame. From seeds sown in March or April good flowering plants will be available for the following year.

Fuchsia: A valuable old-fashioned flower that should be represented in every greenhouse. It makes an excellent bushy pot plant. Fuchsias are also good for pillars, hanging baskets, or for training to the rafters, while as standards they are very effective. There are both double- and single-flowered varieties, and the hybrids of *F. triphylla* have long, graceful, hanging blossoms, chiefly in flaming tints of orange, scarlet and bright red.

SPECIES. Outside botanical gardens few types are grown except, perhaps *Fuchsia splendens* (scarlet and green, Mexico), *F. fulgens* (scarlet, Mexico) *F. triphylla* (crimson, West Indies), and *F. procumbens* (an orange and purple small-flowered trailing species from New Zealand). The *triphylla* hybrids are quite distinct, and they embrace Coralle (a lovely shade of coral red), Mary (coral red), Heinrich Heinkel (salmon pink with dark red leaves) and Gartenmeister Bonstedt (deep glowing red). Florists' varieties can be obtained in a great range of superbly lovely flowers. For a lengthy period the florists' fuchsias lost much of their former popularity, and with the decline of the art of growing huge, trained specimen plants, which were a conspicuous feature of last century's shows, many old favourite varieties were all but lost. Happily, there has been a notable revival of interest in the fuchsia in recent years. The formation of a Fuchsia Society has been very helpful in this direction, and numerous good varieties have been rescued from oblivion and brought back to wider cultivation. A number of nurseries specialise in fuchsia production and new and improved varieties are constantly appearing in their catalogues, including many striking introductions from America.

CULTIVATION. There is no difficulty in growing the fuchsia, its chief requirements being good soil and plenty of moisture when growing. A suitable compost consists of fibrous loam (2 parts), leaf-mould (1 part), and dry rotted manure (1 part) with a sprinkling of silver sand. They can also be grown very successfully in the John Innes mixtures and the new loamless composts. The pots should be moderately drained and the soil made fairly firm around the roots.

After flowering, usually about October, the plants will be allowed to rest. No doubt they would continue to bloom for a few more weeks, but at this period their space will be more profitably occupied by other subjects. During the resting period they can be stood beneath the greenhouse stage or in a frostproof frame. Very little water is needed at this stage, and they should be kept quite cool, to prevent the appearance of premature growth.

In February they must be examined and pruned. As a rule they can be cut back fairly hard. After pruning, arrange the plants in a warm house, syringing them daily with tepid water, and keep the compost just moist. Repot when growth appears, removing as much of the old compost as possible. When the roots take possession of the fresh compost the conditions of an ordinary greenhouse will be best. This will keep the shoots short jointed. Avoid any dryness at the roots and feed with liquid fertiliser when the plants are well established.

The fuchsia gives good results if allowed to develop naturally except for an occasional stopping in the early stages. They are also very effective as pyramids. If these are desired, tie the main shoot to a stick and encourage the formation of side growths from the top of the pot upwards. It may be necessary to stop the leader, where side growths are few. When the latter break out, another leader can be taken up to replace the one that was pinched.

The making of a standard begins directly the cutting is rooted. Select stout, straight specimens and grow on till the required height is attained. During this period all side shoots are removed. When the stem is tall enough, pinch out the centre. Side growths will then emerge near the top, and these will be pinched occasionally with the object of producing a well-balanced head. Standards ought not to be dried off so severely in winter, and to preserve them from injury they should be stored on a stage.

PROPAGATION. Effected by cuttings, which can be rooted in early February, March or September. Old plants furnish plenty of growths suitable for cuttings which are taken from the tips of the shoots and should be free from flowers. They can be about 3 to 4 in. long. They will soon form roots in sandy compost and a little peat. Pot off singly when rooted into 3-in. pots and give further shifts as required.

Cuttings rooted in September will be potted off in 3-in. pots and just kept growing during the winter months. These will make finer plants the following summer than those rooted in the spring.

Fuchsias are also raised from seeds sown in spring in pans of light soil. Place in a temperature of 16°C (60°F). Transplant the seedlings in small pots and give the same treatment as cuttings. Most of the plants will bloom during the late summer and autumn months.

Gardenia: Beautiful evergreen shrubs which require the conditions of a warm house. They are highly prized for their fragrant double and single white flowers, which are very desirable for buttonholes, sprays, and bouquets.

SPECIES. The most useful species and varieties are: *Gardenia citriodora* (from Natal, with lemon-scented single flowers), *G. jasminoides* (from China) and its varieties *florida* (double), *fortuniana* (large flowered), Mystery (very large flowered) and *veitchiana* (winter flowering), and *G. thunbergia* (South Africa, winter flowering).

CULTIVATION. The compost consists of fibrous loam and sandy peat. In February the plants can be pruned into shape, and the general repotting will take place in March. Pots should be well drained. A summer temperature of 18–27°C (65–80°F) is essential. From September to March the temperature should be 13–16°C (55–60°F). Shade from strong sunshine, and give ventilation carefully to prevent cold draughts and a sudden fall in the temperature. Plenty of humidity is required. Young plants of one and two years old flower best. A daily spraying is beneficial but not when flowers are present, throughout the summer.

PROPAGATION. From cuttings of young wood inserted singly in small pots containing a mixture of equal parts peat, loam, and sand, and placed in a warm propagating frame where the temperature is 24–30°C (75–85°F). January is the best month for propagating to produce good flowering specimens for the following winter. Cuttings can also be rooted at other seasons to form a succession. Gardenias, if neglected, are soon attacked by mealy bug and other pests. An occasional spray with an insecticide is advisable.

Geranium, see Pelargonium

Gerbera: These have daisy-like flowers of orange, yellow or red produced one at a time in succession over a long period; some of the latest hybrids are white and pink. They are excellent for cutting. *G. jamesonii*, the Barberton daisy, is the species most commonly grown.

CULTIVATION. Gerberas can be tricky to grow. They particularly resent root disturbance and dampness. A frostproof greenhouse is adequate, although in Cornwall plants can be grown outside in a bed at the base of a south-facing wall. Young plants, while still small, can be planted out in beds in the greenhouse and the soil should be gritty and well drained. They can be grown in pots, but over-potting must be avoided. Gerberas can also be grown successfully in sand if fed regularly with liquid fertiliser. Watering must be done very carefully. Little is needed in winter, but adequate supplies should be given in summer to ensure good growth.

PROPAGATION. Seed germinates quite well in gentle heat and it should be sown fairly early in the year so that the young plants can be potted up or planted out in May. Flowers can be expected in the second year after sowing. Plants can also be increased from cuttings taken with a heel of older wood in the spring. Heat is necessary for the cuttings to root successfully.

Gesneria, see Smithiantha

Gloriosa: Showy and beautiful climbing plants for a heated greenhouse. The petals of the flowers are reflexed and crimped at the edges. The tendrils that appear at the ends of the leaves enable the plants to cling to suitable supports.

SPECIES. *Gloriosa superba* with deep orange and red flowers will succeed in a greenhouse with a minimum temperature of 7°C (45°F) *G. rothschildiana* has crimson and yellow flowers but needs a little more warmth to do really well. Another attractive species is *G. simplex*, which has orange and yellow flowers.

CULTIVATION. The plants have large tubers which are at rest in the winter. These should be repotted in March, and several tubers can be grown in a 10-in. pot. A compost consisting of equal parts of loam, peat and sand gives good results, or the John Innes mixture can be used. The plants should be kept in the warmest part of the greenhouse, and as growth becomes active, supplies of water must be increased. To see the flowers to their best advantage the stems should be trained under the greenhouse roof. The foliage will begin to turn yellow in late summer, and this is when the water should be withheld gradually until the compost is completely dry. Keep the tubers in the pots during the winter in a dry, fairly warm place, with a temperature of not less than 13°C (55°F). *G. superba* requires least heat of the three, and is almost hardy.

PROPAGATION. Offsets can be removed carefully from older tubers when they are repotted in the spring. Plants can also be raised from the seed, which is best sown singly in small pots in 24°C (75°F) in February or March.

Gloxinia: These are handsome, tuberous rooted plants with large, trumpet-like flowers, available in a great variety of colours. Correctly, they should be called *Sinningia*, but *Gloxinia* is still the name by which they are commonly known. Some good modern forms are: Blanche de Mera, pink, bordered white; Defiance, bright red; Diana, frilled light rose to deep pink; Emperor William, blue edged white; Mauve Queen; Prince Albert, violet-blue; Snowdrift; Roi des Rouges, dark red, and the tigrina forms, flowers spotted in many colours.

CULTIVATION. Best raised from seed each year, either in February or July, a temperature of 18°C (65°F) being essential. A peaty compost should be used and it must be very fine. Do not cover the seed, simply press it into the moist surface of the compost. Prick out and pot off as required, ultimately putting plants into 5-in. pots of light peaty compost. They like shade and a moist atmosphere.

After blooming dry off slowly and store undisturbed in their pots, keeping them in a temperature of not less than 10°C (50°F).

Start old corms into growth in February, again using a peaty compost, and grow on as suggested for seedlings.

When ready, pot singly in 4-, 5-, or 6-in. pots, according to size of tubers. The compost consists of fibrous loam, leafmould, rotted manure, and peat in equal parts, with a sprinkling of silver sand.

Press the compost fairly firm, and do not quite bury the corm.

Give plenty of light, but shade from strong sunshine. Avoid overwatering, and when the flower buds appear give weak liquid fertiliser once each week. From the time growth starts until flowering keep the temperature as near as possible to 16°C (60°F).

PROPAGATION. By sowing seed, and leaf cuttings inserted on a bed of warm sand, placed in a propagating frame and kept moist.

Grevillea: A large genus of foliage and flowering plants, a few only of which are grown in the cool greenhouse.

SPECIES. One is most popular. This is *Grevillea robusta*, the silk bark oak, with beautiful fern-like foliage. Native of Australia it is easily grown. Other forms occasionally quoted in catalogues are *forsteri* (with large bright red trusses of flowers), and *thelemanniana* (syn. *preissei*) with bright deep pink flowers, yellow at tip, height 3 to 5 ft.

CULTIVATION. They thrive quite happily in the John Innes composts, but require good drainage. Any repotting necessary is carried out in March.

Grevillea robusta should be grown to a single stem and not pinched. The others will need a little pruning to keep them in shape and within reasonable limits for a greenhouse; *forsteri* grows naturally to about 15 ft. and *thelemanniana* to about 5 ft. Water carefully. Dryness at the base will cause the loss of the lower leaves, and the other extreme will soon produce unhealthy plants. They require the ordinary conditions of a greenhouse, with a winter temperature of 7–13°C (45–55°F).

PROPAGATION. *G. robusta* is raised from seed sown February to April. This will germinate in a temperature of 16–21°C (60–70°F) if sown in sandy compost. The seeds are large and flat, and should be placed point downwards or sideways but not flat. Pot off singly when the seedlings are large enough. Keep near the glass and shade from strong sunlight. Gradually harden to the conditions of the greenhouse, and pot on when needed. If the tops are removed from old plants, they will produce side shoots suitable for cuttings.

The other species are increased by cuttings during the spring months.

Hardenbergia: A small group of flowering plants of twining growth, evergreen. Native of Australia, they have purple flowers.

SPECIES. The best are *Hardenbergia comptoniana* and *H. violacea* (syn. *H. monophylla*), purple. A white variety of the latter is *H. v. alba*. The flowers are pea shaped and are borne during spring or early summer. Hardenbergias are commonly known as the Australian sarsaparilla trees, or Australian lilac.

CULTIVATION. Provide an open compost, 2 parts peat and 1 part loam, with a sprinkling of sharp sand and finely powdered charcoal to render the whole porous.

Repot in spring. Maintain a winter temperature of 7°C (45°F) and no shade at any time. Hardenbergias can be planted out in a prepared border, if they are required to cover a back wall or rafters.

PROPAGATION. By seeds and cuttings. Sow the former in March and germinate in a temperature of 16°C (60°F). Cuttings are made from young side shoots in April and rooted in a heated propagating frame.

Hebe: Several of the hebes make useful plants for a cool greenhouse, and most of them produce their flowers during the early weeks of autumn.

SPECIES. The kinds generally chosen for indoor cultivation are forms of *Hebe speciosa*, obtainable in shades of rose, mauve, pink, red, purple and near blue. They usually go under such names as *rubra* and Blue Gem. Another fine species is *H. diosmifolia*, a small-growing slender shrub with pale lilac-coloured flowers. The gem, however, for pot work is *H. hulkeana*, a loose-growing shrubby plant with long panicles of lilac flowers produced during the spring months. A well-grown example is a joy to the grower.

CULTIVATION. Pot on as required, in loam with a little leaf-mould, and pinch again when the growths are a few inches in length. About May stand the plants in the open, cease pinching, and encourage vigorous growth by regular applications of weak liquid fertiliser. In September return to the greenhouse.

It is advisable to keep up a young stock; old plants will require large pots, and they are not really satisfactory unless they have a liberal root run.

PROPAGATION. All forms are readily increased by cuttings in August. Select partially ripened shoots, insert them in pots of sandy compost and place in a cold frame. When rooted, pot off singly, pinch out the centre of each plant, and grow in a cool greenhouse or where frost is excluded.

Hebeclinium, see Eupatorium

Hedychium: Most of the species require stove treatment, but there are two exceptions which will thrive in an ordinary greenhouse with a winter temperature of 7°C (45°F).

SPECIES. *Hedychium coronarium*, with snow-white, scented flowers; native of East Indies. It reaches a height of 4 or 5 ft. *H. gardnerianum* is a fine species with spikes of bright yellow flowers which are very fragrant. Height 3 to 5 ft. These plants develop broad leaves which are also highly ornamental, and they are often planted out of doors for summer bedding in the same way that cannas are.

CULTIVATION. Hedychiums need fairly large pots. After the flowering season remove the faded flower spikes and keep the roots on the dry side until February. Then the plants are repotted in 3 parts fibrous loam, and 1 part turfy peat, and a little coarse sand. Water freely when the plants are in full growth.

PROPAGATION. By division of the crowns in spring.

Heliotropium: The principal species is *Heliotropium peruvianum*, a native of Peru, and is the common heliotrope or cherry pie. The flowers are violet or lilac in colour. There are numerous varieties in commerce, chiefly of Continental origin, and some are remarkable for their dark coloured foliage and delightfully fragrant flowers. The form known as Florence Nightingale belongs to this class, and others are Lord Roberts, President Garfield, Swanley White, Princess Marina and Chatsworth.

CULTIVATION. If heliotrope is kept growing through the winter, it may be had in bloom more or less throughout the year. The best plan is to allow the plants to take a partial rest in winter. Where it is desired to clothe walls or pillars, the plants should be put out in a well-drained border or bed. Temperature in winter should be about 10°C (50°F).

For those grown in pots the John Innes No. 2 potting compost or one of the loamless mixtures will be quite suitable. About February examine the old plants, remove dead wood, and cut hard back all the side branches. When growth begins, repotting or topdressing should be carried out. Very little pinching or stopping will be needed with old plants unless a shoot begins to grow strongly and rob other parts of the plant. Such growths must be pinched in the early stages.

The making of a standard begins at the cutting stage. Allow the plants selected to develop until the required height is attained except for the early removal of all side growths, then stop the leading shoot.

PROPAGATION. Named varieties are increased by cuttings of young shoots in spring or early autumn, the former for preference, but if plants for bedding are required the autumn-rooted cuttings give the best results. Fill well-drained pots or pans with light, sandy soil, and arrange the cuttings in a close propagating frame until rooted. Pot off singly, and each one should be pinched two or three times in the early stages to form a bushy base. Cuttings chosen for standards are not pinched until they have attained a height of 3 ft. or a little more if taller stems are needed. Selected forms and mixtures are also raised from seed sown in March in pans of John Innes seed compost and germinated at 16–18°C (60–65°F).

Helipterum (Rhodanthe): These are charming annual everlasting flowers suitable for pot cultivation. They are useful for winter decoration, with their incurved, crisply petalled flowers in clusters.

SPECIES. Among these is *Helipterum manglesii* (rose). There is also a double form known as *flore-pleno*. In many seed catalogues rose, crimson, white, and mixed varieties are offered.

CULTIVATION. Seeds are sown in September or March. They germinate in a warm greenhouse with a temperature of 10°C (50°F). Careful watering is necessary during the early stages, otherwise the plants will damp off. If seedlings are raised in September they should be grown during the winter months on a shelf where the temperature is about 7°C (45°F). Keep the compost just moist, and if greenfly appear syringe them slightly with a weak solution of quassia extract or derris. Never fumigate helipterums. Pot on as required in a mixture of loam and leafmould. When the plants are well rooted weak liquid fertiliser can be given whenever water is required.

PROPAGATION. By seed only, as above described.

Hibbertia: Slender growing, evergreen flowering climbers, which bear yellow flowers during the summer months.

SPECIES. The favourite is *Hibbertia dentata*, a native of Australia. The deep yellow flowers are very effective against the dark coppery foliage. Another Australian species occasionally met with is *H. volubilis*, to 4 ft., rather trailing, the largest flowered of the genus. The blooms are yellow and the leaves dark green. *H. perfoliata* is a dwarf grower with pale yellow flowers.

CULTIVATION. Although it will grow successfully in pots, *H. dentata* should be planted out in a confined border whenever possible. Any repotting should be done early in March, and the compost consists of turfy peat and loam in equal parts. To this must be added a liberal sprinkling of silver sand and finely broken brick. This can be put through a quarter-inch sieve. The rooting medium must be kept sweet and wholesome at all times. The pruning of weak and stray growths will be done directly the days begin to lengthen. Plants growing near the roof will need training and tying in position from time to time, so that the shoots will not be over-crowded. Well-rooted specimens will require plenty of water in sum-mer, but in winter the compost is kept just moist. Insect pests must be eradicated directly they are seen, otherwise the plants will soon become unhealthy. Cleanliness is a very important cultural factor.

PROPAGATION. Hibbertias are propagated by cuttings in May. They should be semi-ripe and about 3 in. long. They will form roots in pots containing peat and sand. Place in a propagating frame and shade from strong sunshine.

Hoffmannia: The most interesting species is *Hoffmannia ghiesbreghtii variegata* which has unusual and handsome foliage. On the upper surface the long-pointed leaves are velvety green in colour with blot-ches of red and silvery grey. Underneath they are red.

CULTIVATION. A temperature of 16–18°C (60–65°F) is needed to grow this plant well, and in the spring and summer it will grow rapidly in a moist atmosphere. Plants can be raised from cuttings of young shoots, which should be rooted in sandy compost in a warm, moist propagating case. A compost consisting of equal parts fibrous loam, moist peat and coarse sand is satisfactory, and good specimens can be had in 6-in. pots. Plenty of water is needed during the growing season, but in winter the plants should be watered spar-ingly. Once well established in their final pots feeding with liquid fertiliser is beneficial.

Hovea: A genus of handsome, half-hardy, pea-flowered evergreen shrubs.

SPECIES. The best members of the family are *Hovea celsii* (deep blue), *H. chorizemifolia* (purple), *H. longifolia* (purple) and *H. pungens* (blue). With the exception of *H. longifolia* which grows to 8 to 10 ft. the average height is from 1 to 4 ft.

Hoveas are remarkable for their intensely coloured flowers, the shades of blue being very pronounced. All are spring flowering.

CULTIVATION. Repotting, when required, should be done after flowering. Press the compost firm, and avoid over-potting. The most suitable compost consists of fibrous peat and a little sand. A light position in an airy greenhouse will suit these plants throughout the year. The roots must never become dust dry, but very little water will be needed during the winter months.

PROPAGATION. Either by seeds or cuttings, the latter being rather difficult to strike.

Seeds are sown in spring, in pots of fine peaty compost, and germinated in a temperature of 13°C (55°F). When large enough transfer the young plants to small pots, and grow on in a temperature of 10–13°C (50–55°F). They need a peaty compost. Pinching must be resorted to when the seedlings are a few inches high to induce a bushy habit. Careful watering must be the rule. When the young plants are nicely established cooler surroundings should be allowed, somewhat similar to old plants.

Hoya: An old-fashioned quaintly beautiful evergreen climbing plant, suitable for training on wires under the roof of a greenhouse where a winter temperature can be maintained at about 10°C (50°F). The flowers of hoya are wax-like in appearance, star shaped, rather small and borne on slender stalks in loose hanging clusters. Their colour is flesh pink with a dark reddish centre. They are borne on long trailing growths furnished with thick, smooth-surfaced leaves in pairs at regular intervals. The blossoming period extends over the greater part of summer.

SPECIES. The species most suitable for greenhouse cultivation is *Hoya carnosa*. There is another named *H. bella*, which is white with a crimson centre, but this requires a much higher temperature to maintain it in good health during winter.

CULTIVATION. *H. carnosa* grows in a compost of equal parts fibrous peat and good loam, with the addition of a little charcoal and sufficient sand to keep the whole porous. Plants may be grown in large pots, but growths have to be trained around a framework of canes or wire. They may also be planted in a well-prepared bed at the foot of a pillar or against trellis work at the back of the greenhouse. A good method is to place a large pot or tub in the corner of the house, and lead up the shoots until they reach wires strained about 9 in. below the roof glass. Train the branches to the wires after the manner of vine growths.

The plant enjoys good light and sunshine, shading only being necessary in the very hottest part of summer. Foliage should be freely syringed morning and evening, and the roots should be well supplied with moisture from spring to autumn. Weak growths may be cut back or crowded shoots removed during February. When flowers fade the foot stalks should not be cut away because secondary growths will appear and further blossoms will be produced upon these.

One trouble with hoya is that it easily falls victim to mealy bug, and a sharp watch should be kept for signs of this pest and action taken immediately.

PROPAGATION. Cuttings of shoots of one-year-old growth should be inserted in well-drained pots of sandy peat, and placed in a propagating frame some time between early March and late May. Where long trailing growths break from the main plant near enough to the ground to enable them to be pegged down, such shoots may be layered during summer. A good method is to fill a well-drained pot with sandy peat and raise it to a convenient height under the branch to be layered. Make a small incision in the bark on the underside of the stem close to a joint, and secure the cut stem to the compost by means of a bent wire or hooked peg. Keep the compost in the pot comfortably moistened and leave undisturbed until the following spring, when the stem may be severed between the layering point and the parent plant, potting on the separated layer into a pot of convenient size.

Humea: A miscellaneous group of plants seems to be not quite complete without a few representatives of this genus.

SPECIES. One only, *Humea elegans*, a biennial with scented leaves and tall drooping panicles of brownish-pink flowers; it is sometimes known as the incense plant, on account of its fragrance. It is native of Australia, and attains a height of 4 to 6 ft. An elegant and graceful plant, in bloom from July to October, but it is only suitable for the large greenhouse.

CULTIVATION. Plants can only be raised from seeds, which are sown from April to July. The compost should be light and finely sifted, and owing to the minuteness of the seeds they will only require the merest covering. The pots or pans must be well drained, and the compost may be well watered a few hours before sowing takes place.

When trained along a roof or to a wall, the full beauty of the summer-flowering climber Lapageria rosea *is revealed*

Cover the containers with a pane of glass or paper, and place them in a cold frame. Germination may be somewhat irregular, so if only a few seedlings appear at first they should be carefully removed with as little disturbance as possible. Transfer the seedlings to pans or small pots and return to the cold frame. Until germination is effected, and during the early stages of growth, the frame should be kept rather close. Afterwards plenty of air is essential.

The next move will be to 3-in. pots. When these are comfortably filled with roots, pots 5 and 6 in. in diameter will be needed. In these the plants will pass the winter, in a cool greenhouse fully exposed to the light. Provide ample drainage, and grow in John Innes No. 1 potting compost. Always stand the pots on a cool base. Careful watering is essential, and in winter, when growth is almost nil, only sufficient moisture need be given to keep the foliage rigid.

In March the largest plants can be placed in 9- or 10-in. pots, but smaller examples are given a 7 in. with a further shift in May if needed. Do not disturb the ball of compost when repotting. Make the compost fairly firm. Humeas have a tendency to die off suddenly for no apparent reason, but it is usually caused by over-watering. A mistake in this respect proves fatal. When the pots are filled with roots and the flower spikes show, weak liquid fertiliser can be given. If the sun is very bright during the late spring and summer, a thin shading will be beneficial.

Hydrangea: A genus of shrubby plants of varying interest and value, coming from China, Japan and America. Some are only suitable for planting in shrubberies, but *Hydrangea paniculata* is sometimes used for forcing.

SPECIES. For the average amateur *H. macrophylla* (syn. *H. hortensis*) is the one of importance, and apart from the type a large selection of named cultivars will offer abundant choice.

The range of colours includes beautiful shades of blue, pink, red, and white, and some of the pinks and reds can be turned blue. A few good cultivars are Holstein (pink or blue), Madame Mouillière (white), Sensation (bright red), Eldorado (dark pink), Europa (deep pink) and La France (bright pink).

CULTIVATION. Hydrangeas may be raised each year and brought into flower when a little over a year old, or they may be grown as larger shrubby specimens several years old.

Old plants may be repotted in February or March, in John Innes

Top left: Mandevilla suaveolens *Top right:* Medinilla magnifica
Bottom: Mimosa pudica

No 1 or 2 compost from which the ground chalk has been omitted.

Hydrangeas are gross feeders and will require regular feeding while in active growth. During summer and autumn stand the plants outside in full sunshine and keep them well supplied with water.

Towards the end of October remove the plants to a frostproof greenhouse. The water supply is then gradually reduced, and when the foliage falls an occasional watering will suffice. For plants two or more years old a season of rest is essential. Afterwards the grower can either allow the plants to develop in an ordinary greenhouse temperature of 7–13°C (45–55°F) or gently force a few at a time, thereby prolonging the flowering period.

If the latter is chosen a start can be made early in the year. Select specimens with prominent flower buds and place them in a temperature of 13–16°C (55–60°F). Water sparingly for a start, but as growth increases much more moisture will be needed. A thin shading from strong sunlight will be needed when the plants are in bloom. Good specimen plants can be obtained in pots 6 and 7 in. in diameter.

BLUE-FLOWERED HYDRANGEAS. The flowers of some of the red and pink varieties can be turned to blue, by watering the plants with hydrangea colourant every 10 days, from when growth begins until the plants are almost in flower. For this purpose professional growers use aluminium sulphate at $\frac{1}{2}$ oz. to 1 gallon of water. They also add 4 oz. per bushel of the same substance to the compost for the plants which are to be treated.

PROPAGATION. Plants are increased from internodal cuttings in spring, or they can be rooted in August, but these will not flower for 20 months or more.

Insert the cuttings singly in small pots filled with sandy compost, and arrange them in a close propagating frame where the temperature is between 10 and 16°C (50 and 60°F). Admit a little air when roots are formed, and after a few days transfer them to a shelf to get hardened. Pot on as they fill their containers with roots. The best plants will produce a fine head of bloom in 5- and 6-in. pots. Keep them growing freely till the end of October, and although during the winter less moisture is needed, these plants ought not to be kept quite so dry as two- or three-year-old specimens. Plants from cuttings rooted before the end of March will produce several heads of flower the following spring. Those rooted later should be grown without any stopping to produce a single head of flower.

Impatiens: The balsam, *Impatiens balsamina*, is a gay and fine annual from India, and if well cultivated it will produce a grand display throughout the summer and autumn months.

The Camellia-flowered is the best strain, and in addition to mixed varieties they can be obtained in salmon pink, white, rose, violet, and scarlet. A good flower should be similar to a perfect camellia. The plants attain a height of about $1\frac{1}{2}$ ft.

CULTIVATION. Seeds should be sown from the third week in March till the first week in May. Sow the seeds in boxes or pots of rich sandy soil, and germinate in a temperature of 16°F (60°F). When the seedlings appear, keep them near the roof glass, and gradually admit a little air.

As soon as the first rough leaves appear the plants should be potted off singly in 3-in. pots, allowing the seed leaves to touch the compost surface. Provide plenty of drainage, and use John Innes No. 1 potting compost. Do not starve the plants in the early stages and when roots touch the sides of the pots transfer them to 5- or 6-in. containers.

Do not pinch or stop in any way, and if fine specimens are required a few branches may need staking.

Grow the plants in the greenhouse near the glass, and see that the roots are well supplied with water. A lack of moisture is the main reason for failure. Frequent overhead spraying is beneficial until the flowers begin to open. When the flowering pots are filled with roots, liquid fertiliser can be given two or three times each week. Continue to remove dead flowers, and prevent the formation of seed vessels; then the flowering period is considerably prolonged.

Ipomoea: Close kinship exists between the well-known convolvulus of the garden and various species of the genus *Ipomoea*, which are natives of hot countries and grow better under greenhouse treatment than in the open. Some of these are of remarkable beauty and make gorgeous greenhouse climbers, where they can be trained around a few pea-sticks or used to clothe a pillar. Strictly speaking they should be called *Pharbitis* these days, but the name *Ipomoea* is so firmly established it seems a pity to change it.

SPECIES. The best is *Ipomoea rubro-caerulea* Heavenly Blue, and if the early flowering strain is obtained the plants will bloom in four months from the time of sowing the seeds.

CULTIVATION. Sow seeds at intervals from the end of February till June, but for general greenhouse work a March or early April sowing is best. Place the seeds singly in small pots of sandy compost, and allow a temperature of 16°C (60°F). If it is lower than this, the seeds will germinate, but the first leaves will be yellow and the seedling will gradually die. Bright sunlight produces the same condition. The soil should be just moist, so that little or no water is needed until the seedlings appear, otherwise the seeds may decay. When sufficiently rooted move the plants into 3-in. pots, using a compost of loam (3 parts), leafmould (1 part), and a little sand. The flowering pots will be from 6 to 8 in. in diameter. They should be well drained and the compost made moderately firm. When the seedlings are a few inches high they should be pinched, after which no further stopping is required. This ipomoea will succeed in an ordinary greenhouse from May onwards. It is also known as morning glory, because its beautiful flowers are fully open in the forenoon and close after midday. *I. learii*, the blue dawn flower, is a beautiful perennial climber for a warm greenhouse.

There is also a perennial, tuberous-rooted, white-flowered ipomoea. It bears the common name sweet potato, its tubers being edible. *I. batatus* is its botanical name. Plant singly in 6-in. pots of good mixed compost in February. Water sparingly at first, but liberally throughout summer, gradually drying off in autumn for a complete winter rest. Propagate by division of tubers at time of potting, or by cuttings of young growths in April.

Isolepis, see Scirpus

Ixora: These are hothouse, evergreen flowering shrubs. There are numerous forms of *Ixora coccinea* having scarlet and orange flowers, apart from *I. lutea* with yellow flowers and *I. fulgens* with red flowers, all growing to about 3 or 4 ft.

CULTIVATION. Although this plant is often used for room decoration it really needs a greenhouse with a hot, moist atmosphere to do well. A minimum temperature in winter of 13–16°C (55–60°F) is necessary, but from October until February conditions must be kept drier and water should be given sparingly. Mature plants can be pruned into shape in February, which is also a good time for repotting. A mixture of 2 parts fibrous loam, 2 parts peat, and 1 part coarse sand is satisfactory. Given a temperature of 18–21°C (65–70°F) and moist atmospheric conditions growth will be made rapidly. The colourful flower heads appear during the summer months.

PROPAGATION. Cuttings made from moderately firm shoots will root in a mixture of sand and peat during the spring and summer. They should be inserted in small pots and stood in a propagating frame with a temperature of 18°C (65°F).

Jacaranda: A native of Brazil, *Jacaranda ovalifolia* has dark green, fern-like foliage. Although it does have blue flowers, these are rarely seen in this country as the plant is grown primarily for its attractive foliage, and grows eventually into a shrub about 10 ft. tall.

CULTIVATION. To obtain graceful plants 2–3 ft. tall, it is best to raise new ones from seed or cuttings each spring. This can be done in a propagator, provided a temperature of 18°C (65°F) can be maintained. To obtain cuttings old plants can be cut back to induce side shoots to form. Rooted cuttings or seedlings should be potted into 3-in. pots and later moved on into 5- or 6-in. pots. Plants will grow happily in John Innes compost and they like a light position in a warm greenhouse. During the summer, however, plants can be stood outside in a sheltered sunny place, and if they are kept in small pots you may be lucky enough to have some flowers.

Jacobinia: Most of the species require stove treatment, but the interesting *Jacobinia carnea* is an exception. This is an excellent subject for producing a display in early autumn. Well-grown plants will possess fine heads of fleshy pink flowers. Although it will attain a height of 6 ft. if planted out, fairly dwarf flowering examples can be had in pots from 6 to 8 in. diameter. It is a native of Rio de Janeiro. Another attractive species is *J. pauciflora*, whose red and yellow flowers are produced in winter on a plant 2 ft. tall. It is evergreen and, like *J. carnea*, can be grown in 6- to 8-in. pots.

CULTIVATION. A suitable compost is fibrous loam, good peat, and leafmould in equal parts with a little sand added. Pinch out the points of the shoots soon after cuttings are rooted, and again when the growths are about 6 in. in length. No further stopping is needed.

Plants may be grown on a second year. After flowering reduce the growths to fairly firm wood, and during the winter give only enough water to prevent withering. Maintain a temperature of about 10°C (50°F) in winter. Repot in February, and give the same treatment as advised for cuttings. It should be noted that *J. pauciflora* is watered normally in winter while flowering, but is given a rest during August and September, after gradually drying off, and is stood out of doors at that time to ripen the shoots thoroughly and ensure good flowering the following winter.

Jacobinia carnea is occasionally planted out to cover the back wall of a greenhouse.

Red spider is sometimes troublesome to both species, unless the top growth is sprayed with clear water daily during the summer.

PROPAGATION. Raise from cuttings in the spring. Insert singly in small pots filled with sandy compost and arrange them in a close propagating frame. When rooted, gradually harden; further treatment consists of potting on as required until the plants are in 6- to 8-in. pots.

Jasminum: These are almost evergreen and more or less climbing in habit. Hence they are useful for covering a wall.

SPECIES. *Jasminum grandiflorum* is a fine one with white flowers, which are highly fragrant. *J. primulinum* is pale yellow. The former is autumn, and the latter winter flowering. The last named will make a good pot plant, but growth is more free if consigned to a well-drained border.

CULTIVATION. Weak, straggly shoots are removed after flowering, and fresh compost given in March. This consists of fibrous loam (3 parts) and leafmould (1 part). Specimens growing inside must be syringed daily when the weather is bright and the roots kept well supplied with water. Pot plants can be placed in the open from May till September. Liquid fertiliser may be given to healthy and well-rooted examples about once a week.

PROPAGATION. By soft young cuttings in spring. They should be removed from the old plant with a heel, inserted in sandy soil, and placed in a propagating frame where the temperature is about 16°C (60°F).

Kennedya: These are twining or prostrate perennials, and are known as the Australian bean flower. They are excellent for covering walls, trellis work, or pillars, but unfortunately they are subject to attacks of scale and mealy bug. Probably this accounts for their being so little grown, but the beauty of the flowers would warrant them being represented in most collections.

SPECIES. *Kennedya prostrata major*, a twiner, with scarlet

flowers and, moreover, owing to the downy nature of the leaves and stems, it is seldom attacked by insect pests. Other desirable species are *K. coccinea* (scarlet), *K. nigricans* (deep violet-purple), and *K. rubicunda* (red). These are in bloom from March till August.

CULTIVATION. For best results, kennedyas should be planted in a well-drained bed or border. The rooting medium consists of loam and peat in equal parts, with a liberal addition of sharp sand and finely broken charcoal. Train the shoots thinly, and in such a way that their removal is an easy task. If at any time they become infested with insects, they should be taken down and thoroughly cleansed. Frequent syringing during the spring and summer months will help to keep the foliage clean. In the autumn cut out all dead wood and shorten any growths that have overrun the allotted space. During the winter they need a temperature of about 7°C (45°F), and water in small quantities when the plants are at rest.

These delightful climbers can also be grown in pots, and the repotting carried out in March. They require plenty of water in spring and summer, when growth is freely made.

PROPAGATION. Increase stock by seeds sown in spring or summer. They will germinate in a temperature of 16°C (60°F). Cuttings, if made from fairly firm side growths, will form roots in peaty compost if placed in a close propagating frame with a little bottom heat.

Laelia, see Orchids

Lagerstroemia: A genus of handsome evergreen plants.

SPECIES. *Lagerstroemia indica* (the Cape myrtle) is a native of China, and will attain a height of 6 to 10 ft. Under cultivation quite small plants will furnish plenty of blossoms. It bears bright pink flowers in terminal panicles during the summer. The variety *alba* is pure white.

CULTIVATION. During winter the temperature should be about 10°C (50°F), and only enough water need be given to prevent the compost becoming dust dry. With the approach of spring and summer more water can be applied, and a few degrees more warmth will be beneficial. Repot annually in March in equal parts of peat and loam. Remove as much of the old compost as possible, and do not over-pot. Syringe daily, and give weak liquid fertiliser occasionally when the pots are filled with roots. The growths are cut back fairly hard a few weeks before repotting takes place.

PROPAGATION. Stock is increased by cuttings in March or April. Select young shoots, and insert them in pots of sandy compost, or pure sand. Place in a propagating frame where the temperature is 18–21°C (65–70°F). Pot off singly when rooted, and pinch out points of shoots when the plants are nicely established to encourage a bushy habit.

Lantana: In this genus the natural species are not important to the gardener, being inferior to the named varieties with their large verbena-like heads of richly coloured flowers. These may be had in bloom during the greater part of the year.

SPECIES. *Lantana camara,* pink or yellow to red or orange, growing to 6 to 8 ft.; *L. nivea,* white, 2 to 3 ft.; *trifolia,* red, 3 ft. All American. They are chiefly interesting as the parents of hybrids of greater merit than themselves.

Among the varieties available will be found Cloth of Gold, Peach Blossom (salmon pink), Pink Supreme, Montevidensis (deep lavender), Professor Raoux (red) and Snow Queen.

CULTIVATION. For best results, lantanas must be given a liberal diet. They will grow quite happily in John Innes No. 2 potting compost or one of the loamless mixtures. Make the compost moderately firm. Cut back old plants about the middle of February. Each shoot can be reduced to within 3 in. of its base. Provide a temperature of about 16°C (60°F) and syringe daily with tepid water. When the plants break freely into growth they must be repotted. Remove most of the old compost, and see that the pots are well drained. Keep warm, and use the syringe twice daily, morning and evening. When established in the new compost, cooler conditions should prevail, and if needed the growths should be pinched. After flowering, a partial rest is allowed, but sufficient moisture is given to keep the wood rigid.

PROPAGATION. Named varieties are increased by cuttings during March or August. A little bottom heat will greatly assist in the formation of roots. When ready, pot off singly, and frequent stopping of the shoots is necessary to secure bushy specimens.

Lantanas may also be raised from seeds, and from a reliable strain some good forms will be secured. Sow in pans of John Innes seed compost and place them on a hotbed or in a temperature of 27°C (80°F).

Lapageria: These plants are among the most beautiful of greenhouse climbers, but a somewhat shaded position is required.

SPECIES. There is only one natural species, *Lapageria rosea*, with rich rosy-crimson flowers. These are large and pendulous, so their full beauty is revealed when the growths are trained to a roof or on a wall. It is a native of Chile, and this species is very variable, some forms being far superior to others. There are several named varieties, such as *albiflora* (pure white and very chaste), *superba* (rich brilliant crimson – a great improvement on the type), and *ilsemannii*, larger, very bright crimson.

CULTIVATION. Lapagerias may be grown in pots, but wherever possible they should be planted out. Choose a position where the plants can be shaded from strong sunshine and the roots kept cool and moist. Thorough drainage is necessary, and the compost consists of 3 parts good fibrous peat and 1 of loam. To this should be added a liberal sprinkling of sand and charcoal. Plant early in March. See that no slugs are brought in with the compost; they are very partial to the young shoots. During the spring and summer the roots must be well supplied with water, and the growths should be syringed daily. Attend to the training and tying of the shoots. Little pruning is needed beyond the removal of weak growths. In winter less water is needed, and it is not advisable to allow the temperature to rise above 10°C (50°F). Lapagerias enjoy plenty of air in summer and early autumn. Plants in pots should be given fresh compost in March and the same treatment as those planted out.

The growths are occasionally infested with greenfly, thrips, red spider, and mealy bug unless measures are adopted to keep them clean. Spraying with an insecticide and fumigation will hold insect pests in check.

PROPAGATION. Effected by layering the shoots. Fill a large pot or box with sandy peat and arrange so that growths can be pegged down on the compost. The shoots may be coiled around over the compost if needed. Roots will form at each leaf joint, and eventually young growths will spring up. When ready, sever the shoot and place singly in small pots of light, peaty compost.

Limonium: There are several species and varieties of the sea lavender suitable for the greenhouse, but they are not so easily grown as many subjects. However, if due attention is paid to watering, most of the difficulties will be overcome.

SPECIES. *Limonium imbricatum* (blue), *L. macrophyllum* (blue), *L. profusum* (white and purple), *L. suworowii* (lilac pink).

CULTIVATION. Winter temperature of 7–10°C (45–50°F) is needed to keep plants healthy, and throughout the dull period of the year only give enough water to keep the roots just moist. In spring, when signs of renewed activity are evident, the plants may be repotted. Limoniums will succeed in the John Innes potting composts. When root action is vigorous they will take copious supplies of water.

PROPAGATION. Is from seed or from cuttings. Place the old plants in a temperature of 13°C (50°F) early in March and encourage the formation of side shoots. When they have made five or six leaves they should be removed and inserted singly in small pots filled with sand or sandy peat. Place them in a close propagating frame where a temperature of 21°C (70°F) can be maintained. When rooted stand the plants outside the propagating frame for a few days and shade from strong sunlight. Then place them in 3-in. pots, using a J.I. compost, and remove to a cooler house; when nicely established pot on as required. Seeds are sown in a sandy compost in early spring with a temperature of between 13 and 16°C (55 and 60°F).

Lippia: A plant with sweetly scented foliage, suitable for training up the pillar of a cool greenhouse or as bush plants in pots. In mild districts it is hardy outside.

SPECIES. *Lippia citriodora*, native of Chile, is also known as the lemon-scented verbena. The leaves, especially when rubbed, are agreeably scented, and the terminal panicles of small flowers are lilac or pale pink. It is deciduous. If the fallen leaves are collected they will be found to keep their lemon fragrance for a considerable time. Oil of verbena is distilled from them.

CULTIVATION. This plant can be kept to any size by pruning in early spring. Cut all the last year's growths back to two or three buds, and when growth is evident any plants that need it can be repotted. Water freely in summer, and little in winter after the leaves have fallen. It will thrive in any standard compost.

PROPAGATION. By cuttings in spring made from young shoots 4 in. long with a heel of the old wood attached. Sandy soil and a little heat are necessary.

Lomatia: These are evergreen shrubs, and worthy of cultivation for their foliage. They are mostly native of Australia.

SPECIES. *Lomatia ferruginea*, a handsome plant with graceful fern-like foliage, covered with a rusty-coloured down. Height up to 10 ft. Native of Chile. *L. longifolia*, 10 ft., very narrow leaves to 8 in. long, from New South Wales.

CULTIVATION. The compost should consist of equal parts of loam, peat and sand. Ample drainage must be provided. Cut back any straggly shoots in February, and repot during the following month. During the spring and summer syringe daily, and keep the roots well supplied with water. Less moisture is needed in winter, and the temperature should be about 10°C (50°F).

PROPAGATION. By cuttings of well-ripened shoots placed in a warm propagating frame. The temperature should be about 21°C (70°F); even so they form roots very slowly. Propagation is effected during the summer months.

Luculia: Greenhouse shrubs with pretty foliage and flowers.

SPECIES. The one usually met with is *Luculia gratissima*, a shrubby plant which will in time attain a height of 10 ft. or more, which makes them too large for the average greenhouse. The large heads of sweetly scented pink flowers are produced during the late summer and autumn months. *L. pinceana* has larger and more fragrant white flowers, which change with age to a rosy hue. It resembles the preceding species in general habit, but is not quite so tall.

CULTIVATION. Luculia may be grown in pots, but grows better planted out in a bed or border in the greenhouse. It succeeds in a compost of fibrous loam, peat and a little sand. If the loam is on the heavy side, add broken charcoal. Good drainage is essential. Plenty of water is needed during the summer, and the syringe can be used freely while growth is being made. Cut back the shoots after flowering, usually about December, and then keep the roots on the dry side, with a temperature of not less than 7°C (45°F) until April, when the plants are restarted into growth. They need a rest for two or three months.

PROPAGATION. By seeds when available, but the seedlings require two or three years' growth before they flower.

Cuttings of young shoots can be inserted in sandy compost and placed in a warm propagating frame. Shade from strong sunlight. Luculias are rather difficult to increase by cuttings.

Macleania: A small family of pretty evergreen flowering shrubs, more or less trailing in habit.

SPECIES. *Macleania cordifolia*, brilliant scarlet with yellow points; native of Ecuador. Owing to its decided trailing habit, this plant should be grown suspended from the roof or on a shelf. *M. insignis* is remarkable for the brilliant red tints on the young foliage. *M. Longiflora*, red; height 5 ft., from Peru. *M. pulchra*, yellow and deep scarlet; long drooping branches; native of New Grenada. All flower during the spring and summer months.

CULTIVATION. These plants will need careful training owing to their straggling growth. It is best, however, to allow them to grow as naturally as possible.

Provide ample drainage, with compost consisting of fibrous loam and peat. They enjoy a fair supply of water during the summer months and rather less in winter. The winter temperature should be from 7 to 13 °C (45 to 55 °F).

PROPAGATION. Effected by cuttings of young shoots in the spring. Insert them in pots of a mixture of equal parts peat and sand and place in a propagating frame to root.

Mandevilla: Only one species, *Mandevilla suaveolens*, is in general cultivation. This is a beautiful deciduous climber, bearing large pure white flowers during the summer months. They are sweetly scented, and produced in great profusion when the plant is in a suitable position. It is ideal for pillars, trellises, and training up the rafters of a cool greenhouse or conservatory, where it receives plenty of light and air, but is obviously on the large side for the ordinary greenhouse.

CULTIVATION. If possible *M. suaveolens* should be planted in a bed or border; it rarely succeeds in pots after a couple of seasons. The compost consists of loam, 3 parts, and 1 part peat or leafmould with a liberal sprinkling of sharp sand.

Use the syringe freely during the spring and summer months, and give ample ventilation in the autumn to ripen the growths thoroughly. Pruning should be carried out during winter. The strong growths must not be cut back, but weakly side shoots can be reduced to within 2 in. of their base. This plant needs plenty of water when growing freely but very little is required during the winter months when it is resting.

PROPAGATION. By cuttings made from side shoots about 3 in. long. Insert in pots of sand and place in a close propagating frame until rooted. Suitable growths are usually available in April or May. Seeds are sometimes available. These should be sown in sandy peat and germinated in a moist temperature of 18°C (65°F).

Maranta: These are warm house subjects grown for their ornamental foliage, and are now very popular as house plants. The leaves are of various shapes, and while the lower sides are greyish, purple, or rose, the upper part is beautifully green and blotched, dotted or streaked with yellow, purple, rose, or brown. Marantas are commonly known as the prayer plants, because the leaves lie flat during the day, but become erect at night.

SPECIES. *Maranta arundinacea variegata*, dark and light green, and greenish-yellow; *bicolor*, dark and light green leaves above, purple below; *leuconeura*, white, green, and purple, and several varieties from this species.

CULTIVATION. The compost must be composed of peat and loam in equal parts, with sand added. Drainage is important and essential to the good development of the foliage. Shade is required.

During spring, summer, and autumn these plants require plenty of water and constant humidity, but this must be reduced considerably during winter, though the plants must still be kept in a warm temperature of not less than 10°C (50°F).

PROPAGATION. By division of the roots in summer.

Masdevallia, see Orchids

Maurandia: A small genus of Mexican trailing or climbing plants.

SPECIES. *Maurandia barclaiana*, violet-purple, rose or white; *M. erubescens*, rose and white; *M. scandens*, violet-purple.

Maurandia barclaiana is the favourite. It is a trailing plant, and is useful as an edging to the stage, also ideal for baskets. The flowers are produced during the summer and autumn months. It will bloom in quite small pots.

CULTIVATION. Pot in light sandy loam and leafmould. Plenty of water is needed during the period of activity but very little in winter. In the spring cut back the growths nearly to their base, and when new shoots appear repot.

PROPAGATION. *M. barclaiana* is raised from seeds and is

usually treated as an annual. Sow in sandy compost about March, and germinate in a temperature of 16°C (60°F).

Cuttings of young shoots will also root freely in the spring if given sandy compost and placed in the propagating frame.

Medinilla: Although rarely seen outside botanical gardens, *Medinilla magnifica* is one of the most beautiful of all hothouse shrubs. The huge, deep pink flower clusters, nearly 12 in. long, appear in May and they are surrounded with large pink bracts.

CULTIVATION. A temperature of 16°C (60°F) in winter, and higher in summer, is needed to grow medinillas well, and during the spring and summer they like a hot and moist atmosphere. Plants usually grow about 3 ft. tall and they are evergreen. After flowering bare stems can be cut back to keep the plants shapely, and as new growth develops repotting can be done, using a compost of moist peat, fibrous loam and coarse sand in equal proportions. Good specimens can be grown in 8-in. pots. Some of the old compost should be shaken from the roots so that new compost can be added when plants are repotted in the same pot size. Once good new roots have been made water should be given liberally for the rest of the summer with weekly feeds of liquid fertiliser. Water plants sparingly in winter.

PROPAGATION. Medinillas can be increased from moderately firm side shoots. It is usual to insert them singly in small pots in a mixture of peat and coarse sand. The pots should be stood in a humid propagating frame, having a temperature of 18–21°C (65–70°F). Once rooted pot the cuttings in 3-in. pots and gradually repot them on into 5- and 8-in. pots as they develop.

Miltonia, see Orchids

Mimosa (Sensitive Plant): *Mimosa pudica* is the botanical name for the curious sensitive plant with light green, feathery leaflets which fold together and hang down together with the midrib when touched. After a short time the foliage returns to its normal horizontal, rigid state. Apart from the unusual foliage the species has small, globular, lavender-coloured flowers. It grows 1 to $1\frac{1}{2}$ ft. tall.

CULTIVATION. Plants are not difficult to grow, but they do best in a warm, sunny greenhouse and, although perennials, it is usual to treat them as annuals by raising fresh plants from seed each spring. This will germinate readily in a propagating frame with a temperature of 16–18°C (60–65°F). After germination place the seedlings separately in small pots and later move them on into 5-in. pots.

Mimulus (Musk): This is a popular and was at one time a very fragrant plant. Although the musk has lost its scent it is well worth growing for its flowers alone.

SPECIES. *Mimulus moschatus* (common musk); the stronger form known as Harrison's Musk is more usually grown. Both bear yellow flowers.

CULTIVATION. Repotting of stock plants is carried out in March. During the growing season the plants need copious supplies of water. In winter, directly the growth dies down, the compost should be kept just moist enough to preserve the roots. If the growths are not numerous enough to make a bushy plant, the shoots can be pinched back when 2 in. high. Weak liquid fertiliser may be given when the pots are filled with roots. A few neat twigs will keep the plants erect.

PROPAGATION. Musk is easily raised from seeds in the green-house, and a close watch should be kept for any sign of the lost scent. Harrison's Musk is increased by cuttings taken in March from stock plants.

Another race of mimulus is the large-flowered, blotched or spotted *M. variegatus*, of which good strains of garden varieties are available, embracing many peculiar and beautiful combinations of colours, chiefly shades of red, crimson, and maroon on a yellow ground. These plants are raised from seeds in the manner already described. The seedlings should be potted on by easy stages until 5- or 6-in. pots are reached, in which they will flower for many months in a cool greenhouse with some shade.

Mitraria: This genus contains one species, *Mitraria coccinea*, the scarlet mitre-pod, a shrubby plant of rather straggling growth. It is evergreen, and bears a quantity of bright scarlet flowers from May till July. Native of Chile.

CULTIVATION. The plant will thrive in a peaty compost with a liberal sprinkling of sand. Repot in March and provide ample drainage. Select a cool, shady part of the greenhouse, and use the syringe freely during the spring and summer months. Plenty of water is necessary during the greater part of the year. In autumn slightly cut back the shoots, and keep the roots moderately dry until February. A temperature of not less than 7°C (45°F) in winter is advisable.

PROPAGATION. Effected by cuttings of young shoots during the spring and summer months. Place them in sandy peat, pot off when rooted, and pinch the shoots a few times to produce a bushy habit.

Monochaetum: Pretty, free-flowering evergreen plants, of easy cultivation and valuable for autumn and winter flowering.

SPECIES. *Monochaetum alpestre*, pink-purple; *M. bonplandii*, purple rose; *M. hartwigianum*, pale rose purple; *M. humboldtianum*, purple. They are mostly natives of Central and South America, being shrubs of 1 to 2 ft. high.

CULTIVATION. Grow the plants at the warmest end of the greenhouse, where the winter temperature does not fall below 10°C (50°F). After flowering keep slightly drier at the roots. In spring the growths are cut back, and when new shoots appear repot in a mixture of 2 parts peat, 1 part loam, and 1 part leafmould. From July till September the plants can be grown in a cold frame. Water freely while growth is active.

PROPAGATION. Cuttings of young shoots root about March if placed in sandy compost. Arrange in a close propagating frame until rooted. Pot off when ready, and pinch off the points of each shoot occasionally until early in August, when stopping should cease. The final potting will take place in July. Keep them near the roof glass, and syringe the foliage daily when the sun is bright.

Monstera: The most popular species is *M. pertusa* (syn. *M. deliciosa borsigiana*) which has large green, perforated leaves. These are very attractive, and the plant is now a very popular house plant. Given hot, moist conditions in a greenhouse, however, growth is rapid, though less so in the average living room.

CULTIVATION. The plant produces aerial roots and it should be trained against supports covered with moss to which the roots can cling. During the summer it is happy in a temperature of 18–21°C (65–70°F), provided a moist atmosphere is maintained by syringing and damping down with water. Plants can be grown in large pots, but they are better planted in a border of good soil where they will produce finer leaves. Plenty of water is needed when plants are growing actively in the summer, but much less should be given

Top left: Paphiopedilum *Claire de Lune Top right:* Monstera pertusa
Bottom left: Pilea cadierei *Bottom right:* Nepenthes

in winter. It dislikes draughts and should be kept reasonably warm in winter, with a temperature of not less than 10°C (50F).

PROPAGATION. Cuttings made from pieces of stem will root readily in the spring and summer if they are placed in sandy compost in a propagating frame with a temperature of at least 21°C (70°F).

Moschosma: A small genus which contains one species suitable for greenhouse embellishment. This is *Moschosma riparium*, a native of South Africa, with nettle-like foliage and pinkish-white flowers. They are borne in spiraea-like panicles during the autumn and winter. Height 2 to 3 ft.

CULTIVATION. This plant succeeds under the same treatment as for *Salvia splendens* and similar plants. After flowering the shoots are cut back, and the plants are placed in a warm and moist house to encourage new growth. The best of these plants may be grown on for another year. Shake out the old compost as much as possible and repot in a compost of loam, 3 parts, and 1 part leafmould with a little sand. Encourage them to grow steadily in the greenhouse, but from July to September a cold frame will provide suitable accommodation.

Keep the roots moist. After the final potting in July, when 8-in. pots will probably be required, liquid fertiliser can be given. The pots should be well filled with roots before feeding begins.

PROPAGATION. Maintain the stock by rooting a batch of cuttings in March. Young shoots will readily form roots in a close propagating frame. Pot off when ready, and if kept on the move nice flowering examples will be available in 6-in. pots. Pinch the tops out of the shoots two or three times to produce bushy specimens. This should, however, cease in July.

Musa (Banana): These are rarely grown for their fruit in this country as much heat and a lofty greenhouse are required. *Musa cavendishii* is grown in the Canary Isles and elsewhere for its fruit, and there are also many forms of *M. paradisiaca sapientum* that are grown abroad for the fruits. Occasionally species such as *M. ensete* and *M. basjoo* are grown in this country for planting outside in the summer for tropical bedding displays, as the large green leaves are attractive. *M. basjoo* will thrive outside permanently in favoured districts if it is protected in the winter. *M. cavendishii* is a dwarf species growing to about 6 ft. high and fruiting fairly regularly.

Cymbidiums are cool-house orchids and, despite their exotic appearance, they are easy to grow

CULTIVATION. Most of the fruiting kinds have no seeds and these are propagated from suckers that appear at the base of old plants. The species that are grown primarily for their ornamental leaves can, however, be increased from seed which should be sown singly in small pots in the spring. A temperature of at least 16°C (60°F) is needed. The young plants can be potted into 5- and 6-in. pots as they develop, and they need to be grown in a hot, moist atmosphere. Before planting outside they must be gradually acclimatised to cooler conditions and hardened off. At the end of the summer old plants are usually discarded and young ones are raised from seed each spring.

Myrtus: A general favourite, and a plant that many would like to include in a collection of cool greenhouse subjects.

SPECIES. *Myrtus communis*, the common myrtle. Several varieties of this strongly scented shrub exist and are all worth growing. The flowers are white, and the type attains to a height of anything up to 10 ft. Native of Southern Europe. The myrtle is not a difficult subject, and large specimens only require fresh compost every third or fourth year. Two parts loam and 1 part peat with sand is an excellent rooting mixture. Shoots can be trimmed into shape in February, and repotting may be carried out at the same time.

From the end of June till September the plants are best outside in a partially shaded situation. Water freely in summer.

PROPAGATION. By cuttings in autumn of side shoots taken with a heel. Insert in sandy compost, keep shaded, and place in a temperature of 16°C (60°F).

Nandina: *Nandina domestica* is the only species, and this makes an elegant evergreen shrub from 2 to 5 ft. high. The size of the leaflets will vary according to the health and vigour of the plant. The flowers are white with yellow anthers. Native of China and Japan. It is very attractive at times when the young foliage assumes almost scarlet tints. A cool greenhouse will suit it.

CULTIVATION. Nandinas grow best in a mixture of equal parts loam, peat and sand.

PROPAGATION. By cuttings of ripened shoots in early autumn. Insert in pure sand, and place in a propagating frame in a cool house.

Nepenthes (Pitcher Plants): These are curious hothouse plants with pitchers, each with a lid, hanging from the ends of the leaves on long stalks. The pitchers are usually mottled with brown, green, red, white and yellow, and in nature their purpose is to attract insects by means of honey glands. Once inside, the insects fall into a liquid at the bottom of the pitcher where they drown, and their decomposing remains help to feed the plant. There are a great many species and hybrids, many of which are rarely seen in cultivation.

CULTIVATION. The pitcher plants are not difficult to grow where temperatures of 21–27°C (70–80°F) and a humid atmosphere can be maintained in the summer; a minimum of 16°C (60°F) is needed in winter. Plants are best grown in teak baskets suspended from the greenhouse roof. A mixture of 2 parts peat fibre and 1 part sphagnum moss, with a little charcoal, is ideal and it must be kept moist all the year round. The plants must be shaded from strong sunshine in the summer. To encourage the development of large pitchers pinch out the tips of the shoots when a few leaves have formed.

PROPAGATION. Cuttings can be made from one-year-old shoots, but they are not inserted into a pot in the normal manner. Each cutting is placed through the drainage hole of a small inverted pot, which is stood on a bed of moist peat in a propagating frame with a temperature of 21–24°C (70–75°F). When good roots have been made the young plants can be potted separately in moist peat and sand and they should be kept in a warm, shady part of the greenhouse.

Nephrolepis, see Ferns

Nerium (Oleander): The oleanders are showy summer-flowering shrubs, with rather thin, willow-like stems. They are somewhat loose growing, but can be kept in order by judicious pruning.

SPECIES. *Nerium oleander* is the common type with rosy flowers. It is native of the Mediterranean region, where it makes a small tree-like shrub, and will attain a height of 6 to 12 ft. There are a number of fine varieties, such as *alba* (white), *splendens* (bright red double), *roseum* (double rose), and others of equal merit. They are largely grown on the Continent, where many fine forms have originated.

CULTIVATION. The plants enjoy full sunshine, and need plenty of water throughout the spring and summer months. After flowering, keep the roots rather dry, and in a few weeks prune all the young shoots back to two eyes near the old wood. Repot in early spring in a fairly rich compost. Place in a warm greenhouse to start growth, when a temperature of 16°C (60°F) will suffice for the summer, and from 7–10°C (45–50°F) in winter. Any plants not repotted should be fed liberally with liquid fertiliser.

The flowers are produced on well-ripened shoots, and it will be necessary to remove any small growths that develop just below the flower buds. Otherwise the blooms will be hidden by foliage, and, moreover, quality will suffer. Use the syringe freely to keep down red spider and mealy bug.

PROPAGATION. Stock is raised by cuttings of matured shoots. They will form roots if placed singly in small pots of sandy compost and given a warm temperature during spring or summer. Quite small plants will furnish a head of blossom. It should be noted that neriums are very poisonous in all parts to humans and warm blooded animals generally.

Nierembergia: Grown as a biennial. *Nierembergia caerulea* makes a grand pot plant which, when covered with its mauvy-blue flowers an inch or more across, somewhat flat or saucer-shaped, gives a most effective display from June to September. These flowers have the added virtue of remaining fresh for a considerable time. As a conservatory subject it is ideal, growing to between 6 and 12 in. tall.

PROPAGATION. Sowing seed in summer or autumn will provide young plants which will develop early in spring into specimens large enough to be potted into 5- or 6-in. pots. Slight support is necessary, but very thin twigs must be used so that they are unobtrusive, and any raffia or twine should be thin and green.

Odontioda, see Orchids

Odontoglossum, see Orchids

Oncidium, see Orchids

Ophiopogon: Known as the Japanese hyacinth on account of the slender spikes of miniature hyacinth-like blue or white flowers. The more permanent beauty of the plants, however, lies in the brightly variegated and graceful foliage. They can be grown in the cool or cold greenhouse as they are quite hardy.

SPECIES. The best one is *Ophiopogon japonicus intermedius* (or *O. spicatus aureo variegatus* of catalogues), with yellow variegated foliage much used in decoration. Another useful plant is *O. jaburan variegatus*, whose leaves are margined with white. Both are native of Japan and grow about a foot high. Annual repotting is not required, but such work must be carried out in the spring when the plants become potbound. If they are too large, the roots can be divided. They will succeed in the John Innes mixtures. Give plenty of water when growing freely, and a moderate supply in autumn and winter. Syringe the foliage daily when the sun is bright. Established plants will appreciate weak liquid fertiliser once or twice each week when the plants are active.

PROPAGATION. By division when repotting.

Oplismenus, see Panicum

Orchids: Orchids are a large and varied group, embracing genera specially adapted to cool and warm house treatment. It will be impossible to deal adequately with this important class of plants in the space at our disposal. I therefore refer readers to the many excellent reference books on this well-researched aspect of greenhouse gardening, publications which will provide beginners and more advanced amateur orchidists with a wealth of valuable information in varying degrees of depth.

To be successful with orchids, houses should be devoted to their exclusive cultivation with a minimum temperature of 7–10°C (45–50°F), and another with a winter temperature of 13–16°C (55–60°F). The day temperature will rise 5°C (10°F) or more according to the weather.

SPECIES. Not many of the natural types find a place in present-day collections of private growers. Improved forms, varieties of British origin and hybrids, are so much finer and more attractive.

A selection for a cool house would include all the odontoglossums, especially the hybrids, of which there is a wonderful series to select from. I have not given a list of names because they are so numerous. One could fill a house with forms of *Odontoglossum crispum* among the species, and *O. eximeum* of the hybrids. Bright reds are not to be found among the odontoglossums, but that lack is supplied by the odontiodas. In general outline they are identical with the odontoglossums except colour. A few good forms are

Odontioda bradshawiae, charlesworthii, Elpheon, Ruby Glow and Trixie.

A few oncidiums may be included in a collection of cool house orchids. *Oncidium concolor, O. macranthum, O. tigrinum,* and *O. varicosum rogersii,* all in shades of yellow, being delightful in their dainty gracefulness. The scarlet dwarf *Sophronitis coccinea* and *Zygopetalum mackaii* are other desirable plants, also the pleiones, while those who like quaint and unusual flowers would grow the masdevallias. Most of the cypripediums and paphiopedilums would thrive in the cool house including the varieties of *Paphiopedilum insigne.* Cymbidiums, too, are cool-house orchids, of which there are many grand hybrids of recent introduction, including Cambria, Castle Hill, Pauwelsii, Rosanna Westonbirt and *insigne sanderae.*

For the warm house we have quite a different type of plant, and such a structure would be mostly filled with cattleyas and their allies. They are characterised by their large showy flowers and strong constitution. There are both species and hybrids among the cattleyas, also brasso-cattleyas, noted for their fringed and gorgeous lips. The laelias and laelio-cattleyas are all desirable.

CULTIVATION. Dendrobiums succeed suspended from the roof. Many of the miltonias would be at home on the staging, both require warm house conditions. The sophronitis hybrids are like miniature cattleyas, but much brighter in colour. There are other genera suitable, but enough has been said to give an idea of the wealth of material to be found among the orchid family.

The flowering period of a mixed collection of orchids is extended over the whole year, consequently the plants will be in different stages of growth at any given time. Therefore no season can be stated for general repotting. No plant should be disturbed unless it needs a larger container, or where the compost has become sour. Any repotting should be carried out when the new growth is about to start and the plants show signs of making fresh roots. If this rule is strictly adhered to, there will be few failures. Use clean pots, and fill them to one-fourth of their depth with drainage. The rooting medium consists of osmunda fibre (3 parts) and clean fresh sphagnum moss (1 part). The former is cut up into pieces about 1 in. long; the dust must be removed. All rubbish is picked out of the sphagnum, and it is then chopped up fairly fine. Good quality fibrous peat is occasionally used instead of the osmunda fibre. For strong rooting subjects such as cymbidiums a little fibrous loam is recommended. Press the compost fairly firm, and trim neatly with a pair of scissors or shears.

Newly potted plants need careful watering, the greatest quantity being required when top growth and roots are active. When at rest a smaller quantity will suffice, but enough must be given to keep the pseudo-bulbs rigid. Careful ventilation is essential to prevent cold currents of air passing over the plants. Shade from strong sunshine and maintain a moist atmosphere. A light spray overhead is beneficial when the weather is hot and dry, but this must not be a deluge, and it should be carried out sufficiently early for the foliage to dry before sunset.

Give due attention to the temperatures, and keep the plants free of insect pests. Thrips are sometimes troublesome, but periodical fumigations will hold them in check.

PROPAGATION. Effected by division at the time of repotting, also by seeds if new varieties are required.

Palms: Few foliage plants can equal the noble appearance of certain species of this highly decorative group. Some of them attain large size, making fine specimens for tall conservatories and halls, while others even in a small state are ideal plants for room decoration.

SPECIES. Suitable for the average greenhouse are: *Chamaerops humilis, Howea belmoreana* and *H. forsteriana, Livistona australis, Phoenix roebelenii,* and *Trachycarpus fortunei.*

CULTIVATION. Palms of small size are frequently starved either of water or compost. When grown for table or room decoration it is necessary to keep them in small pots. This, however, cannot be carried on indefinitely, so if plants are needed for this purpose they must be young. When palms become too large for the greenhouse, they should be discarded and replaced by smaller, younger specimens. When the roots have to be restricted, liquid fertiliser should be given twice each week. The best time for potting up is the early spring, but with young plants such work can be done at any time, provided they have filled their containers with roots. Good drainage is essential. A suitable compost consists of one-third good fibrous loam, one-third peat and one-third good sharp sand. When the plants have become fairly large specimens annual repotting is not needed. In fact, they can remain in the same pots for several years, but it will be advisable to give a topdressing of fresh compost in the spring, and to feed the roots with liquid fertiliser.

Palms need partial shade in spring and summer and plenty of water. Even in winter the compost must never become really dry. Syringe the leaves freely morning and late afternoon when the weather is bright and hot. The winter temperature should be from 7–13°C (45–55°F), and in summer about 18°C(65°F). The foliage will need sponging occasionally to remove accumulations of dust and insect pests. Plants in rooms will need attention in this respect more frequently.

PROPAGATION. The chief method followed is by seeds. High temperature is needed. It is better for the gardener to buy young plants and grow them on. In repotting care must be taken not to over-pot, because a large mass of compost would become sour before the roots could take possession.

Pandanus (Screw Pine): These are tropical or hothouse plants with ornamental foliage. The long strap-like leaves have sharp spines along the edges and they are striped with green and white or yellow. *P. veitchii* is the most commonly grown species.

CULTIVATION. Plants are not difficult to grow, but in a hot, moist atmosphere they soon develop into large bushes, too large for the average size greenhouse. They have a tendency to push themselves almost out of their pots and large specimens form thick buttress roots. However, small plants are very attractive, and when they become too big they can be discarded as it is not difficult to raise new plants. This is done by removing offsets from the base of old plants. They will grow well in a mixture of equal parts loam, moist peat and coarse sand. Plenty of water is needed in the summer, but it should be given sparingly in winter.

Panicum: Although the plant referred to in this note is generally known as *Panicum variegatum*, its correct name is *Oplismenus burmannii variegatus*. It is a pretty free-growing trailing grass from tropical Asia, with green foliage striped with white, and often tinted with pink. When well grown the long trails are useful for decoration, while plants can be grown in pots for draping the margins of the stages. It is also suitable for hanging baskets or growing on a shelf when it will look very attractive.

CULTIVATION. Readily propagated, and may be grown in small pots. The best method is to place three to five cuttings in a 3-in. pot filled with sandy compost. Root them in a close propagating frame. When they are slightly hardened, and the pots are filled with roots, transfer to 5-in. containers without dividing. A suitable compost consists of fibrous loam (3 parts) and leafmould or peat (1 part), with a little sand. During the winter the plants should be kept in a house where the temperature is about 10–13°C (50–55°F).

PROPAGATION. By cuttings only, as described above.

Passiflora: These are vigorous climbers commonly known as the passion flowers. They are of more than average merit, and are suitable for covering rafters, walls, and pillars of large houses where they will bloom throughout the summer months.

SPECIES. The best are *Passiflora caerulea*, blue; Lady Constance Elliot, white; and *racemosa*, purple. *P. belottii* is a large and showy hybrid with delicate rose and flesh-coloured flowers. Another hybrid is *P. allardii*, a very free-flowering form bearing almost pure white flowers with a flush of pink; the filaments of the corona are deep cobalt blue; other good kinds are *P. alato-caerulea,* and *P.* Imperatrice Eugénie.

CULTIVATION. Passifloras are not particular about soil or compost as long as drainage is good. They will succeed in pots or a border if the roots are somewhat restricted. Both repotting and planting can be done in March. A suitable compost consists of fibrous loam (3 parts) and peat (1 part) with a liberal sprinkling of sand. A very rich rooting medium would produce a lot of growth at the expense of flowers.

Overcrowding can be prevented by the removal of weak shoots as they appear, and a few of the best growths will be allowed to hang down from the roof. During the winter months any necessary pruning can be carried out. It consists of cutting out weak and useless growth, reducing others to two eyes, and regulating the main shoots. When the plants break into activity a few of the shoots can be rubbed off if they are likely to cause overcrowding. Supply plenty of water throughout the growing season, and the foliage should be syringed freely during the spring and summer months to keep down red spider. A winter temperature of 7–10°C (45–50°F) will suffice, when the roots are kept just moist. Frequent pinching of the shoots, often practised to keep the plants within bounds, is a great mistake. Few flowers are produced by such treatment.

PROPAGATION. Effected by cuttings of young shoots from 4 to 6 in. in length during the spring months. They should be taken with a heel, although this is not absolutely essential, and inserted in sandy compost. If placed in a close propagating frame, they will soon form roots.

Pelargonium: This is an extensive and important family of plants which should be one of the most prominent groups of plants in the private gardener's greenhouse. They flower throughout the summer, are beautiful and varied in appearance and habit, very easily grown, fragrant, and require only sufficient heat in winter to keep the frost out. They are relatively free from pests and diseases, but usually suffer from the physiological disorders of over-feeding and over-watering. In this respect, it should be remembered that they are natives of South Africa, where they are acclimatised to little water, a lot of heat and light, and generally poor soil.

The genus embraces several groups of quite distinctive character. In each of these groups, except the scented-leaved pelargoniums, it is garden-raised varieties and hybrids that are grown rather than natural species. Some particularly good kinds are – **Regals:** Carisbrooke, pale pink with magenta blotches; Aztec, strawberry pink and white; La Paloma, white with pale mauve blotches; Stardust, pale lavender with purple blotches; Senorita, bright red; Grand Slam, red. **Zonals:** Gustav Emich, vermilion; Maxim Kovaleski, orange; King of Denmark, pink; Eric Lee, magenta. **Fancy-leaved:** L'Elegante, white variegated ivy leaf; Mrs H. Cox, yellow, red, brown and green leaves; Golden Orfe, copper zone; Mrs Parker, white variegated leaves; Mme Butterfly, cream leaves with green markings; Bronze Corinne, yellow leaf with bronze zone; Crocodile, white veins on green background. There are many more to be found in specialist nurserymen's catalogues. For many years pride of place was held by the Regal pelargoniums which produce their brilliant, somewhat trumpet-shaped blooms in colours ranging from the deepest maroon to shades of red, pink, and pure white, from May to July. Many of them are semi-double, with attractive blotches and markings on the petals.

The Zonal pelargonium must now be acknowledged to have outstripped the regals in widespread popularity. This is the class which is so generally spoken of as 'Geranium', and not only are its varieties widely used for summer bedding, but both single and double flowered varieties are popular as pot plants, as they may be had in bloom during the winter as well as in the summer months. The name *Pelargonium zonale* was given as indicative that each rounded leaf has a zone of dark brown copper running horseshoe fashion through the middle part of the leaf. In many varieties of the section, however, the zone is missing. There are sub-sections of the zonal class known as 'silver-leaved', with white margins to the leaves, 'bronzes', with distinctive bronze zones on a yellow ground leaf, and 'tricolors', in which yellow, bright red, and green make up wonderfully effective variegations.

The Ivy-leaved pelargonium is another excellent group. This has shining, thick, brittle leaves, five pointed, resembling the ivy in shape, and grows prostrate, with stems attaining considerable length. In pots the stems may be trained climber-fashion by tying them to supports, or the plants may be suspended in hanging baskets, allowing the growths to hang gracefully down. Most of the varieties bear semi-double or double flowers in well-formed trusses, the colours embracing salmon and rose pink, scarlet, red, purple, and whites of varying degrees of purity.

The Scented-leaved pelargonium embraces a number of species, most of which have beautifully cut or crimped and fimbriated leaves which emit distinctive and pleasing odours. The blossoms are for the most part small, and it is usual to pinch out the buds to throw all energy into the foliage.

The principal species are *P. capitatum* (rose scented), *crispum* (lemon scented), *fragrans* (nutmeg scented), *odoratissimum* (sweet scented), *quercifolium* (oak leaved), the most familiar of the section; and *tomentosum* (peppermint scented).

CULTIVATION OF REGAL PELARGONIUMS. After flowering take the plants outside and reduce the water supply. In a few weeks this will be withheld, and the plants will be thoroughly dried for a fortnight or three weeks. If the weather is wet during this period, lay the pots on their sides. Early in August all the growths are cut back, leaving one or two joints at the base of each. Spray them occasionally to encourage fresh growth. Repot when new shoots are formed. Remove most of the old compost, trim the roots, and place in pots that will just take the roots. A moderate amount of drainage is necessary. The John Innes composts have proved quite satisfactory for these pelargoniums. Small plants may require two more shifts, but older plants will only need one, which is given about January. After the first potting arrange the plants in a cold frame, syringe overhead occasionally, and ventilate freely. Keep free of greenfly by syringing with a good insecticide. Early in October place the plants in a cool greenhouse, from which frost is excluded. Cool treatment produces the best results. With the approach of spring transfer to a position on the greenhouse stage near the roof glass. Plants that are well rooted can be fed with an approved liquid fertiliser until the flowers begin to expand.

PROPAGATION. Effected by cuttings during July or August. Place them in pots filled with sandy compost. They will form roots in a cold frame if the lights are kept close and slightly shaded. Pot off singly when ready. Stop the shoots two or three times, and move on as they fill their pots with roots.

CULTIVATION OF ZONAL PELARGONIUMS. As a rule plants begin to bloom about six months after the cutting is rooted, but the flowering period can be determined by pinching the shoots and the removal of the flower buds until a few weeks before flowers are desired.

Insert a batch of cuttings for winter flowering early in March. They will form roots in a cool greenhouse. When ready, pot singly in 3-in. pots, and grow on in a cold frame. Pinch the shoots occasionally until August to produce bushy plants. Later on they must be given 6-in. pots. Make the compost moderately firm. Remove all blooms until the end of September. During the summer months stand the pots on a bed of ashes in the open. Keep the roots moist, and when the pots are filled with roots they should be fed with liquid fertiliser. Feeding is preferable to having the plants in large pots. In mid-October arrange the plants on the stages of the greenhouse, allow plenty of space, and admit air whenever the elements are favourable. When the nights become cold a little heat will be needed to dispel damp.

For summer flowering, cuttings are rooted in August, and at this season no difficulty is experienced in rooting them. Select ripened shoots, about 3 in. in length. Use a sharp knife, and make a clean cut immediately below a joint, removing the two bottom leaves. They should be laid on the potting bench for a few hours for the cut surface to dry. Insert three cuttings round the edge of a 3-in. pot of John Innes seed compost, make the compost firm, and arrange them on a shelf or greenhouse stage. Shade from strong sunlight, and keep the compost just moist. It is best to leave the cuttings intact until the days begin to lengthen in early spring, when they are potted off singly.

Three-inch pots will be large enough, using John Innes No. 1 potting compost. A warm shelf near the glass will be best for them, but they will need ample ventilation when the weather is mild. Pinch out the centre of each plant, and give water in moderation. Pot on as required, and the plants can be allowed to bloom in 6-in. pots. Feed the plants when well rooted. Keep these plants fairly dry through the following winter, and cut hard back in early spring. Directly growth is active they should be repotted, shaking most of the old compost away from the roots. Such plants will make fine specimens during the summer months.

PROPAGATION. By cuttings of firm, short-jointed growths cut clean just below a joint and inserted in pots of sandy compost, with good drainage. This is clearly explained in previous directions. Stock may also be raised from seeds sown in a mixture of loam and leafmould and placed in a warm greenhouse. Transfer seedlings to small pots and later to larger ones. Grow on a shelf, give plenty of air, and pinch points of shoots to induce bushy habit. It is always rather uncertain what the flowers of seedlings will be like, but inferior ones should be discarded and the best retained for propagation by cuttings.

CULTIVATION OF IVY-LEAVED KINDS. They need similar treatment to the Zonal pelargoniums, except that large plants require stakes, and the growths must be tied in position. Specimens are kept on the dry side in winter, pruned fairly close in the spring, and then given fresh compost. Basket plants are treated the same.

PROPAGATION. As for Zonal pelargoniums.

SCENTED–LEAVED PELARGONIUMS. There is no material difference in the cultivation or propagation of these from the methods advised for the Zonal kinds. As the plants are usually grown for foliage rather than for flower they may be encouraged by the aid of frequent feeding with weak liquid fertilisers. Cuttings may be rooted at almost any time except mid-winter, when growth is at its lowest ebb.

As there are now numerous varieties available in the various sections the best plan is to consult a good nurseryman, and find out what he can supply and which he recommends.

Pentapterygium: There are several species, but *Pentapterygium serpens* is the one that is usually cultivated. All the species are very similar to agapetes (it has been suggested that they should be transferred to this genus) and have drooping stems with beautiful tubular flowers. These are red in *P. serpens* with deep V-shaped markings, and they hang in clusters from the underside of the stems. Each is about $\frac{3}{4}$ in. long.

CULTIVATION. A compost of moist peat with the addition of coarse sand to ensure good drainage suits these plants. They can be grown in pots or in teak baskets. The flowers appear in the winter when water should be given sparingly. In the summer a warm, moist atmosphere is desirable. Feeding during the growing season will help to encourage good growth.

PROPAGATION. Cuttings of firm shoots can be rooted in small pots filled with peat and sand. They should be stood in a warm, moist propagating frame.

Pharbitis, see Ipomoea

Philodendron: A genus of evergreen foliage plants which are best grown in a warm greenhouse, although some of the species succeed reasonably well in a living-room.

SPECIES. *Philodendron scandens* is perhaps the most popular climbing species with attractive dark green, heart-shaped leaves. *P. leichtlinii* has unusual, perforated leaves which can be 12 in. long. A shrubby non-climber is *P. bipinnatifidum* with large, deeply indented leaves.

CULTIVATION. The climbing species are best trained up moss-covered pillars or tree branches. They produce aerial roots which will adhere to the supports. In a warm, moist atmosphere they will grow rapidly. Plants are not difficult to cultivate, and they will succeed in a compost of equal parts loam, peat and coarse sand.

PROPAGATION. Layers root readily or pieces of stem with several joints will soon form roots in a propagating frame with a hot, humid atmosphere.

Phyllitis, see Ferns

Phyllostachys, see Bamboo

Pilea (Artillery Plant): This makes a good green decorative plant for mixing with other subjects. Fern-like in appearance, it remains in good condition for a long time. The flowers are insignificant, but when the hand is brushed over the plant, a mass of pollen is discharged in what looks like white smoke, hence the name of artillery plant.

SPECIES. *Pilea microphylla* is the one already referred to; a more recent introduction is *P. cadierei*, totally different in appearance, with attractive, silvery white patches between the leaf veins and much grown as a foliage house plant.

CULTIVATION. *P. microphylla* is raised from seed sown in spring, the plants soon reach a useful size, and it can then be propagated by cuttings taken in spring and throughout early summer. The plant enjoys a warm, close atmosphere, but one established will grow quite well in any greenhouse throughout the summer. The plant enjoys a warm, close atmosphere, but once estab-propagated from cuttings in spring. It can be kept bushy by pinching back the growing tips. While growing, it requires a lot of water.

Pimelea (Rice Flower): These belong to the hard-wooded section of plants, and are natives of Australia and New Zealand. They usually flower in May, and vary in height from 1 to 2 ft. They are quite attractive, the flower heads being freely produced at the points of the shoots.

SPECIES. Good kinds are *Pimelea ferruginea*, sometimes quoted in catalogues as *P. decussata*, with rosy-red flowers; *P. rosea* (rose); and *P. spectabilis* (white and pink). All are shrubby.

CULTIVATION. After flowering remove old blooms and a little growth where needed to keep the plants in shape. When fresh shoots are starting, repotting should be carried out. Good drainage is essential, and the compost consists of fibrous peat and a sprinkling of silver sand. Firm potting is necessary. Grow in a light, airy house where the winter temperature is from 7–10°C (40–50°F).

Pimeleas require plenty of water and syringing during the summer months, and a moderate supply in winter. Where the young growth has a tendency to become straggly, or if any shoots grow more freely than the majority, they should have their points removed. Red spider mite must be kept down, otherwise the plants will fail.

PROPAGATION. Effected by cuttings made of young shoots about 2 in. in length. Insert them in pots or pans filled with silver sand and a little fine peat, and cover with polythene or a frame. Keep moist and shaded in a temperature of 16°C (60°F). Suitable cuttings are usually available about April.

Platycerium, see Ferns

Pleione, see Orchids

Plumbago (Cape Leadwort): A climbing shrubby plant that is well worth growing for its blue flowers that appear in the summer. It may be grown in a large pot or tub, but where possible it should be planted out in a well-drained bed or border for clothing a back wall, pillars, or rafters. It is usually deciduous, so does not shade other plants during the winter.

SPECIES. *Plumbago capensis* (blue) and *P. alba* (a white form) are native of South Africa.

CULTIVATION. After flowering keep slightly on the dry side. In spring the shoots must be cut back to within 9 in. of their base, unless a few growths are needed for extension. Directly new growth appears the repotting and topdressing should be carried out.

Plumbago will thrive quite well in the John Innes composts. When dealing with pot plants, remove some of the old compost, then a slightly larger container will suffice. A copious supply of water is needed from March to September, and the foliage may be syringed daily when the weather is bright. Well-rooted plants will appreciate liquid fertiliser twice each week. Although this plant needs plenty of light, a little shade from the midday sun will be beneficial.

PROPAGATION. When new shoots are 3 in. long they can be removed with a heel and used as cuttings, generally in late March or April. Insert them singly in small pots filled with sandy soil, and arrange in a close propagating frame. Pinch the shoots occasionally when rooted, and pot on as required.

Cuttings may also be rooted in July.

Polygala: The polygalas are evergreen shrubby plants. Native of South Africa, they are distinct and easily grown.

SPECIES. *Polygala myrtifolia grandiflora* (rich purple) is good. It grows to a height of 4 to 6 ft. and makes a sturdy shrub. *P. oppositifolia* (purple and yellow) is from 2 to 4 ft. high. There is a form known as *P. dalmaisiana* with rich purple pea-shaped flowers. It is probably a hybrid between the two species quoted above. The flowering season is from April till June.

CULTIVATION. After flowering prune shoots to within 4 in. of their base; other straggly growths may also be reduced.

Regal pelargoniums can provide a brilliant show of colour during the summer months and Begonia semperflorens *is a good plant for a hanging basket*

Repotting should be done in the spring, using a compost of equal parts loam, peat and sand. See that the pots are clean and well drained. Do not over-pot. Keep them near the roof glass, and spray the foliage morning and late afternoon when the weather is bright, except when in bloom. A little shade from midday sun will be beneficial. From early July till September keep the plants in a cold frame, and admit air freely.

Keep the roots well supplied with water during the growing period, but from October to February smaller amounts will be sufficient. Maintain a winter temperature of 4–10°C (40–50°F) and remember that polygalas do not require a high temperature at any time.

PROPAGATION. By cuttings of the young shoots about 3 in. long taken in spring. Fill small pots with sandy peat or pure sand, and set one cutting in each pot. Place in a propagating frame at a temperature of 16°C (60°F). Keep them just moist, and shade lightly until rooted.

Polystichum, see Ferns

Primula: The various forms of primula are invaluable for the greenhouse during the winter and early spring months. They are well adapted for small houses from which the frost is excluded. *Primula auricula* is also a very attractive little plant requiring slightly different treatment to the general run of primulas, so is treated separately.

SPECIES. *Primula malacoides*, *P. obconica*, *P. sinensis* (all of Chinese origin), and *P. kewensis* (a hybrid). British-raised varieties of each species are finer in flower and embrace a wider range of delightful colours than the original types.

A popular and free-flowering primula is the Star or *stellata* group. They are very graceful, and produce their moderately sized flowers in tiers for several months. The colours range through pink, white, lavender, blue and ruby.

The Giant *sinensis* varieties with their large, perfect flowers and attractive foliage, are also worthy of consideration. Both these and the smaller flowered varieties of the species can be obtained in a variety of colours, such as blue, crimson, rose, scarlet, white and pink.

Since the introduction of the dainty *P. malacoides*, considerable improvement has been made in both size and colour of flowers.

Top left: Thunbergia alata *Top right:* Strelitzia reginae
Bottom: Zantedeschia aethiopica

There are now several distinct varieties which come true from seeds. The original form has pale lilac flowers, but now it can be had in white, rose and pink shades. There are also deep purple, red and salmon varieties and several good doubles.

Great improvement has also been made in *P. obconica*. The flowers are larger and more varied than formerly and, moreover, the flowering season has been extended. The pink, blue, and mauve shades are very pleasing.

Quite distinct in colour and foliage is the beautiful yellow *P. kewensis*. It is a colour that is absent among the other groups quoted, and for this reason a batch should be grown. It is very floriferous, and remains in full beauty for several weeks.

The double-flowered primulas are not so easily grown, and are best left alone by the gardener until he has gained experience with the other members of the genus. They can be raised from seeds, but the usual method is by cuttings and division.

The plants, however, have one drawback. The leaves and stems of one species or another, when touched by some people are injurious to the skin, producing a sore and irritating rash of greater or lesser severity, although some gardeners are immune. This difficulty can be overcome if the grower wears a pair of gloves when potting plants or handling them in any way.

CULTIVATION. There is no need to differentiate between these groups regarding general cultivation; they all require much the same treatment. Primulas enjoy cool and somewhat moist surroundings, once the seedlings are potted off. To keep up a good display, two sowings of the *stellata, sinensis*, and *malacoides* varieties should be made, one early in April and another towards the end of May. *P. malacoides* may even be sown some weeks later with excellent results. As a rule one sowing of *P. obconica* and *P. kewensis* will be sufficient for most gardeners. About the end of March or early April is the best time to sow.

Use well-drained 4-in. pots carefully filled with John Innes seed compost, and water them a few hours before sowing by immersing each one in clean water up to its rim until the surface begins to stain with moisture. Sow thinly and evenly, and cover very lightly with finely sifted soil. Place the pans in a warm propagating frame for the seeds to germinate, covering each one with a small sheet of glass and keep shaded from the sun.

When the seedlings appear, slightly tilt the glass for a few days, and finally remove it. Until the young plants are large enough for potting or pricking off they should remain in the propagating frame. After pricking off or potting in thumb pots keep in a warm greenhouse for a fortnight or three weeks, and then gradually harden to a cold frame. When nicely established, pot into 3-in. pots, and stand them on a bed of ashes in a cold frame. Admit air whenever the weather is mild both day and night, and keep just moist.

At this stage many growers make a mistake by allowing the plants to become starved in the small pots. They should be comfortably filled with roots and then placed in 5-in. pots. With the exception of strong examples of *P. obconica*, which need 6- or 7-in. pots, all the primulas can be flowered in pots 5 in. in diameter. Provide a little drainage. The John Innes mixtures have proved quite satisfactory for growing all the primulas. They also grow quite well in the loamless mixtures. Hard potting is not advised, but the compost should be made quite firm with the fingers.

Whenever any repotting is done, the leaves should be brought down to the compost. No harm will accrue from covering the stem; in fact, it will form roots when buried in the compost. If this is carried out there will be no necessity for staking the plants when in bloom.

A cold frame is the best accommodation until September or October if the weather is favourable. Allow plenty of space and ample ventilation. Shade from strong sunlight, especially in the summer, and avoid over-watering. Keep a close watch for greenfly, and remove any premature flower spikes that may appear. With the approach of cold nights remove to a cool, airy greenhouse where the temperature fluctuates between 7 and 10°C (45 and 50°F). When the pots are filled with roots, weak liquid fertiliser can be given until the flowers begin to open.

PROPAGATION. With the exception of the double kinds, all the primulas should be raised from seeds, no good purpose being served by retaining old plants, however healthy they may appear. Double primulas can also be raised from seeds, cuttings and division. When the plants cease flowering, three or four weeks' rest is allowed. When growths appear they can be removed and treated as cuttings. Place them singly in thumb pots filled with very sandy compost, and arrange in a warm, shaded house or frame. Pot on when rooted, and gradually inure to a cold frame. Give the same treatment as advised for *P. sinensis*.

Primula auricula (Auricula): It may appear strangely out of place today, to include auriculas among the range of plants which are to be considered legitimate subjects for the greenhouse. Present-day custom is to grow a bed of alpine auriculas in mixed colours, treating them as we treat beds or drifts of the polyanthus. It is with recollection of the days when the show or stage auricula was the highly prized favourite that they are mentioned here.

A small collection of these delightful plants is ideal for the unheated greenhouse. They can be brought into the greenhouse while in flower and kept in frames for the rest of the year.

The race is divided into sub-sections, known as white-edged, grey-edged, green-edged, and selfs. Under the heading of Fancies will be found some very showy varieties which do not conform to any of the other groups. All of these are coated with white farina.

CULTIVATION. Auriculas need cool conditions. They are best grown in a cold frame facing north, except during their flowering period, when they may be placed in a greenhouse without heat except to keep out frosts. Shade from bright sunshine is necessary to preserve the flowers from withering prematurely.

A medium pleasant atmosphere, neither too dry nor damp, is best for developing the flowers. The truss may need a neat stick, and some fresh green moss on the soil in the pots will conserve moisture and improve the appearance.

The usual time for repotting is immediately after flowering. Turn the plants out of their pots, remove some of the old compost, cut off a piece of the old stem to living roots. Remove any offsets. Place the old plants in well-drained pots that will just comfortably take the roots. A convenient size will be $3\frac{1}{2}$ or 4 in. diameter.

Auriculas will grow successfully in the John Innes No. 1 potting compost, but the classic formula is 4 parts loam, 1 part rotted cow manure, and 1 part leafmould or peat, with a sprinkling of coarse sand or crushed oyster shell. After potting arrange in a cold frame, and shade from full sun for a few days.

Aftercare consists of free ventilation, the prompt removal of decaying leaves, and watering when dry until October. During autumn and winter give only sufficient water to prevent the foliage from drooping. Watch for greenfly and fumigate when necessary.

At the end of February signs of renewed activity will be evident, and more water will be required. Pick out 1 in. of topsoil, and replace with fresh compost. This will improve the flower spikes.

PROPAGATION OF NAMED VARIETIES. Effected by side growths taken off at the time of repotting, or in July if any are available. If possible they should have a few roots attached. Place singly in small pots, and treat similarly to old plants as described in the cultivation notes above.

Pteris, see Ferns

Rehmannia: Although the rehmannias are termed half-hardy herbaceous perennials, they are excellent subjects for the greenhouse. They produce fairly large, drooping incarvillea-like flowers throughout the spring and summer months. The plants succeed best under cool treatment.

SPECIES. *Rehmannia angulata*, a native of China and Japan. The type has purplish flowers, somewhat variable in form, but garden selections of brighter colour are now available.

The most popular is *R*. Pink Perfection, a variety of *R. angulata*. The stems are from 4 to 5 ft. high, furnished with large, drooping pink flowers. *R. kewensis* is of hybrid origin with large, yellowish flowers blotched with crimson on the upper segments. It is a fine companion to Pink Perfection. Other interesting rehmannias are *R. briscoei* and *R. henryi*.

CULTIVATION. No difficulty is involved in growing fine plants of rehmannia if they are given a good compost such as John Innes No. 2 potting mixture in their final pots. They need ample supplies of water during their period of growth, and liquid fertiliser when the pots are filled with roots.

Keep slightly on the dry side in winter.

When new shoots appear – usually about March – break up the old plants, remove the strong, basal growths, and place them in 4-in. pots. Rehmannias will bloom in 6- and 7-in. containers. Until the flower spikes appear keep the plants in a cold frame.

PROPAGATION. Many growers discard old plants and raise a batch annually from seeds. These are sown during February or March in pots of light, sandy compost and germinated in a warm frame or greenhouse. Pot off singly when large enough, and keep the plants growing steadily in a cool frame.

Rhodanthe, see Helipterum

Rhodochiton: This genus contains one greenhouse species, an elegant climber from 10 to 15 ft. high. *Rhodochiton atrosanguineum* (syn. *R. volubile*) is a native of Mexico. It has reddish-purple flowers, produced during the summer months. Recommended only for large greenhouses.

The plants can be grown in pots, tubs, or planted out in a bed or border. Thin and cut back the shoots in February. Tie the main growths to the wire supports, and then allow the slender side shoots to hang down. This will achieve a graceful effect. For further cultural details, see maurandia and similar plants.

Rhododendron (Azalea, see p. 98): At one time greenhouse rhododendrons were very popular, especially the hybrids which were in bloom the greater part of the year. They are not easily grown, and unless their cultural requirements are fully understood and strictly carried out very poor sickly specimens will result. One cause of failure is a very low temperature in winter.

SPECIES AND HYBRIDS. A few species are very fine, but plants of hybrid origin have more pleasing colours and the flowers are often of large size.

The javanico-jasminiflorum hybrids need a minimum winter temperature of 10°C (50°F); it is better if it is kept nearer 16°C (60°F). They also enjoy a somewhat moist temperature at all seasons. A few hybrids of merit are: Aphrodite, Brilliant, Indian Yellow, Ne Plus Ultra, Princess Royal, and Triumphans. The Himalayan rhododendrons require cooler treatment, and the winter temperature should range from 4–7°C (40–45°F). They are a very showy section and embrace such beautiful plants as *fragrantissimum*, Countess of Haddington, Lady Alice Fitzwilliam, *dalhousiae*, *thomsonii* and *veitchianum*. Another small group are known as the *balsaminaeflorum* hybrids. They include *album*, *aureum*, *carneum*, and *roseum*.

CULTIVATION. Some of the above grow into large specimens, an example is *fragrantissimum*. Good drainage is essential, and the best rooting medium is a turfy peat chopped up with a spade, and a liberal quantity of silver sand. They will succeed in rather small pots and repotting should only be carried out when really necessary. This can be done immediately after flowering. Avoid over-potting and make the compost firm. Water must at all times be given with discretion, and especially immediately after repotting and whenever a plant exhibits signs of ill-health. On the other hand, dryness at the root is equally fatal. Rain water ought always to be used, as water containing lime will harm the plant and can produce yellowing (or chlorosis) of the leaves.

Remove all seed pods after flowering, and keep the house rather close while growth is being made. Rhododendrons need ample ventilation during the summer months, and particularly after they have made their growth. Little or no pruning is necessary, and those hybrids that grow somewhat straggly can have their shoots neatly trained round two or three stakes rather than cut back. Avoid overcrowding; an occasional syringing between the pots will be beneficial.

PROPAGATION. By grafting on to vigorous seedlings. This requires considerable skill, so amateurs are advised to purchase their plants from a nurseryman. Most of the rhododendrons can, however, be increased by cuttings, using medium-sized, half-ripened shoots in March or early April. Insert in pots filled with sandy peat and plunge the pots in a close propagating frame, preferably where there is a little bottom heat. Some plants, such as *veitchianum* and others, set seeds freely and these provide a ready method of propagation. Sow in pans of peaty soil and raise the seedlings in a warm house.

Rivina (Blood Berry): This is a small decorative greenhouse shrub, easily grown and making a splendid decorative subject when its flowers are followed by red berries about the size of a red currant. The brilliance of the berries when the plant is well grown is most attractive. As these plants are at their best in autumn, when most things are passing out of bloom, they add colour and variety to the display.

SPECIES. Only one appears to be grown, that being *Rivina humili*, 2 ft. tall with inconspicuous whitish flowers from January to autumn.

CULTIVATION. Seed is sown in March in a temperature of 16°C (60°F) and the seedlings pricked off at the earliest possible moment, so as not to become drawn. Pot on into loamy compost and grow in a cool house or frame all the summer. Keep well syringed to prevent red spider mite spoiling the foliage. Feed frequently when in full growth, and, above all, never let the plants become dry.

PROPAGATION. By seed or cuttings, sown or taken in spring.

Rochea, see Crassula

Rosa: The forcing or cultivation of roses under glass can safely be attempted by the gardener. Excellent blossoms can be obtained during the early spring months if the greenhouse is light and well heated. It all depends whether he thinks it is worth the time and greenhouse space that will have to be devoted to them.

VARIETIES. There are many varieties for forcing, particularly among the hybrid teas. The gardener will be well advised to buy the bushes for this purpose from a good nurseryman and seek his advice as to what will be suitable.

CULTIVATION. Roses may be grown in pots varying in size according to vigour and the varieties chosen. Hybrid teas succeed in 6-, 7-, or 8-in. pots, but ramblers generally require larger containers. Plants can be lifted and potted from the open ground, or purchased already established in pots. The best time to obtain the latter is early September. If the pots are full of roots, the plants may immediately be moved into larger ones.

A suitable rooting medium consists of good turfy loam of medium texture (3 parts) and well-rotted manure (1 part), with a little sharp sand. A 6-in. potful of bonemeal to each medium-sized barrowload of compost should be added. Mix the whole thoroughly a few days before it is required. Or John Innes No. 3 can be used. Provide free drainage, and make the compost firm, but not too hard, otherwise the growth will be stunted.

Pot roses should be overhauled annually in September or early October. Repot those that need it, and topdress others. In all cases see that the drainage is clear. Well-established specimens will be the first to be placed under glass. Ordinary plants should be bought as early in the lifting season as possible and potted up immediately after their arrival. It must, however, be borne in mind that these cannot be forced the first season, but must be allowed to flower naturally.

It will pay to take a little trouble in preparing the site for climbing roses. The chief essential is drainage, and to make sure this is perfect the soil should be dug out about 3 ft. deep. If needed, place 4 in. of broken bricks in the bottom, over which is arranged a layer of rough turfy loam to ensure a free outlet for water. Fill in with loam and a little rotted manure. A light sprinkling of bonemeal may be mixed with the soil. A border 2 ft. wide and 4 or 5 ft. long is usually sufficient for one plant. Make the soil firm, and water in.

PRUNING. Plants lifted and potted in the autumn will need hard pruning, cutting back the growths to the second dormant basal bud. Thin, spindly shoots should be cut out entirely. This will be done in January. These remarks apply to hybrid teas and floribundas. Climbers recently put in pots will be pruned to within 6 in. of their base.

Climbers planted out must be pruned during the dormant period. It consists of thinning out the weakest shoots to prevent overcrowding, and reducing other growths to 4 or 6 in. All shoots on the dwarf polyanthas are cut back to within two or three buds of their base.

Roses, after being repotted, should be plunged in ashes outside until the end of November, when the first batch can be arranged in a cool greenhouse. Select the best plants – those with fairly strong wood and plenty of roots. A temperature of 10°C (50°F) by day and 7°C (45°F) at night will be ample for the first few weeks. When growth is evident, this can be raised to 16 or 18°C (60 or 65°F), giving an inch or so of top ventilation when wind and weather are favourable. Lightly spray the plants daily when the temperature is on the upward grade. Weak liquid fertiliser can be given when growth is free. Watering will need careful attention, and the water should be tepid, or at the same temperature as the house. Avoid over-watering, also dryness at the roots.

Cold currents of air will produce mildew, which must be checked by spraying with dinocap or sulphur. Greenfly must also be destroyed. Any weakly growths that form can be rubbed off, and when the flower buds are visible on the hybrid teas disbudding should be carried out.

After flowering a cooler temperature will suffice, and the plants are gradually hardened so that they can be stood in the open in May. Plunge the pots in ashes, keep the roots well supplied with water, and syringe each afternoon when the weather is bright. Here they will remain until September or October, when the annual repotting takes place.

Climbers planted out under glass will need daily syringing to keep them free of insects. After August admit plenty of air to ripen the wood.

PROPAGATION. Roses for pot cultivation may be budded in the

ordinary way in the open ground, and lifted for potting during the autumn following their first flowering season. This is the simplest method for the private grower to adopt. They may, however, be budded in pots. Briar stocks for this purpose are potted in autumn and plunged in the open ground until the following summer, when they are budded at the base of the stem. The tops should be cut off in January and the pots at once removed to a cool house to start the buds into growth. Heat may be gradually increased as growth advances. Trade growers propagate also by grafting, but that is a procedure demanding expert skill and a properly constructed propagator. Roses struck from cuttings of ripened wood may be grown on for pot work.

Saintpaulia (African Violet): *Saintpaulia ionantha* is the only species known, and it is a native of East Africa. It is a charming dwarf plant with rather fleshy leaves and intensely violet flowers. The golden anthers are an additional charm. The whole plant is only about 3 in. high, and the flowers are freely produced from August till March, in several flushes. It is known as the African violet, and needs the conditions of a warm house until flowering begins, coming, as it does, from tropical regions near the coast. There are now also a large number of named varieties in a range of flower colours and forms.

CULTIVATION. When the plants are about to flower, a temperature of 10°C (50°F) will be warm enough. Careful watering is necessary; if given in excess, the roots soon decay. If the plants are kept growing steadily they will bloom in six or seven months from the time of germination, and in a warm, growing atmosphere they soon become established. The new loamless composts appear to suit them better than those of the John Innes type, and they make excellent root growth very quickly in the former without rotting off. A humid atmosphere is most important, as they appear to absorb almost more moisture through the thick leaves than they do through the roots. After flowering has finished, less water should be given, and the plants should be encouraged to rest for a few weeks. When starting into growth again, they can be divided, making sure that there are some roots on each piece. A good light is required for flowering, but really strong sunlight will bleach the leaves and flowers.

PROPAGATION. *S. ionantha* is raised from seeds. The seeds are very minute, and should be given the same treatment as seeds of begonias. They will germinate in a temperature of 16–18°C (60–65°F). When the seedlings are large enough, transplant them an inch apart in 3-in. pots. Keep them near the roof glass and shade from strong sunlight. In a few weeks they can be potted off singly in 3-in. pots or three at equal distances apart in a 6-in. pot. Provide good drainage. The compost consists of fibrous loam (1 part) and 3 parts in equal proportions of leafmould and peat, with a sprinkling of sand, or the loamless composts previously mentioned.

Leaves can also be used for propagation. A leaf with its stem is removed and inserted upright in a mixture of equal parts peat and sand, rather shallowly, in spring, in warmth. Rooting takes about three weeks, and flowering of rooted leaves is 10 to 12 months later.

Salvia: For autumn and early winter flowering the salvias are almost indispensable, especially the scarlet varieties. They are ideal for small houses, and are easily grown. They vary in height from 1 to $2\frac{1}{2}$ ft.

SPECIES. The best is *Salvia splendens*, native of Brazil. It bears fine spikes of bright scarlet flowers. Others are *S. azurea grandiflora* (blue), *S. involucrata bethelii* (pink), *S. patens* (bright blue), and *S. rutilans* (scarlet). A useful shrubby species is *S. grahamii*, which produces its scarlet flowers in summer and autumn.

CULTIVATION. When young plants are potted off grow on in a cool greenhouse, and in June transfer the plants to a cold frame. After a week or two admit air freely. Keep the roots moist, and syringe overhead before sundown. A further pinching will be needed, and premature flowers should be picked off.

Pot on as required until the plants occupy containers from 6 to 8 in. in diameter. John Innes No. 2 is a suitable potting compost. After the final potting, liquid fertiliser can be given to well-rooted examples once or twice each week. At the end of September remove to the greenhouse, where the right temperature will be from 10–13°C (50–55°F). Here they will bloom.

If whitefly is troublesome the plants should be sprayed or dipped in a solution of malathion.

PROPAGATION. Most salvias are increased by cuttings during spring months, but several varieties of *S. splendens* are readily raised from seeds. After flowering a few of the best plants should be retained for stock purposes. They will pass safely through the winter in a temperature of about 10°C (50°F) if given just enough water to keep them healthy. About February or March introduce them to a warm house, and syringe daily with tepid water. Directly the new shoots are about 3 in. in length they can be removed and used as cuttings. Insert them in pots filled with sandy compost, and place in a propagating frame until rooted.

Seeds are sown in March in pots or pans of light compost, and germinated in a temperature of 16–18°C (60–65°F). When the seedlings are large enough, and the cuttings have formed roots, they should be potted off singly in 3-in. pots. Pinch out the points of the shoots directly the roots are established.

Sansevieria: Although popular as room plants the sansevierias grow best in a warm greenhouse. *Sansevieria trifasciata* has long, narrow leaves, pointed at the ends, and with light and dark green mottling. *S. t. laurentii* has two yellow bands running the length of the leaves and it is the most popular form.

CULTIVATION. Light, sandy compost is needed with good drainage. Regular repotting is not required, and before this is done the pot should be full of roots. Water very sparingly in winter, but when in growth keep the compost comfortably moist. Sansevierias like a light position, but a little shading from very strong sunshine is advisable. They dislike cold very much, and die quickly at the base if subjected to it, hence the winter temperature should not fall below 10°C (50°F).

PROPAGATION. The simplest method is to detach rooted offsets or suckers from the base of the plants. Leaf cuttings will also root in a heated propagating case, but as *S. t. laurentii* will lose its yellow banding if raised from leaf cuttings, it is best propagated from offsets.

Saxifraga: Only one member of this genus is described here, *Saxifraga stolonifera*, variously known as Aaron's Beard, Roving Sailor, Mother of Thousands, and Wandering Jew. It is a pretty little plant, with long trailing, slender shoots studded here and there with tiny plantlets, which make it very effective. A useful subject for hanging baskets and front of stages in the cool greenhouse. Native of China and Japan.

The variety *tricolor* is more compact, with beautifully marked foliage. The green leaves are blotched with creamy white and crimson. It is not quite so easily grown as the type.

CULTIVATION. They are useful plants for small hanging baskets, and can also be grown in small, well-drained pots in John Innes No. 1 potting compost. Repot in March or April. The pots can be suspended from the roof by attaching a wire around the pot. Cultivation in baskets is the same as for achimenes, selaginellas, and other basket plants.

Careful watering is essential, and during the winter months keep the soil just moist, only giving water when absolutely necessary. The variety *tricolor* needs a few degrees more warmth in the winter than the type.

PROPAGATION. There is no difficulty in increasing stock of *S. stolonifera*. Remove the plantlets from the creeping stems or runners in spring or summer, and place them singly in small pots. Keep shaded, and the surroundings moist until they are established.

Scirpus: Only one species calls for notice, *Scirpus cernuus*. This is an Indian plant with grass-like, hanging foliage, suitable as an edging to the stage or in suspended baskets. It is also known by the common name Job's tears, and grows to a height of between 6 and 12 in.

CULTIVATION. Repotting should be done in March, using fibrous loam, peat, and leafmould in equal parts. It needs a copious supply of water at all times. The warm greenhouse is best for this plant, and during the winter months the temperature ought not to fall below 10°C (50°F).

PROPAGATION. By division at the time of repotting and from seeds. These are sown in the spring in pans of light, sandy compost and germinated in a temperature of 16–18°C (60–65°F). Pot off singly when large enough. This plant does not require large pots; good specimens can be obtained in 4-in. containers.

Selaginella: A large and varied genus containing several species which enjoy the conditions of a cool greenhouse. Owing to their preference for shade they will succeed if given similar treatment to ferns. A few species are erect and fern-like in habit, and are suitable for pot cultivation. Others are dwarf and dense, excellent for shallow pans, while those of a drooping character are ideal for baskets, rockwork, or trailing over the front of the stages, and some will even thrive beneath the stages, an example being *Selaginella kraussiana*.

SPECIES. Among those usually chosen for a greenhouse are *S. caulescens amoena*, a foot high and a pleasing shade of green, and *S. martensii*, 6 to 12 in. This is a fairly common plant, with many varieties, a variegated one of which is named *robusta*. *S. involvens*, 2 to 6 in., and *S. denticulata*, 6 in., are also grown. A dwarf creeping species is *S. apus* (or *S. densa* of catalogues), from 1 to 4 in. high. A fine trailing species is *S. uncinata*; it is largely grown for its long and graceful stems of a bluish tint, changing to bronze and gold when fully grown. Another desirable plant is *S. kraussiana*, with trailing stems. Its varieties *aurea*, with yellow leaves, and *variegata* ought also to be included.

CULTIVATION. Selaginellas thrive in light compost such as peat, leafmould, and loam in equal parts. Silver sand and fine charcoal will help to keep the compost open. Good drainage must be provided and the roots kept moist at all times. Shade from strong sunlight is also essential. March is a suitable time to overhaul the plants for repotting. A winter temperature of 7–10°C (45–50°F) will suffice. Large pots or pans are not necessary.

PROPAGATION. All species are readily increased by cuttings at any time except winter. Insert the upright growing kinds in pots of sandy compost and place in a little light extra warmth. When rooted transfer them to pots or pans, not singly, but several should be arranged in the containers to form a specimen. The dwarf kinds are placed in small pans, half an inch apart. Pot on without dividing the cuttings. Old plants can be pulled to pieces and repotted when needed.

Sinningia, see Gloxinia

Smilax, see Asparagus

Smithiantha: This plant used to be known as *Gesneria* and *Naegelia*, but only one species commonly available is still known as gesneria, and that is *G. cardinalis*, which has beautiful cardinal red flowers in a terminal cluster on a stem 12 to 15 in. tall. It flowers in autumn. Apart from the tubular flowers on handsome spikes 1–2 ft. tall, the heart-shaped leaves of smithiantha are extremely attractive, being velvety and sometimes patterned in other colours than green. It is not surprising that they have been tremendously popular for over a century; they are commonly known as temple bells. They require stove greenhouse cultivation.

SPECIES. Commonly cultivated species are *Smithiantha cinnabarina*, orange-red in summer and purplish-red leaves; *S. multiflora*, creamy white, summer; *S. zebrina*, red and yellow, purple variegated leaves. All are 2 ft. or more tall. There are a great many named hybrids and selected forms such as Abbey, peach and white; Carmell, white, spotted red; Dairy Maid, yellow and salmon; Pink Domino, rose pink and white; Primrose Dame, olive-green leaves; Shirley Carmine; Vespers, orange and pale orange-red. Others will be found in nursery catalogues.

CULTIVATION. Plants are grown in a similar manner to achimenes from scaly rhizomes, but they prefer a temperature of 16–30°C (60–85°F) when growing. Minimum winter temperature should be in the region of 13–18°C (55–65°F). Two or three tubers can be placed in a 6-in. pot in the spring and they should be covered with about an inch of compost. When they are in full growth they must have plenty of water with frequent feeds of liquid fertiliser. A warm, moist atmosphere is needed, but the hairy foliage must not be sprayed with water otherwise it will be marked badly. When the flowers have faded and the foliage begins to wither water should be withheld gradually and the compost must be kept dry in the winter. For autumn flowering the rhizomes should be potted in May, and for winter flowering, in June.

PROPAGATION. The rhizomes should increase naturally, but new plants can be raised from cuttings of the young shoots. These need to be rooted in a mixture of moist peat and sand in a propagating frame with a temperature of 18–21°C (65–70°F). Species and selected forms can also be raised from seed sown in shallow pans of John Innes seed compost in April and germinated at 18°C (65°F).

Solanum: A valuable and varied genus, which contains both climbing and dwarf berry-bearing species suitable for the greenhouse. The latter are cultivated for their brightly coloured fruits in winter, while the climbers are highly decorative when in flower. The two sections are quite distinct, and their cultural requirements also differ.

SPECIES. *Solanum capsicastrum* (winter cherry), native of Brazil, 1 to 2 ft. high. *S. pseudocapsicum weatherillii*, with oval berries. *S. jasminoides*, a trailing or climbing species with trusses of white flowers; a variety of this species named *floribundum* has large and more effective trusses. *S. wendlandii*, a climber with trusses of effective lilac-blue flowers, native of Costa Rica.

CULTIVATION. The climbers include *S. jasminoides*, bearing clusters of white flowers with a slight blue tint. It is an excellent subject for a pillar or wall, and should, whenever possible, be planted out. *S. wendlandii* is also a fine species with large clusters of lilac-blue flowers. It is a vigorous climber and a good plant for pot cultivation. When grown as a climber it should be planted out in fairly rich soil. If cuttings of young shoots are rooted in sand early in the spring they will produce a fine head of bloom in the autumn. A close propagating frame is needed, and directly roots are formed the plants should be potted off singly in $2\frac{1}{2}$-in. pots. Grow in an ordinary greenhouse where the minimum temperature is about 10°C (50°F), and when ready place in $4\frac{1}{2}$-in. pots. Both species require a fibrous loam with a sprinkling of leafmould added. Firm potting is advised. During the winter months remove any decayed shoots and other old growths to prevent overcrowding. Retain just enough new wood to cover the allotted space.

The red-berried plant so popular at Christmas time and called winter cherry is *S. capsicastrum*. Seeds should be sown in pans of light compost and placed in a temperature of 18°C (65°F) about the end of February or early March. Directly the seedlings are large enough transfer them to single pots filled with good compost. Pinch out the centre of each plant when it is a few inches high to induce bushy growth. Pot on before the plants become starved. After the first potting gradually harden to the temperature of a cool greenhouse, and at the end of May transfer to a rich plot of ground in the open, where they may remain till the autumn. Plant them 15 in. apart, and give plenty of water in dry weather. The growth will need pinching twice; at the beginning of June, and early in July. Lift the plants during September, with a liberal ball of soil, and place in pots that will just take the roots. Make the soil firm, water in well, and shade from sunlight. Neatly stake out the growths to produce a well-balanced specimen. When the roots have recovered, arrange the plants in a greenhouse where the temperature is from 7–13°C (45–55°F). These solanums may also be propagated by cuttings in March. An old plant or two should be set in a warm house and syringed daily. When the new shoots are 2 or 3 in. in length, they can be removed, inserted in pots of sandy compost, and placed in a temperature of 18°C (65°F). When rooted

Top: Clivia miniata
Bottom left: Cyclamen persicum *Bottom right:* Crinum powellii album

pot off singly, and give the same treatment as seedlings. There is also a variegated form, *S. c. variegatum*, which although it does not produce its red berries quite as freely, has interesting yellow and green leaves.

Sollya: A small genus of evergreen twining plants, suitable for covering trellises at the end or back wall of a cool greenhouse. They are native of Australia. They flower freely during the spring and summer months.

SPECIES. The best known is *Sollya fusiformis* (Australian bluebell creeper) which attains a height of 6 or 8 ft. *S. parviflora* (*S. drummondii* of catalogues) is about the same height, and bears small deep blue flowers. Both make good pot plants with their growths trained around wire supports formed in the shape of a balloon.

CULTIVATION. Repot in March and use a compost of peat (2 parts) and loam (1 part) with a liberal sprinkling of sand. They are sun-loving subjects, and should be syringed freely each day during their period of activity.

PROPAGATION. Effected by cuttings of young shoots removed with a heel in spring. Insert in sandy peat, or sand, and root in a frame or under polythene.

Sophronitis, see Orchids

Sparmannia: This genus contains one plant for the greenhouse. *Sparmannia africana* is an evergreen shrub from South Africa, and in bloom the greater part of the year. The flowers are white. Height anything up to 10 ft. but plants 3 to 4 ft. high flower well. There is a variety *flore-pleno* with double flowers. Cool greenhouse temperatures suit it well.

CULTIVATION. In February plants need hard pruning. When new growth appears repotting should be carried out. The compost consists of fibrous loam (3 parts) and leafmould or rotted manure (1 part). Keep the roots well supplied with water, and apply liquid fertiliser when the pots are filled with roots. In July the plants can be stood outside, and remain there till September.

PROPAGATION. This plant is increased by cuttings in sandy compost. Place in a close propagating frame with a temperature of 18°C (65°F) till rooted.

A fine collection of foliage plants which shows a varied and striking range together with varieties of impatiens

Spiraea, see Astilbe

Statice, see Limonium

Stenotaphrum: This small genus is sometimes referred to as *Stephanophorum*, and the species as *glabrum* instead of *secundatum*. It is a pretty and graceful variegated grass suitable for baskets or pots.

The species in cultivation is *Stenotaphrum secundatum variegatum*; it will be found in catalogues as *Stephanophorum glabrum variegatum*. Height 1 ft.

CULTIVATION. Its cultural requirements are few. It needs shade, good compost and plenty of water except through the winter months. A winter temperature of 10°C (50°F) will suffice.

PROPAGATION. By cuttings during the spring months.

Stephanotis: The species most commonly cultivated is *Stephanotis floribunda*, and it is a very fine evergreen twiner for a greenhouse with a minimum temperature of 13°C (55°F). The pure white scented flowers are produced freely in clusters in May, and they are in demand by florists for bouquets.

CULTIVATION. It is best to grow plants in beds filled with good soil, although they can be grown in large pots provided regular feeding is carried out in the summer. The shoots can be trained horizontally along wires beneath the greenhouse roof. A warm, moist atmosphere is needed to encourage good growth, and shade from strong sunshine should be given. Little growth is made in winter when water should be given sparingly. Plants in large pots do not need repotting each year, but it is wise to remove some of the old surface compost each spring and to topdress with fresh compost.

PROPAGATION. Cuttings taken in the spring from the previous year's growths will root in sandy compost if they are placed in a temperature of 16–18°C (60–65°F).

Strelitzia: There are several species in this remarkable genus, but only one is recommended, which hails from the Cape of Good Hope.

Strelitzia reginae (the bird of paradise flower) is a magnificent subject. It has large leaves about 1½ ft. long on stems of the same length, and stout spikes of very striking blue and orange flowers.

Height about 5 ft. The flowering period is spring and early summer, and the blooms remain in full beauty for several days.

CULTIVATION. To flower this gorgeous plant, pots 8 or 10 in. in diameter are needed. Make the compost fairly firm around the roots, and water carefully until the plant is established. Provide good drainage and a compost of sandy loam, 3 parts, and 1 part in equal proportions of peat and well-rotted manure. Add plenty of sand if the loam is on the heavy side. Repotting is best done in the spring.

Strelitzia reginae is a sun-loving plant, and should be afforded the lightest position in the house. Copious supplies of water are necessary during active growth, but at other seasons the compost is only kept moderately moist. A winter temperature of 10–13°C (50–55°F) is advised, but in summer these figures can be exceeded by 5 or 10°C (10 or 20°F) with sun heat.

PROPAGATION. One or two plants are usually sufficient, and the best plan would be to purchase them from a nurseryman.

They may be raised from seeds (set by hand pollination), but high temperature and bottom heat are necessary. The principal method is from suckers or by division of old plants. This should be carried out in spring, and when the portions are potted up they should be kept in a warm, moist house until well rooted.

Streptocarpus: Since the first hybrid Cape primrose was raised from *Streptocarpus rexii* and *S. saundersii* many years ago considerable progress has been made by cross-breeding and selection, which has resulted in a magnificent strain with a vigorous habit. They are perennial, and remarkable for the abundance and almost continuous succession of large flowers, in many beautiful shades of colour. There are distinct shades of pink, blue, rose, violet, red, rosy purple, and white. Moreover, the flowers are produced on stout stems well above the foliage.

SPECIES. A few which come from South Africa are *S. dunnii* (rose), *S. galpinii* (mauve and white), *S. parviflorus* (yellow) and *S. wendlandii* (violet-blue and white). With the exception of *S. parviflorus*, the species mentioned produce only one immense leaf.

Most gardeners, however, will ignore the species and concentrate on the beautiful series of modern hybrids. For general purposes a good mixed strain of giant hybrids will give the greatest satisfaction. Although a few flowers are open the greater part of the year, the normal flowering period may be termed summer and autumn, and again in early spring if all the blooms are cut off in October.

CULTIVATION. First obtain some seeds from a reliable source, and then sow thinly and evenly in pans of John Innes seed compost in January or February. The seeds are minute, and they are barely covered with finely sifted compost. They need exactly the same treatment as begonias, gloxinias, etc. and thrive in the John Innes composts or one of the loamless mixtures. When the plants are small the compost should be fairly fine, but for the last potting it may be rougher. Hard potting must be avoided, just make the compost firm with the fingers.

About June the plants will be ready for 4-in. pots, and the temperature should not fall below 13°C (55°F). Keep the roots moist, and shade when the weather is bright. Admit air freely. A further and final potting will soon be needed, and this time containers 5 and 6 in. in diameter should be chosen. Provide ample drainage. A few stray flower scapes will appear in the early part of the summer, which are best removed. This will encourage the building up of strong plants, and, furthermore, liquid fertiliser will be beneficial when the pots are comfortably filled with roots. Do not forget to keep shaded from bright sun. In August, if all goes well, the plants will begin to flower freely, when they are taken into the greenhouse. Watch for greenfly, and fumigate directly this pest is seen.

Seed can also be sown in July and the seedlings wintered in 3-in. pots, being kept on the dry side from November onwards. In early March they can be moved into 5-in. pots, where they will make fine plants, flowering over a long period.

PROPAGATION. Any special plants that the grower wishes to retain should be kept slightly on the dry side in winter and repotted in March. Remove most of the old compost; large specimens with several crowns may be divided. Such plants can also be increased by portions of matured leaves. Insert them in equal parts peat and sand and place in a propagator until growth is apparent.

For ordinary purposes seed of a good strain will provide the simplest means of raising stock as described above.

Streptosolen: A genus that contains one species which should be in every greenhouse. *Streptosolen jamesonii* is a free-flowering climber or pot plant, bearing clusters of bright orange flowers from April to July and often later. It is excellent for clothing a back wall, where it is very effective when covered with a mass of bloom. It is also very fine when grown as a standard or bush specimen.

CULTIVATION. Plants should be overhauled in spring and repotted in John Innes No. 2 potting compost or one of the loamless composts. After potting, syringe the plants daily until flowers appear. Allow plenty of light and ventilation during the spring and summer months. Well-established plants will need plenty of water, and liquid fertiliser can be given directly the pots are filled with roots. Immediately after flowering the annual pruning should be done, cutting the shoots back fairly hard. Maintain a winter temperature of 7°C (45°F) and keep the roots slightly on the dry side.

PROPAGATION. Easily done by cuttings of young shoots during the spring or summer months. Insert them in pots of sandy compost and place in a close propagating frame till the cuttings are rooted. Pot off singly, and pinch out the points of the shoots to encourage bushy growth. If standards are required, select a few of the best plants, and grow them on without pinching until the required height is attained. Remove side growths as they appear.

Swainsona: These belong to the Pea family (Australian).

SPECIES. The most popular species is *Swainsona galegifolia*, which bears sprays of deep red flowers but it has been found in the wild varying through all shades of blue, pink, mauve, red and yellow; the variety *albiflora* is white. They produce flexuous branches, and when well grown reach a height of several feet. They are useful for greenhouse embellishment and for cutting purposes, especially the white variety, which is the one most largely grown. The flowers appear during the summer months.

CULTIVATION. Swainsonas can be planted out in well-drained soil, but the plants must be a good size before they are turned out of pots. They will also succeed in pots or tubs, and the compost consists of sandy loam and peat in equal parts, with a sprinkling of fine charcoal. Repotting or topdressing should be done in March, but the plants must be pruned into shape a fortnight before the roots are disturbed. Train and tie the growths to neat stakes, and pinch any straggling shoots. Syringe the foliage daily, and keep the roots moist. When the flowers begin to open, cease using the syringe. During the autumn admit a little more air, and see that the plants get plenty of light to ripen the growths. In winter less moisture at the base is needed, and a temperature of 7°C (45°F).

PROPAGATION. Swainsonas are easily raised from seeds sown in March. Place in a temperature of 18–21 °C (65–70 °F). Cuttings of young shoots will form roots from April till July if arranged in a close propagating frame. Pot off singly, when rooted, in sandy peat, and gradually harden to the conditions of a greenhouse. Pinch the shoots occasionally, remove all flower buds, and pot on as they fill their containers with roots.

Thunbergia: As a rule the thunbergias need hothouse conditions, but one species will thrive in the greenhouse.

SPECIES. *Thunbergia alata*, Black-eyed Susan, has attractive orange-yellow flowers with a deep brown eye; height about 4 ft. It is an elegant twiner, suitable for hanging baskets or pots for draping the front of the staging.

CULTIVATION. Its cultural requirements are few. It needs shade, pots of light compost in March or April and to be placed in a temperature of 16–18 °C (60–65 °F). When large enough for removal place singly in small pots. As growth advances transfer to 5-in. pots or baskets in which they will bloom. Thunbergias enjoy a fairly rich compost. Give plenty of water during the summer months. After flowering the plants should be discarded.

Tibouchina: *Tibouchina semidecandra* (syn. *Lasiandra macrantha*) is an evergreen hard-wooded plant which bears magnificent, large, rich, violet-blue flowers during the summer months. It is native of Brazil.

CULTIVATION. This plant will grow in pots or planted out. It flowers much more freely when the plants have reached a good size. For this reason they should be planted out whenever possible. The position must be well drained, and the compost consist of rough peat and loam in equal parts with a sprinkling of sand. Fresh compost should be given in March, and this is also a suitable time to overhaul pot plants. Little pruning is needed beyond a general trim up or the removal of straggly shoots before the end of February. By careful pinching of the shoots during the growing season, the plants can be kept in bounds as bushy specimens. Give plenty of water to plants that are well rooted, except in winter, when the supply is naturally much less. Maintain a winter temperature of 10 °C (50 °F).

PROPAGATION. Cuttings made from young shoots in the spring

should be inserted singly in small pots filled with sandy peat. Place them in a close propagating frame until rooted. Pot on as required, and do not pinch the shoots. These will be cut back the following spring.

Cuttings of side shoots will also root in July and August in a cool frame.

Trachelium (Throatwort): On account of its free flowering qualities and easy cultivation the only representative of this genus should be grown by all greenhouse owners. It is *Trachelium caeruleum*, a native of Italy and Spain, with large dense heads of small blue flowers during the summer and autumn months. It grows from 1 to 5 ft. high, and will develop into a fine exhibition specimen. The size of the plants will depend on when the cuttings are rooted or the seeds are sown. There is a white variety known as *T. c. album*.

CULTIVATION. Sow seeds in spring. Germinate in a warm greenhouse. When large enough pot off the seedlings singly, and pinch the growths occasionally to produce a bushy habit. Much larger plants are obtained by sowing seeds in July, when they will germinate without difficulty on the greenhouse stage if kept well shaded. Remove the shading as soon as growth appears above the soil, and when the young plants are large enough they should be potted off separately. Use small pots of John Innes No. 1 potting compost or a similar mixture. For the final potting add a little rotted manure. The plants should be kept growing steadily in a cold frame until October, when they can be removed to a light, airy, cool greenhouse. Pot on as the pots become filled with roots and pinch the points of the shoots three or four times. This ought only to be done when the roots are established and not at the time of repotting. Make the compost fairly firm. The flowering pots of the best plants will be from 7 to 8 in. in diameter. The pots should be tolerably filled with roots before any manurial assistance is given.

PROPAGATION. By seeds as previously described.

Trachelospermum: A small genus also known under the name of *Rhynchospermum*.

SPECIES. One only, *Trachelospermum jasminoides*, which hails from Shanghai and is an evergreen climber of easy cultivation. This plant, commonly called Chinese jasmine, bears small trusses of very fragrant white flowers in July and August. It will attain a height of 10 to 15 ft. A variety, *angustifolium*, has smaller and narrower leaves than the common type. This plant is excellent for covering a back wall, clothing a pillar, or any support for the greenhouse. If used for either of these purposes it should be planted out in March, starting with good strong plants. Small examples may be given pot cultivation when the shoots are trained around stakes or a wire balloon.

CULTIVATION. Sandy loam and peat in equal parts make a suitable compost. Repot in March. During the spring and summer months see that the roots never suffer from drought, and a daily syringing with clear water will promote healthy growth and keep down insect pests. Shade from strong sunlight. A cool greenhouse temperature will suffice. Pruning should be done immediately after flowering. It consists of thinning out and trimming the plants into shape so that they will be kept within bounds.

PROPAGATION. Easily effected by cuttings of firm shoots during the summer months. Insert them in sandy peat and arrange in a propagating frame until rooted. Shade during bright weather.

Tradescantia: Although these plants used to be grown in stove houses they will thrive under cool greenhouse conditions, and are of course now very popular as house plants. They are useful for draping the front of stages, clothing spaces beneath where few plants will thrive, covering the soil of large pots or tubs, and hanging baskets.

SPECIES. *Tradescantia fluviatilis*, leaves striped with green and white; *T. blossfeldiana*, dark green and purple fleshy leaves and stems.

CULTIVATION. Provide ample moisture, a little shade, and a temperature of not less than 7°C (45°F) for *T. fluviatilis* and 10°C (50°F) for the other species, and no difficulty will be experienced in growing the tradescantias.

PROPAGATION. By cuttings placed in a close propagating frame. When rooted and slighly hardened transfer to a larger pot or basket, or wherever it is intended to grow them.

Tropaeolum: Several members of this showy genus are also known under the name of nasturtium, especially the fibrous-rooted section. This is the group most largely grown.

SPECIES. Tuberous kinds include *Tropaeolum azureum* (blue), and *T. tricolorum* (scarlet, black, and orange). They are in bloom from June to October and are natives of Chile. The fibrous-rooted species and varieties embrace *T. peltophorum*, Brilliant, Lucifer, and Ball of Fire, all of which are shades of vivid scarlet and crimson and orange. Double scarlet and double yellow are also well worth growing.

CULTIVATION. The tuberous-rooted section will thrive in sandy peat, and loam in equal parts, with a liberal sprinkling of sand. The pots should be clean and well drained.

Potting must be done while the tubers are dormant. Owing to the delicate roots, careful handling is essential when shaking out the old compost. As a rule they are grown singly, one root or tuber being placed in a 5-in. pot, but several may be arranged in larger containers covering the tubers with about 2 in. of compost. Until growth is visible very little water is needed – in fact, moisture must be applied in strict moderation until growth is fairly well advanced. The shoots will need some supports, and these may be in the form of a trellis, wire balloon, or stick from a birch broom. These tropaeolums succeed best under cool treatment; a minimum temperature of 10°C (50°F) in winter will suffice.

The fibrous-rooted varieties should be grown for winter and early spring flowers. With this object in view, the plants ought to be established in their flowering pots by October. Seeds of the single varieties should be sown in July, and cuttings of the double forms rooted in heat about this date. Pot off singly when ready, and grow in a cold frame till early September, when they are removed to the greenhouse. The plants will flower freely in 6-in. pots of John Innes No. 1 potting compost. To secure blooms with long stems and firm texture the growths must not be overcrowded. Pillars or rafters are suitable supports, but the growths may also be trained to strings reaching from the roof to the stages.

PROPAGATION. By dividing the tubers when repotting, also by seeds and cuttings. The latter should be fairly firm and short jointed. Place them singly in small pots filled with sandy compost. A close frame and shade are needed until roots are formed.

Zantedeschia (Arum Lily): A popular and easily grown plant, valuable for a variety of purposes. The flowering period is spread over several months, the actual time of blooming being governed by the amount of heat at command. In addition to the well-known white arum lily there are both yellow and pink species, some of which have mottled foliage.

SPECIES. The typical arum lily, *Zantedeschia aethiopica*, is white and grows about 2 ft. high. There are several varieties such as *childsiana*, The Godfrey, and Little Gem, the last-named being about half the size of the ordinary type. Other species are *Z. elliottiana* (yellow, with dark green leaves spotted with white), *Z. angustiloba* (deep yellow with purple-brown blotch at base, leaves green), *Z. rehmannii* (rose), and light pink to violet forms of this.

CULTIVATION. There are slight differences between the species. The common arum and its varieties claim first attention.

As a rule blooms are not in great demand after the end of April, they are more valuable in winter and early spring. To obtain these results the plants should be gradually dried off in May, and allowed to rest with the pots on their sides until early in August, during which month those required for Christmas flowering should be repotted. The old compost should be shaken out, and if the tubers show signs of disease the damaged portions must be cut off. Dust the cut ends with green sulphur. Pots 6 to 10 in. in diameter may be used. The former will take one tuber and the latter four or five. Provide ample drainage and a fairly rich compost. This consists of fibrous loam, 3 parts, and 1 part dried manure or the remains of an old mushroom bed. A 6-in. potful of fine bonemeal to every two bushels of the mixture will be beneficial.

After the repotting is completed stand them in the open until mid-September or October if there is no frost. Keep the roots moist and the soil free of weeds. Arrange the plants in the greenhouse and for a week or two little if any heat will be needed. Afterwards the temperature is gradually increased until it fluctuates between 13 and 16°C (55 and 60°F). Both top growth and root action will be vigorous, and the plants must not suffer from drought. When the pots are nicely filled with roots, liquid fertiliser may be given regularly. Greenfly is sometimes present as the days begin to lengthen, but aphids are easily destroyed by an occasional light fumigation. Where a temperature of 16°C (60°F) cannot be maintained the flowering will be later. The plants will not suffer in health.

The remaining species, of which *Z. elliottiana* may be cited as an example, require a winter temperature of 13°C (55°F), and from 16–21°C (60–70°F) at other seasons. Repotting is done in February, and the compost consists of loam 2 parts, and 1 part each of peat and silver sand. Afterwards place the pots in a warm house and give water in moderation until growth is well advanced. Flowers are produced during the summer months. After blooming the plants are gradually dried off, and the compost is kept dry until the time arrives for repotting.

PROPAGATION. Achieved by offsets taken at time of repotting. They may be placed in pans, or small pots, and grown on under similar treatment to old plants.

Zygopetalum, see Orchids

CHAPTER EIGHT

Annuals and Biennials in Pots

Growing annuals in pots has always been a fairly quick and easy way of providing colour in the greenhouse. The choice of subjects is very wide indeed with a tremendous variation in form, habit, colour, and flowering season.

If one wished to do so, the greenhouse could be filled with annuals for most of the year but most people will be satisfied with the spring and early summer display which owes much of its colourfulness to the use of such brilliant annuals as clarkia, schizanthus, annual chrysanthemums, and the like. Most annuals are adaptable to houses with low temperatures, and a good cultivator with an unheated house can quite easily have the same spectacular display in spring as his neighbour with the heated house – though this may be a little later.

The majority are sown in autumn and carefully watered throughout the winter, potted into larger pots in early spring, and allowed to develop in cool conditions. There is, however, one point to observe – namely, that there must be no casual cultivation or laxness on the part of the grower for, though annuals are easy to grow, they soon show their resentment of poor conditions, bad treatment, and over-watering.

Sowing of most of them should take place about the beginning of September, though there are a few exceptions to this, notably the salpiglossis which makes a delightful pot plant but requires sowing in early August.

All the ordinary annuals should be sown in two or even three batches – say, at the beginning of September, the third week in September, and the first week in October. There are two main reasons for this. One is that with care it will extend the flowering period and the other reason is that the seedlings have a tendency to damp off should the weather be too hot and close, and so with the two or three sowings one can assume with some certainty that one of the batches will survive. However, with careful sowing in John Innes seed compost which has been watered with Cheshunt Compound, this trouble can be kept at bay.

The cold frame is the best place in which to raise the seed, but, failing this, a greenhouse shelf is the next best, so long, of course, as one is willing to watch the young seedlings all the time in respect of watering, shading from very bright sunshine, and ventilation. The last mentioned is of paramount importance because, from the moment the seedling shows itself above the compost, every effort must be made to keep the plant dwarf, sturdy, and strong. Once a young annual weakens it may be counted as the end, so this rather small but important point should be borne in mind from the very first.

Once they are large enough to handle, the seedlings should be pricked out into a well-drained compost and still given all the light and air possible. Within a few weeks they will be ready for their first pots, and it will be in these that most of them will spend the winter. Well-drained compost must be the keynote of this move, for annuals are the fussiest of all plants in the winter. They do not mind cold air temperatures, but they do resent a cold and badly drained compost, and few will pass the winter safely in such a mixture. The free-draining, well-aerated properties of John Innes No. 1 potting compost make it an ideal mixture for this purpose. The earlier this potting up is done the better, because the weather tends to make rooting difficult as the year dies.

Some plants are grown three or more in a pot, and this is usual practice with *Linaria maroccana*, nemesia, *Phlox drummondii*, and *Helipterum manglesii*. In such cases the plants will be put in around the edge of the pot.

Once this potting is over and the new roots have formed in the compost, there will be little to do other than pay the particular care to watering already mentioned. In very cold weather the compost may become almost dry without any damage to the seedling. Coupled with this must be the careful ventilation which plays such an important part in the growing of annuals. Air should be given on every possible occasion though one should obviously note the difference between draughts and the correct method of giving fresh air.

At the same time, keep the plants away from heated pipes, and at all times give them a place in the lightest part of the house. Obviously a greenhouse shelf suggests itself as the ideal spot and, except in the severest weather, it can be counted as ideal – partly because it offers all the light possible and partly because the circulation of air is better on a shelf than on a staging. Once the winter is over – say, mid-February – a start can be made on potting on the various subjects to their final pots, though perhaps a few may take another move after the February one.

The potting compost must now be richer, and the John Innes No. 2 potting compost is ideal – or at least it can be taken as a guide. Crock the pots well and pot firmly, and whatever you do only bury the stem of the plants to the same point as it was in the previous pot. Deep or low potting is a most prolific cause of trouble and many growers fail to realise this.

The plants will grow very rapidly and something in the way of support must be given. Always use canes or sticks that are strong enough to support the fully grown plant, but avoid unsightly or unpainted sticks. Many annuals may be supported simply by four thin canes or hazel twigs placed around the edge of the pot with a circle of raffia tied round the four. This is unobtrusive but perfectly satisfactory.

Annuals may also be sown in warm houses during January and February, and the plants grown on quickly to give a display between the time the autumn-sown ones finish blooming and the time the outdoor kinds are in flower. There are one or two which do better from a spring sowing than from an autumn one, notably those which seem to resent the winter conditions – such as nicotiana, phlox, nemesia, nasturtiums, zinnias, and scabious. The term 'warm houses' indicates those with a minimum winter temperature of 13°C (55°F). Very few annuals, except those belonging to the 'tender group' – such as celosias, cockscombs, exacum, torenia – will need a high temperature for germination or afterwards, but those just mentioned will require a consistent temperature of 16°C (60°F) or more to do well and, what is more, such temperatures should be as steady as possible. The tender annuals of all kinds should be sown in spring rather than autumn.

Some annuals for pot cultivation may be sown in April for providing a summer or autumn display, and the four just mentioned will be found ideal for such a purpose. Another annual for this late flowering is the zinnia. Sown in May, grown on quickly in pure loam, all the side shoots should be removed to allow only one flower to develop on the main stem. In this way it is possible to get a flower as big as a dahlia in a 6-in. pot. They require as much sunshine as possible and every particle of fresh air that can be given.

Here are a few of the outstanding and most useful annuals for pot cultivation responding to cool house treatment: calendula (especially the variety Orange Cockade); candytuft; carnation (annual); chrysanthemum (annual); clarkia (a great favourite, which may be had 6 ft. high in spring); cornflower; dimorphotheca; echium; godetia; *Gypsophila elegans*; helipterums; larkspur; lavatera; *Mentzelia lindleyi*; mignonette; nasturtium; nemophila; nicotiana; *Phlox drummondii*; salpiglossis, scabious; statice; stocks; ursinia; viscaria, and zinnia.

Perhaps of all the pot annuals for the cool house the schizanthus is one of the most important and it is certainly one that lends itself to cultivation by most gardeners, even if they do not possess a warm greenhouse. It is easy to raise from seed – and it makes a good shaped plant and is probably covered with more flowers than any other greenhouse plant we know. Moreover, the colours are so varied and so beautiful and the shape of the flower so quaint, that it almost demands cultivation in every type of greenhouse. There is now a dwarf strain for the cooler greenhouse known as Dwarf Bouquet.

Up-to-date shades of all colours are available and the flowers have been so improved that they are large and fleshy and last a good deal longer than they did in the days gone by.

Its cultivation is fairly simple, seed being sown in August, the plants pricked out into boxes and ultimately, in November, being potted into 3-in. pots; it is in these that the plants stand the winter. Schizanthus will stand a degree or two of frost, but it is far better if kept in the region of 7°C (40°F) all the time.

In February potting on is done into final pots. A light compost will not give a bushy or well-grown plant, therefore a somewhat heavier, richer mixture should be used (the John Innes No. 2 potting compost is quite suitable) to encourage the development of a sturdy specimen.

On account of its sweet perfume certain kinds of the popular annual mignonette, *Reseda odorata*, are largely grown in pots. These include Machet, Red Monarch and other giant forms which attain a height of $1\frac{1}{2}$ ft. For general treatment, see the preliminary remarks in this chapter. The following may also be helpful to the beginner.

If tall standard specimens are required, seeds should be sown about midsummer. Sow the seeds in small pots filled with John Innes seed compost. Reduce the seedlings to the strongest plant, pinch once or twice, but keep the plants erect, and pot on as required.

Mignonette is more generally cultivated for late winter and spring display. Seeds should be sown in August and September in the pots in which the plants will flower. These are usually 5 in. in diameter. They should be clean and well drained. John Innes No. 2 potting compost or one of the loamless mixtures will be quite suitable at this stage. Make the compost tolerably firm. Place the pots in a cold frame on a bed of ashes until October, when they can be grown with clarkias and other annuals. When large enough, thin the seedlings to 1 in. apart. Never subject the plants to a high temperature or a close, stuffy atmosphere, and water carefully at all times.

This list by no means includes all the subjects that can be grown in this way, and it is an interesting experiment to sow a number of ordinary garden annuals and await the result when treated as pot plants. Some of the plants included in this list have already been dealt with in other parts of this book.

BIENNIALS

In the days when gardeners were more patient they did not mind waiting a good time for the ultimate display of colour from pot-grown subjects, but today the interest seems to be centred around the quick-growing material rather than anything else. A pity this, as one tends to forget some of the biennials, which might make a truly useful addition to greenhouse colour.

Wallflowers, for instance, make grand pot plants, and to have only one or two in a house during the cold days of winter is worth a great deal if only for their delightful perfume. Sown outdoors in April, transplanted in June, potted up and stood in frames in September, they make bushy plants which, with the slightest warmth, come out in January, February and March.

Forget-me-nots may be treated in the same way, and what delightful colour they bring, to mix with the bulbs of March. Avoid damp conditions in winter, for though we are apt to think of them as ditch-loving plants, they resent the cold, stagnant moisture of

A conservatory in May with abutilon, coleus and two popular annuals
for greenhouse cultivation, schizanthus and salpiglossis

winter when in pots. Three or four plants will usually make a good potful.

The lovely *Campanula pyramidalis* is another of those biennials which must be grown in a pot if it is to be seen at its best. The blue or white spires of open bells bring a particular richness to the summer greenhouse. Always use a rich and rather loamy soil.

Canterbury Bells, *Campanula medium*, potted from the open ground in September or October and wintered in frames, will make splendid April or May subjects. They are quite easy to grow, and so long as they have enough root room and are given occasional feeds to avoid starvation the result should be fine.

Gilia rubra, another beauty, has tall spikes of tubular flowers, with the petals turning outwards at the tips. The colour is a most vivid scarlet and the foliage is thin and feathery, thus making a delightful combination. Sow in June, pot off singly, and keep in a cool but frostproof house for the winter, potting on in March. Three in a 6-in. pot or one in a 5 in. will make grand decorative specimens.

The biennial stocks make beautiful plants in pots, notably the best type of East Lothian, Brompton, the Intermediate sorts and of course the modern column stocks. A good time for sowing is early July and again in early August, potting the plants into small pots at the earliest possible moment, and then wintering them in frames till February, when they can be potted on and given a slightly warm house in which to encourage development. Avoid sharp heat at all times.

Those near relatives of the mulleins, *Celsia arcturus* and *C. cretica*, should both be treated as biennials, and from a June sowing a bright display may be assured during the following late spring and summer. *Exacum zeylanicum* is another good biennial sown in late summer, for flowering the following spring.

Top: Lilium auratum
Bottom: Haemanthus coccineus

CHAPTER NINE

Bulbs and Allied Subjects

Bulbs add a great deal to the greenhouse display, especially during winter and spring. In general, their cultivation is easy and does not require much in the way of artificial heat. In fact, the use of heat can be detrimental, and it is certainly the cause of many failures and disappointing results. Only the practised hand should use heat, and so the beginner might be well advised to stick to the cool or cold treatment until he has mastered the finer points of bulb forcing.

All the ordinary spring flowering bulbs found in the garden can be grown in pots and, so long as they are considered as hardy subjects, and not as exotic plants, their cultivation is not difficult, even for the novice.

The main requirements are a good, thoroughly drained compost, well-crocked pots, and good-quality bulbs. It cannot be expected that second-rate bulbs will provide a first-class display, and therefore a few pence more on a dozen might be considered money well spent. Certain bulbs are treated so as to flower earlier than the main batch and these should be given preference.

Moreover, it is just as much trouble to grow a poor variety as a good one, so consider this point too. This is especially true of the narcissus family, where practically any sort will grow and bloom in a pot, but by a careful choice of the larger and better-coloured varieties, the display will be of the highest order and far more pleasing to the grower.

Another point which applies to spring flowering bulbs is that if they are wanted early they must be potted correspondingly early. Late potted bulbs may, by artificial means, be brought into bloom very quickly, but the flowers are usually thin, the stems weak, and the lasting quality almost non-existent. Flowers from early potted bulbs, on the other hand, will last a considerable time longer and will be far more fleshy and more developed than the late ones.

Where certain families allow it, a careful choice of varieties to provide a succession of bloom should be obtained, and this is easily understood by considering the tulip and narcissus families which have certain sections that could be termed 'early', 'mid-season', and 'late'.

Watering is an important part of bulb growing, especially in the spring when so many roots have been made that they will require far more water than is usually given to pot plants at this time of the year, but dryness is fatal.

Most bulbs require covering with ashes, peat, soil or straw, immediately after potting, the depth of ash being decided by the bulb; 4 or 5 in. is the usual depth, though small bulbs will only require 2 or 3 in.

The following are some bulbous plants suitable for pot cultivation in greenhouses according to their heating capacity.

Achimenes: A large genus of tuberous rooted plants, adapted for pot or basket cultivation. They can be had in bloom throughout the summer and autumn by starting the tubercles in batches from February till the end of May. The flowering stems grow to about 1-2 ft. long. Some grow erect and others more or less pendant. Blossoms are very freely borne and comprise many shades of red, blue, purple, white, yellow and orange.

SPECIES. The species are not so readily available these days, but there is a very wide choice of hybrids and named varieties in the catalogues. A good strain of seed will produce plants in a variety of colours.

CULTIVATION. The first batch of tubercles can be started into growth in February. Shake them from the old compost, and arrange them in shallow boxes containing a layer of light sandy compost. Just cover them with the compost and place in a temperature of 16°C (60°F). Water sparingly. When the shoots are about 2 in. high, they are carefully transferred to well-drained pans or pots 5 to 8 in. in diameter. The small tufts are set 2 or 3 in. apart.

For basket cultivation line a basket with weed-free moss, start at the base, and as the basket fills up insert a few plants so that the growths will push through the wires. Fill up with compost, and finish off with a few plants on the surface. Suspend the basket from the roof rafters.

John Innes No. 1 potting compost is a suitable mixture for growing achimenes. Hard potting is not advised, but the soil must be moderately firm. Arrange the plants near the roof glass, and shade from strong sunshine. Maintain a moist growing atmosphere, and until flowering starts the temperature should be about 16°C (60°F). After this a cool greenhouse will suffice. Water freely during active growth and give a weekly application of liquid fertiliser when the pots are filled with roots. Plants in baskets will be allowed to grow naturally, but those in pots will require a few thin neat stakes to maintain a nicely balanced effect.

After flowering gradually reduce the water supply, and withhold when the stems are dried off. Store the pots on their side where the temperature will not fall below 10°C (50°F).

Thrips, red spider mites, and greenfly will be troublesome if the atmosphere is too dry, but an occasional fumigation will destroy these pests.

PROPAGATION. By seeds, leaves, cuttings, the tubercles mentioned at the beginning, and scales from the tubercles, which are rubbed off and sown as one would sow seeds. For propagation by any of these methods a temperature of 18°C (65°F) and John Innes seed compost will meet their requirements; early spring is a suitable time for all.

Allium: A large family of bulbous plants, with only a few suitable for the greenhouse. They are useful for early forcing, flowering in March–April, but their beauty is somewhat discounted by the accompaniment of a disagreeably pungent odour.

SPECIES. *Allium neapolitanum* from Southern Europe is the best of the white-flowered species.

CULTIVATION. Bulbs are potted when dormant, and can be allowed to almost touch each other. Plunge in ashes to a depth of 3 in. till growth begins, when they are removed to a cold frame for a few weeks prior to being taken into the greenhouse. They will stand a temperature of 16°C (60°F) when growth is advanced. Water freely when well rooted, and gradually dry off after flowering.

PROPAGATION. Any offsets can be taken off at potting time and grown on in the garden until they attain flowering size.

Amaryllis: Most of the gorgeously coloured bulbous plants which formerly were known as *Amaryllis* are now known (by decision of the botanists) by the name *Hippeastrum*, but *Amaryllis belladonna* still retains its familiar generic name, and although this is a hardy plant which thrives and blooms in many gardens which provide warm, sheltered and sunny situations, it is also a good plant for cultivation in an unheated greenhouse. This one species has lily-like flowers on sturdy erect stems. They are exquisitely coloured in delicately tinted shades of pink on an almost white ground. The pink reaches quite rosy hues, and the flowers are sweetly fragrant. Outdoors, they bloom about August or September, but in an unheated greenhouse can be considerably earlier.

CULTIVATION. This is not difficult. The best time to pot bulbs is shortly after they have finished flowering. Large pots are required, and the bulbs should rest on a thin layer of fibrous loam over a layer of crocks. Compost should be good loam, peat and well-rotted manure with enough sharp sand to ensure reasonable porosity. Pot firmly, see that the compost is never allowed to be really dry, but nearly so during the resting period, increasing moisture supply as fresh young growth appears. Allow plenty of ventilation, never trying to hasten growth by maintaining a close, stuffy atmosphere. Feed regularly with liquid fertiliser from the time when the flower buds appear.

PROPAGATION. Is best effected by offsets from the bulbs, but if pots are of ample size it is unnecessary to shake out, divide, and repot more than once in three years.

Chionodoxa: These miniature beauties are best grown in 3-in. pots filled with sandy compost. Five or six bulbs can be placed in each pot, putting them in during September and keeping them in the plunge bed till November. After that, keep in absolutely cold frames and do not attempt forcing till, say, February, when very slight warmth will bring out the flowers.

Clivia: These are beautiful bulbous plants for a spring display. They can be obtained in various shades of orange, yellow and scarlet, and grow about 2 ft. high.

SPECIES. The pure species have been largely superseded by a brilliant set of hybrids. The former embrace *Clivia gardenii* (orange, yellow, South Africa), *C. miniata* (scarlet and yellow, Natal), and *C. nobilis* (yellow and red, South Africa). There are several new varieties and hybrids of *C. miniata* which are a distinct improvement.

CULTIVATION. Clivias bloom more freely when in a pot-bound condition, but if larger plants are desired, then repotting must be carried out occasionally. This should be done in February, using a compost of fibrous loam with a sprinkling of leafmould and sand. A 7-in. potful of coarse bonemeal can be added to every 3 bushels of soil or they can be grown quite successfully in the John Innes mixtures.

Throughout the growing period, from February to September, give plenty of water, and no shade except during very bright weather, when the sun is scorching. Ventilate freely, and feed well-rooted examples with liquid fertiliser.

Reduce the water supply in autumn and throughout the winter just give enough moisture to prevent the compost becoming dust dry. A temperature of 7°C (45°F) will be ample, and admit a little air whenever possible. Unless the plants receive a rest under dry and airy conditions they will not flower so freely in the spring. About February they should be given more water and a few degrees more warmth, to assist in the development of the flower spikes.

PROPAGATION. Plants are raised from seeds, which germinate in a warm house. Seedlings are kept growing until they attain flowering size and never dried off, but this is a slow process which will try the patience of all but the very keen. Named varieties are increased by division when repotting. Owing to the mass of thick fleshy roots this is difficult to carry out without a certain amount of injury to the roots. However, pieces can usually be extracted with a few live roots attached, and if they are potted up, and grown for a while in a warm house, they will soon develop into nice specimens.

Crinum: Although in favoured areas crinums are more or less hardy, in most districts they need the accommodation of a cool greenhouse. They are handsome and bold bulbous plants, with large arching leaves and tall flower stems. The flowers somewhat resemble a lily.

SPECIES. The following are the chief: *Crinum longiflorum* (white, tube greenish); *C. macowanii* (white and purple); *C. moorei* (white and red); *C. m. schmidtii*, (white); *C. powellii* (white and rose), and *C. powellii album* (pure white).

CULTIVATION. The roots of crinums are numerous, and in consequence need large pots or even tubs. When the plants are of flowering size there is no necessity for annual repotting. The rooting medium consists of 3 parts turf loam, and 1 part leafmould with a little sand. Repotting, when necessary, should be done in the spring.

During their period of activity water freely, and pot-bound examples can be assisted with liquid fertiliser twice a week. Grow them in a light position. Most of the crinums mentioned are autumn flowering though *C. moorei* may flower in spring or autumn. *C. macowanii* will be the last to flower. After the spikes have been removed during the winter, the bulbs will rest, and water should be partially withheld. Expose the plants to all the light possible.

PROPAGATION. Effected by seeds and offsets. The former are large, and should be sown directly they are ripe. Sow singly in small pots and germinate in a temperature of 18°C (65°F). Offsets are secured in March when rather small, potted singly, and grown on as the mature plants.

Crocus: This family, by virtue of its early flowering species, may be had in bloom in January in a house with no heat at all, but the majority of growers will concentrate on the larger and later hybrids. These should be put in during September or October, covered with 3 in. of ashes for five weeks, and then kept in a cold frame till January when they can be brought into slight warmth. To attempt early forcing in sharp heat usually defeats one's object, as the foliage becomes long and thin, with no blossom to speak of. Gentle forcing is best.

Cyclamen: For a winter and spring display a well-grown batch of cyclamen has few equals. The marbled and marked foliage is charming in addition to the variously coloured flowers in salmon, pink, scarlet, magenta and white. Some of the latter are very vivid even during the dull days of winter.

SPECIES. *Cyclamen persicum* (syn. *C. latifolium*), a native of Asia Minor, bearing white flowers with a purplish-red base. It is the parent from which the greatly improved and brightly coloured modern varieties have been evolved.

CULTIVATION. Cyclamen are raised from seeds, and the best time to sow is in August or September. Good flowering plants cannot be obtained from late sowing, although the result may be fair. Fill well-drained pans or shallow boxes with a light rich compost placing the seeds about half an inch apart and a quarter of an inch deep. Place the pans in a temperature of about 16–18°C (60–65°F) and cover the surface with paper or a pane of glass until the seedlings appear. When two or three tiny leaves have been formed transfer singly to thumb pots, using a mixture of loam (2 parts) and leaf-mould (1 part) with a liberal sprinkling of sand. Place the plants on a shelf, shade from strong sunshine, and keep the atmosphere moist around the pots. Here they will remain with the temperature about 10°C (50°F) till March or early April, when they are repotted in 3-in. pots. Make the compost fairly firm, and keep the plants growing steadily. Stand the pots on a shelf or staging on which is spread a layer of ashes to maintain a moist base. Careful watering should be the rule.

About June or early July they will be placed in their flowering pots, usually the 5- or 6-in. size. Well drain the pots and use the John Innes No. 2 potting mixture with an extra part peat added. Take care not to bury the corms too deeply. Gradually harden the plants, and then set them in a cold frame on a cool base of moist ashes. Shade from bright sunshine, admit plenty of air, and see the roots do not suffer from drought. Freedom from insect pests is essential.

About the end of September remove the plants to the greenhouse. The stage should be covered with coke breeze or fine gravel. When the buds appear give weak liquid fertiliser once a week until the flowers are fully developed. A free circulation of air is advised, but cold draughts must be avoided. Watch for damp, and if leaves or flower stems are affected they must be removed right down to the corm to prevent further damage.

Cyclamen can be grown on for a second or third year with good results. After flowering, water is partially withheld, and the plants are stood in a cold frame. When there is no danger from frosts they can be given a shady position outside and enough water to prevent the soil becoming dust dry. Here they will rest till about the middle of August. Clean off dead foliage and repot. Reduce the ball of soil and place in pots that will just take the roots. After potting stand the plants in a cold frame, and keep the lights some-what close and the interior fairly moist. Spray the corms daily. In a few weeks growth will be active, when any that need it can be transferred to larger pots. Aftercare is the same as for seedlings.

PROPAGATION. By seed, as in the preceding cultural directions.

Endymion: *Endymion hispanicus* is not usually grown in pots, but it does make one of the loveliest displays provided the bulbs are not hurried into blossom. They are like very improved woodland bluebells (*E. non-scriptus*). The stems, however, are harder and consequently they keep perfectly upright. Pot in September or October, grow absolutely cold and do not attempt any forcing until the beginning of March, and even then only about 13 °C (55 °F) should be given, otherwise the stems will become thin and spoil the display.

The outstanding blue is Excelsior, but the whites, pinks, and rosy forms are all worth a place in the greenhouse.

Eucharis: This is a stove house bulbous subject belonging to the amaryllids. It is often called the Amazon lily, and is probably one of the whitest and most beautifully scented of all bulbs.

SPECIES. The favourite species is *Eucharis grandiflora*, often called *E. amazonica*, which will bloom at frequent intervals from March to October and sometimes later still.

CULTIVATION. Much depends on the right type of compost being used which should be made up of 2 parts loam, 1 part peat, a little rotted manure, and some coarse sand. Bulbs should be potted in spring, putting 6 to a 10-in. pot and carefully watered until roots are being made. In potting, the compost must be made quite firm, and the bulbs should not be covered completely until growth has obviously started; frequent syringing must follow until about November when only a little syringing or watering will be required, thereafter, until spring.

In spring more water must be given and generous quantities will be needed all the summer, together with much syringing. During winter the bulbs are partially at rest and consequently need little water. Feeding with a liquid fertiliser is essential during the growing season. A humid atmosphere and considerable warmth are required at all times, with a minimum winter temperature of 13 °C (55 °F).

PROPAGATION. By means of offsets taken from the old bulbs in spring and potted up singly at first in a 6-in. pot, then placed three or four in a larger pot. Seeds (if obtainable) can also be used for this purpose but they require a very hot, moist temperature to germinate.

Freesia: Since the advent of the beautifully coloured hybrids these charming bulbous plants have become extremely popular.

SPECIES. The old types are still highly prized for their fragrance, and they include *Freesia refracta* (yellow), *F. refracta alba* (white) and *leichtlinii* (cream and deep yellow). Glorious hybrids which are noted for their strong growth and robust constitution rank now amongst the most important recent additions to greenhouse plants. Among the named hybrids are Buttercup (primrose yellow with orange shading, highly scented), Carnival (red), Orange Sun, Sapphire (violet), and Show Queen. In addition, there are strains which contain primrose and yellow shades mixed, also new hybrids mixed, which include varieties of rose, pink, salmon, orange, apricot, mauve, lavender, etc. All are free flowering and produce branching sprays of sweetly scented blossoms, most fragrant when they are white or yellow.

CULTIVATION. Bulbs – or corms, as they should technically be called – are available from July onwards, and can be potted from August to October. Pots 5 and 6 in. in diameter are usually chosen and well provided with drainage. The compost consists of fibrous loam, 3 parts, and 1 part leafmould, dry rotted manure and sand, in equal proportions. Six or eight full-sized corms are enough for a 6-in. pot, and their tops should be about an inch below the surface of the soil. A good depth of compost is important, and for this reason some growers use boxes rather than pots, to ensure really good growth.

Stand them in a cold frame, water in, and shade. Keep the compost moist and admit plenty of ventilation. Here they will remain until the end of September when they can be removed to the greenhouse. If flowers are desired at Christmas the bulbs potted early in August must be gradually inured to a temperature of 13–16°C (55–60°F). Successive batches will be introduced to gentle warmth, and so keep up a display for a lengthened period. The compost is kept moist, and when the pots are filled with roots freesias benefit by weak liquid fertiliser at alternate waterings. Supports will be required, as the leaves will be up to 12 in. high, and the flowering stems are longer and tend to be rather floppy. After flowering the bulbs are allowed to dry off naturally on a shelf, but the roots will require moisture until the foliage dies down. A rest in a sunny place with no water is then allowed till the end of July, when the corms are shaken out of the old compost and graded. Flowering bulbs are potted up, and the next size can be placed thickly in pans or boxes to be grown on.

PROPAGATION. Named varieties can only be increased by off-sets in the manner above described, as that is the only sure means of keeping the stock true to character.

Freesias are also easily raised from seeds, and it is now estab-lished practice among commercial growers to raise them from seed sown in April. This could be a very interesting exercise for the enthusiastic amateur particularly if he wishes to produce freesias as cut flowers for the house. The seeds have a hard coat and will germinate more quickly if soaked in water for twenty-four hours before sowing. They are best sown singly where they are to grow, as they produce a long tap root and breaking this is a severe check to growth. As with the corms, six or eight seeds can be placed in a 6-in. pot. Place in a propagating frame at 18°C (60°F) and after germination move them to a cooler part of the house. In June they can be stood out in a cold, shaded frame, and treated as for corms. Flowering from seed-grown freesias can be expected from October onwards.

Gladiolus: The dwarf types of the colvillei group are ideal for early blooming in pots. They should be potted in September, kept in frames, and brought into a warm house during March. This is another bulb which resents hard forcing. The large-flowered group and the primulinus types are also grown in pots but in this case large pots, say 8 or 9 in. in diameter, will be necessary. Compost should be loamy and rich. Pot up in October or early in the New Year. It is not necessary to plunge these bulbs in ashes.

Haemanthus: Bulbous rooted plants from South Africa and, like most other Cape subjects, they enjoy plenty of sunshine.

SPECIES. The chief are *Haemanthus albiflos* (white), *H. coccineus* (scarlet), *H. katherinae* (deep red), *H. natalensis* (green and orange), *H. puniceus* (orange-scarlet), and *H. tigrinus* (deep crimson). They mostly grow to between 1 and 2 ft. tall. Chiefly spring and early summer flowering, but much depends on the cultivation. *H. nata-lensis* flowers in February.

CULTIVATION. After flowering bulbs make their annual growth; during this period the roots must be well supplied with water. Well rooted specimens can be stimulated with weak liquid fertiliser. Any repotting is done immediately after flowering, but annual disturbance of the roots is not desirable. The compost is made up of sandy loam and fibrous peat in equal parts. Keep the bulbs well down or quite buried in the compost. When growth is completed the plants are gradually dried off. Give a decided rest and expose the bulbs to full sunshine. *H. coccineus* requires a minimum winter temperature of 13°C (55°F), the others are happy with cool greenhouse temperatures.

PROPAGATION. Stock is increased by offsets, removed when the plants begin to grow, and potted off singly. Careful watering is essential until root action is vigorous. Young plants can be given a higher temperature, which will encourage them to attain flowering size more quickly.

Hippeastrum (Amaryllis): These are among the most showy of all bulbous plants. Under what may be termed normal greenhouse conditions, their large and spectacular trumpet-shaped flowers appear in spring and early summer but where heat is available for forcing, plants can be had in bloom as early as January and February.

SPECIES. *Hippeastrum ackermannii, H. aulicum,* and *H. pardinum* are occasionally seen but these have been largely superseded by the varied and brilliant hybrids of recent years. There are varieties which can be found in nurserymen's catalogues, some of which currently available are: Beautiful Lady, light orange-red; Bouquet, salmon; Easterflower, pink; Ludwig's Dazzler, white; Picotee, white, apple-green throat, red spots; Wyndham Hayward, dark red. Unnamed seedlings are also available at a reasonable price.

CULTIVATION. Hippeastrums need rest under cool, dry conditions from October till February unless very early flowers are desired.

While at rest the temperature should be about 10°C (50°F), and water will be almost entirely withheld. With the arrival of February examine the stock weekly and those showing signs of flowering should be arranged in a temperature of 16°C (60°F). Give a thorough watering with tepid water, and clean off loose scales around the bulb. By this method a succession of bloom is kept up.

Another plan often adopted is to divide the stock into three batches, and then introduce them to more warmth at intervals of three weeks, beginning at the end of February. Well soak the roots, and then apply water sparingly until the flower spikes are visible. An average temperature of 16°C (60°F) is ample.

Frequent or annual repotting is not advisable, but an inch or so of topsoil can be removed and replaced with a rich compost. The best time for this work is the spring, just when the plants are starting into growth. Good drainage is essential, and a few pieces of loam fibre should be placed over the crocks to ensure a free outlet for water. The compost is made up of good turfy loam with a sprinkling of rotted manure and sharp sand. Pot firmly, and when the operation is completed the bulb should be partially out of the compost.

After the flowering period the plants will need warm, moist conditions to enable them to complete their season's growth. During this time the roots will require plenty of water, moderate ventilation, and a thin shading when the sun is very bright. By the end of the summer growth will be nearly completed and somewhat drier conditions should prevail.

The drying off must be gradual. When growth is finished place the plants in a frame fully exposed to the sun. This will help in ripening the bulbs. Afterwards a decided rest is allowed in a cool house, and here they will remain until the flowering season.

PROPAGATION. Special varieties are increased by offsets when repotting. Pot up singly, and give the same treatment as to old plants.

Many growers cross-fertilise fine varieties and save their own seeds with a view to obtaining improved forms. Such seeds should be sown directly they are ripe in well-drained pans filled with sandy compost. Place them in a propagating frame or in a temperature of 18°C (65°F) and cover the pan with a pane of glass until the seedlings appear. When large enough the young plants should be pricked off in pots or pans an inch or so apart. Keep them growing steadily through the winter in a temperature of 16°C (60°F) and give enough water to maintain the foliage in healthy activity. In the spring they will be potted off singly, and until the bulbs approach flowering size no decided drying off is recommended. If, however, any plants show signs of resting, the supply of water should be reduced.

Hyacinth: These are great favourites and one of the easiest bulbs to force so long as one follows the common-sense of not being in too great a hurry. The earliest to bloom are the Roman hyacinths, which, if potted in August and plunged under the ashes for five weeks, can then be placed in cold frames for a time before being taken into a slightly warm house in November. If subjected to sharp heat in early December they should be in full bloom at Christmas. The larger flowered types will come later, though here again, by potting early and bringing them into good heat by easy stages, the majority can be made to bloom at the end of January, and by putting in enough bulbs it allows a succession of bloom right into April. By using pre-treated or prepared bulbs these can now also be brought into flower by Christmas.

Like all bulbs, hyacinths resent too much water when first potted, but as roots become numerous, plenty may be given so long as the pots are well drained. Plunge the bulbs in ashes as soon as potted for five or six weeks, and when taking out of the plunge bed and putting into frames keep the bleached crowns darkened for a week or so, giving light gradually until the normal green colour appears in the crown.

Best grown three or more in a pot, it is important to use the same variety in the pot otherwise a slight variation in time of blooming will spoil the effect.

As to varieties, there is a very long list to choose from in a wide assortment of colours, and any good bulb catalogue will give the grower a selection specially suitable for pot cultivation. The 'prepared' bulbs should be chosen for the flowering period following the Roman type, as these come into bloom very early in the year with very little forcing.

Iris: There are a vast number of species which respond to pot cultivation, notably those which bloom in the first months of the year with no heat whatever. These are widely used as pot subjects for alpine houses, but the owner of a mixed greenhouse should also include them in his collection for the show they give with no trouble and without much warmth being necessary. These sorts are mainly dwarf and grow only a few inches high. Six to eight bulbs can be placed in a 4-in. pot, and if potted in September and given frame treatment all the time until January they are quite easy to grow. These early species include *Iris reticulata* (blue) and its various forms, *I. histrioides* (blue), *I. histrio* (porcelain blue), and *I. danfordiae* (golden yellow).

Another useful winter iris is *I. tingitana* which, potted in early September, may be made to bloom in December if given slight warmth at the beginning of that month. This is a delightful blue, with a heavy splash of orange on its 'falls', and reminds one of the Spanish iris.

Dutch and Spanish irises are amongst the easiest of all to grow and make a grand show in April. Plant in September and keep cool till March, when the slightest artificial heat will bring them into bloom. The colours in both groups are delightful, embracing purple, blue, white, yellow, lilac, and heliotrope and lilac.

None of these should be plunged in ashes, but rather allowed to grow naturally.

Ixia: These beautifully coloured flowers, with their wiry stems and grassy foliage, do not get the attention they should from gardeners. They are not difficult to grow and need the same treatment as freesias. One of the main points to observe is to avoid over-watering, especially in winter, and they are best grown cool and should not be forced if the best results are to be obtained. They bloom at the end of April as a rule in a cool house.

Lachenalia: This family, known as the Cape cowslip, is one of the most beautiful of all pot-grown bulbs, and in recent years much progress has been made with it, so that there are now many named varieties of more than average merit. They are very effective in hanging baskets as well as making good pot plants. While it does not require much heat, it will not be happy in a purely cold house. The temperature during winter should be round about 7– 10°C (45–50°F). Perhaps the best known of all species is *Lachenalia aloides nelsonii*, a rich golden yellow, which blooms so freely and is so adaptable to pot cultivation. The leaves of many varieties are beautifully marked or spotted, while the flowers embrace strikingly contrasting colours which melt into each other in a fascinating manner.

Another good sort is *L. aloides* itself, with reddish bells suffused with citron and green, and there are also a number of hybrids of both these species which are delightfully coloured and respond so freely to pot cultivation.

The secret of growing good lachenalias lies in getting them potted early, and early August is probably the best time. The bulbs should be planted 2 or 3 in. apart, with their tops covered to a depth of about half an inch, using a rich but open compost. Put the pots into a shaded frame until growth begins, when all the light available (other than exceptionally fierce sunshine) should be given. Grow them in winter near the light and again pay special attention to watering.

After flowering the bulbs must be allowed to dry off gradually and then spend the summer on a greenhouse shelf, still in the compost where they will 'bake' and ripen, ready for potting in August. They can easily be propagated from seed, or by offsets, and treated in the same way as freesias. They can also be grown from leaf cuttings.

Lapeirousia: A small genus of pretty little bulbous perennials from the Cape of Good Hope.

SPECIES. The principle species is *Lapeirousia cruenta* (recently changed to *L. laxa*). Flowers scarlet, with crimson blotches, during July and August. Height about 9 in. Other species are *L. juncea* (bright pink) and *L. grandiflora* (red and yellow).

CULTIVATION. Place several bulbs in a 5- or 6-in. pot, in a mixture of loam and leafmould with plenty of sand. Repot when dormant, and directly growth is visible keep the roots well supplied with water. After flowering and when the foliage has died down, a thorough rest is allowed. Expose the pots to full sunshine, and withhold water until early spring.

These plants can also be grown in a cold frame and on a warm sheltered border.

PROPAGATION. By seeds, in spring in a warm house, and by small bulbs at the time of potting.

Leucocoryne: This bulb, introduced from Chile many years ago, is one of the loveliest of all pot bulbs. Its clear blue flower with a white centre and a number of golden anthers issuing from the funnel-like throat is most attractive, and several of these are borne on long thin wiry stems during spring. It objects to hard forcing, but responds to a little gentle heat. It has a pleasing fragrance which adds much to its charm, and it well deserves the name of Glory of the Sun. There is only one species grown here, *Leucocoryne ixioides odorata*, and it requires the same treatment as freesias.

Lilium: Although most members of this beautiful genus can be grown in pots for greenhouse decoration, there are a few that are especially valuable for the greenhouse or conservatory.

SPECIES. Among the best is glorious *Lilium auratum*, a magnifi-

Top: Tritonia crocata
Bottom left: Nerine sarniensis *Bottom right: Hippeastrum*

cent plant which produces its gorgeous flowers in August and September. It grows from 3 to 5 ft. high. *L. longiflorum*, with its varieties *giganteum* and *harrisii*, both white, are excellent for forcing. The most popular, perhaps, is *L. speciosum*, with its varieties *album*, *magnificum*, *melpomene* and *rubrum*. They constitute a charming group, whose flowering period can be extended over several months. With little or no forcing, beyond being in a greenhouse, the plants will be in bloom from July to September.

If only one lily is grown it should be *L. regale*, the royal lily, from Western China. It produces sturdy stems 3 to 4 ft. high and several large trumpet-shaped flowers. It is more or less white, with the centre flushed with yellow. Externally the blooms are streaked with brown.

Lilium sulphureum is a tall grower with large, tubular white flowers and rich yellow throat. This plant grows best if planted out in a greenhouse bed or border. From these two species a series of seedlings has been raised, and they are known as sulphurgale hybrids. These show considerable variation.

Lilium henryi has been described as the orange-yellow *speciosum*, and it succeeds fairly well in pots, but still better when planted out. There are a large number of lilies which, though ordinarily grown outside, will make ideal pot plants. Amongst these are *L. brownii*, *L. monadelphum*, *L. szovitzianum*, *L. testaceum* and *L. willmottiae*.

CULTIVATION. Always make a start with good bulbs, and they should be potted in the autumn or early winter. The size of the pot will depend upon the circumference of the bulb. Most of them will go in 6-in. pots, or three bulbs in the 10-in. size. Many of them will bloom in these containers, but strong growers, such as *L. auratum*, *L. henryi*, and some of *L. regale*, may need potting on when growth begins. Good drainage must be provided. The compost consists of turfy fibrous loam (2 parts), leafmould or peat (1 part), and rotted manure (1 part) with a sprinkling of gritty sand. Make the compost fairly firm, and place the bulbs sufficiently low in the pots to allow space for topdressing. This will be done when the stems start to push out roots. Many lilies are what is known as stem rooting, because they send out roots from the lower part of the stem as well as from the base of the bulb.

After repotting stand them in a cold frame, and if possible protect from frosts. Keep the compost just moist. If overdone with water basal roots will fail to develop, and poor flowers will be the result.

This lovely spring conservatory scene includes primulas, daffodils, poinsettias, ferns and cinerarias displayed on tiered staging

When growth begins in the spring a few of the most forward can be brought into the greenhouse. The pots should be filling with roots, consequently more water will be necessary. Keep them near the glass, and attend to topdressing and repotting where this is advisable.

Further batches should be introduced to the greenhouse later on, and in May the remainder left in the frame may be stood outside. Plunge the pots in ashes. Here they can remain until the flower buds are visible. By adopting the above method the season of flowering will be considerably prolonged.

From the time the pots are well filled with roots until the buds begin to open weak liquid fertiliser should be given.

When in the greenhouse lilies enjoy plenty of light and a free circulation of air. They must also be kept clear of greenfly.

Do not neglect the plants after flowering. Stand them in the open, but keep the roots moist until the foliage dies down. It is essential to keep the basal roots healthy, so even when no top growth is visible the soil must not be allowed to become dust dry.

Old bulbs should be repotted early in winter; remove all the old compost possible, but do not destroy any living roots.

PROPAGATION. Lilies may be raised from seeds. They can be sown either in the autumn or spring, and will germinate in a warm greenhouse or cold frame. Sow in boxes of light compost and when the seedlings have made their third leaf they must be pricked off in boxes or in a frame. A light compost 3 or 4 in. deep is needed, and the seedlings should be 2 in. apart. If kept growing steadily either in pots or in a partially shaded border, they will begin to bloom about two years after sowing the seeds. Some species produce bulbils in the axils of the leaves towards the end of the growing season. These can be removed just before the stems die down and treated the same as seedlings.

Bulbs grown in the open ground increase in a natural manner by offsets, but pot-grown plants have not the same freedom for development. Propagation by scales is practised by experts; that, however, is scarcely a task for the average gardener.

Muscari: The grape hyacinth makes a perfect pot plant so long as one is patient. It will force, but it never makes the good specimen potful that it does when allowed to develop slowly in only slight warmth. The dark blue spikes of *Muscari botryoides* make a grand contribution to the early March display, and the lighter Heavenly Blue is a good companion. Pot in September or October and plunge them in ashes, though they do not need to be in the plunge very long and a month is usually quite enough. After that, grow them in a cold house or frame, and avoid any damage to the foliage which adds so much to their beauty. Give slight heat from mid-January onwards and the result should be more than satisfactory.

Narcissus: Here is one of the largest families used for growing in pots, and one of the easiest. Every one of the divisions or groups into which the family is split will provide numerous species or varieties for this purpose, and it would take far more space than can be allowed here to give a full list of either. The grower should consult a comprehensive bulb catalogue, where he will find out those specially useful for this purpose and choose his own colours and types.

For early flowering he will choose the old sorts like Paper White, Soleil d'Or, and Grand Monarque, which come out at Christmas time with only the slightest warmth, but after that he has the whole range of other sorts open to him, especially the Trumpet and Barri groups, which probably contain the gems of the family. In the first of these there is the popular King Alfred, one of the grandest daffodils for greenhouse decoration, but there are very many others as well, especially the newer and larger white trumpets and the bicolours. It is rather a question of one's own taste as to what is chosen. Pre-cooled bulbs of some of the established favourites are available which brings them into flower two to three weeks earlier than ordinary bulbs.

All narcissi should be potted in August and September, using a compost that is about 4 parts loam to 1 of peat. It should be rich and, if possible, full of fibre so as to avoid soil clogging during winter. The John Innes No. 1 potting compost is quite suitable, so are the loamless mixtures. Pot the bulbs firmly and put them at once into the plunge bed, covering the larger pots with 5 in. of ashes. Here they will stay for six weeks, by which time they will have filled their pots with roots and made an inch or two of foliage. From the plunge bed put them into frames and shade for a week till the spears of foliage turn greenish, and after that expose to light and air all the time. The earliest sorts may be taken into slight warmth at the end of November and the rest in successional batches until March, by which time even the latest group – the poeticus – should be coming into bloom quite naturally.

Avoid premature forcing, and wait until the bud is well out of the bulb before giving anything in the way of sharp heat. Never allow the roots to dry out, especially as the spring days become warm. Stake early to support the foliage. After flowering, the bulbs should be put outside to ripen, leaving the foliage and roots intact and undisturbed. Such bulbs will be useful in the garden, but are no use for forcing two years running.

Nerine: Nerines are among the most beautiful of greenhouse bulbous plants, and recently they have become very popular, owing to the introduction of many fine hybrids. The species are natives of South Africa. The flowers are produced in umbels of six to upwards of twenty blooms, on stout stems from 1 to 2 ft. high. All flower from August to October.

Among the best are *Nerine fothergillii major* (brilliant salmon red, shaded scarlet) and *N. sarniensis*, Guernsey Lily (crimson, light red, pink). There are several varieties of this fine plant, such as *venusta* (scarlet) and *corusca major* (fiery orange-scarlet). There are many named hybrids in brilliant and attractive colours. Moreover these are strong growers and free bloomers. A few especially noteworthy are Mrs H. J. Elwes (delicate shell pink), Carolside (salmon pink), Lady Cynthia Colville (blush white), Rotherside (rosy orange), and Lucifer (deep crimson-scarlet). Mixed unnamed seedlings of more than average merit can be obtained at a reasonable cost. Newly introduced named varieties can be obtained from nurserymen who specialise in them.

Nerines do not require great heat, and may be grown in any greenhouse from which frost is excluded. Their chief requirements are ample ventilation and plenty of sunshine. These plants flower most freely when well established, so repotting will only be necessary every third or fourth year. This should be done in August, just as growth begins. The compost consists of sandy loam (3 parts), well-rotted manure (1 part), and a little sand, or they will grow satisfactorily in the John Innes mixtures. Provide good drainage, and half bury the bulb when repotting takes place.

One average-sized bulb will need a 3- or 4-in. pot, but if there is plenty of stock, three to five bulbs can be planted in pots 5 and 6 in. in diameter. Immediately after flowering the growing season begins, and continues till about May. During this period keep the roots well supplied with water, and feed established plants with liquid fertiliser. A temperature of 4–8°C (40–45°F) will suffice.

When the foliage begins to die off, gradually reduce the water supply, and finally withhold until autumn, when the flowering season begins. While at rest expose the pots to the sun. A greenhouse shelf is just the position, and failing this a cold frame. If stood outdoors they are liable to get soaked with rain.

Nerines need a good growing season and afterwards a thorough ripening. Propagation is by offsets removed when repotting. They should be treated the same as older plants, but it may take two or three years before they attain flowering size. New varieties are obtained from seeds which are sown directly they are ripe. They will germinate in a warm propagating frame. Prick off when large enough, and encourage as much growth as possible, the first year.

Ornithogalum: An extensive genus of bulbous plants, chiefly native of South Africa. A few are useful for a cool greenhouse.

SPECIES. *Ornithogalum arabicum*, S. Europe; *O. biflorum*, Chile and Peru; *O. longebracteatum*, South Africa.

Ornithogalum arabicum is the Arabian Star of Bethlehem, a good decorative, free-flowering plant. The fragrant flowers are borne in umbels about 6 in. in diameter. They are large and pure white with a black centre. It is easily forced into bloom, or may be allowed to flower naturally in the greenhouse.

CULTIVATION. Pots should be well drained. Compost consists of loam and peat in equal parts. Place six to eight bulbs in a 5-in. pot. Arrange in a frostproof frame until growth begins, and then transfer to the greenhouse near the roof glass. Give plenty of water during their period of activity, and afterwards gradually dry off. Similar treatment suits other species, but *O. longebracteatum* should be potted singly in 5- or 6-in. pots.

PROPAGATION. By offsets when dormant.

Oxalis (Wood Sorrel): It is surprising that at least a few of the species of oxalis are not more largely grown. They possess an elegant habit of growth, and produce flowers of great beauty. They are tuberous or bulbous rooted, and more or less deciduous. Grown as basket plants, they are very effective, while they may also be placed in pans and suspended from the roof. As pot subjects they are also an acquisition to greenhouse or conservatory.

SPECIES. The best are *Oxalis purpurata bowiei*, with large deep pink flowers and deep green handsome foliage, August flowering; *O. cernua*, the Bermuda buttercup, yellow, spring; *O. tetraphylla*, purplish violet, June; *O. rosea*, rose, spring; *O. variabilis*, white or rose, according to the variety, autumn flowering; and *O. versicolor*, crimson, in winter. *O. rosea* and *O. floribunda* may often be seen flowering profusely in cottage windows.

CULTIVATION. All are easily grown in John Innes composts. The general potting time is September, but the August-flowering species may be potted later, any time to March. Five-inch pots or baskets are employed. Place the bulbs half an inch deep and about half an inch apart. When potted give a thorough watering, and then keep just moist until growth is well above the soil. Arrange the pots in a cool greenhouse. Well-established plants will benefit by an occasional application of liquid fertiliser while in active growth.

After flowering, when the foliage shows signs of decay, gradually reduce the water supply. When fully dried off remove the dead leaves, and keep perfectly dry until the period arrives for repotting.

PROPAGATION. Effected by seeds, or by offsets when roots are dormant. The latter are potted up and treated the same as full-sized corms or tubers. Seeds may be sown in pans of light compost and germinated in a warm greenhouse. Prick off in pans when large enough, and be careful not to overdo the watering. If given ordinary care and attention they will soon attain flowering dimensions.

Pancratium: The subjects here referred to are handsome bulbous plants suitable for pot cultivation in a cool greenhouse.

SPECIES. *Pancratium illyricum* bears snowy-white fragrant flowers. Height 2 ft. *P. maritimum* is also white and delightfully fragrant. Height about 2 ft. Both are summer flowering.

CULTIVATION. Frequent repotting is not needed; the plants bloom more freely when well established and pot bound. When fresh compost becomes a necessity it should consist of 3 parts loam and well-rotted manure with a little sharp sand. Repot in spring. They need plenty of water throughout the growing season, and little when at rest. Plants that have not been disturbed for several years will benefit by liquid fertiliser during the summer months. A winter temperature of 4–10°C (40–50°F) will be ample.

PROPAGATION. By offsets in spring or whenever the plants are repotted.

Polianthes: These are the tuberoses noted for their sweetly scented flowers. They can be had in bloom for several months of the year.

The main species grown is *Polianthes tuberosa*. There are two kinds – the double American dwarf or Pearl tuberose, and Early African. Both are white flowered. Bulbs of the American Pearl are available from January to April, and those of Early African in October.

CULTIVATION. Bulbs may be potted at frequent intervals if a continual supply of bloom is required. If only a small quantity is grown, one bulb should be placed in a 3-in. pot but, to economise space, three or four can be set in a 6-in. pot with equal success. The pots must be well drained, and the compost made up of fibrous loam (3 parts) and leafmould (1 part), with a little sand. After potting they are often plunged in bottom heat in a temperature of 16°C (60°F) until growth is well advanced. The amateur, however, would do better if he placed the pots in a warm greenhouse 10–13°C (50–55°F), and then gave each pot a watering with tepid water. Allow the compost to dry again before more moisture is applied. This treatment is continued until root action is evident by the plumping up of the bulbs. Avoid over-watering in the early period of growth.

At this stage a few of the most forward plants can be introduced to a temperature of 16°C (60°F), when the roots are kept moist. Later batches are more easily dealt with because the weather is more congenial and the greenhouse much warmer.

After flowering the growth will gradually die down, and the bulbs should be rested in a temperature of 13–16°C (55–60°F). Early in the spring they can be repotted, but they will not produce such fine spikes as the first season.

PROPAGATION. By offsets, but it is far better to purchase fresh bulbs annually.

Scilla: The small *Scilla sibirica*, grown four or five in a 3-in. pot or several in a shallow pan, makes a delightful contribution to the spring greenhouse display. The small blue flowers on 3- or 4-in. stems are no trouble to produce, but it is wise to buy the very best type, as some of the newer sorts, like Spring Glory, are great improvements on the ordinary sibirica.

Tritonia: The tritonias are South African corms from the Cape, rather like montbretias in appearance, and not as generally grown as they might be, as there is no difficulty about cultivation; they bloom when most of the other spring flowering bulbs have just finished. They grow about a foot high, and are excellent for a cool greenhouse.

Species and varieties commonly grown are *Tritonia crocata*, orange-red, Prince of Orange, Orange Delight, and White Beauty.

During November, put five corms in a 5-in. pot, using a compost consisting of loam (2 parts) and peat (1 part), with plenty of sand to ensure the good drainage that they like. Arrange the pots in a cold frame, and when growth is well advanced place in a cool greenhouse where they will receive plenty of light. Moderate watering while in growth is required, less when dying down, and eventually they should be kept dry until January or whenever growth starts again. Annual repotting is not needed – in fact, better specimens are obtained if they are not disturbed for several years. They will force slightly, but much better results are obtained if they are allowed to develop at their own pace in a cool greenhouse. They are almost hardy and therefore do not like much in the way of artificial heat.

Propagation is by offsets removed when repotting, or by seed.

Tulipa: Here is another family as large and useful as the narcissi, for with the right choice of types and varieties the tulip may be had in flower in pots from Christmas till the end of May.

The earliest to bloom are the small Duc van Thol sorts, which are so familiar at Christmas time in florists' windows, followed by the early species and the early Dutch sorts such as Mon Tresor, Artus, General de Wet, Prince of Austria, Vermilion Brilliant, etc., these being followed by the Mendel and Triumph groups, then the Darwins, and ultimately the May-flowering and Cottage sorts. It will be seen that by making a judicious selection one can have tulips for nearly six months.

In one sense the tulip is most accommodating, for it can be forced or grown cold, but it is almost best to grow them cool where possible, because the flowers last longer and have a much more fleshy texture than if forced.

The early tulips should be potted in September, but the others can all wait until November if other work prevents them being potted before. For the earlies a light sandy mixture is best, but for the later ones a slightly heavier one is better. In fact, the May-flowering and Cottage types like a really heavy compost so long as it is reasonably well drained.

To force tulips early, it is necessary to pot and plunge them in September, and when taken out of the plunge, the pots should be placed in a frame and kept dark. This continual darkening – or partial darkening – will cause the foliage to 'draw', and this encourages the bud to leave the bulb, so once this has happened the pots can be placed in sharp heat and still kept partially dark. Soon the flower buds will be seen developing and swelling and they can then be put into a lighter place to open properly.

The later sorts do not need this darkening process, but with very little heat will develop naturally in any slightly warm house.

The later ones must be kept near the light, otherwise the stems may be weak, and some are very definitely better if allowed to remain in the frames until the buds are opening.

Apart from the groups of what may be called the florists' tulip and its various hybrids, there are a number of serviceable species which make grand pot plants, and all are best if grown in frames and given slight warmth when coming into flower. The following may be considered as particularly useful: *Tulipa biflora* (cream), *clusiana* (white, streaked with red), *dasystemon* (creamy white with yellow eye), *eichleri* (crimson/scarlet), *fosteriana* (very brilliant scarlet), *kaufmanniana* (creamy white, streaked yellow with red margins), and *praestans* (brilliant scarlet).

Vallota: This is the Scarborough lily, known botanically as *Vallota speciosa*. It is probably one of the easiest bulbs for the gardener to grow, and looks rather like a small hippeastrum in flower. The lily-like blooms are an intense red, produced in spikes during August and September. There are several varieties such as *eximia*, large flowered to 4 in. wide, *minor*, smaller in all parts, and *delicata*, salmon pink. It is a native of South Africa.

Bulbs can be bought growing at any season of the year, but spring or summer are the best times to buy loose bulbs for potting and flowering in late summer – early autumn. One bulb is put in a 4- or 5-in. pot, or three in a 7-in. size, being nearly buried and the compost made fairly firm. The compost can consist of 3 parts loam and 1 part peat, with a little sand added, or the John Innes No. 2 potting compost is equally good. The pot is then put in a temperature of 10°C (50°F) and a sunny position. Little water is given until root action starts and growth is apparent, and then the plant is watered moderately. After the flowers have faded and have been removed, watering is increased while the bulb makes its main growth, but once the leaves begin to die down, less water is given until growth ceases altogether, when just enough water should be given to keep the compost barely moist.

Vallotas should be grown undisturbed for several years, but when repotting does become necessary, it should be done in early summer. Feeding with a liquid fertiliser during the growing season will be necessary after the first year; in winter a high temperature is not necessary or advisable, but it is best not to let it fall below 4°C (40°F).

Propagation is by offsets removed at potting time, and grown on in small pots with one of the composts mentioned previously.

Veltheimia: A small genus of bulbous plants that usually flower during the winter or spring months. The leaves are broad and about 10 in. long, sometimes much waved at the margins, while the flower scapes attain a height of 1 or $1\frac{1}{2}$ ft.

SPECIES. The best is *Veltheimia viridifolia* (green leaved), with flesh-coloured flowers, which are produced between August and February. *V. glauca*, with glaucous foliage, is red and yellow, and flowers in early spring. There is a variety *rubescens* with reddish blossoms.

CULTIVATION. Both new bulbs and old plants can be repotted in autumn, and they will thrive in a mixture of loam and peat with a little sand. Grow in a cool house where there is plenty of light. Frequent repotting is not advised. Give plenty of water when in full growth, after flowering a less quantity will suffice.

PROPAGATION. By offsets when repotting plants, or by leaves. These are pulled off close to the bulb and placed in pots of sandy soil similar to cuttings. They will eventually produce small bulbs at their base.

CHAPTER TEN

Shrubs for the Greenhouse – for forcing or early flowering

Hardy flowering shrubs are largely employed for decorative purposes from Christmas until March or April. The time of flowering will depend on the amount of heat employed, but even in a cool greenhouse many shrubs can be had in bloom several weeks in advance of those growing in the open. It will of course depend entirely on the greenhouse owners interests and the size of the greenhouse whether he forces shrubs or not.

One of the best shrubs for early work is *Forsythia intermedia spectabilis*, a free-flowering plant with bright golden blooms. It should be grown outside, lifted just before Christmas, and placed in the greenhouse. With very little warmth the flowers will start to open and, if there are sufficient plants to draw on, a supply of flowers can be kept up till they appear outside. It is ideal for cutting in bud. After flowering, plant out in the border, and in two years they will be well budded and ready again for the greenhouse.

Another good plant is the yellow *Jasminum primulinum*. Others are *Amelanchier lamarckii* (white); *Corylopsis pauciflora* (pale yellow); various hybrid cytisus; *Daphne mezereum* (pink); *Kalmia angustifolia* (rose); *K. latifolia* (pink); *Laburnum vossii* (yellow); lilac in variety, both white and coloured; *Olearia stellulata* (white); *Osmanthus delavayi* (white, fragrant); *Prunus persica* (pink, double); *P. pseudocerasus* (white); *P. triloba* (peach pink, double, in large pots); *Rhododendron praecox* (rosy purple); *R. racemosum* (rosy pink); *Spiraea arguta* (white); *Staphylea colchica* (white); *Viburnum farreri* (white, fragrant); *V. carlesii* (white and rose); *Wisteria multijuga* (pale rose tipped purple); and *W. sinensis* (lilac).

For later flowering the large-flowered kinds of rhododendrons are suitable, Pink Pearl being one of the best. All the rhododendrons need a peaty soil free of lime. Strong, young, and well-budded plants should be bought or lifted from the open ground in October and placed in pots that will just comfortably take the roots. A loamy compost should be used, and after repotting plunge the pots in ashes in a sheltered, but not shaded, situation outside. Here they will remain until they are brought into the greenhouse.

After the bulk of the chrysanthemums are over there is usually a little space for a few shrubs. In December as many as possible should be placed inside, and for the first fortnight the temperature ought not to rise above 7 or 10°C (45 or 50°F). After that time it can be increased gradually to 18 or 21°C (65 or 70°F) by day. Keep the roots moist and syringe the plants daily with tepid water. The water should also be warm when applied to the roots. When the flowers begin to open a temperature of 13°C (55°F) will be ample and spraying should cease. Further plants can be introduced at intervals of three weeks or a fortnight.

As the forced plants go out of flower a little pruning will be needed. Cut out weak and straggly growths and reduce the shoots that have flowered. Gradually harden off and stand outside in May. Plunge the pots to their rims, supply plenty of water, and keep the foliage free from insect pests. Liquid fertiliser will be beneficial once or twice each week until growth ceases. When not subjected to hard forcing the plants can be grown in pots for several years if they are repotted or topdressed with fresh compost in the early autumn. This remark applies especially to wistaria, kalmia, cytisus, prunus and olearia. Where very early flowers are desired it is best to have two sets of plants and force them in alternate years.

Lilacs are strong-rooting subjects, and in a few years they become too large for pots. They can, however, be planted in a border about June and after two years lifted and potted up.

To get good results from shrubs that are kept in pots for several years they must receive due attention throughout the summer months, especially in regard to watering and feeding during their period of growth. When repotting the compost should consist of fibrous loam, 2 parts, and 1 part in equal portions of leafmould and rotted manure, with a little sand. The John Innes No. 3 potting compost is also suitable. Firm potting should be practised.

Some of the plants, such as forsythia and jasmine, are readily increased from cuttings in the spring. Select young side shoots and place them in a close propagating frame. When rooted harden off and plant outside. It will take several years before they are large enough for pots. It is better to buy specimens of flowering size.

CHAPTER ELEVEN

Vegetables for the Table

Quite apart from the capabilities of greenhouses to provide pleasure and interest in ornamental plants, there has always been a lot of interest in them for more practical purposes. This was increased 30 years ago during the Second World War when it was vital to produce as much food as possible from all sources. The degrees of success and failure were widely varied, but the ultimate result is that vastly more private gardeners are now alive to the utility value of glass than ever before. For this reason it has been considered necessary to include a section dealing with this aspect of greenhouses in the garden.

It is fully realised that not every gardener is sufficiently keen on growing food crops under glass to think of erecting special types of greenhouses for the purpose. This, of course, is the essential for maximum and economical production. In this section, therefore, houses of purely utilitarian character will first be described, whilst the more limited possibilities of growing food crops in the ordinary amateur's greenhouse will be dealt with for the benefit of those who wish to make the most of the facilities possessed.

Apart from such crops as mushrooms and the vegetables which require darkness for the purpose of blanching, it must be emphasised that the vital necessity in any house which is to produce food crops is maximum daylight. The provision of adequate means of admitting fresh air, without cutting draughts, may well be coupled with the need of daylight. A further requirement is that the structure of the house shall provide every possible foot of growing space, with little room that will require filling with warmth and humidity without adding to production.

Dutch lights

One thing that wartime privations taught us was to economise in building materials by dispensing with everything that could be spared without detriment to the inmates of the structure. That, undoubtedly, was the powerful factor that brought favourable consideration of the type of glasshouse generally described as the Dutch light greenhouse. Dutch lights actually are frame lights composed of large-sized sheets of glass edged with a light frame of wood, instead of our customary heavy end and side pieces with several thinner rafters to hold rows of small sheets of glass. For a Dutch light greenhouse a framework is constructed with eaves at the exact height to enable the top end of a vertical light to rest against and be held to it by a turn button, while the bottom end rests on a basal plate with a ridge to prevent it slipping from position. The two side walls are separated by the exact width to allow two rows of the same sized lights to form a span roof, the centre ridge rafter being held by uprights at the correct height to give a reasonable slope to the roof.

The advantages of such a house are that there are no side walls to cast shade over the root-run in the house; no need for foundations; the length of a house can be extended at will by simply removing an end and adding more lights to sides and roof, and the whole structure can be dismantled and removed to a fresh site should the soil bed become contaminated with plant diseases or otherwise rendered infertile. Small, portable heaters and easily fixed hot-water pipes are made for moderately heating such houses, and whether they are heated or not, the Dutch light type of glasshouse offers more serviceable equipment for cultivation of food crops, other than grapes or tree fruits, on a scale suitable for the amateur cultivator.

The situation for such a house should be in the open, where the sun can reach both sides in turn, the ideal direction in which its ends should stand being north and south in preference to east and west.

Frames

It is sound policy always to provide a few frames as accessory to a greenhouse. These, also, may be of Dutch lights. At certain seasons of the year the frames will accommodate young plants for successional crops at times when there is no room in the greenhouse. At other seasons the frames will themselves mature useful produce, thus bridging over periods when there would be gaps between supplies. A point which should be kept constantly in mind is that the principal object in utilising glass for growing food crops is that there shall be a continuous succession of vegetables and salads for table use in fresh enjoyable condition.

Successional cropping

Owners of greenhouses which are mainly devoted to a miscellaneous assortment of flowering plants are usually content to grow a few tomatoes in summer, or perhaps a cucumber plant or two. Those who have had little experience in that direction will require information on various points of importance. An effort is made to provide that information, but short-sighted conversion of the mixed greenhouse is scarcely enough to turn it into a real utility greenhouse. For that reason the first part of this section of the book is devoted to the greenhouse production of crops during all seasons of the year.

With the type of house already described, if equipped for moderate heating, something of real food value can be produced practically the whole year round. The year can begin with forced seakale and rhubarb. Choice may range between early carrots, radishes, lettuces, chicory, cress, salad onions, early cauliflowers, peas and french beans, vegetable marrows, and extra early new potatoes. Tomatoes or cucumbers will, in the majority of cases, be the choice for summer and autumn crops, although a batch of pot strawberries may have a stronger appeal to some. For late autumn and early winter, salads again come to the forefront.

Soil

For all or any of these crops the first and foremost consideration must be the healthy state and fertility of the root-run provided for the crops. Dutch light houses are primarily constructed to enable crops to be rooted in mother earth. It is quite practicable to fix staging and shelving in this type of house in order to grow plants and crops in pots or boxes. That phase of the subject is dealt with separately, but our present task is concerned with floor beds under glass. It is desirable, whenever possible, to erect the house where the ground has already been well cultivated, but it should also be free from troublesome pests and destructive diseases. It should be as well dug and as judiciously manured as any outdoor ground, and another important point is that it should be well drained. The easy portability of a Dutch light house is of greatest advantage, because it enables the soil bed to be uncovered and exposed to winter's weather when this becomes necessary for sweetening and recuperation.

Tomatoes: So much has been written about tomato cultivation that it seems almost superfluous to attempt to condense into the limited space available the routine principles involved in it.

The general idea of gardeners is to take a summer crop of tomatoes from houses which are occupied by other subjects in late autumn, winter and spring. In such circumstances the main consideration is to get plants well advanced in time to place them in fruiting quarters, but to steer clear of getting plants in good form before those quarters are ready for their reception. Checked or starved and stunted tomato plants get so sadly handicapped that valuable weeks are lost in their recovery and later unchecked plants surpass them in setting, developing and ripening fruit.

Where utility and economic value are studied seriously, the general view is that earliness of ripening fruit is the great factor. That means use of artificial heat, the cost of which has to be offset against the cash value of tomatoes gathered. Where a house is utilised for forcing other crops, it is usually possible to accommodate some tomatoes to replace gathered crops of other kinds, but not many gardeners will find it policy to heat a greenhouse purposely for the production of early tomatoes for home use.

Root-run is a matter for important consideration. In a house that is staged for plants of other kinds, it is usually wisest to utilise boxes or pots for tomatoes. Eight-inch pots will produce good crops, whilst a box that will permit 2 in. of rubble drainage and from 6 to 7 in. depth of compost will be adequate for plants which can have a rooting area of a square foot. That is reckoning that a single row will be grown and trained from the back of the stage up under, but not touching, the roof glass. Needless to say, a tomato house should have a sunny position.

Where a house lends itself to cultivation in floor beds, it is, all things considered, wiser to make up beds above ground level than to dig the soil of the floor itself. Boards, a foot wide, can be placed on edge and held by stakes to form the sides and ends of beds. A layer of drainage can be overlaid with good soil to a depth of 8 in. or thereabouts. Plants can then be trained to perpendicular

Aphelandras, begonias, anthuriums, ferns, columnea, Euphorbia splendens *and* E. pulcherrima *in a warm greenhouse setting*

strings as recommended for climbing beans. The one point I would emphasise is that planting too closely is avoided. Those who have opportunity to see commercial growers' tomato houses at the height of the season are apt to form the idea that the greater the number of plants that can be crowded into available space the better. It requires the skill of experience to grow tomatoes thus. The average gardener will obtain more fruit by allowing plenty of space for air and sunlight between plants. A good plan is to plant double rows at $1\frac{1}{2}$ ft. apart, with 3 ft. between pairs of rows. The plants are then approachable from the wide alleys.

COMPOSTS. For raising plants from seed use sterilised compost of the type known as the John Innes seed compost. Seed can be sown in heat – 16°C (60°F) – in February, and the young plants pricked out and grown on in a temperature of 18–21°C (65–70°F), gradually dropping to 13°C (55°F) at night as the plants grow. Planting out or final potting can be undertaken in about the middle of April, and a little heat may be required at night from then until mid-May to ensure that the temperature does not fall below 10°C (50°F). Fruit should be ready for picking from July. For a cold house, plants are brought in during late April and will ripen from early August. For beds, boxes, or pots, it is an advantage if all soil can be sterilised, if not, use good, fresh, turfy loam, to the extent of 60 per cent.; granulated peat (thoroughly moistened), 30 per cent.; old rotted stable or farmyard manure, passed through a 1-in. mesh sieve, 10 per cent. Alternatively the J.I. potting compost No. 3 can be used. The proportions of these should vary in accordance with the character of the loam and manure. Chemical fertilisers can be used later, either as topdressing or as liquid feeds. Firm planting is essential.

GENERAL CULTIVATION. Cultural instructions have been disbursed of late years with such bewildering freedom that one is reluctant to devote space to more. The chief points are: good ventilation without cutting draughts; water in quantity sufficient to prevent flagging at any time, but never to reach saturation; overhead syringing in the mornings in dry weather; prompt attention to pinching side shoots from axils of leaves; feeding whenever foliage and stems show tendency to weakening, thinness, or paling of colour, but not to cause gouty thickening of stems or coarse flabbiness of leaves. Keep watch for pests and diseases. If an odd plant collapses suddenly, uproot it, and drench the soil from whence it came with a

Top: Echeveria agavoides
Bottom: The compact and showy mammillarias are good cacti for a grower who is short of space

solution of permanganate of potash, using a level teaspoonful of crystals to a gallon of water. Defoliation is sometimes advocated, and this is of value where leaves are shading the trusses, particularly near the base of the plant, and if they are withered or yellowed and of no use; no part of their stalks should be left on the plant.

RING CULTURE. During recent years a successful new system of growing tomatoes has been devised. It is called ring culture, as the plants are grown in bottomless, composition rings which are stood on a base of weathered cinders or shingle. Two different root systems are encouraged to form, fibrous roots in the rings of compost and coarse water roots which penetrate to the cinder base. The main advantage to be gained from this method is that tomatoes can be grown where the ordinary greenhouse soil is contaminated with diseases, such as wilt, or pests, such as eelworms, which affect the root system of the plants.

A bed of weathered ash is laid down to a depth of 4 to 6 in. The ash must not be too fine; $\frac{1}{4}$ to $\frac{1}{8}$ in. is about the right particle size. Unweathered ash must not be used as the sulphur which it contains can cause many troubles. The rings should hold about 14 lb. of compost, and John Innes No. 3 potting compost can be used. Each one should be spaced $1\frac{1}{2}$ ft. apart on the ash base. The young plants can then be placed in the rings as if they were being potted normally in large pots. Water must be given sparingly in the rings at first to encourage roots to penetrate into the ash base. When this occurs watering in the rings should cease and the ashes must be drenched with water daily. However, the compost in the rings should not be allowed to dry out. Suitable tomato feeds for ring culture are available at garden shops, and the recommended amount should be given to the rings only at weekly intervals. Most tomato varieties can be grown successfully by this method.

CULTIVATION ON STRAW BALES. Another system of tomato growing has also been advocated during the last few years, when soil is badly contaminated with pests and diseases, in which the plants are grown on straw bales. For this, wheat straw is best, and the bales are laid flat, on polythene sheeting, and soaked with water, using a total of 9 gallons in several applications over two or three days. The bales should be put in position about 16 days before planting. Fertilisers are then applied to help in the decomposition of the straw, using $1\frac{1}{2}$ lb. nitro chalk to each 56 lb. bale, sprinkled lightly on, and watered in. Another application of 1 lb. is given

3 days later, with a final dressing 3 days after this of: 12 oz. nitro chalk, 18 oz. potassium nitrate, 10 oz. triple superphosphate, 3 oz. ferrous sulphate and 4 oz. magnesium sulphate per bale. They should not be allowed to dry out at any time. Planting can take place when the temperature within the bales has fallen below 38°C (100°F), into a small quantity of potting compost placed in the centre of the bale.

CULTIVATION IN PEAT COMPOST BAGS. This system has been introduced very recently and is easy to follow. The peat compost bags can be bought at garden centres. They should be laid on the greenhouse floor, opened up and the tomatoes can then be planted in them and grown on in the conventional way.

Varieties of tomatoes are so numerous and ever changing that I make no attempt to give a list of names. Any good seedsman's catalogue supplies names in plenty.

Cucumbers: It is not easy to grow cucumbers in a mixed house. In the first place, a considerably higher temperature is required than in the case of tomatoes, whilst the atmosphere must be humid and ventilation in consequence must be restricted.

There are certain kinds of plants that will grow in conjunction with cucumbers; these include gloxinias (sinningias), smithianthas, achimenes, warm house ferns, selaginellas, cannas, and begonias.

If the house is a span-roof structure it is best to place the cucumbers on the shady side of the house, training them up to the apex of the roof, leaving the other side free for pot plants. Training wires should be trained up the side and under the roof at a foot from the glass.

The plants must occupy a bed or ridge of compost on the stage, slates, boards, or corrugated iron being placed over the latticed staging to hold the soil. A compost consisting of rough, turfy loam, rotted stable manure, a liberal sprinkling of bonemeal, and if possible some ashes from the garden rubbish fire, will suit cucumbers. About a bushel of this material will be required for each plant. It should be built in the form of a mound, and about 2 ft. wide at the base. It is necessary that the compost should be thoroughly warm before young plants are introduced.

If the house is well heated and there are hot-water pipes passing close under the stage, the compost will reach a suitable temperature in about two days, but it may be advisable to heat some bricks and then bury these in the soil a few hours before planting, removing them when they have disbursed their heat. Alternatively electric soil heating wires can be put in position before planting.

PLANTING AND TRAINING. Young plants must be healthy, clean, and by no means pot-bound or starved at the time of planting. See that they are well watered with tepid water the day before they are turned out of pots. Make a hole in the centre of the mound just large enough to take the root ball, and gently press the fresh compost around, but not roughly to cause bruising or breakage of the tender roots. Soak the mound of compost with warm water, place a stick to each plant and secure it to the first wire, loosely tying the plant to the cane. Always be careful not to damage the leaves of young plants, but encourage them to grow by frequently syringing with warm water; maintain a good temperature until sunshine reduces the necessity for artificial heat.

Remove side shoots from the lower part of the stem until the wires are reached. Proceed to train the main stem of the plant in a straightforward direction up the roof till the apex is reached, when the growing point must be pinched out. In the meantime side branches should be trained out horizontally on either side. In due course two kinds of flowers will be produced on these side branches; on some of these tiny cucumbers will be visible at the back of the flowers. These are the female flowers and should be retained, the others are male and if the time can be spared should be removed, otherwise seeds form in the fruit, and they become bitter. Generally speaking, it will be advisable in a mixed house to stop the side shoots after two fruits have set, but if the plant is still vigorous and healthy, sublaterals may be allowed to grow from the last joint of each lateral. If growth becomes crowded the number of branches must be reduced, and when these sublaterals have set a fruit each their points should be stopped and further growth pinched out as soon as it can be handled. In other words, one healthy plant can be allowed to produce 10–15 fruits.

WATERING. After a week or two's growth, when white roots will be observed on the surface of the mound of compost, a top-dressing of good loam, and short manure must be spread entirely over the mound to bury these exposed roots to a depth of 2 in. or so, the whole being settled by a good watering with a rosed can.

Cucumbers require an abundance of water, and must never be

allowed to dry at the root; at the same time the foliage must be syringed at least once a day, and when the weather is fine and warm syringing should be carried out both in the morning and afternoon. When the sun gains power it will be advisable to give slight shading by whitewashing the outside of the glass above the plants. As soon as the first fruits begin to develop feeding must commence; this will take the form of weak liquid fertiliser.

VENTILATION AND TEMPERATURE. Ventilation must always be carefully considered; it will be harmful to open ventilators on a cold day when the atmosphere inside the house is heated to a high degree, but when the outside temperature is fairly warm top ventilation will be beneficial, so long as the inside temperature can be maintained at about 24°C (75°F).

As summer advances more ventilation will be required, and the house need not be closed until an hour or so before the sun passes from the roof.

When nights are cool, however, the house should always be closed in time for a good degree of warmth to be attained before sundown, and in conjunction with the rising temperature there should be a sufficient distribution of water on floors and stages to create a humid as well as warm atmosphere.

The greatest checks to successful progress are cold atmosphere, cutting draughts, and lack of moisture, but whilst the latter is very detrimental it must always be carefully observed that stagnation will have disastrous results. First signs of damage from this cause will be a yellowing of the foliage, followed by mildew and decay of leaves. Any foliage that commences to rot must be immediately cut away, and dry flowers of sulphur must be sprinkled about the house. Steps must be taken to raise the temperature sufficiently to allow for ventilation to sweeten the atmosphere and thus restore the plants to a healthy condition.

VARIETIES. For the most part, the needs of a private household for cucumbers are insufficient to justify devoting the whole of a greenhouse to a crop, and the most that need be done is to grow a plant of such a variety as Telegraph in a frame on a hotbed. Cucumbers, in general practice, are kept in close conditions with high temperature and moisture-laden atmosphere, and few other plants, except ferns, can tolerate the close, moist conditions and dense shade under their large spreading leaves.

Of recent years a cucumber has gained popularity by reason of its capability of growing happily in the freer ventilation and comparatively drier atmosphere of a greenhouse occupied by a general assortment of greenhouse plants. The name of this cucumber is Conqueror, and that is the variety I recommend to the gardener who wishes to grow a few cucumbers for home use to select. I have grown it for some years past, and find it excellent in every way for a cold house.

My plan is to grow a couple of plants from seeds sown early in March, and a further couple sown at the beginning of May. I use round cheese boxes (9-in. whalehide containers would be excellent) in which to plant, and provide large-meshed netting supported on canes for the plants to climb. That saves the shading of the stages that would result from training the growths under the roof glass. The cucumbers occupy one end of the greenhouse, and get the benefit of some sunshine, the end being glazed to stage level. The soil is lighter than that used for tomatoes, more manure and some leafmould being used. The syringe is used freely and frequently on the plants, but the house is freely ventilated for the benefit of its other occupants. I have cut good cucumbers from the first plants early in July, and the later plants have provided last fruits in October, the total number from four plants exceeding three dozen, some of which have been over a pound in weight. No other cucumber I have tried as an item in a mixed house has been anything like so successful.

My plants have the growing point pinched out when four good leaves have formed. The growths from the leaf joints are then carried up the netting. Laterals from these are pinched at one leaf joint from an embryo fruit. Sublaterals are again pinched at a leaf beyond the appearance of a fruit. Male blooms are nipped out before fully opened, as I dislike the flavour of fertilised cucumbers. Another point is that cucumbers should not be cut while too young; they are bitter in flavour, but the bitterness passes off as the fruits reach full size. The roots of cucumbers must never be allowed to become dry. Start them with no more than an inch of compost covering the pot ball of earth. Give a mulch of another inch of rich light compost whenever white roots become visible at the surface. Contrive to get the spray of the syringe to the back as well as to the surface of the leaves, otherwise there is risk of attack by red spider, the chief enemy of the cucumber plant.

OTHER CROPS FOR GREENHOUSE CULTIVATION

Aubergine: The egg plant is not often grown in this country, but the purple fruits are delicious when cooked.

It is an annual, and seed can be sown in a temperature of 16°C (60°F) in February. After germination the seedlings are transferred to small pots and gradually potted on until they are in 7-in. pots. Cultivation and temperatures are very similar to those for tomatoes, remembering that they like to be on the warm side. They like a sunny part of the greenhouse and plenty of water when well established. The tip of the main shoot should be pinched out when it is about 6 in. tall, and when fruits have formed on the side shoots these also should have their tips removed. It should be noted that the fruit is purple in colour from the time it is formed, and does not, as is sometimes thought, change from green to purple as it matures. When the fruits begin to swell, feeding with liquid fertiliser at regular intervals is beneficial. The fruits should be picked before they are mature, otherwise they become tough.

Beetroot: Small early beetroot must be reckoned a luxurious addition to a salad in winter and early spring. Summer and autumn crops grow satisfactorily in the open ground, and the last crop of the year will be well enough accommodated in a frame. For the earliest crop, in a warmed greenhouse, a globe variety of deep colour should be grown. Cultural requirements are rich compost, a temperature not above 10°C (50°F), all the daylight possible, and ample watering.

Carrots: For earliest cropping, intercropping between slower growers, the best type of carrot is the very short, small, but tasty early forcing or early frame carrot. This type may be found under various varietal names in different seed merchants' catalogues, but the name is of less importance than the character of the carrot, which should be nearly round or 'wooden-top' shape. This ensures rapid development near the soil surface instead of deep penetration into earth which is cold in the winter months. Seeds of these small, earliest carrots may be sown in January, and with slight heat they will begin to yield succulent young roots for tasty dishes in spring. If broadcast thinly in a bed of well-enriched soil there will be little need for thinning until the largest can be pulled to be cooked whole. Where intercropping is practised – and it certainly should be done within reasonable limits under glass — it is customary to sow these earliest carrots between newly planted cauliflowers.

For a second or later crop, carrots of the stump-rooted type, such as Early Nantes, are best to use. These are best sown in rows which, to economise space for a short-season crop, need not be more than 6 or 7 in. apart, the plants in the rows being thinned to 3 in. at an early stage of growth. Half an inch depth is sufficient at which to sow the seed, and any water used should be tepid.

French Beans: These may be considered among the most important of greenhouse crops. It should not be overlooked that there are climbing varieties as well as dwarfs among french beans, and for practical purposes the climbing haricots and wax pod beans may also be included. The climbers are best adapted for floor bed planting because their pods are lifted nearer to the roof glass and daylight. The dwarfs are more suited for cultivation in pots or boxes, enabling them to be grown on stages instead of at greater distance from the roof.

A friend who grows climbing french and haricot beans with conspicuous success, sows seed in January in a raised bed on the floor of a span-roof greenhouse. Vertical strings are fixed from horizontal rods just above ground level to other rods under the roof. The plants are grown on a double row system with 15 in. between the paired rows and 3 ft. between pairs. This plan makes gathering an easy task and crops have proved heavier than from closer planting; 16°C (60°F) is high enough temperature; anything below 10°C (50°F) is too low. Watering should be ample for unhindered growth, but not sufficient to provoke mildew or decay of foliage. Water should always be tepid, and on days when the atmosphere is lively and dry, overhead syringing should be practised at least once a day.

The root run for beans should be well nourished with rotted stable manure. If during cropping, supplementary feeding is deemed requisite, let it take the form of liquid fertiliser in liberal quantity. By gathering beans young cropping is increased and prolonged.

For pot cultivation there are varieties of small-seeded beans which produce usable pods very quickly. They are serviceable where an extra early dish or two may be required, but bigger crops, although a little later, can be obtained by growing such varieties as Masterpiece, The Prince, or some other speciality of a leading seed merchant. Some growers allow a considerable number of plants to grow in a pot. It is probably wiser to use the best selected strains of seed and to allow two plants to a 6-in., three to a 7-in., or four to an 8-in. pot. The compost should be half good fibrous loam, the other half being made up with good leafmould and rotted manure, rubbed through an inch-mesh sieve, with a good sprinkling of fertiliser.

Give the plants no more artificial heat than is necessary to keep them growing. Allow plenty of ventilation, and lose no chance of moving and turning the plants round, never letting them become overcrowded.

Peppers: These are an increasingly popular vegetable grown a good deal on the Continent. They have spread to this country no doubt as a result of the increasing number of people who have Continental holidays nowadays. Seed is sown in a temperature of about 16 °C (60 °F) in March, and germinates about 10 days later. The John Innes seed compost is suitable. Pot the seedlings up singly into 3-in. pots, and pot on as required till the 7-in. size is reached, using the J. I. potting compost No. 1. They can be planted straight into the greenhouse border also, and in either case feeding with a liquid fertiliser will be required, with shade from strong sun, and a humid atmosphere; overhead spraying is beneficial when established. Flowers will start to appear when the plants are about 8 in. tall, and it is advisable to hand pollinate. In general their cultivation is similar to that of tomatoes.

Potatoes: In the ordinary way it would be farcical to suggest that potatoes are to be considered a profitable crop to grow in a greenhouse. As a means of producing specially early dishes of new potatoes it may certainly be urged that it is worthwhile to grow one of the earliest of varieties, either in large pots or in a portion of the floor bed.

I have seen a greenhouse bed dug and manured in December, then well soaked with water. Tubers have been sprouted ready for planting in January, and good crops have been lifted by Easter, enabling the bed to be planted with melons or some other summer crop. It is not, however, wise policy to grow potatoes in soil which is to take tomatoes as the following crop. The better course would be to grow potatoes in 10-in. pots, keeping them away from the soil in which tomatoes are to be planted.

Always remember that potatoes enjoy a light, rich soil with plenty of leafy material of rotted manure and vegetable compost. It is more necessary for these semi-forced potatoes than for those grown out-doors, and quite indispensable for those grown in pots. The potting compost should contain good leafmould and thoroughly rotted manure. The proportions must be regulated according to the texture of the loam.

The planting set should rest at about midway between the bottom and the rim of the pot. It is as well to start with only an inch of compost above the top of the tuber. That enables topdressing by easy stages, adding fertiliser to the topdressing mixture as conditions of progress dictate.

Early varieties under glass are unlikely to need spraying against attack by *Phytophthora infestans* (potato blight), but they are liable to attack by greenfly. The best measure is to spray weekly, before aphids appear, with some suitable insecticide, such as derris or malathion.

Some of the most serviceable varieties of potato for indoor cultivation are May Queen, Sharp's Victor and Di Vernon. A few seedsmen still offer an improved, reselected, and rejuvenated Ash Leaf. The original Myatt's Ash Leaf, if not absolutely extinct, would be very difficult to obtain; moreover, it is so old that its vitality is not comparable with modern varieties. The new Ash Leaf varieties are worth trial, because in particular varieties of Ash Leaf rapid development combines with distinct flavour and sterling qualities.

Turnips: In the general routine it is scarcely necessary to occupy space in a greenhouse to grow turnips. A frame is adequate protection for most of even early batches. There is, however, something to be said in favour of the earliest of all, to be grown in gentle warmth, quite in the opening weeks of the year. For this purpose there are varieties which are grown regularly on hotbeds by French intensive gardeners, and those varieties are the best for greenhouse cultivation, because they make comparatively small leaf growth and develop tender, sweet-flavoured roots very rapidly. Little Marvel and White Milan are two which are most frequently used by English growers for earliest crops. Turnips respond to the same treatment as forced carrots, except that more growing space must be allowed them. The rows should be not less than 9 in. apart, plants in the rows being thinned to 6 in.

Vegetable Marrows: An enterprising gardener of the writer's aquaintance annually devotes a greenhouse to an early crop of tender young marrows, choosing small-fruited varieties of trailing habit of growth. The plants are trained to wires under the roof glass, after the manner of training cucumber plants. The whole object is to secure very early marrows, which are appreciated by many who care nothing for the later, outdoor produce. To this end seeds are sown in January, starting them in a temperature of 16°C (65°F) or thereabouts. Make up mounds or a ridge of turfy compost, with a liberal amount of manure intermixed, and keep the whole root-run constantly damp, using tepid water. Train main stems to the wires until the ridge of the span roof is reached. Stop laterals at one leaf joint beyond the embryo fruit. Fertilise the female flowers, and as soon as fruits begin to grow feed the plants with liquid fertiliser.

Marrows should be but a short-season crop, the plants being displaced in time for a crop of tomatoes to fruit in summer and autumn.

WINTER AND SPRING SALADS

Many gardeners who would not attempt to grow the vegetable crops aforementioned will find much interest in growing salads at the season when they are both scarce and costly.

Mustard and Cress: This can be grown in shallow trays on the stages of any greenhouse where a temperature of 13–16°C (55–60°F) can be maintained.

Radishes: These make a good intercropping subject where bigger, slower-growing crops are given floor bed space, but where no such crops are grown it is still possible to have winter or early spring radishes by sowing such varieties as French Breakfast or Sparkler in boxes capable of holding a 6-in. depth of good rich compost, maintaining temperature as recommended for mustard and cress.

American Cress: This is another serviceable winter salad crop, and presents no cultural difficulties where the seed can be sown in a bed, the seedlings being thinned to 3 in. apart. When the leaves of neighbouring plants meet, cut out alternate plants for use. Thereafter the leaves of remaining plants can be cropped as required. High temperatures are not required so long as frost does not reach the plants.

Salad Onions: These can be available throughout winter and spring by sowing seeds where a temperature of 16°C (60°F) can be maintained. Varieties like White Lisbon, Silver Skin, and one of the Rocca tribe will serve the purpose, and if a continuous supply is the aim, it is advisable to make small sowings at intervals of about three weeks.

Lettuce: This must be reckoned the most important of the greenhouse salad crops. For winter and very early spring use, the cabbage-hearted type is far ahead of any cos variety. Numerous named varieties are styled as 'good for forcing'.

Cheshunt Early Giant is one of the best for artificial heat. Cheshunt Early Ball is better for unheated houses or frames. Other good lettuces are May King, Mayfair, Delta, Kloek, Kwick, and Knap.

Some experience and practice is necessary to ensure an unbroken supply of lettuces throughout winter. The root run should be a bed of good rich compost, raised above ground level, and well drained. A long-cherished idea is that the correct procedure is to sow seeds in shallow trays and transplant the young plants, thus reducing the number of weeks the whole area of growing space lies practically idle. Experiments of late years have proved that young lettuces left with roots undisturbed make much better progress than transplanted seedlings do. This is particularly so in the cold, dull winter period and the hottest of summer weather.

An excellent plan is to scratch lines half an inch deep, against a straight-edged batten, at 9-in. intervals both ways throughout the bed. At each point where these lines cross sow two or three lettuce seeds. As soon as the seedlings are well up, pull out surplus plants, leaving one at each station undisturbed. At the same time as sowing the lettuce, sow radish seeds, about three in a patch, one patch in the centre of each square and one patch midway between the crossings where lettuces are sown. The radishes will be ready for use before the lettuce leaves cover the ground.

Quantities of lettuces grown must be governed by the numbers in demand at one time, but it is wiser to sow small batches at frequent intervals than to rely upon fewer and bigger batches.

It has been proved that where requirements are small it is sound policy to grow winter and spring lettuces in 5-in. pots, small batches being accommodated on the stages of the greenhouse. Only one lettuce can mature in each pot, but as the pots and compost can be freed in a period of three months this is not an extravagant method.

Forcing Rhubarb and Seakale: The essential condition for forcing either of these crops is total darkness, hence the reason for coupling them in these notes. The most convenient place to provide the necessary accommodation is under the greenhouse stage. If this happens to be made of the usual slatted battens with spaces between the woodwork, the first step is to cover the stage with sheets of corrugated asbestos, the grooves of which can be filled with sharp sand or shingle, to form a level base on which to stand pot plants. The front of the stage can then be curtained with canvas or with sheets of thick brown paper. Place a thin layer of manure on the floor. Upon this stand the selected crowns of rhubarb, packing them as close as can conveniently be arranged. Then fill the spaces between the roots with sifted soil, bringing this up to the level of the crowns. The finishing task is to soak thoroughly with water and, after a reasonable time for drainage, put on more soil to make good any hollows caused by washing the soil into cavities between the roots. Having done that, all that is required is to adjust the curtain, making sure that no holes or creases are left to admit daylight.

It will depend upon the temperature maintained in the house how quickly rhubarb develops stalks fit for pulling. If heated water pipes run along under the staging it is possible that rhubarb may be obtainable in a fortnight. In an unheated house it will take three or four weeks.

Roots lifted for forcing should have been growing in well-nourished ground three years before attempting to force them. When the best stalks have been pulled bring out the roots, leaving some of the weaker growths on every crown. These roots may be divided and replanted in freshly prepared ground. Pull no stalks from these the following year, but leave all to die down, returning their nourishment to strengthen next year's crowns. The third year they may be lifted for forcing again.

Rhubarb roots force better if they can be frosted before housing. In any case, December is soon enough to begin the forcing process. If desired, a second batch of roots can be placed under the stage to replace roots removed. These should carry on supplies until outdoor rhubarb is available.

Seakale: Forcing crowns of this delightful vegetable should be strong roots about $1\frac{1}{2}$ in. in diameter and 6 to 8 in. long, and should show stout growing points. Lift carefully, trim off all fang roots, reserving the stoutest of these for propagating as root cuttings. Take the trimmed roots and with a thick dibber make perpendicular holes in a bed made up as for rhubarb. The holes should be just deep enough to receive the roots, leaving the crowns at soil level. Press the soil closely round each root. A distance of 6 in. between roots is sufficient to allow good head growth without undue tangling of neighbouring stalks. The seakale requires one good watering and should require no more, unless there are hot-water pipes near enough to the bed to dry the soil.

Seakale may be cut when the stems are 7 or 8 in. high. Cut with a thin slice of the actual root, thus preventing the stem falling apart.

Forcing may be done in successional batches from November to the end of January. The roots, after forcing, are not worth replanting.

Crops from Mixed Houses

From the foregoing paragraphs it will be clear to the reader that where the requirements of a small family would not justify running a house solely for production of food crops, it is quite possible to grow something edible, provided the house is well lighted and ventilated and care is taken not to spoil either utility crops or ornamental plants by overcrowding. A few tomatoes, in large pots or suitable boxes, may be grown on the sunny side of a house where begonias, fuchsias or other plants which enjoy partial shade are grown. Salad onions, mustard and cress or American cress can be grown in shallow wooden boxes on the greenhouse shelves, or the house may be useful to raise early beans, peas, marrow plants, etc. for planting out as soon as weather conditions permit.

Another plan is to use the glasshouse as accommodation for a collection of late chrysanthemums in their flowering season and to fill it with such a utility crop as tomatoes or cucumbers in summer. There will be plenty of room, early in the season, for propagation of the chrysanthemums, and for raising seedlings of other plants for transference to the open garden. The summer crops will occupy all the house.

CHAPTER TWELVE

Fruits for the Table

Utility houses must embrace some fruits, particularly grapes, peaches, melons, and pot strawberries. There are many private greenhouses in which a grape vine is already installed, but the management of such vines often leaves much to be desired. Many a lean-to house has a peach or nectarine tree trained on the back wall. Again, many of these would produce far better crops if their management were improved.

Melons can be grown successfully in many amateur's houses if only the principles of good cultivation are grasped, and the production of a few early and delicious strawberries is a possibility within range of most owners of a greenhouse. These, consequently, are the subjects dealt with in this book.

Grapes: Assuming that a house already contains a vine with its rods extending under the roof of the house, there are various reasons why a good crop of grapes may never be obtained. The usual course for instructors is to begin by urging that the vine border and root system is in sorry state and must be the first point of attention. In fact it is of rare occurrence that this can be thoroughly carried out in a satisfactory manner. If the vine border is really self-contained with bricked and cemented walls and floor, nothing less than a complete clearance and refilling with fresh compost can be effective, and this, besides being a laborious, expensive task, will probably be so damaging to the roots that the wiser plan would be to clear out the old vine and make a completely fresh start.

The probability is that the roots of a long-established vine have long since strayed far beyond the confines of any made border, and the feeding roots are now likely to be a long way beyond the confines of the greenhouse. Starting point at renovation of an old vine is more wisely made with the rods, and the season to start

287

is as soon as all leaves have fallen in late autumn, and at any rate before Christmas. The first step is to prune away all growth of the current season, leaving only the basal eye of each branch from the rod. Next, strip off all loose, old, perished bark from the rods and the main stem of the vine. Then carefully spray the rods with a tar oil winter wash, taking care not to damage other plants.

If the vine, during a period of neglect, has made a new rod near an old and decrepit one, cut out the latter from its starting point and lay in the new young rod in its place, but ensure that there is at least a yard of space between the rods as tied to the wires. The only other task for the winter is to wash the whole interior of the house with water containing a disinfectant, and to lime-wash the brick walls. The vine can then be left to itself until new growth starts in the New Year.

The date of that start will be governed by the temperature maintained in the house. From the amateur's point of view, a cool temperature delaying the start, is better than an earlier start induced by an artificially heated atmosphere. When the start is made work begins, and thereafter prompt attention to small details spells the difference between real success and mediocrity.

TRAINING. As soon as the number of starting eyes can be discerned, go over each rod carefully, select shoots alternately placed to right and left of the rod, and as near as possible 1 ft. apart; rub out all other starting shoots. This task must be repeated at intervals of a few days until surplus shoots cease to appear. Syringing the rods should now commence, using tepid water twice daily, before and after direct sunshine through the glass. The selected shoots will grow rapidly, and by the time they are 6 in. long, a strand of raffia should be looped over their soft, growing ends and tied with a bow to the wire so that the growth points in the direction the lateral is required eventually to travel. Extreme care must be taken not to put pressure on the shoot in tying or it will peel out from its base. The reason for fastening the loop with a bow is that, from time to time, as the wood gains firmness the bow can be loosened and the shoot drawn downwards a trifle by shortening the loop. Properly done, the lateral can ultimately be brought parallel with the wire. It is a case of what can be done gradually with patience, cannot be done hastily without disaster.

In due time, the tiny clusters of buds which are to develop into bunches of grapes will appear. The lateral should be allowed to grow

Top: Gasteria, the file aloe
Bottom left: Agave americana marginata *Bottom right:* Sarracenia tolliana

on beyond that point until two more leaf joints are formed. When the two leaves can be seen, the point of growth just beyond the second leaf should be nipped out, using the thumb-nail for the operation. Be prompt to attend to this, because if an unnecessary length of stem is allowed to grow nourishment will be wasted which should have gone into the development of a finer bunch of fruit. Moreover, if the stem is allowed to thicken before the severance sap will exude from the end for days. This escape of sap is termed 'bleeding', and it robs the grapes of nourishment to a serious extent.

The stopping of the lateral will result in secondary shoots starting from every leaf joint. These are termed sub-laterals. Each of these should be allowed to make one leaf and then the point of growth should be stopped before a second leaf unfolds. The one leaf is necessary to maintain proper functioning of the sap-course. More than one leaf per sub-lateral means wasteful utilisation of sap. A further shoot will, in due time, appear from the joint of the one reserved leaf. This, again, should be stopped when it has opened one leaf. After that very little further leaf growth will be made except for increase in the size of the foliage permitted to remain. The larger these leaves become the better. To this end daily syringing must be maintained until the grapes become coloured, and the root-run should never be allowed to suffer from drought.

THINNING. The next important task is thinning the grapes. This should be started when the berries are about the size of pearl barley. Most amateurs are afraid of cutting out too many berries, but nothing is gained by leaving too many on the bunch. Begin at the bottom of the bunch. Leave the lowest berry and clip out those next above it all round the bunch. Most branches of the fruit stalks carry three berries; cut out both side berries of the triplet, leaving only the central one. Any berries which point towards the centre of the bunch should at once be clipped out, otherwise they will become quite hidden and crowded until they decay.

By the time the berries attain the size of green peas, examine each bunch carefully a second time. Wherever two berries touch cut out the one that has least room. Also, cut out any which show a tendency to grow inward or to rest on a berry below.

The scissors used should be the proper grape thinning scissors with blades which taper, equally, to a neatly pointed end.

While thinning, if any lateral is seen to carry two bunches, cut the weakest or the most awkwardly placed bunch away. There is

The large, spectacular flowers of the epiphyllums give the genus the common name of the water lily cactus

no advantage in allowing two bunches to mature on one lateral. Their combined weight will not exceed the weight that one bunch might have achieved.

MANAGEMENT. Points in management to consider important are as follows: cleanliness of both vine and vinery, top ventilation throughout the growing season, day and night through hot weather. Syringing morning and evening from· start of growth until grapes are coloured. Pinching or stopping before unwanted stems and leaves have to be removed. Thinning early and adequately. Watering whenever the root-run is dry, using an abundance of water thoroughly to soak the soil. Remember, also, that nearly a month must elapse after colouring is complete before the grapes have attained sweetness and full flavour.

STARTING A VINERY. To those about to make a start on grape cultivation the following points should be considered: first, the best type of house is a lean-to with a good length of roof from front to back. An outdoor vine border is preferable for the private gardener, with the stem of the vine passing through a hole in the front of the house. If the subsoil is clay and is badly drained, a vine border should be excavated to a depth of 4 ft., a width not less than 5 ft., and the length of the house. Build up the sides with bricks, cement the bottom, allowing a slight slope to an escape drain for surplus moisture. The bottom of the pit should be covered with 3 or 4 in. of porous rubble, and this layer of drainage rubble covered with inverted turves before filling in with good soil and manure, with a 6-in. potful of coarse bonemeal to each barrow-load of soil. Allow some weeks for settlement before planting the vine.

The vine should be transferred from its pot while leafless, preferably during late November or December. Secure the stem vertically up to the eaves (inside the house). Cut off the stem at that point. Select the two strongest shoots of young growth near the severed top and train these, horizontally to right and left, along the top of the side lights. These will form main limbs from which, next year, rods will issue. Select the shoots which will run up under the roof at about equal distances – say, 4 ft. apart. Rub out all other shoots. Next pruning season shorten these rods to half length. Use the topmost shoot of the young growth to form an extention of the rod. Stop other shoots below this extending rod at the fourth leaf. Next season prune back these laterals to the basal eye, and the following season the strongest of the laterals on each rod may bear one bunch of grapes. The year after that it should be possible to produce a bunch from each strong lateral if these are not closer on the rod than a foot apart.

VARIETIES. The number of varieties of grapes in cultivation is large, but for the amateur the wisest course is to select varieties which will thrive and mature either without artificial heat altogether, or at any rate with only a moderate amount and a minimum demand upon skilful management.

Black Hamburgh. This is the one to be most strongly recommended to the novice. It produces medium-sized bunches of large, black berries. Growth is vigorous; it will grow and ripen either with or without heat. Ripens in September and hangs safely in a cold house through October.

Black Prince. A long, tapering bunch of oval berries, sweet, juicy, and will stand travelling well. In season September.

Foster's Seedling. A pale yellow grape. Medium size; tender and delicious fruit. Good grower. Ripens September, but lasts only a short period in good condition.

Madresfield Court. One of the best of grapes for quality combined with easy management. Purple-black; tough skin; splendid flavour. For September use.

Royal Muscadine. A round-berried grape, otherwise like a Muscat. Amber colour, in long, tapering bunches. Sweet flavour; growth vigorous. Ripens in August.

Peaches: A ripe peach is so delicious that it is no cause for surprise that a peach tree is to be seen in many an amateur's greenhouse, either trained to the back wall or under the roof of the house. Failure is, however, more common than conspicuous success with this fruit, the chief reason being erratic pruning and training. Reluctance to cut away superfluous wood too often results in hopeless overcrowding and production of far greater numbers of fruits than the tree can develop properly.

WINTER PRUNING. Possessors of old trees which do not fruit well should decide to be severe at pruning time. Attack this task while the tree is in a leafless and dormant state. Cut away entirely the oldest branches where wood is most crowded, leaving younger growth to be trained in such a manner that the finished tree presents the appearance of an evenly balanced fan. Even after that, if it is found that in placing a reserved branch in an obviously appropriate position some of its side shoots will crowd against those of neighbouring branches, cut out more of the weakest and most awkwardly placed; it is essential that every trained-in piece of growth shall get a reasonable share of space and daylight when in leaf.

Apart from this drastic pruning of an old and overgrown tree, the regular winter pruning is a simple task if certain principles are kept in mind. First, fruit is borne on the young wood of the previous year's growth. On these shoots are two kinds of buds: growth buds are oval and almost pointed at the end; fruit buds are rounder, fatter, and not pointed. At intervals three buds nestle together, and are known as triple buds. Those at either side are fruit buds, the centre one being a growth bud. Shorten each selected shoot to one of these clusters, or to a growth bud, as a new shoot will be required from that point. If any small growth beside the pruned shoot cannot be given a clear 4 in. of space on either side, cut it right out.

SUMMER PRUNING. Perhaps even more important than this regular winter pruning is summer pinching. Look at each new growth. A new shoot should be extending from the triple bud at its end. Leave that to grow at will. About midway between that and the base of that young branch find a starting shoot on its lower side. Leave that to grow. Then at or near the base of the young branch leave one new shoot on its upper side. All other new shoots on that branch should be pinched out with thumb-nail pressure before the stem gets too hard for such removal.

POLLINATION. Peaches can be grown in entirely unheated houses, but earlier crops can be secured if a house can be kept comfortably warm — say around about 10°C (50°F) from the time of starting growth at the beginning of the year. Measures should be taken to ensure adequate pollination, as the peach flowers too early in the year when grown under glass for the bees to be about; either hand pollination with cotton wool, or daily spraying with clear water in the mornings are necessary. As fruit begins ripening a slightly higher day temperature will be helpful, with a fall back to 10°C (50°F) at night. Never, however, seek high temperatures by denying the house good ventilation.

FRUIT THINNING. This is another important task which is too seldom carried out thoroughly. First go over the tree when the fruits are no bigger than hazel nuts. Pick off all that are obviously useless and those which are badly placed, pressing against the wall or the branches. Give a second look round for further unwanted fruits when about an inch in diameter, and at the final thinning, leave no more than one peach to a square foot of space or one nectarine to 8 or 9 in. The length of time during which thinning is started and completed is about three weeks.

Nectarines are managed in the same way as peaches.

PLANTING YOUNG TREES. To start young peach trees in a greenhouse, choose a spot against a plain wall where the sun reaches the tree and where a good root-run can be provided.

Perfect drainage is essential, and above a porous rubble base there should be a 2-ft. depth of good, well-enriched soil. In addition to well-rotted manure put in bonemeal of coarse grade at 4 oz. per sq. yd. of surface area, if the soil is acid.

Buy young trees with about half a dozen branches trained fan-wise, but with no central, perpendicular branch. Plant just as deeply as the tree was previously planted, but no deeper. Roots should be well spread out and the soil trodden firmly around them.

Allow a little time for settlement before tying in the branches. October or early November is the best season for planting. One tree is sufficient for a wall-breadth of 14 to 16 ft. Let no fruit mature the first year after planting, and only one per branch the second year. By allowing more the future of the tree is sadly handicapped.

VARIETIES. Good peaches are Duke of York, Hale's Early, Peregrine, Royal George, and Bellegarde. These cover the season in successive order from earliest to latest.

Nectarines, also, may begin with Early Rivers, followed by Lord Napier, Elruge, Humboldt, and Pine Apple.

GENERAL CARE. To keep peaches clean syringe freely and regularly, and spray periodically with nicotine, derris, or malathion, as red spider mite tends to be a nuisance on indoor peaches.

Cut away and burn any withered or diseased shoot, and pick up and burn any unhealthy leaves.

Besides pruning, other winter treatment should consist of the addition of a compound general fertiliser, containing nitrogen, phosphorous and potash, in January. After pruning, if possible, leave all ventilators and doors open, for a month or so, to ensure that the tree has a complete rest. When it starts into growth again, a very heavy watering is required to ensure that the subsoil is thoroughly soaked, followed by the fertiliser dressing.

A mulch of rotted manure after fruit set is also helpful, and make quite sure that sufficient water is given while fruit is swelling.

Melons: The melon (*Cucumis melo*, family *Cucurbitaceae*) is a native of the warmest parts of Asia, and was introduced from Jamaica into this country about the year 1570. The fruits, when well managed, are greatly valued for dessert and other purposes, and the average season is from May until October. The season, however, may be extended to Christmas under the best conditions and management.

The finest fruits are obtained from heated greenhouses where a fairly constant temperature of 18°C (65°F) can be maintained. They can, however, be grown quite successfully from April to September in garden frames placed on well-constructed hotbeds, while the more hardy kinds, such as the Cantaloupe, may be grown under Dutch light protection from June onwards by the aid of solar heat only.

SOWING THE SEED. To avoid any undue check to the plants later on the seeds are best sown singly in 3-in. pots, plump seeds only being chosen. Melon seedlings are not fastidious as to compost. Good loam, which should be broken up finely and sterilised, 3 parts, and well-rotted manure, 1 part, with just sufficient crushed rubble to keep the compost open, make up a mixture which will suit them well. The pots should be clean and then filled with the mixture, the rougher portions being placed in the bottom to ensure drainage. With the finger and thumb gently press the seed, hilum or scar end downwards, into the compost to the depth of not more than half an inch, and cover it with fine soil.

Place the pots in a propagating frame, where a bottom temperature of 21°C (70°F) can be maintained. Immediately the seedlings have pushed through the compost they should be raised to a position where they can obtain all the daylight possible, but that high temperature is still essential until the first true leaves have developed. Water should be given with great care, but they should never be allowed to become root dry or stunted through starvation in those small pots.

REPOTTING. Melon plants are subject to a form of canker which attacks the stems close to the soil, causing the plants to collapse just as the fruits are approaching the netting stage and, of course, they are rendered useless. Water thoughtlessly applied to the plants during their adult stage, particularly to the stem at soil level, is the prime cause of this disease.

In order to minimise the risk of contracting this disease the seedling plants should be transferred from the 3-in. pots to bottomless pots, 5 or 6 in. in diameter. Later, when they are being set out on the prepared beds, plant them with the pot intact, the rim of the pot being 2 in. above the surrounding compost. Ordinary pots, with the bottom knocked in, will answer the purpose admirably. The same compost mixture as recommended for seed sowing will answer quite well with the addition of some reliable fertiliser, such as the John Innes base fertiliser mixture. The rougher portions of the compost should be placed in the bottom of the pots as drainage, instead of the ordinary crocks, which would impede the roots entering the bed from the pots after planting.

The greatest care should be taken to prevent the plants being checked in any way; water when given should be tepid, and the plants should be repotted in the propagating house, the compost being warmed previously.

SOIL. A good, strong, fertile loam, inclining to the heavy side rather than light, invariably produces best results in both growth and size of fruit. The top 3 or 4 in. of good pasture land is best. It should be cut and stacked, grass side downwards, during November. During the stacking process, the alternate layers of turf should receive a good sprinkling of lime or chalk, and the other layers some bonemeal and a good shovelful of bonfire ash to the square yard. When required for the melon beds in March or later, the stack should be cut down with keen-edged spades from top to bottom to ensure a perfect mixture. This should then be placed, in a continuous ridge, about 14 in. deep and $1\frac{1}{2}$ ft. wide, on the greenhouse border. It is important to ensure that the latter is well drained. The mixture should be made quite firm to the extent of using a brick as a rammer. The interior of the house, where the melons are to grow, should be wired lengthways, the wires being 9 in. apart and not less than a foot from the glass.

PLANTING. Allow the compost time to get warmed thoroughly – this may take twenty-four hours or more. The house should be closed and the heating turned on. The soil temperature, 4 in. below the surface, should be as near 21°C (70°F) as possible. Indeed, a soil temperature of less than 18°C (65°F) may cause serious root troubles, and it may be necessary to use electric soil warming wires.

The crest of the ridge should be rounded somewhat to facilitate the insertion of pot with plant intact, the rim of the pot being 2 in. above the surrounding soil. The distance between the plants should be 2 ft. A neat stake should be inserted in the bed behind each pot and tied securely to the first wire. To this stake the young plant should be tied loosely.

TEMPERATURE. During the early stage in the development of the plants the night temperature should not fall below 18 °C (65 °F), and there should be a steady rise of 5 °C (10 °F) at least during the day. Ventilation should be given when the temperature reaches 27 °C (80 °F) with sun heat, and increased steadily as the temperature rises. On such occasions the artificial heat can be lowered or turned off altogether, as not only is it unnecessary but excessive heat may cause an attack of red spider mite. Heat can in fact be cut out altogether during the summer months.

WATERING AND SYRINGING. Water should be given to the young plants in the pots until the roots are well established in the bed. Pot watering should cease gradually, and water should be applied more copiously to the bed of soil.

The foliage should be syringed, somewhat forcibly, twice daily. On dull, sunless days, one syringing would suffice. Normally the first should be about 8 a.m., and again about 4 p.m. The pathways, walls, and borders may be sprayed several times daily, the only exception being during the mornings when the plants are in flower. Otherwise dry atmospheric conditions should be avoided until the fruits are approaching the ripening stage, when both watering and syringing should be discontinued.

TRAINING. The usual custom with melons grown in greenhouses is to run the plants on unstopped until the single stem attains a length of about 5 to 6 ft., then the growing point is taken out, and this results in diverting the energies of the plant to the laterals issuing from the lower joints. It is from these that fruits are obtainable. By adopting this method no more than 15 in. of space is required between plants, and the fruits produced from a house under this system will be as numerous and weightier than if one plant is given more space and allowed to carry two or more vines.

As the laterals advance, it will become apparent which are capable of carrying good fruit. These are laced up in a more or less horizontal position and allowed to grow on until fruit has set, but some attention will be required in stopping laterals where they show a tendency to extend themselves without producing female flowers. A strong plant may be capable of maturing four good melons; weaker growers may perhaps carry only three. Experience teaches what it is wise to leave, but for safety's sake it is advisable to set more fruits than it is intended to leave for development because accident or unexpected causes may spoil the chances of several embryo fruits in the very early stages, and these can be removed as soon as it is seen they will be useless. If one finds that too many good examples have been left it is an easy matter to reduce these before they have unduly sapped the plant of energy. One should aim at even distribution of the fruits which are left. It is better to have one near the base, two well separated in the middle of the plant and one near its end than to get them huddled together.

A point of importance is that one should aim at getting several female flowers open and ready for fertilisation at about the same time. If one or two blossoms are fertilised on one date and others are not ready for a considerable time, the latter stand a very poor chance of development because the earlier fruits will exert the greatest draw upon the sap flow of the plant.

A good deal may be done to encourage production and opening of the flowers required by watching the lateral growths and pinching them where they show a tendency to make rank, rapid growth without producing female flowers. Often the first break from the main stem will go on and on if left unchecked, covering too much space and making too many leaves before yielding blooms, but if stopped a sub-lateral is produced and the check given to the plant seems to waken it up to its natural purpose in life of producing female blossoms for the reproduction of its species. Never get into the practice of stopping all the growths throughout a house at given intervals. The wiser plan is to watch each individual growth and pinch one here and there whenever it is noticed that it is going ahead rapidly without revealing the desired flower buds.

POLLINATION AND FRUITING. All this time the plants must be kept warm, the atmosphere humid, and the foliage frequently dewed by spraying with a very fine nozzled syringe using only tepid water. The next important point is to watch the opening of flowers. When this occurs there must be some reduction in the amount of water sprayed on to them so that the pollen may become free and tolerably dry. When the female flower is well expanded and its stigma prominent, the pollen must be transferred from the male blossom. For this purpose there is no better plan than to pick off a fully developed male bloom, tear away its petals and thrust the stamen cluster into the centre of a female flower.

As with cucumbers, a topdressing of rotted manure may be given when white rootlets show on the surface of the soil but, provided the bed was properly prepared in the first place, no other feeding will be necessary.

Once the fruits begin to swell appreciably, it is a good idea to support them in netting, suspended from the wire framework. The fruit is ready for picking when the stalks begin to crack close to the fruits, and there is a distinct smell of ripe melon in the air.

Strawberries: It is possible, even in a greenhouse stocked with an assortment of other plants, to grow a batch of early ripening strawberries if a shelf can be provided upon which plants in pots can stand with 2 ft. of space between the foliage and the roof glass.

Start by transferring young plants from small pots to those of 6 in. diameter. September is the month for this task. When potted the best place for plants is a plunge bed in a frame. Cover and shade the frame until the plants show that they are thriving, then remove the lights, except in bad weather. January is soon enough to place the plants in a gently warmed greenhouse. Even then it is best to introduce a few plants at a time, allowing an interval of a week or so between batches. Temperatures may range from 13°C (55°F) to 5°C (10°F) higher, but 18°C (65°F) should be the maximum allowed with artificial heat.

Keep the plants well watered with tepid water. Feed with liquid fertiliser when fruits begin to develop. Thin flowers if they are found to be too numerous. It may be taken as a rule that twelve or fourteen fruits are as many as a plant in a 6-in. pot can develop and mature properly. Fruit can be expected to start ripening in April.

At present a more important point than name of variety of any strawberry grown is assurance that plants are from runners of a vigorous disease-free stock. Virus diseases have played havoc of late years with many stocks of strawberries, but it is good to know that the task of propagating healthy stocks has been taken seriously in hand at places like East Malling, John Innes Institute, Long Ashton, and elsewhere. Nurserymen are now able to offer clean, healthy stocks of known good varieties, and that is the important consideration for all amateur growers.

Figs under Glass: A strangely neglected fruit, the home-grown fig, well ripened and eaten fresh from the tree is, to those whose taste is attuned, a supreme luxury. Probably, we have here an outstanding example of the unhappy effect of popularising an imported product for since it became customary to import huge quantities of foreign figs in a dried and pressed form, which could be sold at extremely low prices, the fresh, home-grown fig has been so far neglected that the great majority of the British public will confess to never having tasted a fresh fig. Yet, from a health-promoting point of view, fresh figs are of exceptionally high merit, and it certainly may be stated that the general outcome of a fair trial results in an acquired taste which speedily develops into a cordial appreciation of the superb qualities of the fruit.

Figs are so nearly hardy in this country that many old trees live indefinitely in warm corners of old walled gardens, and where some degree of knowledgeable care in cultivation is given quite good crops are frequently produced out of doors.

It is, however, in the hope that figs may become more generally and systematically cultivated in England that it is here advocated that they should be grown by amateurs in greenhouses, either planted in a prepared floor bed or in pots. A fig tree may be grown without artificial heat, or may be subjected to gentle forcing in the early months of the year. Three sets of fruit are formed within twelve months by a flourishing tree. Outdoors in England one set only can be brought to the stage of ripening, but under glass two crops should be secured, and in some cases a limited number of fruits of the third set will be matured.

PLANTING. The first consideration should be to secure the snuggest, warmest position in the greenhouse; preferably against the back wall of a lean-to house where the branches can be secured to the wall climber fashion. Next point is to contrive to restrict root-run, because a fig fruits more freely when its roots are confined.

Take out a cubic yard of soil; build up the sides with bricks and cement. Put into the bottom a foot depth of brick rubble and stones; then fill in with turf loam, sand, lime, and a moderate addition of bonemeal and shells of oyster, cockle, or winkle. Let the whole have time to settle and plant firmly in early spring. Water freely throughout growing period. Keep tolerably dry in winter.

When growth becomes vigorous pinch out young shoots where too numerous. If this task is too long delayed and larger shoots have to be cut out, bleeding of milk-white sap will be excessive.

The first crop is borne at the joints of the young stems of the previous year's growth. The second crop comes on the strongest of the current season's growth. On young trees it is advisable to reduce the number of these where a stem forms a larger number of small fruits. A third set of fruits will often appear on the branches approaching two years old. It is these that should be reduced to two or three per branch.

Always syringe freely, except during winter. Feed with liquid fertiliser while a fruit crop is swelling. Gather fruit by gently twisting when the fig is soft and obviously ripe. Take care not to use pressure which will burst the skin.

Pruning time is March or early April. Cut out complete branches when old and producing only weak new shoots. Pinch points of young growths which show signs of too much vigour. The rest of the pruning should be done by pinching out young growths at the start as mentioned before.

FIGS IN POTS. Figs may be grown in pots of large size − 10 or 12 in. in diameter. Once established the trees seldom require repotting. Potting may be done between November and April but nearer the first-named than the spring month. Compost should be mainly turfy loam, with some rubble, shell (crushed), bonemeal, or hoof and horn. Ram firmly. After treatment corresponds to that for planted-out trees, except that branches should have the points pinched when not longer than 9 in. One crop per season is enough for pot plants to mature. Rub off other embryo fruits as they form. It is as well to plunge pots in the open after fruit is gathered, housing again in winter.

Figs in pots require liberal quantities of water and liquid fertiliser throughout the growing season; little or none when resting.

FRUITS IN MIXED HOUSES. Many houses have grape vines trained under the roof, with other plants on the stages. This is a feasible proposition so long as the plants are of kinds which will thrive under the shade of expanded vine leaves, will not resent the daily syringing the vine requires from the starting of growth to colouring of grapes, and − a very important point − plants are avoided which are prone to attract and harbour pests and diseases which may spread to and cause trouble among the grapes. Plants which attract red spider, mealy bug, bees or wasps should be avoided.

Strawberries in pots can be grown on the shelves of greenhouses otherwise occupied by cacti, succulents or other sun-loving plants.

CHAPTER THIRTEEN

Cacti, Other Succulents and Carnivorous Plants

Cacti are, with one or two exceptions, succulent plants but all succulents are not cacti. The latter term is confined to the members of the natural order of *Cactaceae*. A cactus may be defined as a herb or sub-shrub, with soft flesh and copious watery juice, a small root system, a branching or single stem which may be flattened or roundish, smooth, channelled, or tubercled; generally leafless, but often clothed with keen-pointed spines, and bearing areoles, i.e. buds with spines, hairs or bristles on them, which are peculiar to the *Cactaceae*. Flowers may be showy or insignificant, many petalled, are (with one exception) always borne singly, stamens numerous, pistil one, fruit pulpy and full of small, usually black, seeds. Any cactus-like plant not fitting this general description is not a cactus. The euphorbias mimic cacti closely, but are promptly distinguished by their milky juice.

Cultural Requirements

Cacti are for the most part desert plants, exposed to scorching sun and withstanding long periods of drought, but they also pass through a period of torrential rain with a hot, steamy atmosphere. At such times they plump up with sap, make their growth, and perfect their flower buds; thereafter they 'sit tight' and conserve what they possess. The root system serves chiefly as anchorage, worming its way into crevices and cracks in the rocky soil they affect. For this reason over-potting is an evil to be avoided, as also is frequent repotting; while a plant is thriving, leave well alone.

Potting

A suitable soil for spiny cacti – and these favour the native conditions above described – is good fibrous loam (6 parts), coarse silver sand (1 part), and broken brick rubble in fragments the size of hazel nuts. Let the pots be clean and dry internally and well drained. Non-spiny cacti – epiphyllum, phyllocactus, and rhipsalis – prefer less extreme conditions and do well in loam (4 parts), peat or good leafmould (1 part), and coarse sand (1 part). Phyllocacti are the most normal of the family and they appreciate a richer soil. A small amount of well-rotted manure added to the above formula will suit them. These are also the most showy flowered of the family, and are often seen well grown in cottage windows. Cacti generally need no manurial stimulants, but phyllocacti and epiphyllums in full growth – June till the end of August – are benefited by weekly waterings from liquid fertiliser. Repotting should only be done when really necessary, and then in March and April. If a plant overturns and its pot is broken between August and March, simply drop the ball into another of like dimensions and make good with as little root disturbance as possible. Pots should be well drained, using small pieces of broken clay pots and filling the lower third of the pot's depth; cover with fibrous compost. Make the compost firm. Do not bury the base of the plants or decay is very possible.

Watering

Not required during the winter months November to March, but with nice weather in April a good soaking should be given, using tepid, or, at least, not cold, water. After that and during May, June and July, liberal watering may be practised in hot weather, even damping the house floor during heat waves. Reduce the supply from the end of July, and give every ray of sunshine possible to ensure thorough ripening in August and September; with the coming of October let watering cease unless a bad case of shrivelling appears, with tiny plants or with the phyllocacti, when give one watering to relieve the distress.

Sunshine

Cacti cannot receive too much, and particularly when ripening. The non-spiny kinds appreciate moderate shade or a moist atmosphere while the new growth is tender, but must have full exposure afterwards.

Temperature

Cacti will withstand a low one during winter if the plants, soil, and air are thoroughly dry, but it is not well to risk frost; rather keep the winter scale to 4°C (40°F) as a minimum, rising to 13 or 16°C (55 or 60°F). During growth in summer 27°C (80°F) is not too high, and 21°C (70°F) with dryness is a good ripening warmth. Phyllocacti will do with a minimum temperature, but epiphyllums and rhipsalis are not happy in less than 16–18°C (60–65°F) during winter.

Pests and Diseases

Cacti come off rather lightly as regards enemies. Mealy bug, scale insects, and thrips are their worst foes, and it may be said that the first two are the result of general neglect. If these pests are allowed to infest greenhouse plants, then the cacti will come in for a share. Owing to the spine tufts cacti are difficult to cleanse by hand, and it has been found a good plan to immerse the plants, head downwards, in a solution of soft soap, 3 oz. to the gallon, heated to 47°C (120°F). Immerse the plants for only twenty seconds. Touching the insects with a small paint brush dipped in methylated spirit or petrol may be tried.

When potted too deeply or over-watered, decay of the roots and base of stem may take place. The treatment is to remove the plant from the compost, cut away the decayed roots, and carefully repot in the smallest size that will take what are left. When the stem has rotted, the damaged part must be cut away and then the plant be tied to a stick, which is thrust into a pot of very sandy compost or of sand alone, so that the new base just rests on the surface. Give no water till new roots are produced.

Propagation

This is mostly a simple operation. Where offsets are produced these can be broken away, and if laid on sand or very sandy compost will soon produce roots and can then be potted. Those which yield branches may have these broken or cut at the socket and then treated as cuttings. Where there are neither offsets nor branches, but a tall stem, the upper 2 or 3 in. may be treated as a cutting.

Grafting is easily done, slicing the top of the stock like an inverted V. (∧) and splitting the scion to fit over like a letter A, the latter being kept in position with a spine pushed through itself and the stock. If more convenient the scion may be cut wedge shape and the stock notched to receive it, securing with a spine and a few strands of raffia or worsted in each case. Pendant kinds make nice standards grafted on tall cereus stems or those of pereskia; epiphyllums are commonly so grown.

A Small Selection

Aporocactus flagelliformis: Practically the only species commonly grown, this is known as the rat's tail cactus, with clusters of long hanging stems, bearing red-brown spines, and crimson flowers in April and May.

Cereus: A large genus, with showy flowers which has, however, been much split up amongst other genera. All are easily cultivated. *Cereus peruvianus* is columnar stemmed with white flowers, and its variety *monstrosus* is grotesquely contorted.

Echinocactus: Globose plants, sometimes very large, and chiefly noted for their spines. *Echinocactus grusonii*, a popular species, the 'golden ball', covered with white or yellowish wool, and yellow spines; flowers yellow.

Echinocereus: Dwarf plants, formerly classed as *Cereus*; flowers showy, and roundish. *Echinocereus cinerascens*, clustered stems, white spines, red flowers. *E. enneacanthus*, prostrate stems, bright red flowers. *E. engelmannii*, large clumps of erect stems, purple flowers. *E. polyacanthus*, erect, cylindrical stems, pink or red flowers. *E. reichenbachii* (syn. *E. caespitosus*), clustered stems, spines coloured, flowers light purple, fragrant.

Echinopsis: Globose plants of moderate size, remarkable for large white or whitish, tubular, fragrant flowers. *Echinopsis eyriesii* and *E. ozygona* should both be grown.

Epiphyllum: Flat, large-pointed stems, almost spineless, flowers all shades of pink, rose, and red, many hybrids also, with white or yellow flowers. Plants grow to about 2 ft. tall and bear large, spectacular flowers, giving them the common name of the water lily cactus. Compost needs to be slightly richer than for desert cacti, and they do better with more water. Staking is a necessity. They like a little shade, and should be shielded from great heat in summer, and are altogether easily cultivated. *Epiphyllum ackermannii* (scarlet); *E. anguliger* (white), scented; *E. crenatum* (cream and bronzy green), fragrant; *E. phyllanthus* (pink and white). Some good named varieties are: *cooperi* (lemon and white, fragrant); Gloria (orange-salmon); Innocence (white); London Lady, dark pink; Niobe, orange; *peacockii*, cerise-violet.

Ferocactus: Round or cylindrical bodies, with prominent ribs and strong spines. *Ferocactus colvillei*, red and yellow flowers; *F. latispinus*, very strong broad spines, pink to purple flowers; *F. lecontei*, yellow or red flowers freely produced, long spines.

Heliocereus: Showy plants, rather like epiphyllum in flower; *Heliocereus speciosus* with stout roundish stems and scarlet flowers, has been crossed with epiphyllum to produce some brilliantly coloured hybrids.

Mammillaria: A very large genus, now much split up into other genera, but species are given here under *Mammillaria* with new names in brackets. Plant bodies round, occasionally cylindrical. Small flowers arranged in a ring around the top of the plant. *Mammillaria echinus* (*Coryphantha echinus*), globular, yellow flowers, likes warmth; *M. baageana*, carmine red; *M. micromeris* (*Epithelantha micromeris*), white or pale pink; *M. pusilla* (*M. prolifera*), pale yellow flowers, very easily cultivated.

Opuntia: Flat-jointed plants of variable size, sometimes very spiny or with few spines; flowers mostly yellowish. *Opuntia microdasys* (very fine golden spines), *O. dillenii*, *O. rafinesquei* (hardy).

Pediocactus: Much like the echinocactus; *Pediocactus simpsonii*, pink flowers and globular body; spines brown.

Rhipsalis: Called mistletoe cacti owing to the round white fruits borne. Plants slender, small jointed, non-spiny. Flowers small. Warmth needed. *Rhipsalis cassytha*, creeping or hanging stems, flowers green and white; *R. grandiflora*, erect, bush-like, white flowers; *R. myosorus*, (*Lepismium myosorus*), creeping stems, pinkish white flowers.

Schlumbergera: Epiphytic, pendulous plants, much branched, with short, flat, notched leaf-like joints. *Schlumbergera truncatus*,

Christmas cactus, red fuchsia-like flowers at the ends of the stems in winter. *S. gaertneri*, Easter cactus, similar, but flowers slightly larger and produced in late winter and early spring. Easily grown, with a period of rest and warmth from May to August.

Selenicereus: Formerly included in *Cereus*, these are slender climbing plants with aerial roots and nocturnal flowers. *Selenicereus grandiflorus*, white strongly scented flowers, about 12 in. long. Sometimes called Queen of the Night. Should be grown fairly warm, with stems twined round a pole.

Trichocereus: Dwarf plants, producing their flowers at night on columnar bodies. *Trichocereus candicans*, white scented flowers, spines yellow and white.

SUCCULENTS

Succulents that are not cacti are members of many families, sometimes taking in the whole of a genus, as agave, aloe, and sempervivum; at other times only a section, as in euphorbia. All have fleshy, succulent leaves or stems, sometimes coloured or spiny or warted; some are showy flowered, but most of them are grown for their general appearance.

Agave (American Aloe): Mostly of large growth, with fleshy leaves armed with fierce spines and arranged in rosette fashion. Flowers borne on a tall stem, the plant dying after their production. *Agave americana* (blue-green leaves), *A. a. marginata* (broad yellow margin), *A. a. mediopicta* (yellow central stripe), *A. filifera* (thread-bearing leaves), and *A. victoriae reginae* (leaves white-margined).

CULTIVATION. Agaves are of easy cultivation in loam (3 parts), coarse sand and crushed mortar rubble (1 part), and leafmould (1 part). Water freely during warm summer weather, but give little in winter, especially in low temperatures. Repot in May or June when necessary.

PROPAGATION. By offsets removed when repotting or detached and treated as cuttings. A minimum winter temperature of 4–7°C (40–45°F) suits them.

Aloe: A numerous genus of large and small plants with stems bearing spirally arranged fleshy leaves or in alternate pairs; the plants do not die after flowering. *Aloe variegata* (partridge-breasted aloe or mackerel plant), dark green leaves barred with white, flower stem up to 1 ft. *A. vera* and *A. succotrina* are similar, grey-green leaves, with inflorescence 2 to 3 ft. tall. *A. aristata*, narrow leaves with hair-like point; *A. ferox*, spiny all over.

CULTIVATION. Simple. A temperature of 10°C (50°F·) suits them, with a sunny position. Water freely when in growth; give much less in winter. Repot as necessary in early summer in turfy loam (3 parts) and old mortar rubble, broken brick, oyster-shell, and coarse sand mixed (1 part).

PROPAGATION. By offsets or tops of tall plants treated as cuttings.

Gasteria (File Aloe): Leaves tongue-shaped and arranged in two ranks; plants dwarf and free flowering. *Gasteria verrucosa*, white warts on leaves; *G. carinata*, spiral growth and warty foliage; *G. lingua*, broad tongue-like foliage, *G. nigricans*, dark green or purple leaves with pale green blotches.

Haworthia (Pearl Aloe): Small rosette-like plants with pointed leaves, having warted surfaces or smooth. *Haworthia margaritifera*, warts large; *H. attenuata*, warts small; *H. arachnoides*, fringed leaves.

CULTIVATION. Gasterias, haworthias, and apicras (separated from haworthia by some) thrive under like treatment. They are of slow growth, and do well in small pots thoroughly drained; for compost use sandy loam with plenty of broken brick and old mortar rubble added. Water freely in summer and moderately in winter. Shade from hot sunshine May to August.

PROPAGATION. By suckers or by leaves cut off and laid on sand till plantlets develop.

Klenia (Cacalia): Blue or grey leaved plants, the most interesting being *Klenia articulata* (Candle Plant). This has grey stems with fleshy leaves when young, later being bare and looking like a series of small jointed candles. *K. tomentosa* has white stems and fleshy leaves; *K. repens*, blue foliage.

CULTIVATION. The candle plant thrives in sandy loam. It should not be dried off, though little water is needed while leafless. With other klenias syringing or overhead watering should be avoided, or the leaf colouration will be spoilt.

PROPAGATION. By sections of the stem or by sucker shoots.

307

CRASSULA AND ALLIES

Bryophyllum pinnatum: An interesting plant with leaves having dented or crenate margins. Any piece of leaf broken off and laid on soil or elsewhere soon develops plantlets along its edge. Treat as for Echeveria.

Crassula and Rochea: These are very ornamental plants, chiefly dwarf and shrub-like, the stems and leaves both being rather succulent. The flowers are usually produced in terminal heads, but occasionally in loose cymes. They are chiefly native of South Africa.

SPECIES. First choices are *Crassula cooperi* (pale flesh colour, summer flowering and dwarf), *C. coccinea* (now known as *Rochea coccinea*), bushy plants 1 to 3 ft., summer flowering in scarlet, with closely set non fleshy leaves in two double ranks. Hybrid rocheas in white, rose, etc., are similar in habit to *coccinea*. *C. falcata*, thick irregular shaped leaves, dotted and grey in colour, flower heads scarlet; *C. jasminea*, a small grower with white flowers in heads, in spring; *C. lactea* has thick oval leaves in opposite pairs and heads of white flowers in winter, a good spreading plant 1 to 2 ft. high; *C. lycopodioides*, tree-like with square stems and insignificant flowers – a plant mimic; *C. marginalis* and *C. spatulata*, both summer and September flowering, and good for hanging baskets.

CULTIVATION. Repot in March. Compost consists of 2 parts loam and 1 part crushed bricks and sharp sand. Small pieces of brick are also ideal for drainage purposes. Careful watering is the chief factor in the successful cultivation of crassulas. They ought never to be really wet, and must be protected from drips.

The small growing species need extra care. They all require plenty of light and a winter temperature of 4–7°C (40–45°F). *Rochea coccinea* deserves to be grown in quantity and old plants will flower profusely every second year. After flowering the plants need cutting back to keep them shapely. The old stems will push out plenty of new shoots, but they will not be strong enough to bloom till the following year. It is always advisable to prune half the stock each season and thereby have a batch in bloom every year.

PROPAGATION. By means of cuttings inserted in sandy compost and placed in a sunny shelf in the greenhouse. They will form roots during the late spring and summer months.

Echeveria: Once included in the genus *Cotyledon*, the plants given are now nearly all called echeveria. Some are tree-like in growth, others distincly rosette in form. In many cases the foliage is glaucous or mealy white, the latter needing careful handling not to mar their beauty. *Echeveria agavoides* (syn. *Cotyledon agavoides*), pale green and brown; *E. gibbiflora* (syn. *Cotyledon metallica*), grey-green flushed red or purple, and *E. g. metallica*, bronze with red edges; *E. glauca* (syn. *Cotyledon secunda glauca*), blue-grey with reddish margin, much used for bedding; *E. peacockii* (syn. *Cotyledon desmetiana*), bluish-white with red edges; *E. pulverulenta* (syn. *Cotyledon pulverulenta*), mealy white; *E. secunda* (syn. *Cotyledon secunda*), pale green to red, valuable for winter flowering. These are all rosette-like.

CULTIVATION. These plants are easily grown. A compost of 2 parts turfy loam and 1 part sand and broken brick suits them well. Water freely spring to autumn, moderately in winter; do not dry them off or many leaves will fall.

PROPAGATION. By offsets and by mature leaves broken off and laid on sand till roots and plantlets appear. A minimum temperature of 4°C (40°F) suits them.

Euphorbia: The succulent euphorbias mimic cacti in form, some being globular, others columnar, and again climbing; some are also very spiny. All can be distinguished by their milky sap. *Euphorbia beaumieriana, E. caput-medusae, E. cereiformis, E. cooperi, E. globosa, E. meloformis, E. obesa, E. splendens*, are all worth growing. The last named is the crown of thorns, very spiny, to 3 ft. tall, and with bright scarlet flowers.

CULTIVATION. These euphorbias do well in a compost similar to that for stapelias, and, like them, also need warmth in winter; keep quite dry at that season.

PROPAGATION. By cuttings, which should be allowed to callus at the base before inserting in very sandy compost; bottom heat aids rooting.

Kalanchoe: A summer flowering genus of succulent-leaved plants, native of South Africa. They are easily grown if not overdone with moisture, and the large branching heads of flowers are always admired. The fleshy leaves are arranged in four ranks.

SPECIES. The best are *Kalanchoe flammea* (orange-scarlet, 2 ft.), the hybrid *K. kewensis* (a fine plant with beautiful heads of rose-coloured flowers), and *K. pumila*, grey-pink leaves and reddish violet flowers. Height from 1½ to 3 ft. *K. blossfeldiana* is an easily grown species responding to cool house treatment, together with its cultivated forms, such as Tom Thumb (red) and Tom Thumb Golden. It has large heads made up of myriads of small crimson scarlet flowers that last; best grown as a biennial, seed being sown in spring for flowering the following winter or spring.

CULTIVATION. During winter the temperature should be about 7 or 10 °C (45 or 50 °F). The atmosphere must be fairly dry, and only sufficient water need be given to prevent the compost becoming dust dry. Wet conditions will cause the stems and leaves to decay.

When the days begin to lengthen, gradually give a little more water, and in March repotting should take place. Kalanchoes will thrive in John Innes potting compost or one of the loamless mixtures. To the former should be added a liberal sprinkling of sand, and where the loam is inclined to be heavy a proportion of crushed bricks will be an advantage. Good drainage is essential.

Keep the plants fully exposed to the sun. The compost is now kept just moist and, when about to flower, well rooted specimens can be given weak liquid fertiliser once or twice a week. A summer temperature of 16–18 °C (60–65 °F) will suffice. Admit air whenever possible, and keep the plants near the glass.

PROPAGATION. This is effected by seeds, which will germinate in a temperature of 18 °C (65 °F). Use sandy compost in well-drained pots or pans. The seedlings will need careful handling to prevent injury, also careful watering. They will thrive best on a shelf in a warm greenhouse, and will flower 10 to 18 months later. All may be increased by cuttings made from side growths after the plants have flowered, also from leaves. Both will form roots in sandy compost in a little warmth. Keep young plants growing during winter.

Mesembryanthemum: A vast genus and most variable in form and habit; some dwarf, succulent, and looking like split pebbles; others fleshy and spiny, tall, bushy, and sub-shrubby, prostrate, or creeping. Leaves are smooth, spiny, warted, or prickly; round, three-cornered, or vari-shaped. Flowers daisy-like and glistening; colours all shades except blues. Because of these variations, it is proposed to split the genus up considerably, but for the time being the species are retained here under mesembryanthemum. Popular kinds are *Mesembryanthemum barbatum* (red); *M. blandum* (pink); *M. brow-*

nii (orange-red and yellow); *M. cordifolium variegatum*, a pleasing, prostrate, or creeping kind, used for summer bedding (purple flowers, creamy white variegated leaves); *M. crystallinum* (ice plant), half-hardy annual with green leaves covered with 'ice', and white flowers; *M. dolabriforme* (yellow and red); *M. falcatum* (pink, scented); *M. spectabile* (magenta); *M. tricolor* (red and yellow), half-hardy annual.

CULTIVATION. Simple in a minimum temperature of 4–10°C (40–50°F) and in a compost of loam (2 parts), leafmould (1 part), and sand (1 part). Avoid over-watering at all times and keep dry in winter without allowing shrivelling.

PROPAGATION. By cuttings or offsets.

Othonna: Only one species will be referred to. This is *Othonna crassifolia*, native of South Africa with yellow flowers in summer. It is a very pretty trailer with inch-long leaves, suitable for hanging baskets or stage front.

CULTIVATION. All the othonnas are of quite simple cultivation. They need a light sunny position and ample drainage. In fact, good drainage is the principal factor in their successful cultivation. The compost consists of loam, 2 parts, and 1 part peat and sand in equal proportions. Repot in March. Supply liberally with water during the spring and summer, especially when grown in suspended baskets. In the winter only a moderate quantity is needed, and the minimum temperature is 4–7°C (40–45°F).

PROPAGATION: Cuttings of young shoots root in spring if inserted in sandy compost and placed in a close warm frame.

Rochea, see Crassula.

Sedum: Sedums or stonecrops are mostly hardy, but one or two make good greenhouse plants.

CULTIVATION. A loamy soil well drained suits them. The deciduous kinds must not be dried off entirely in winter. *Sedum lineare variegatum*, a pretty, small, drooping kind with starry yellow flowers. *S. sieboldii* and *S. s. variegatum*, pleasing hanging kinds, die back in autumn, pink flowers, and yellow central blotch on leaves of *variegatum*; *S. stahlii* and *S. obtusatum* have reddish leaves and yellow flowers. *S. stahlii* flowers August and September.

PROPAGATION. By cuttings or division.

Sempervivum: The houseleeks are mostly hardy, but some need a greenhouse or make pleasing pot plants for the house.

CULTIVATION. They like a sandy loam with crushed old mortar added. Water moderately only in winter. Tall kinds are *Sempervivum arboreum, S. a. foliis purpureis, S. a. foliis variegatus, S. holochrysum,* and *S. tabulaeforme.* All these are now listed by some authorities under *Aeonium*; all have flowers in varying shades of yellow. Dwarf kinds include *S. arachnoideum* and *S. a. tomentosum* (cobweb houseleek), and *S. tectorum* (copper coloured). Sempervivums, like agaves, die with flowering, but usually leave offsets behind.

PROPAGATION. Effected by separating and potting offsets, singly in the case of those attaining large size, and in groups of three, five, or more of the smaller kinds. They may also be raised from seeds sown in well-drained pans of porous soil and sifted mortar and brick rubble.

Stapelia: Known as star-fish flower, toad flower, and carrion flower, these names alluding to shape, colouring, and odour respectively. Pollination in their natural habitat is by flies, hence the very unpleasant smell of rotting meat of some species – not those given here. The plants consist of many four-angled, leafless, fleshy, green stems. The flowers are borne singly and are curiously shaped, marked, and coloured. The species are numerous. *Stapelia gigantea,* pale yellow flowers lined with red, up to 16 in. wide; *S. revoluta,* purple; *S. variegata,* pale yellow, purple spotted, but very variable; *S. verrucosa,* pale yellow, blood red spots, are a selection.

CULTIVATION. The plants need little soil and dislike disturbance. A compost of 2 parts good sandy loam and 1 part crushed oystershell, pounded brick, and coarse sand suits them; good drainage is essential. Grow the plants on a shelf near the glass in a winter temperature of 18°C (65°F). Water freely in growth, but only to prevent shrivelling in winter. A dry atmosphere when flowering is essential.

PROPAGATION. Stems easily broken off root.

CARNIVOROUS OR INSECTIVOROUS PLANTS

A most interesting little group of plants, which for cultural reasons are placed under one heading. They embrace such genera as *Cepha-*

lotus, *Darlingtonia*, *Dionaea*, *Drosera* and *Sarracenia*. The last-named are the most commonly grown, and cultivation for all is similar to that for sarracenias.

Sarracenias: These constitute a pleasing section of the pitcher plants. They have tubular leaves, and produce in early spring attractive and highly perfumed flowers. After flowering the plants make their annual growth. The leaves or pitchers are more or less reticulated and of various tints, and vary in length from 1 to 4 ft. Each one is surmounted with a kind of lid, of large proportions. Their value as decorative subjects covers three parts of the year and, as their cultivation is of the simplest description, one wonders why they are not more largely grown. The sarracenias are known as the huntsman's horns.

Noteworthy species and hybrids are: *Sarracenia chelsonii* (pale green and dark purple); *S. flava* (green with purple veins), *S. f. gigantea* (large); *S. moorei* (green, 2 ft. long); *S. psittacina* (small, veined with purple, nearly horizontal); *S. purpurea* (dark green, suffused and veined deep purple); *S. tolliana* (green and deep purple-red).

The best time to repot is early spring, when the plants are dormant. The compost consists of good fibrous peat and living sphagnum moss in equal parts. A liberal sprinkling of rough sand and finely broken crocks or charcoal should be added to maintain a free and open rooting medium. The pots or pans should be well provided with drainage. Keep the soil fairly moist after repotting, and when growth is active an abundance of water is necessary.

The plants will need a temperature of about 13°C (55°F) and a fairly light position. This will develop the various bright tints on the pitchers. As autumn approaches the water supply will be gradually reduced, and in winter the compost is kept just damp. The temperature will be 7–10°C (45–50°F) when the plants are at rest.

Sarracenias are increased by the division of the crowns at the time of repotting.

Drosera: In addition to our native *Drosera rotundifolia*, there are several species well worthy of cultivation. They are small growing, with rosettes of leaves nestling on the soil. The leaves are ornamented with hairs, which present the appearance of being covered with dew, hence the name sundew plants. Under the influence of

313

the sun's rays most of these plants assume a distinct bright reddish colour, when they are very charming.

A few good species are *D. binata*, *D. capensis* and *D. spathulata*. They will succeed in a greenhouse or with the sarracenias, and require the same kind of compost and treatment. Repotting is done in early March, and shallow, round, well-drained pans are the most suitable containers.

Droseras are increased by seeds, division of the crowns when repotting, and root cuttings. Seeds are sprinkled on a pan of newly potted plants, and careful watering will be needed until the seedlings are removed. Such species as *D. binata* produce strong roots, and if these are cut into pieces half an inch long and just covered with fine peaty compost, new plants will be quickly formed.

Darlingtonia californica: The only species grown. It is closely allied to sarracenia, with a curiously hooded top to the stems or leaves. The latter are white, green, and reddish-pink.

Cephalotus follicularis: An interesting little plant with green leaves and purplish-green pitchers marked with pink. A humid atmosphere is essential, so that the plant should be covered with an ordinary bell-glass. It can be grown with the sarracenias. Keep the crown of the plants slightly above the rim of the pot or pan, and the compost built up so as to form a slight mound.

Dionaea muscipula (Venus's Fly-trap): Full of interest. It produces two lobed green leaves beset with a row of teeth on the margin, and three bristles in the centre of each lobe of the leaf. Whenever a small insect such as a fly alights on the bristles, the outer edges immediately close so that the margined teeth meet and trap the intruder.

The compost consists of peat, leafmould, live sphagnum moss, and sand. Thorough drainage is essential, anything approaching stagnation being detrimental. The plants can be grown in a cool house and covered with a bell-glass if desired. A liberal supply of water is required during active growth, with sufficient to keep the plants plump when at rest, in winter.

CHAPTER FOURTEEN

The Year's Work in a Greenhouse

JANUARY

Maintain a night temperature of 4–7°C (40–45°F) and a day one of 10–13°C (50–55°F). Water cautiously during the month. Repot and start to grow hippeastrums for early flowering. Prune pot roses, also climbing roses, *Plumbago capensis*, and passion flowers. Introduce bulbs into heat to flower in March. Get pots, pans, boxes, and composts ready for seed sowing and inserting cuttings. Pot American tuberoses. Insert cuttings of perpetual flowering carnations. Prune greenhouse climbers. Start begonia and gloxinia tubers and achimenes into growth. Introduce the first batch of roses into the forcing house. Pick over rooting cuttings, removing all decaying leaves.

Plants in Flower: The following plants are available for flowering in the heated greenhouse, temperature 7–13°C (45–55°F), also in the cold house during January.

Arum	Carnations, perpetual flowering	Freesias
Begonias, fibrous rooted	*Cyclamen persicum*	Haemanthus
Boronia heterophylla	*Epacris purpurascens*	*Primula obconica*
B. megastigma	*Erica gracilis*	*P. sinensis*
Bouvardias	*E. hyemalis*	*Rhododendron (Azalea)*
Camellias	*E. willmorei*	*obtusum amoenum*
	Euphorbia fulgens	*R. (Azalea) indica*

Seeds to Sow: About the middle of the month sow seeds of tuberous-rooted begonia, canna, fuchsia, gloxinia, impatiens, pelargonium, petunia, streptocarpus, and verbena.

Cuttings to strike in heated structures: Insert cuttings of chrysanthemums singly in thumb pots, or three in a 3-in. pot, in good gritty compost, plunge the pots in peat in a box and cover with a sheet of glass. Shade from sun. Admit air for a few minutes every morning.

Bedding lobelia may also be rooted for stock by inserting cuttings in trays of light compost, and placing them in the propagator with moderate bottom heat. Remove to a shelf when rooted.

FEBRUARY

Temperature for the month 4–7°C (40–45°F) by night and 10–13°C (50–55°F) by day. Water plants more freely now the days are lengthening. Ventilate moderately during the middle of bright sunny days. Prune fuchsias into shape early in the month and repot towards the end, also begin to repot generally, e.g. ferns, palms and so on. Introduce a fresh batch of bulbs into heat. Repot odontoglossums as they go out of bloom. Pot off rooted cuttings of perpetual flowering carnations. Transfer Regal pelargoniums to larger pots. Introduce a further batch of roses into heat.

Plants in Flower: Temperate house, 7–13°C (45–55°F)

Abutilon	*Chorizema cordata splendens*	*Euphorbia fulgens*
Acacia armata	*Cineraria stellata*	Freesia
A. dealbata	*Coronilla glauca*	Haemanthus
Arum	*Cytisus fragrans*	*Primula stellata*
Begonia	*Daphne indica*	*Rhododendron (Azalea)*
Carnation,	*Epacris purpurascens*	*indica*
perpetual flowering	Epiphyllum	*R. (Azalea) molle*

Plants for Forcing:

Arum	Dicentra	*Philadelphus lemoinei*
Astilbe	Hippeastrum	Polygonatum
Convallaria	*Magnolia stellata*	Tulipa
Deutzia	Narcissi	

Seeds to Sow: Seeds of all kinds of greenhouse plants, e.g. acacia, alonsoa, amaryllis, tuberous and fibrous-rooted begonia, calceolaria (shrubby), perpetual flowering carnation, celosia, celsia, gloxinia, impatiens, salvia, schizanthus, and streptocarpus may be sown. Also seeds of half-hardy annuals and bedding plants. Temperature must average 13–18°C (55–65°F).

Cuttings to Strike: Continue to propagate chrysanthemums. Early flowering kinds for the garden should also be propagated during the month. Perpetual flowering carnations, heliotrope, fuchsia, bouvardia, and salvia will root well this month in a propagating frame.

Potting: Ferns and foliage plants, fuchsia, pelargoniums, and other plants starting into growth may be repotted now.

MARCH

Temperature for the month 7–10°C (45–50°F) by night, and 13–16°C (55–60°F) by day. Admit air when temperature reaches 18°C (65°F). Shade from bright sunshine. Syringe plants, except those in flower, morning and afternoon. Sow seeds of plants mentioned last month; also asters, stocks, and other annuals. Repot plants generally. Keep a sharp eye on pot and climbing roses, spraying or fumigating with a suitable insecticide if greenfly be present. Repot orchids just beginning to grow. Finish propagating perpetual flowering carnations. Stop the leading shoots of more advanced plants of latter. Prune bouvardias that have flowered. Give the first stop to decorative flowering chrysanthemums early in the month.

Plants in Flower: As the year progresses, so do the number of flowering plants which increase the beauty of the greenhouse.

Acacia armata	Cineraria	Haemanthus
A. grandis	*Correa speciosa*	*Primula malacoides*
Boronia	*Cytisus fragrans*	*Rhododendron (Azalea) indica*
Callistemon speciosus	*Epacris impressa*	*R. (Azalea) molle*
Carnations, perpetual flowering	Freesia	Schizanthus

Plants for Forcing:

Arum	*L. harrisii*	Syringa (lilac)
Astilbe	*Magnolia stellata*	Tulipa
Deutzia gracilis	Narcissi	*Viburnum carlesii*
Forsythia	*Paeonia suffruticosa*	*V. farreri*
Hippeastrum	Rosa	*Wisteria sinensis*
Lilium longiflorum	*Spiraea arguta*	

Seeds to Sow: Sow seeds of all the plants advised last month, also of cannas, cacti, fuchsias, geraniums; in fact, of any kind of plant capable of being reproduced from seed.

Cuttings to Strike: Fuchsia, coleus, bouvardia, marguerite, heliotrope, perpetual flowering carnation, and soft-wooded plants generally, can now be readily increased by cuttings in a propagator in the heated greenhouse.

Potting: Any kind of plant requiring additional root room should now be repotted. Have the materials for the compost – loam, leaf-mould, or peat and seed – placed in the greenhouse a week beforehand to get thoroughly warm.

Tuberous begonias and gloxinias that have started to grow should be planted in small pots, shifting them into the flowering pots when well rooted. Keep the crowns of the tubers level with the surface of the soil.

Cacti and succulents that require repotting should be attended to now.

APRIL

Temperature as for last month, except that it may rise to 18°C (65°F) by sun heat. Shade during the day. Syringe roses and other plants, except those in flower. Ventilate early in the morning, and close about 4 p.m. Repot any plants not attended to last month. Transfer bulbs that have flowered to a cold frame to harden off. Gradually withhold water from freesias and hippeastrums that have flowered. Give roses and other plants that are flowering freely weak liquid fertiliser twice a week.

Directly insect pests make an appearance fumigate the greenhouse on a calm evening. Do not water the plants in the afternoon, and try to get the atmosphere as dry as possible.

Stop the first week those varieties of chrysanthemums that are required to produce flowers from second crown buds.

Plants in Flower:

Abutilon	Clivia	Narcissi
Acacia	*Cytisus fragrans*	*Primula obconica*
Arum	*Deutzia gracilis*	Rosa
Astilbe	*Erica persoluta*	Schizanthus
Carnation, perpetual flowering	Freesia (finishing)	Streptosolen
Chorizema cordatum splendens	Hippeastrum	Tulipa (Darwin)
Cineraria	Lachenalia	

Seeds to Sow: Carnations and impatiens in light, sandy soil in well-drained pots, also freesia seed where they are to grow in J.I. potting compost.

Seedlings: Those reared from seed sown last month should be carefully transplanted in a mixture of sifted loam, peat, fine charcoal, and sand.

Cuttings to Strike: Almost any kind of greenhouse plant may be propagated from cuttings this month.

Potting: Repot Indian azaleas and camellias directly after flowering. Pot tubers of begonias and gloxinias as required. Achimenes tubers may also be started in pots.

Fuchsias, petunias, plumbagos, oleanders, and zonal pelargoniums that were pruned early in the year should be transferred to larger pots at once. Repot ferns, palms, aspidistras, dracaenas, and any other plants that require more room.

MAY

Temperature as for April. Water must be freely supplied, the floors damped twice a day, and the stagings and pots syringed to maintain a moist atmosphere. Continue to shade from sun. Encourage Indian azaleas to grow freely by syringing them morning and evening. Admit air freely. Prune shoots of *Rosa* Maréchal Niel that have flowered to within 6 in. of their base, to induce new shoots to form. Transfer carnations to frames.

Flowers in Season:

Abutilon	*Epacris longiflora*	*Lilium longiflorum*
Begonia, tuberous	*Erica ventricosa*	Pelargonium
Calceolaria, herbaceous	Fuchsia	Petunia
Carnation, perpetual flowering	Heliotropium	Rosa
Chrysanthemum frutescens	Hippeastrum	Strelitzia
Clivia	Hydrangea	Streptosolen

Seeds to Sow: Star and large-flowered Chinese primulas for winter flowering. Sow cineraria seeds at the same time.

Cuttings to Strike: Heath, cytisus, and azaleas may be inserted now in pure, clean silver sand, in well-drained pots. Place the pots under a bell-glass or in a propagator.

Potting: Transfer into their flowering pots celosia, petunia, impatiens and other seedlings reared early in the spring for summer flowering in the greenhouse.

Tuberous begonias, gloxinias, and streptocarpus should also be placed in their flowering pots at the earliest moment.

Chrysanthemums, too, should be planted in their flowering pots by the middle of the month, then be stood outdoors in full sun on a bed of cinder ashes or on planks. Syringe the plants every evening.

JUNE

Artificial heat should no longer be required unless the weather becomes unseasonably cold and damp. Give plenty of air, and shade the roof from sun. Water may be required twice a day in hot weather, with frequent dampings down. Gradually harden off forced shrubs and place them outdoors. See that aphids are quickly got rid of by spraying, or by fumigating. Layer Malmaison carnations. Look out for thrips infesting orchids. Transfer cyclamen to a cold frame, and only give sufficient water to keep the soil barely moist. Pinch out shoots of chrysanthemums for the last time in the case of the November-flowering sorts.

Plants in Flower:

Abutilon	Francoa	Pancratiums
Agapanthus	Fuchsia	Pelargonium
Begonia, tuberous	Gloxinia	Petunia
Bougainvillea	Hedychium	Phyllocactus.
Canna	Heliotropium	Plumbago capensis
Celosia	Hippeastrum	Strelitzia
Cestrum	Hydrangea	Streptocarpus
Chrysanthemum frutescens	Impatiens	Streptosolen
Crinum	Lapageria	
Diplacus glutinosus	Mimulus	

Seeds to Sow: Large-flowered and star-flowered primulas and cinerarias for autumn and winter flowering, as advised last month; also calceolarias.

Cuttings to Strike: Rochea and other succulents.

Potting: Chrysanthemums into flowering pots, and moving on young plants of all kinds as their present pots are filled with roots.

JULY

The advice given regarding temperatures, watering and general management for last month applies equally to this month. Pot roses should be placed outdoors on a bed of ashes in full sun to ripen their wood. Indian azaleas, heaths, camellias, cytisus, and acacias may also be placed outdoors in partial shade till September. The greenhouse should be well ventilated during the day. If the interior requires repainting now is a good time to do it, placing the plants outdoors meanwhile. Bud orange and lemon trees. Cut back regal, fancy, and show pelargoniums that are waning. Pinch December-flowering chrysanthemums for the last time.

Plants in Flower:

Begonia	Fuchsia	Petunia
Bougainvillea	Gloxinia	*Plumbago capensis*
Cacti	Hedychium	Rochea
Campanula isophylla	Heliotropium	*Saintpaulia ionantha*
Canna	Hydrangea	Schizanthus
Celosia	Impatiens	Streptocarpus
Chrysanthemum frutescens	Ipomoea	Streptosolen
Clianthus puniceus	Oleander	*Swainsona galegifolia*
Cobaea scandens	Pancratium	Thunbergia
Crinum	Passiflora	Trachelium
Diplacus glutinosus	Pelargonium	

Bulbs and Tubers:

Achimenes	Gloxinia	*L. longiflorum*
Begonia	*Lilium auratum*	*L. speciosum*

Seeds to Sow: Chinese primulas, cinerarias, and herbaceous calceolarias; the latter will succeed better in a shady frame. Also sow mignonette for winter flowering in pots.

Cuttings to Strike: Insert cuttings of hydrangeas singly in 3-in. pots. Choose the ends of well-ripened shoots about 3 in. long, remove the lower pair of leaves, and cut the base off close to a joint. Place the pots in a shady cold frame, and do not give too much air at first.

Potting: Freesias repot at the end of the month. Plant the bulbs 1 in. deep and 2 in. apart, in 6- or 7-in. pots, in a compost of equal parts loam, peat, rotted manure, and sand, J. I. potting No. 2 and place in a cold frame.

Plant zonal pelargoniums reared from spring cuttings in 6-in. pots. Plunge the pots to their rims in cinder ashes in full sun. Nip off the points of the shoots to cause lateral shoots to form, and keep all flowers removed. Such plants will flower freely in autumn.

Plant perpetual flowering carnations in their final flowering pots, and cease stopping the shoots. Grow in a frame exposed to the air, and spray the foliage every afternoon.

AUGUST

See remarks regarding shading, watering, ventilating, and so on in the June calendar. Plants standing outdoors should be well syringed every evening. Feed plants in flower with liquid fertiliser. Remove perpetual flowering carnations to greenhouse from frame. Feed chrysanthemums growing in pots. Vallotas and Guernsey lilies will be commencing active growth, and hence require more water.

Plants in Flower: These are practically the same as last month, with the addition of:

Campanula pyramidalis	*Nerine sarniensis*	Tibouchina
Exacum affine	*Oxalis floribunda*	*Vallota speciosa*
Lantana	*Saintpaulia ionantha*	

Seeds to Sow: Schizanthus, nemesia, and clarkia. Shade from the sun and keep just moist. When the seedlings are well up, thin them out to about five or six in each pot, and plant the thinnings in other pots. Intermediate stock and cyclamen seed can also be sown now.

Cuttings to Strike: Regal, fancy, and show pelargoniums can be increased by cuttings of the firm ends of shoots about 3 in. long, cut off close to a joint, and with the lower leaves removed. Insert each singly in thumb pots in sandy compost, and place on a shelf in the greenhouse.

Potting: Bulbs of many kinds can now be planted in pots. Freesias, for example, plant at the rate of seven bulbs to a 6-in. pot, placing them 1 in. deep. Lachenalias, too, plant half a dozen $\frac{1}{2}$ in. deep in a 6-in. pot. Roman hyacinths, Duc Van Thol tulips, and polyanthus narcissi for forcing, should also be potted early in the month. In each case use a compost of 2 parts loam and 1 of equal proportions of leafmould, peat, rotted manure, and sand. Pot bulbs of winter flowering *Iris reticulata*. Repot cyclamen and *Amaryllis belladonna*.

SEPTEMBER

Artificial heat will be required at night this month. Maintain a temperature of about 7°C (45°F). Plants will require less shade and water. Give air freely during the middle of the day. Remove into greenhouse azaleas, heaths, camellias, and similar plants that were placed outdoors for the summer. Remove chrysanthemums into the greenhouse. Let Maréchal Neil roses have plenty of air this month to ripen their growth.

The seed-sowing season is over for the year.

Plants in Flower: From now onwards for some months the greenhouse will meet with a more welcome appreciation than it has during the summer months. The chief plants in flower will be:

Begonia	Fuchsia	Petunia
Bougainvillea	Heliotropium	Rhodanthes
Campanula isophylla	Ipomoea	*Saintpaulia ionantha*
C. pyramidalis	Lantana	Streptocarpus
Carnations, perpetual flowering	*Lilium auratum*	Thunbergia
Chrysanthemums	*L. speciosum*	Tibouchina
C. frutescens	Nerine	Trachelium
Cobaea scandens	Passiflora	Vallota
Exacum affine	Pelargonium	

Potting: Such bulbs as narcissi, early tulips, hyacinths, and others for early flowering should be procured and potted at the earliest moment. Bulbs of *Lilium harrisii*, too, should be potted singly in a 5-in. or three in a 6-in. pot. Only half fill the pots with compost 2 parts loam, 1 leafmould or peat and sand – leaving the remaining half to be added when the shoots are 6 in. high.

Cyclamen, cineraria and Chinese primulas should also be placed in their flowering-sized pots early in the month, transferring them from the cold frame to a shelf near the glass.

Calla lilies planted outdoors should be lifted and planted in pots in a compost of 2 parts loam, 1 part rotted manure, and 1 part silver sand. Stand the plants outdoors in a shady place till the end of the month, then bring them into the greenhouse.

OCTOBER

Temperature for the month 4–7°C (40–45°F) by night and 13°C (55°F) by day. Water plants sparingly. No syringing required. Discontinue shade. Admit air slightly from 10 a.m. to 3 p.m. on sunny days. Repot roses. Plant climbing roses under glass. Pot hyacinths, narcissi, tulips, and other bulbs for spring flowering. Pot African tuberoses. Gradually withhold water from lilies. Keep oleanders on the dry side from now onwards. Feed cyclamen, cinerarias, primulas and camellias with a good fertiliser in weak solution. Keep the plants near the glass.

Remove pot-grown chrysanthemums into the greenhouse, and feed them twice a week with liquid fertiliser.

Gradually withhold water from tuberous begonias and gloxinias, and when the foliage shrivels keep the soil quite dry. Store the pots under the staging.

Look to heating apparatus to ensure complete readiness for regular winter service.

Prune oleanders, cutting back current year's growths to 2 in. from base.

Plants in Flower:

Abutilon	*Eupatorium micranthum*	*Primula malacoides*
Bouvardia	*Exacum affine*	*P. obconica*
Carnation, perpetual flowering	Freesia	*Saintpaulia ionantha*
Chrysanthemum	Jacobinia	Salvia
Cyclamen	Nerine	Tibouchina
Erica gracilis	Pelargonium, zonal	Trachelium

Potting: Bulbs such as hyacinths, tulips and narcissi may still be potted early in the month, and plunged in ashes or fibre refuse in a cold frame.

Roses established in pots should be repotted early in the month if the pots are well filled with roots. Plants from the open may be purchased now and planted in pots for flowering in spring. Stand the plants outdoors till December.

Such flowering roots as convallaria (lily of the valley), *Dicentra spectabilis*, and astilbes should be procured, potted, and placed in cold frames until December, then be introduced into heat.

African tuberoses should be planted singly in 4½-in. pots, or three in a 6-in. pot, in a compost of 2 parts loam, 1 part rotted manure, and coarse sand. Place in a cold frame till the New Year, then introduce to the greenhouse.

NOVEMBER

Temperature for the month 4–7°C (40–45°F) at night and 10–13°C (50–55°F) by day. Admit air only when sun is shining. Water sparingly. Place August-potted bulbs in forcing house. Retarded lilies of the valley, *Lilium harrisii*, etc., may be started to grow in a temperature of 4°C (40°F) to flower at Christmas. Keep cacti and succulents dry. Finish pruning plumbago, oleander, and datura.

Plants in Flower: These are the same as last month, with the addition of:

Begonia Gloire de Lorraine and vars.	*Eriostemon buxifolia*	*Sparmannia africana*
	Primula kewensis	*Trachelium caeruleum*
Boronia heterophylla	*Saintpaulia ionantha*	
B. megastigma		

Potting: Lilies grown in pots and now at rest should be repotted. Turn the bulbs out of the old compost and remove all dead or decaying scales. See cultural instructions under *Lilium* regarding mode of procedure. Place the pots in a cold frame till growth begins, then remove to the greenhouse.

DECEMBER

Temperature as last month. In severe weather protect the sides and lower part of roof with mats at night to help keep out frost. Give water cautiously, and take special care not to saturate the crowns or collars of primulas, cyclamen, and cinerarias, otherwise decay will be encouraged. Remove dead foliage and avoid all stagnant dampness. Ventilate a little in all but the most severe weather. Remove condensation from inside of glass whenever possible. Prune roses for starting in heat next month. Get pots washed in readiness for use. Cacti need very little watering through the winter. Bring another batch of bulbs into forcing house. Cut down chrysanthemums going out of flower, and then store the pots in a cold frame or in a cool position in the greenhouse.

Deutzias, spiraeas, and *Rhododendron molle* (azalea) may be brought in, preparatory to gentle forcing.

Potting, seed sowing, and propagation should be suspended this month, except for rooting exhibition chrysanthemums.

Plants in Flower: The greenhouse is now the chief centre of floral attraction, and those who are fortunate enough to possess one heated to a temperature of 7–13 °C (45–55 °F) may have the following plants in bloom.

Begonia, fibrous rooted	*Epacris purpurascens*	*Primula kewensis*
Bouvardia	*Erica gracilis*	*P. malacoides*
Camellia	*E. hyemalis*	*P. obconica*
Carnation, perpetual flowering	*Euphorbia fulgens*	*P. sinensis*
Chrysanthemum	Freesia	*Rhododendron (Azalea)*
Correa speciosa	Haemanthus	*obtusum amoenum*
Cyclamen	Poinsettia	*Saintpaulia ionantha*

Forcing House:

Convallaria	*Narcissus* Soleil d'Or	Syringa (lilac)
Hyacinthus, Roman	Paper White	Tulipa Duc Van Thol
Lilium harrisii	*Rhododendron (Azalea) molle*	

Index

d = line drawing   p = photograph following page given

327

INDEX